Above: The Peninsula Model Railroad Club, San Mateo, California, combines superb operation with fine scenery. Club operations often are far more complex than the average home layout, especially on the electrical end.

Inside Back Cover: Colonel Carstens rides the back platform of his railroad inspection car No. 4 Ramsey over the Gorre & Daphetid behind the old gas electric. Built by the late John Allen, Master Modeler; the Gorre & Daphetid was destroyed by fire only a few weeks after the builder's passing. Few pikes in any scale have ever approached the all around perfection of this railroad in miniature, much of it due to the electrical work buried behind the scenery.

PREFACE TO VOLUME II, THIRD EDITION

This two-volume Handbook is intended as a reference manual of the electrical information required by model railroaders. Volume I contains basic information needed on all layouts, Volume II, although including some basic information, primarily covers the more advanced aspects of the hobby such as signaling. The emphasis is heavily on those methods which have been proven effective, particularly on those which have been widely used.

Extensive use is made of cross-referencing including references in this volume to information in Volume I either by section or by figure and chapter. These references to Volume I will remain valid for any future edition of Volume I.

In the interest of preserving some of the history of the hobby and to give credit where credit is due, the earliest known publication or demonstration of an important advance of an electrical nature in model railroading has been included in many cases. If any reader knows of an earlier reference than those cited, the author would appreciate being so informed.

Paul Mallery

OTHER BOOKS BY PAUL MALLERY:

Trackwork Handbook for Model Railroads
Bridge and Trestle Handbook for Model Railroads
Wiring Your Layout
Design Handbook of Model Railroads
Model Traction Handbook
The Complete Handbook of Model Railroad Operations

11 WIRING

11.1 INTRODUCTION

Selecting the right devices and designing the proper circuits so they function is crucial to the proper operation of a model railroad. Nevertheless, to function, everything must be connected together by conductors (called wiring in this Handbook). But wiring is not just the simple connecting together of terminals. It must be done correctly and reliably or trouble will be your constant companion.

Before wiring is undertaken, a schematic diagram should be prepared. It is tempting to skip this step but, in most cases, nothing could be more foolish. Drawing the circuit first saves time because it is easier to make corrections with an eraser than with a soldering iron. Following the diagram when running the wires not only saves more time but also reduces the number of errors. Most important, a schematic diagram is invaluable for later reference when shooting trouble or making changes on additions.

11.2 SCHEMATIC DIAGRAM

Schematic diagrams use standardized symbols and techniques so the wiring and the operation of a circuit can be seen at a glance. Pictorial diagrams such as those in Chapter 1 can show the wiring but they are very difficult to understand.

Unfortunately more than one set of standardized symbols exist for schematic diagrams but the one used by the computer industry, radio, television, the telephone system, the armed forces, and in this Handbook dominates. Unless you have a compelling personal reason for using another set of symbols, this is the one to choose.

Appendix I, Volume I, lists many of the standard symbols useful in model railroading. Others are shown in the appropriate chapters. In some cases alternate symbols exist. In this handbook, for example, two different symbols for switch, pushbutton and relay contacts are used. The particular symbol chosen for a specific figure is the symbol which makes the more understandable drawing.

For maximum clarity not only must standard symbols be used, they also must be interconnected in an easily understood manner. Clutter on the drawing must be avoided. The figures of this Handbook give many examples of good practice. It is recommended that the rules given below be followed for all schematic diagrams.

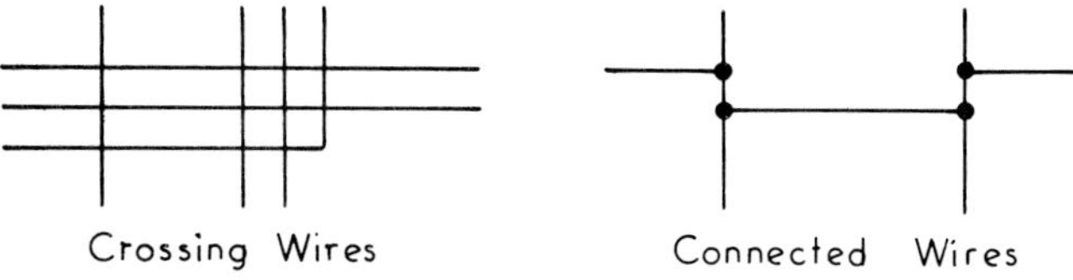

Fig. 11-1 Symbols for wires.

Show wires crossing without connection as straight lines as on the left in Fig. 11-1. Do not use the old "croquet hoop" as this takes longer to draw, adds clutter, and makes tracing a line more difficult. Connected lines should always meet as a T with a dot as on the right in Fig. 11-1. Never place a dot on crossing lines to indicate a connection to avoid any question whether it is a dot or merely a blob.

Use an appropriate symbol (e.g. the ground symbol) or an explicit notation (e.g. -12) to indicate a common voltage connection. This provides immediate identification of that common point and avoids clutter. Never gather a major common point together with a line. Such a line not only adds clutter but also, due to its many connections, forces unnecessary tedious circuit tracing merely to find out that a constant voltage or other common has been reached. Fig. 11-2 illustrates the greater clarity and simplicity of indicating common points with appropriate symbols against gathering these points with lines. On larger drawings, where common points are physically spaced at considerable distances, identification of such points by symbol or notation becomes more important.

Using a self-evident symbol such as 24 for a common voltage point is superior to using some arbitrary symbol such as A or B. The latter must be looked up or remembered for each particular drawing. An exception is an important common point which cannot be given a definite voltage label, a prime example being the common connection within a transistor throttle. Whether this common point is ground or some voltage depends upon the setting of the reversing switch. An

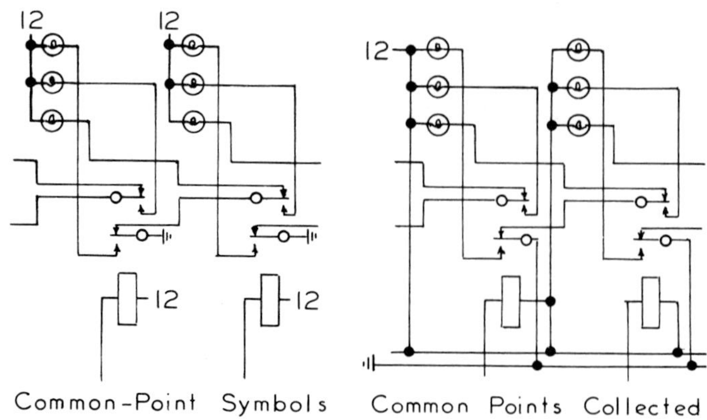

Fig. 11-2 Use symbols for common voltage points.

arbitrary symbol must be used in such cases and so indicated. One such symbol is a "delta" ground as shown in the schematic diagram of Fig. 11-3.

Avoid all clutter on schematics which does not add information (for example the circle often drawn around a transistor symbol, a carry-over from electron tubes, adds nothing to the information). As can be seen in Fig. 11-3, the transistor symbol without a circle is sufficient.

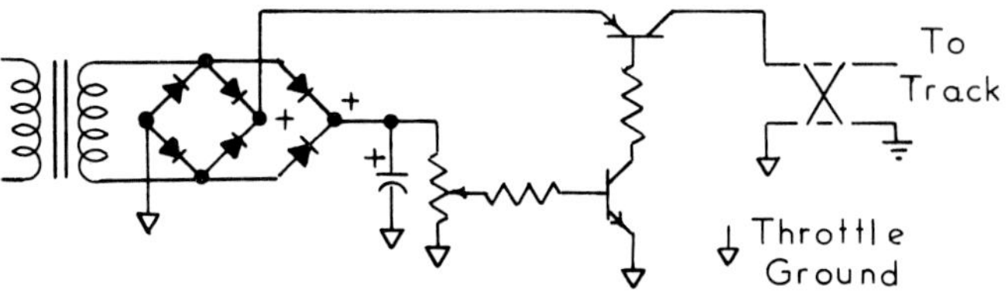

Fig. 11-3 Identify special symbols.

On a simple schematic it may be convenient to locate the symbols in roughly the same order as the devices are mounted. As the drawing becomes more complex, the device symbols should be located to minimize long, involved interconnecting lines. When several leads must be drawn some distance in the same general direction, a "highway", Fig. 11-4, will reduce the clutter.

Integrated circuits became available at affordable prices around 1972 making complex electrical systems practical for model railroads. In particular, synchronous systems with many clock phases, and systems with multi-lead address buses were introduced. Such systems have far more connections common to many parts of the system than the voltage connections and grounds of the older circuits. For all except the simplest of systems made from integrated circuits (ICs), some logical notation must be adopted which clearly shows the source of each common signal, and the points where each such signal is used. Since there may be many using circuits, it is important that the notation specify at the source where each using circuit is located, be it on the same sheet, close or far, or on another sheet. At the using circuit the notation must accurately locate the source. There is no "standard" notation for this purpose. For consistency in this handbook, the system of notation developed and used for many years at The Model Railroad Club is used when such identification is needed.

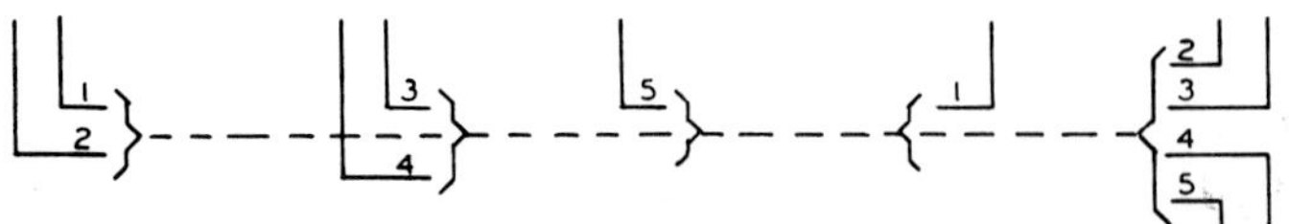

Fig. 11-4 Highways simplify drawings.

Complex systems usually require so many IC packages that it is impractical to include the entire system on one sheet. Even when one sheet will do, often there are so many devices on the sheet that some sort of a cooordinate reference is needed for each symbol. For this purpose The Model RR Club uses coordinate paper with letters A to AJ as horizontal coordinates and numbers 1 to 35 as vertical coordinates. The bottom right corners of sheet 1 and sheet 2 of an IC system are shown in Fig. 11-5. To specify a definite location, the sheet

ELECTRICAL HANDBOOK FOR MODEL RAILROADS

Vol. II

ISBN 911868-43-7

by Paul Mallery

RAIL-CRAFT

C-43

LIBRARY

PUBLICATIONS, INC.

Mailing address P.O. Box 700, Newton, New Jersey 07860.

Located on Fredon-Springdale Road, Fredon Township, New Jersey.

TABLE OF CONTENTS—VOLUME II

VOLUME I

See Table of Contents in Volume I for a more detailed listing and the page numbers.

Scott Wertrands of the Rensselaer Model Railroad Society has good reason to smile as he guides a Rutland RS3 over the club's New England, Berkshire & Western Railroad using a Dynatrol walkaround controller by Power Systems, Inc. NEB&W system was featured in Railroad Model Craftsman's December 1979 and February 1980 issues and can be considered one of the finest model railroad layouts in North America. Many New England landmarks have been incorporated into the scenery of the NEB&W.

Staff photo by Jim Boyd

number is followed by the lettered horizontal coordinate with the numbered vertical coordinate coming last. For example, the cab counter at the left in Fig.11-5 is at coordinate 1AH34. It is not necessary that the device be exactly at the intersection of the coordinates since it is easy to find even if the coordinate is the closest one.

There are four outputs from the cab counter at 1AH34 in Fig. 11-5; they are CC0, CC1, CC2, and CC3. To indicate that these designations are each a common point, they are enclosed by rectangles whose heavy outlines show that these particular rectangles are the sources of the signals. Adjacent to the rectangle, or in this case all four rectangles, the coordinates of all the using circuits are noted. In Fig. 11-5 the using circuits are to be found at 2AI34, 3A4, and 4B10. It is important that the list of using coordinates be complete.

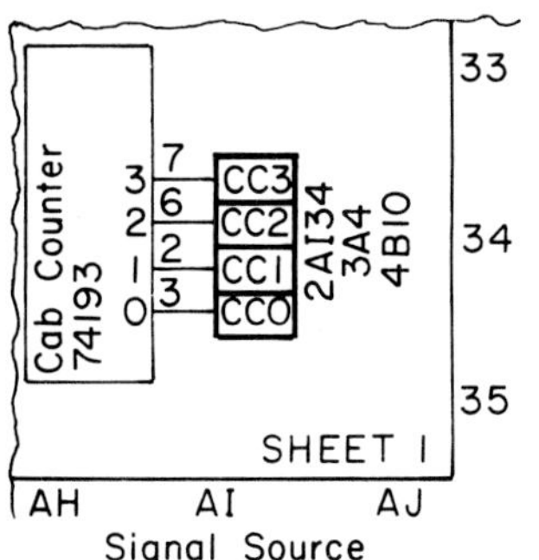

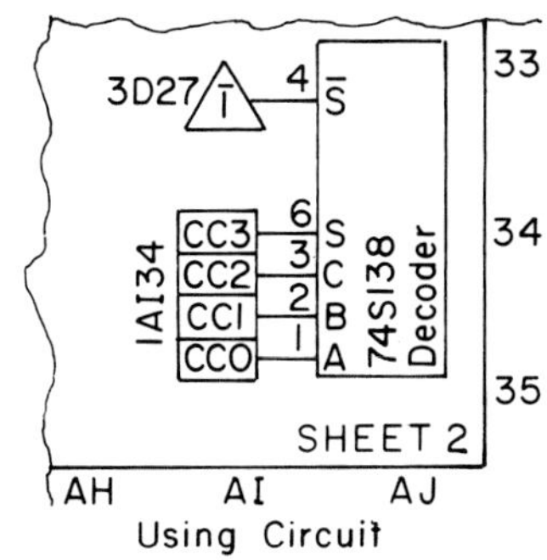

Fig. 11-5 Common connections.

Also shown in Fig. 11-5 is the using-circuit location on sheet 2 (2AI34). Exactly the same symbol appears here as for the source, except the outline is light thereby indicating a using circuit. Only the coordinate of the source symbol, not those of other users, is given at a using symbol, in this case 1AI34.

At The Model RR Club rectangles are used as the general symbol for a common connection. However, if there is a special class of signal for which quick identification by class is helpful, a symbol of a different shape is used. In their case a triangle such as that shown at 2AI33 in Fig. 11-5 represents a strobed signal.

Not only do symbols such as the boxes of Fig. 11-5 simplify the drawings by eliminating many long lines, they also make circuit operations much more obvious. For example, on the right in Fig. 11-5 it is immediately apparent that the decoder is decoding the cycle counter. It is not necessary to trace lines back to sheet 1 to discover this.

Above all make schematic diagrams so that they are permanently legible and file the original for future use. Make copies for current use in wiring or trouble shooting.

On a schematic diagram the connecting lines are drawn considering only the needs for clarity and accuracy. When it comes to duplicating these lines in copper and solder, there are many other things to consider. These are covered in the remainder of this Chapter.

11.3 WIRE

11.31 Wire Size

Since, almost without exception, the wire used for interconnections in model railroading is of copper, wire size is a most important characteristic for size determines resistance and current-carrying capacity. Resistance is important as model railroading voltages are low and currents are often relatively high. Even one or two ohms in a lead would be excessive in wires carrying power to locomotives. Furthermore, a too-small wire size for the current is a fire hazard.

Wire size is specified by number; the smaller the number, the larger the wire. A complete listing of wire sizes of interest with the pertinent data is given in Appendix I, Vol. 1. One convenient rule to remember is that the size of wire doubles for each three numbers (the cross section, not the diameter). For example No. 12 wire is twice as large as No. 15. The commonly used wire sizes in model railroading are Nos. 14, 16, 18, 20, and 22 with even smaller sizes for winding motors and switch machines. The common size for wire-wrap connections for integrated circuits is No. 30. For the leads which carry power to the locomotives nothing smaller than 20 should be used in N, 18 in HO, and 16 in O gauge. Smaller sizes may work quite well on small layouts but they may present a fire hazard under overload conditions.

For HO No. 16 wire has proven adequate even on the largest layouts but, at local retail prices in some areas, No. 14, being a common household wiring size, may be less costly. Mail order houses, such as Sears, normally handle 14 gauge wire in three insulation colors, black, white, and red.

Fig. 11-6 Ground bus simplifies wiring.

Unfortunately, the terminals of most standard electrical items useful to model railroaders, such as toggle switches, are easily damaged by the mechanical force a heavy wire may apply. No. 18 is about as large a wire as is convenient to connect in most cases. Since No. 18 in a 24V system is superior to No. 16 in a 12V system and reduces costs, significant advantages would be gained by adopting the proposal made by Hoyt Haddock in the Sept. 1970 NMRA Bulletin to change HO from 12V to 24V. These advantages are in addition to the virtual elimination of dirty-track problems which can be expected by doubling the voltage and halving the current.

For circuits with currents below 1A (those to operate lamps are examples), Nos. 20 and 22 gauge wires are generally adequate and are less costly than heavier gauges, further, they are easier to install and connect. Gauges smaller than No. 22 are not recommended for conventional interconnections as such wires are easily broken and are difficult to place under screw terminals. The smaller sizes of wire, of course, have other uses on model railroads.

11.32 Wire Types

Wire can be either a single heavy strand (solid wire) or several finer strands twisted together (stranded wire). Size for size they are of equal current capacity. For most purposes solid wire is the better type. It is less costly and easier to connect. Further it can be dressed so it remains in position, important for surface wiring (see Section 11.52). Most important, solid wire produces more reliable and trouble-free wiring than stranded wire since loose strands, particularly at terminals, are a prime cause of short circuits. Also, if the strands are nicked when stripping the insulation, a trouble spot may be formed when these strands break and such trouble spots may be concealed by the unbroken strands. Under similar conditions a solid wire will break completely calling attention to the location of the trouble. For wire-wrap connections, solid wire made for the purpose must be used. Stranded wire should be used only when its greater flexibility is an advantage.

Wire can be purchased either "tinned" or "untinned". See Section 11.43 for a definition of "tinned". Since it is much easier (hence more reliable) to solder to tinned wire, its slight extra cost is more than justified.

11.33 Wire Insulation

Insulation is placed around a wire to prevent a metal to metal contact to another wire or to a terminal thus causing a short or crossed circuit. Since model railroad voltages are low (except for any 110 volt wiring), almost any insulation is acceptable as far as voltage breakdown is concerned. However most wires are subject to abrasion and other forms of mechanical stress. Therefore thin insulations, such as enamel, are unsatisfactory except where the wire is well protected as on the coil of a switch machine.

Insulated wire should be used for all leads (including those for ground) with two exceptions: where the wire is contained so it cannot touch another wire or terminal as in the rail feed wire, Fig. 11-34, and for isolated ground bus wires. Since so many connections are made to the ground bus, using a heavy (Nos. 12 or 14) bare tinned wire or copper braid for this purpose facilitates wiring. Such a ground bus should follow every track route to minimize the complexity of underbenchwork wiring but they must be far enough from all terminals that there is no possibility of the bare bus being dragged against any other connection. Fig. 11-6 shows a ground bus of 1/4″ (6mm) copper braid with two black insulated ground feeders run directly to it from the connectors to the common rail.

An important characteristic of insulation is the ease with which it can be stripped for making a connection. Insulations which are difficult to strip greatly increase the time and effort required to make connections and increase the likelihood of poor connections. Some insulations can be melted by the heat of a soldering iron, these are convenient in some applications (see Fig. 11-11) but present a hazard if used when soldered connections will be made later to nearby terminals.

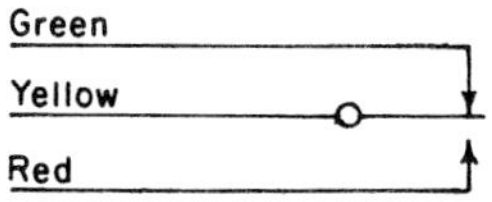

Fig. 11-7 Suggested colors for transfer contacts.

Green
Yellow
Red

Color is an important feature of insulation. It is much easier to trace leads if the wires are of different colors. Certainly if several spools of wire are required, they may as well be of different colors.

For ease in maintenance, common leads which occur often should be assigned a definite color, the most important such lead being ground. Black is generally assigned as the ground-lead color and no lead other than ground should be black. Since so many leads connect to ground, making them all black greatly reduces the difficulty of trouble shooting. An exception to black as ground is for 110V wiring. In such wiring, green indicates physical ground and white the ground power lead.

Another specific, often-repeated application on model railroads is to a transfer contact on a switch machine or other device. Making the three leads to such contacts of standard colors provides immediate recognition of the circuit without tracing to the contacts. Fig. 11-7 suggests green, yellow, and red as, being the colors of a color-light signal, they are easy to remember.

11.4 ELECTRICAL CONNECTIONS

11.41 General

Connections between wires and terminals or rails are among the greatest source of electrical troubles. A poor connection may add ohms to the circuit thus nullifying the advantage of heavy wires or it may introduce a hard-to-find intermittent open circuit. Poor connections are usually the result of either not knowing proper procedures or not using care.

11.42 Removing Insulation

Prior to making an electrical connection, any insulation must be removed, an operation called "stripping". When stripping insulation, it is vital that the wire not be nicked. A nick is an open invitation to a broken lead.

Some types of insulation can be removed by crushing with a pair of long-nose pliers as shown in Fig. 11-8. After crushing, the unwanted insulation is pulled off. Some wire which cannot be stripped by crushing at only one point will respond if the entire length to be stripped is crushed. Ths method of stripping is safe as there is virtually no chance of damaging the wire.

Commercial wire strippers are available. Some use heat to remove plastic insulation and will not nick wire. Others have a cutting tool for one size of wire, a selection of holes to match the wire size, or are adjustable. These tools are rapid and convenient but must be used with care to avoid nicks. Some diagonal cutters and cutting pliers have a wire-stripping notch in their cutting edge. Since these notches are not adjustable in size, it is important to develop skills in their use to prevent damage to the wire.

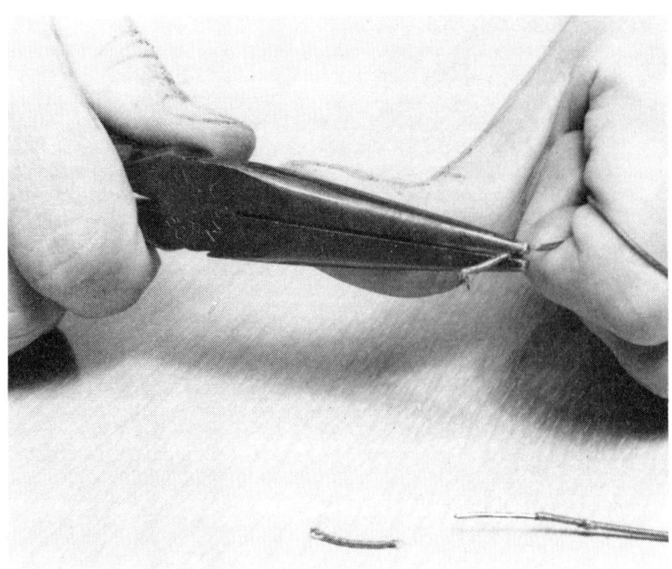

Fig. 11-8 Stripping wires with pliers.

Many types of insulation strip cleanly with no insulation left on the wire. However, some wire has an enamel coating under the outside insulation or, when stripping, some of the insulation smears onto the wire. In either case the wire must be cleaned. Drawing the wire between the two leaves of a folded piece of fine sandpaper is safer than scraping the wire with a sharp tool. It is poor policy to use such wire unless it is available at bargain prices for it wastes time and increases the possibility of a poor connection or broken lead.

For enamel and similar type insulations there are chemical strippers on the market. Their use is not recommended as they may cause trouble at a future date.

There are insulations which can be removed by the heat of the soldering iron when a soldered connection is being made. Such insulations are of two types; one is a special enamel and the other meltable plastic. Although insulations of this type are convenient for special applications, they make it more difficult to assure that a reliable connection has been made compared to insulations which must be stripped. Also, remember that meltable insulations introduce the possibility of short circuits if soldering is required on nearby terminals at a later time.

11.43 Soldered Connection

Since electrical connections are the simplest form of soldering, no model railroader should hesitate to make them.

Before making a connection, both the wire and the terminal or rail, also the soldering iron or gun should be well tinned. Tinned means that there is a layer of solder on the surface of the material to be soldered or on the iron. Without such a layer on the connecting parts a reliable connection is unlikely. Soldering irons used for conventional wiring should be tinned on one side only. This permits them to be used between adjacent terminals without melting the solder of the terminal not involved in the connection being made.

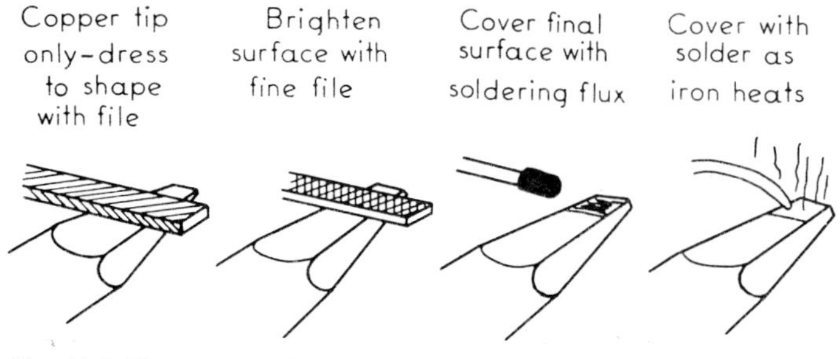

Fig. 11-9 Tinning a soldering iron.

Soldering-iron tips in 1981 were made of many materials including copper and steel. Since steel and some other materials are not dissolved readily by solder, they do not require the redressing and retinning of the copper tip which has to be redressed (filed to shape) and retinned regularly. But regardless of material, the tinning method shown in Fig. 11-9 can be used. A copper tip should be filed to shape first. The *cold* tip then is brightened with a fine file on one side only and covered with soldering flux. This is the only time a flux other than rosin should be used for electrical work. Heat the iron and, as it warms, rub the tip with solder. As soon as the solder deposits on the tip, cover the entire brightened area. This same method can be used for a soldering gun.

Wires, terminals, and rails should be tinned before attempting to make a connection to assure that the solder wets the entire surface and not just where it can be seen. Most solder-type terminals are tinned when purchased and tinned wire is available but, if the tinning looks dull, retin them. Tinning is done by holding a *hot* soldering iron against the lead or terminal and feeding rosin-core solder onto the wire or terminal as on the left in Fig. 11-10. Any stubborn spots which do not wet (solder does not spread out on surface) usually can be handled by rubbing with the tip of the iron but do this while the surface is exposed, not after the wire is in place. This particularly applies to rails.

For tinning and all other electrical soldering of connections, use only rosin-core solder. DO NOT USE ACID-CORE SOLDER OR ANY KIND OF FLUX OTHER THAN ROSIN. Regardless of claims, all fluxes other than rosin are too corrosive and are likely to cause trouble in time. Rosin is unique in that it has the corrosive action necessary to help the solder wet the surface when hot yet is virtually inert when cold. Most rosin fluxes have activators added to assist soldering but, unfortunately, these activators are not inert when cold. Most activated rosin flux is satisfactory for model railroad use, but, if you find a solder which seems to be distinctly easier to use than other solders, the reason is a highly activated flux. Avoid such solders for wiring.

The common solder for electrical work is an alloy of tin and lead. The best is 63-37 which means 63% tin, 37% lead but 60-40 is much more common and quite satisfactory. 50-50 solder is also widely available but when it melts it has a distinct "paste" stage which increases the possibility of the so-called "cold" solder joint.

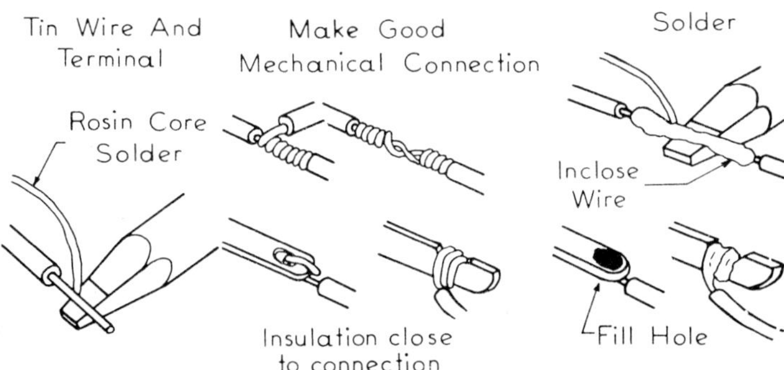

Fig. 11-10 Making a soldered connection.

After the wires and terminals are tinned, make a good mechanical connection as shown in Fig. 11-10. This prevents any movement of the parts being soldered at the time the solder is cooling. Movement at this time is the prime cause of the so-called "cold" solder joint. If two wires are being connected, twist them together well. If a wire is being connnected to a terminal with a hole, run the wire through the hole and bend it back. If the terminal has no hole, wrap the wire securely around the terminal. In all cases bring the insulation on the wire up to the connection so that if the wire is pulled to one side, there will be no chance that the bare wire will strike an adjacent terminal.

For the actual soldering, hold a *hot* soldering iron against the connection and run on enough solder to inclose the wire completely but not so much as to form a blob. If the terminal has a hole, that hole should be completely filled. If it is difficult to fill, look for a piece of insulation blocking the hole. In any connection it is vital that enough heat be applied. Too often connections are "pasted", that is the solder flows but one of the pieces never gets hot enough for the solder to wet its surface. Lack of pretinning also is a major cause of the pasted connection. Observe that the solder wets both parts to be joined. This is particularly important if one part is much larger than the other, as in connecting to a rail, see Fig. 11-34.

When the wire has insulation which is to be removed by the heat of the soldering iron, it is imperative to rub the surface covered by the insulation with the tip of the hot iron. This ensures that the film of insulation is broken and that the molten solder will reach and wet the wire. It is vital to observe that the molten solder is wetting and flowing over surfaces previously covered by insulation.

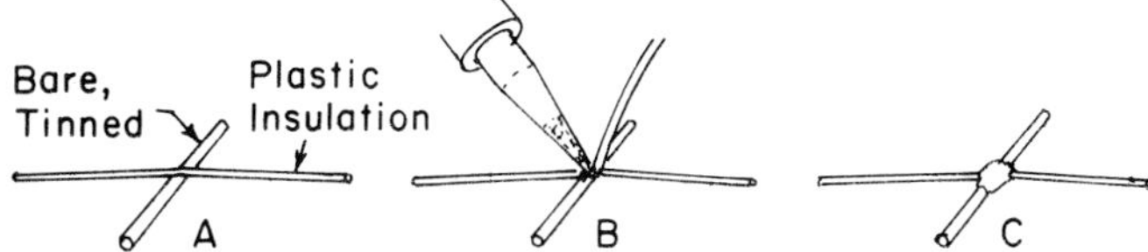

Fig. 11-11 Soldering wires to form ground plane.

Forming a ground plane for integrated circuits is a specific application in which soldering directly through plastic insulation is convenient. As shown in Fig. 11-11, bare, tinned copper wire can be stretched in one direction to serve as ground buses for power to the circuit packages. Insulated wire with meltable insulation, the 30-gauge wire for wire wrap is often of this type, is run at right angles to the bare wire as indicated at A in the figure. To solder these wires together the insulated wire is pressed tightly against the bare wire, as at B; the hot tip of the soldering iron rubbed against the insulated wire and solder is flowed on until it makes an obvious lump enclosing both wires. The final result is shown at C. This type of connection cannot be considered reliable and should be used only when forming a ground plane or similar mesh in which an occasional poor connection will have no significant adverse effect.

11.44 Screw Terminals

Many commercial model railroad devices and terminal strips are equipped with screw terminals. Provided the screws are appropriate to the wire size used, this type of terminal is excellent. Care should be taken that the wire wraps around the screw in the clockwise direction so it tightens around the screw when the screw is tightened, as shown on the left in Fig. 11-12. Since the strands of stranded wire have a tendency to become separated when placed under a screw, it is good practice to solder the strands together first as at the center of the figure or to solder the wire to a lug as on the right. The spade lug shown is convenient when the connection is to be separated on occasion. Other lugs completely encircle the screw. Wires smaller than No. 24 should always be soldered to a lug as such wires are likely to break if placed directly under the screw.

Fig. 11-12 Connecting to screw terminals.

11.45 Wire Wrap

The advent of integrated circuits (ICs) brought the need for making many connections within a confined area, the connections themselves being on close spacing, often 2.5mm (0.1″) on centers. Although printed wiring, described in Section 11.6, can be used, it is always advisable to wire a prototype circuit with individual leads, and to test that circuit before making a printed-wiring circuit. The latter is difficult to change if the design needs corrections. Also, when only one complex unit is to be wired, such as the central processor of a computer cab control system, it is far easier to use individual wires than to make a printed-circuit board. Conventional soldered wiring, however, is almost impossible to use with dense and complex circuits. Although several types of wiring systems have been developed specifically for IC systems, in 1982 wire wrap was the most practical for model railroad use. Wire wrap does require special tools and special terminals, but, if much dense wiring must be done, wire wrap is well worth the investment required. Wire wrap of the type described here is suitable only for light wires such as those needed to connect integrated circuits. This form of wire wrap is not suitable for leads run to panel controls and switch machines, and is particularly not suitable for wires carrying power to the locomotives.

The essentials of a good wire-wrap connection are shown in Fig. 11-13. The terminal must have sharp corners against which the wire can make a gas-tight seal. There must be at least six turns of hard wire tightly wrapped to assure sufficient pressure will be maintained against the corners of the terminal pin. The insulation must come directly to the pin, preferably wrapped one or two turns around the terminal, as shown in Fig. 11-13.

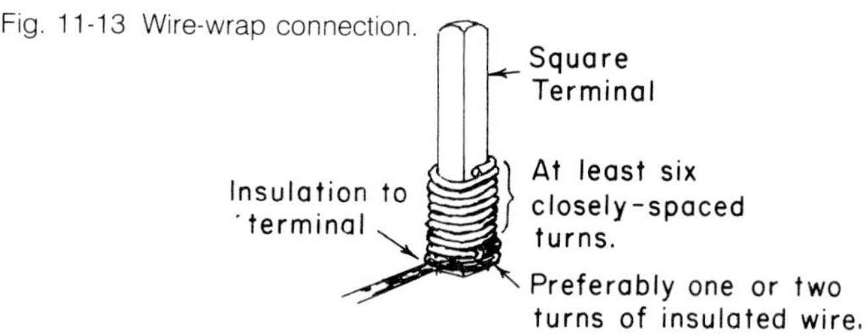

Fig. 11-13 Wire-wrap connection.

An essential for making a wire-wrap connection is a wrapping tool. Although hand wrapping tools are available and useful for making corrections and changes, a power-driven tool not only is more convenient but also is more likely to produce good connections. A power-driven tool is all but a necessity when many connections are to be made. Suitable power-operated tools were available in 1982 starting at $35.

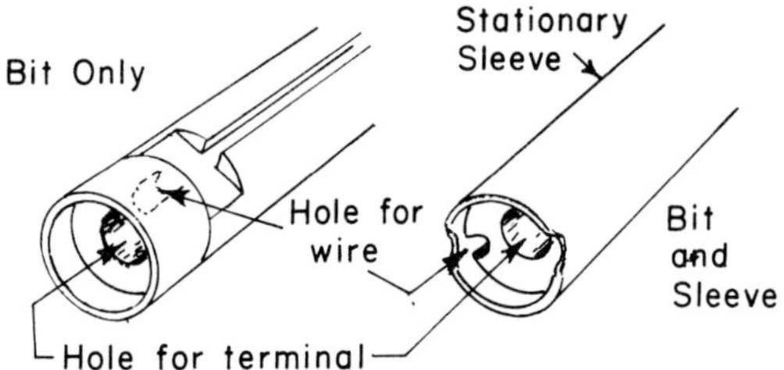

Fig. 11-14 Wire-wrap bits.

Two types of wrapping tools are available, the bit-only type shown on the left in Fig. 11-14 and the bit-and-sleeve type shown on the right. The bit-only in 1981 was used on the less-expensive hand and power-driven wrapping tools, the bit-and-sleeve on the more expensive hand and power tools. A separate bit is required for each size of wire but there is little if any reason to use other than 30-gauge wire.

At the center of the bit is an axial hole which permits the bit to be slipped down over the terminal which is to be wrapped. At the outside edge of the bit is a hole or slot into which the stripped end of the wire is inserted. In most bits this hole or slot is enlarged at its lower end to the depth of about 4mm to accept the wire insulation. About 25mm (1″) of wire is stripped and the stripped end inserted into the wire hole until the insulation bottoms in the enlarged portion of the hole. On the bit-only tools it is often possible to observe that the insulation has been inserted to the full depth of the enlarged hole, but very quickly it is learned to judge by feel.

Once the wire has been inserted in the bit, the wire is bent over the edge of the bit, or in the notch of the sleeve if there is a sleeve. Assure that the insulation remains bottomed in the bit while this bend is made. The loaded bit is then placed over the terminal as shown at A in Fig. 11-15. For bit-only tools it is necessary to have the wire lead directly away from the terminal pin and be held taut. Otherwise there is a strong tendency to wrap the wire around the outside of the bit. For a bit-and-sleeve tool, it is only necessary to assure that the wire is in the notch of the sleeve.

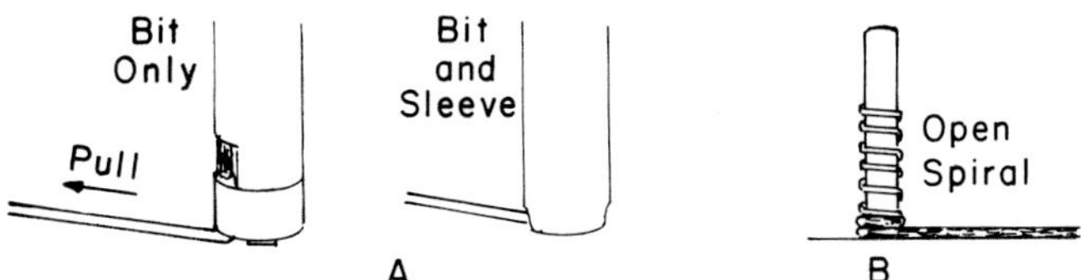

Fig. 11-15 Loaded bits and an improper wrap.

With the loaded bit in place, the bit is rotated a sufficient number of turns clockwise to assure that all of the stripped wire has been wrapped around the terminal. The bit must be permitted to rise as the wrap is made but it must not be withdrawn at a faster rate or an open spiral as shown at B in Fig. 11-15 will be made. If the bit is held down too firmly in an effort to avoid an open spiral, the wire will break. At least one power wire-wrap tool available in 1982 had a spring-loaded bit; the tool itself being held stationary during the wrapping, the bit rising against spring pressure. The author finds no particular advantage to such spring loading as it is easy to gain the skill necessary to permit the tool to back off under hand pressure.

As the tool is being removed after a wrap is made, it is vital that the wrap be inspected for the requirements shown in Fig. 11-13. If the wrap is not tight, if the insulation does not come right up to the terminal, or if there are not enough turns, immediately remove the wrap, strip a new end and rewrap. Never, never, attempt to rewrap the same stripped end! One great advantage of wire wrap is that a connection which looks good is good. This is in contrast to solder connections where a connection may appear excellent but be essentially open.

For short leads, such as between two pins on the same IC socket, it is convenient to strip both ends of a precut lead before making the first wrap. For longer leads most people prefer to make one wrap, measure against the terminal at the other end, cut, strip, and then make the second wrap. If two immediately adjacent pins are to be connected by a bottom wrap, it is convenient to use a bare length of wire bent into a hairpin. If the wire is fully loaded into the bit when the second connection is made, the action of the tool will pull the wire directly between the pins.

Fig. 11-16 Wrapping a string.

When four or more terminals are to be connected by a common lead, often called a *string,* it is important that the wires be added in levels as on the left in Fig. 11-16 rather than as a daisy chain as on the right. Using levels limits the number of leads which must be removed in the event a change is necessary. When doing the initial wiring, try to limit the wires to two levels even though most wire-wrap terminals will accept three, and some even four, levels. Restricting the initial wires to two levels reserves the extra space for later additions or corrections.

In most cases where wire wrap is used, the wires between the terminals will lie in a field of terminals and thus be protected mechanically. Consequently the usual reason for cabling wires for protection does not exist. Therefore wires generally are run directly from terminal to terminal (point-to-point wiring). As explained in Section 11.54, running leads directly rather than in cables is a requirement if high-frequencies are involved, as is almost always the case when ICs are used. Nevertheless all leads not connecting to sensitive circuits (such as timers and oscillators) should be diverted away from the locations of those devices.

Some professional wiremen prefer to make leads taut. It is easier, however, to allow some slack because length measurements are then not critical when a wire is stripped for its second connection. Furthermore, some slack makes it easier to trace a lead later as the wire then can be moved slightly.

Fig. 11-17 Unwrapping tool.

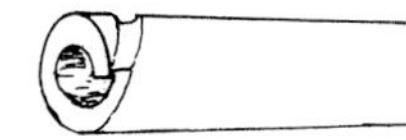

When changes or corrections must be made, an unwrapping tool is almost a necessity. A simple hand tool is adequate for model-railroad use. A shown in Fig. 11-17, unwrapping tools have an axial hole which fits over the terminal and a sharp point to pick up the end of the wrap. When the tool is turned, the wrap is transferred to the outside of the tool. The tool shown is for clockwise wraps, the conventional direction. When starting to unwrap, do not press the tool down on the wrap; this often forces the end of the wire down to where it cannot be picked up by the point.

A wrap can be removed by manipulation of the insulated wire extending from the bottom of the wrap. This is slower than using an unwrapping tool and may be quite difficult if the wrap to be removed is buried under many other wires. When removing only the top wrap of two or more, if possible, it is advisable to remove some or all of the top wrap by manipulation of the wire to avoid the possibility of the unwrapping tool disturbing the next lower wrap.

11.46 Wire Nuts

Wire nuts are a solderless means of connecting two or three wires together. Since they have an insulated jacket, they eliminate the need for tape as is required for a soldered connection. Wire nuts are frequently used for 110V wiring. As shown in Fig. 11-18 the wires are stripped, the nut slipped on and twisted until the insulation

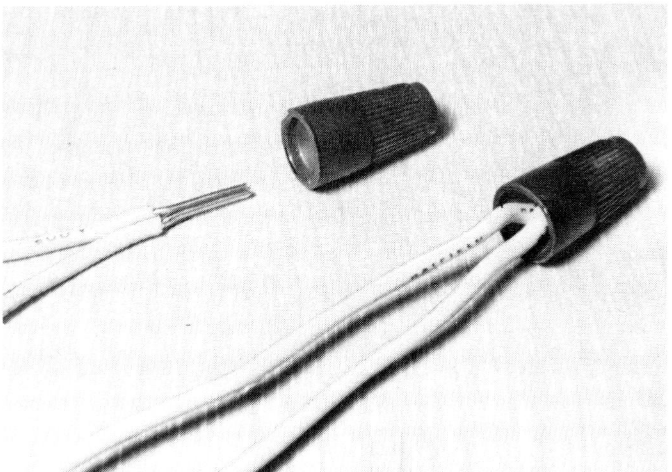

Fig. 11-18 Wire nuts.

is brought up to the nut. The wires may be pretwisted. Nuts are available in various sizes to fit different wire sizes. Soldering rather than wire nuts is recommended for connecting stranded to solid wire or for connecting two wires of widely different sizes.

11.47 Other Connecting Methods

Soldering, screw terminals, and wire nuts are the most useful connections but others exist. Conducting epoxy is available for use where the heat of soldering is undesirable. It is applied like any other epoxy. Conducting paints or inks are useful for low currents, one application in model railroading was to code the receiver in a locomotive to a specific command-control channel. Commercial processes such as welding, reflow and wave soldering require special equipment.

11.5 RUNNING LEADS

11.51 General

The right size and good connections are vital but the way the wires are run is important for reliability and ease of maintenance and changes. Wires run by any convenient method of the moment for conventional wiring will result in a rat's nest easily damaged and difficult to figure out. The cardinal signs of good wiring are neatness and simplicity.

11.52 Surface Wiring

Whenever conventional wiring is done with individual wires (in contrast to cables) the wires should run along the surface of the panel, chassis, or any available support as shown in Fig. 11-19. This serves two purposes. The wires are in the most protected position possible and the terminals and devices are not covered by a cobweb of wires which would make them inaccessible. Often surface wiring is combined with cables, the surface wiring providing the local connections (for example between the controls on a panel) and the cables making the external connections. Solid wire is far more satisfactory than stranded for surface wiring.

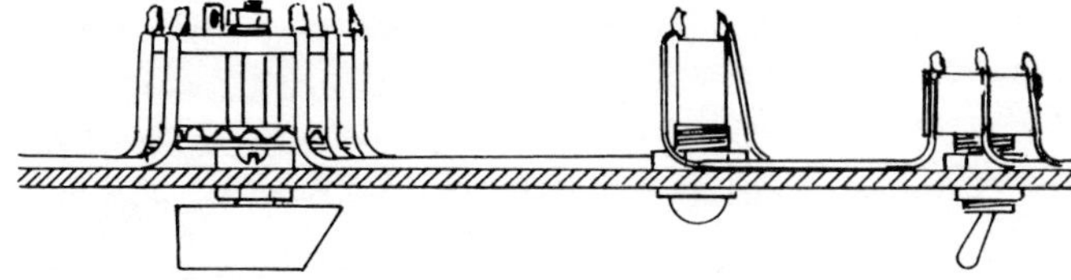

Fig. 11-19 Surface wiring.

11.53 Cabling, Low-Frequency Wiring

Cabling is the grouping of wires going generally in the same direction. The wires mutually support each other against damage and the underside of the railroad or panel is not blocked by a maze of individual leads. Fig. 11-20 graphically illustrates the difference between cables and leads run individually.

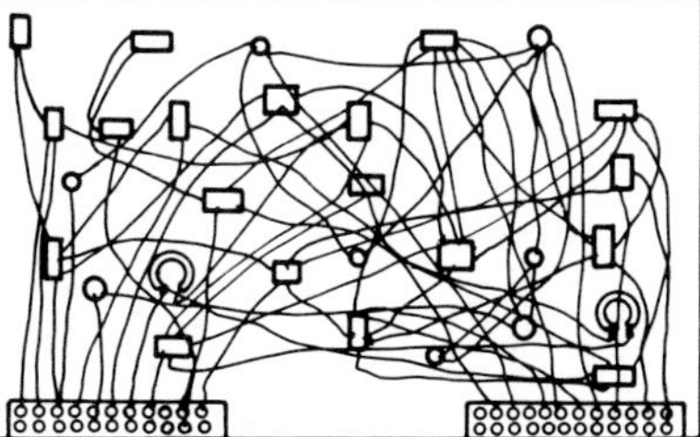

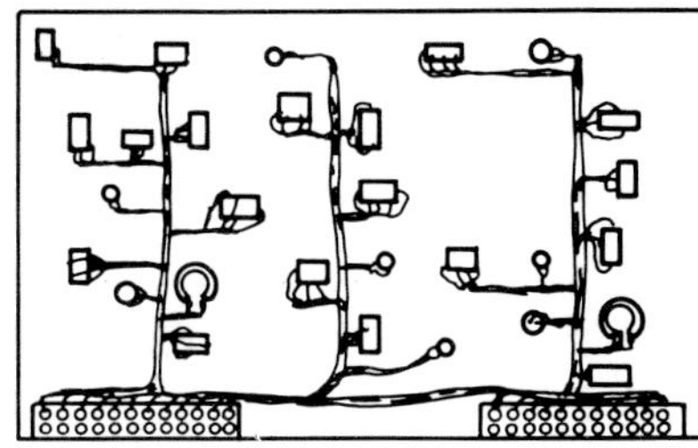

Fig. 11-20 Cabling improves panel wiring.

As can be seen in the figure, a cable can have branches to bring the wires close to their connecting point before they must leave the cable. If more than one wire goes to the same piece of apparatus, they should be formed into a small branch cable.

There are many ways of forming cables. One excellent method for long runs is bridle rings. A bridle ring is like a screw eye but with an opening so a wire can be placed in the ring without pulling it through. Bridle rings are commercially available but can be made from heavy wire such as that of wire coat hangers. Fig. 11-21 shows an under-benchwork cable formed in bridle rings.

Fig. 11-21 Cable in bridle rings.

Any method which allows new wires to be added without dragging them through a series of holes is a satisfactory way of forming cables for long runs. Straps which hook over screws driven into the benchwork and wiring troughs built into the benchwork are methods which have given good service. On small layouts, since most of the wires can be run in initially, it is often satisfactory to lay the wires along the route of the cable then drive staples over the wires to contain them. Fig. 11-22 is the underside of a portable TT layout built by the Model Railroad Club of the Bell Telephone Laboratories in 1950 and cabled in this manner. The staples are not driven down tightly thus permitting the addition of new wires. This layout, con-

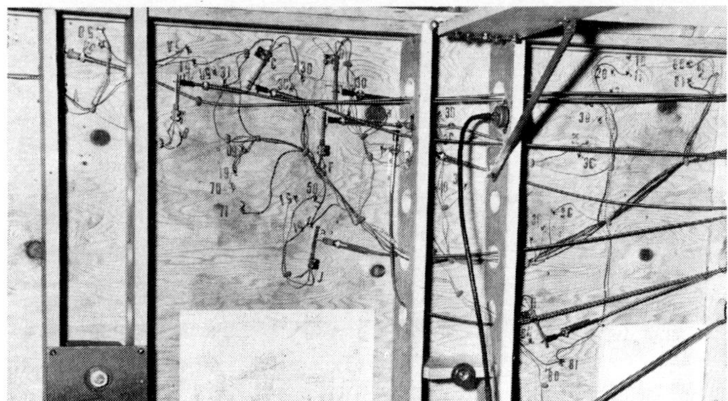

Fig. 11-22 Cable in staples.

verted to N, was still in service in 1981.

When the wires must be contained more closely than is possible using bridle rings or similar devices, as on the back of panels, lacing is a good solution. To make this type of cable, the wires are first run following the path of the proposed cable. An occasional twist of wire can hold the cable together at key points until the lacing is completed. Lacing is started at one end of the cable using a cord approximately three times as long as the cable. Special lacing cord is available but any type of strong cord will do. The steps in lacing are shown in Fig. 11-23. Note that, in making the individual loops around the cable, the running end of the cord comes out under the loop, not over it. Keep the wires well packed and draw up each loop tightly. A loop should be placed at every point where a wire leaves the cable. The cord for a branch cable is attached first to the main cable.

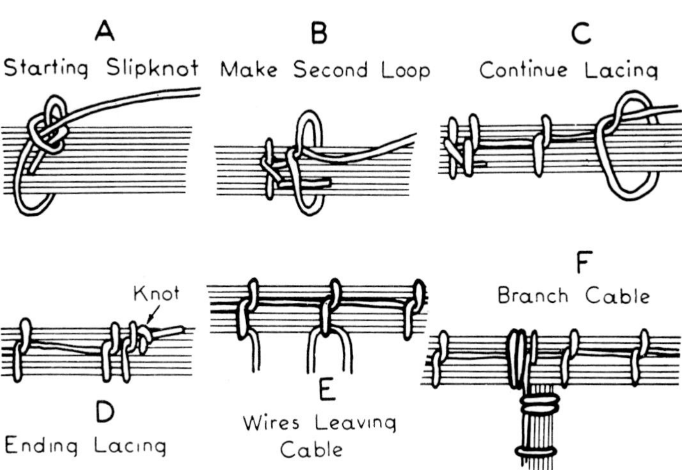

Fig. 11-23 Lacing a cable.

Commercial plastic straps are made which can be placed around a cable and pulled tight as a substitute for the lacing cord.

Fig. 11-24 shows the back of a control panel wired with laced cable by Mike Jensen. Another use of laced cable is shown in Fig. 11-39, where a short cable is used to permit bench wiring of a switch machine to a terminal strip.

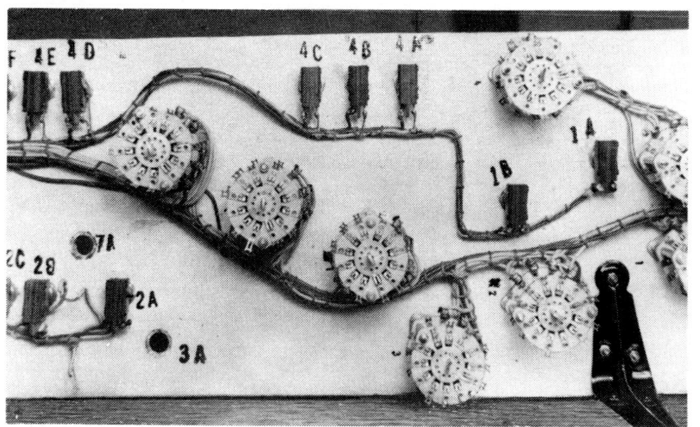

Fig. 11-24 Laced cable on panel.

Cable to a hinged panel should permit movement by twisting rather than by bending. The cable therefore should run parallel to the hinge pins for a distance of 0.6m. (2 feet) or more, as shown in Fig. 11-25. If necessary, the cable can be made as a hairpin to gain additional length. An example can be seen in Fig. 12-2.

When many small-size wires are run a considerable distance (for example to switch machines or for telephone use) commercial cable is convenient. Such cable is often available at reasonable prices from suppliers of salvaged electrical materials, particularly from those specializing in used telephone equipment.

11.54 Wiring for High-Frequency Signals

The advent of integrated circuits introduced model railroading to the need for wiring capable of transmitting reliably, without cross coupling signals with frequency components ranging into the many megahertz. Cables, such as those shown in Section 11.53, while desirable for conventional wiring, are impossible for use with high-

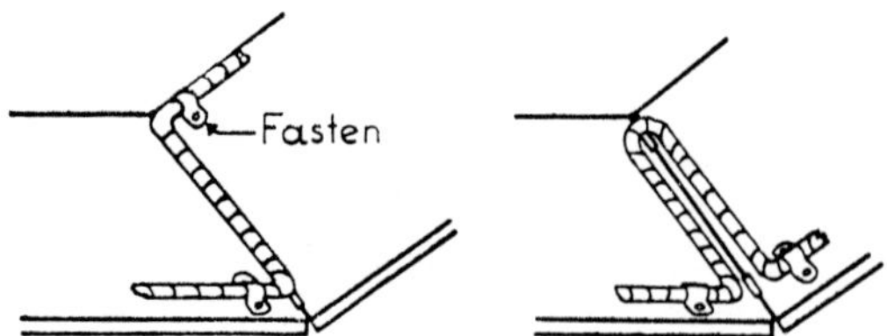

Fig. 11-25 Cable to hinged panel.

frequency signals. The capacitive and inductive coupling between adjacent wires is so great that a signal on one wire will appear as an electrical noise of major proportions on all nearby wires.

The two major forms of cross coupling which must be avoided are shown in Fig. 11-26. At the left is a capacitor formed by two leads running parallel. The capacitance between the two wires is small, but when the signal on one wire changes state rapidly, as on the top wire, a voltage spike of significant amplitude appears on the other wire.

At the right of Fig. 11-26 inductive coupling is illustrated between two loops of wire acting as the primary and secondary of an air-core transformer. A rapid change in the current through one wire will cause a significant noise spike on the other wire.

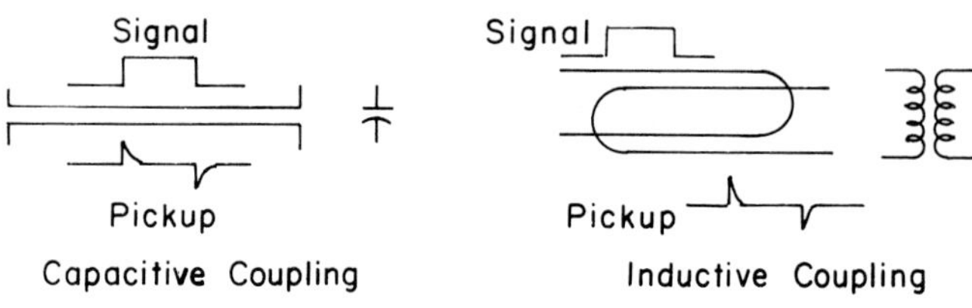

Fig. 11-26 Cross coupling of circuits.

The cross coupling shown in Fig. 11-26 also exists in our conventional circuits but, at the low frequencies involved (60, 120hz), the cross-coupled signals are inconsequential. Even when high frequencies are generated incidentally, say by closing a switch, the devices concerned, such as motors, are so slow in response that short-duration noise pulses are unnoticeable. This is not so with many integrated circuits. If a noise signal is great enough, the circuit will respond to it just as if it were an intended signal.

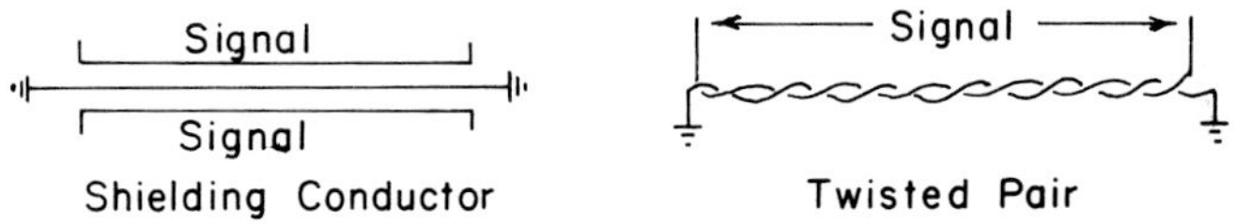

Fig. 11-27 Reducing cross coupling.

Cross coupling can be reduced by running the return path for the signal current immediately adjacent to the signal line. When distances are short (up to 1m), the return path is usually ground. Particularly for printed circuits, it is often satisfactory to decouple two signal lines by running a grounded line between them as shown at the left in Fig. 11-27. Even better is to use a twisted pair as shown at the right in the figure.

For circuits with many signal paths, it is all but impossible to run a separate parallel or twisted-pair ground next to every signal lead. It is far more common to use a ground plane, two forms being shown in Fig. 11-28. On the left a solid sheet of copper, such as the copper foil on a printed-circuit board, is the ground plane. The return currents flowing in this ground plane will be parallel to the separate signal wires above the plane or, for two-sided boards, parallel to the conductors on the opposite side of the board.

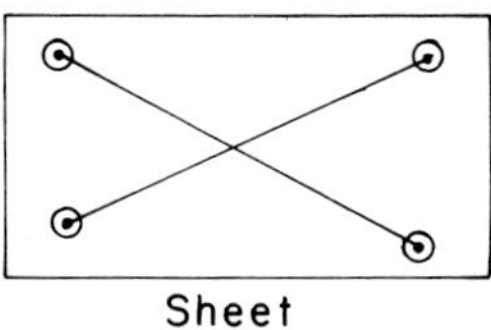

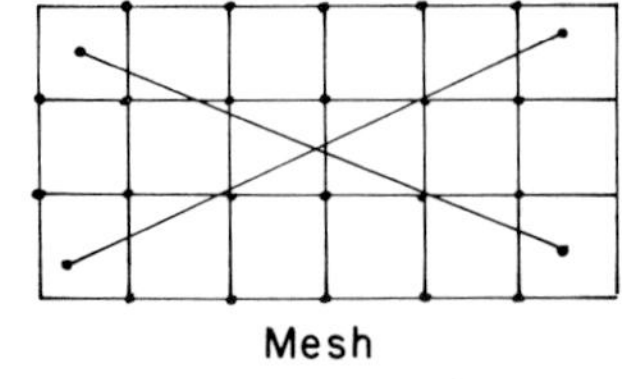

Fig. 11-28 Ground planes.

A ground plane effective with most ICs can be made of wires soldered together to form a mesh as shown at the right of Fig. 11-28 (see also Fig. 11-11). Regardless of the type of ground plane, it is necessary to couple the DC power leads at frequent intervals to the ground plane by decoupling capacitors (.01 to .07uf are usually satisfactory). These capacitors supply the surges of current required when circuits switch. One capacitor about every five IC packages plus one at each critical circuit (such as a timer) usually are sufficient.

When printed wiring is used for anything but a simple circuit, it is often difficult to find a reasonable path from one location on the board to another location, unless there are more than two layers of copper. Multilayer boards, unfortunately, are unlikely to be economically viable in model railroading. A solution is to run a twisted pair line between the points involved, as shown in Fig. 11-29. One side of this twisted pair is grounded at both ends.

The wiring techniques described in this Section are suitable for conductor lengths up to about 1m (3'). To transmit high-frequency signals beyond that distance it is necessary to use transmission-line techniques as described in Section 24.93.

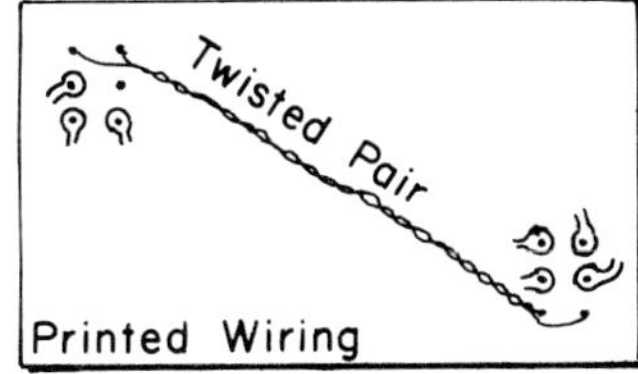

Fig. 11-29 Twisted pair added to printed wiring.

11.6 PRINTED WIRING

The term "printed wiring" started in the thirties with the use of conductive inks which were printed to form circuits but has become the generic term for all types of wiring fixed to flat surfaces regardless of the means by which the wiring is produced. For use by model railroaders only one form of printed wiring was of importance in 1981, laminated copper circuit boards. As shown in Fig. 11-30 a thin copper sheet is attached to one or both sides of an insulator, stiff as fiber or epoxy-glass or flexible as Kapton. Single-sided boards generally are sufficient for all model railroad applications except when a ground plane is needed.

To a model railroader the important specifications for a wiring board are the thickness of the copper, the thickness of the board, and the material of the board. Two weights of copper were generally available, one ounce (.033mm, .0013", thick) and two ounce (.069mm, .0027"). Normally two ounce should be selected.

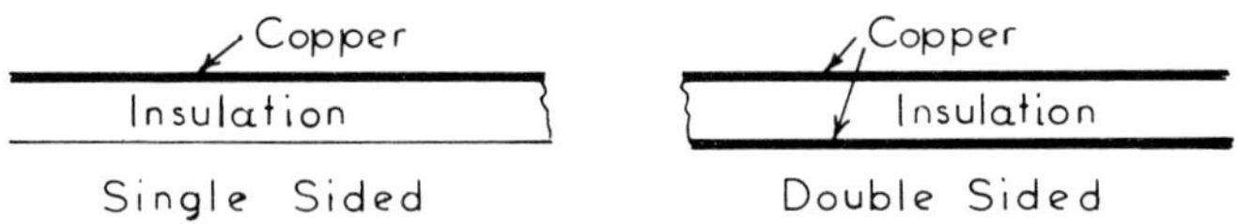

Fig. 11-30 Copper laminate circuit board.

If used on a model, scale dimensions will set board thickness but otherwise 1/16" (1.6mm) should be the thinnest. Thicker would be better as a stiff board reduces the possibility of damage to the conductors. Although epoxy-glass is a better material than fiber, it tends to dull tools.

Printed wiring offers many advantages to manufacturers which can be summed up as increased reliability and decreased costs. The commercial cab-control system shown in Fig. 5, Chapter 9 uses a printed wiring circuit not only as a low-cost way of manufacturing a complex circuit but also to make low-cost slide switches. To the individual modeler printed wiring will save time and errors if there are many replications of a single circuit (for example a block-signal system). If the circuit is complex, a transistor throttle for example, use of a printed circuit will contribute to neatness and uniformity, even if not enough samples are required for an economic or time saving. On a model a printed circuit might be the best solution to carry power through the floor to motors, lamps, etc. even if only one was required.

To create a circuit, the copper foil is separated into conductors by removing unwanted copper by etching (usually) or mechanically. A printed circuit can be designed by laying out the conductors as shown on the left in Fig. 11-31 or by laying out narrow strips of insulation as on the right. Although the latter is not as obvious, it is the better method for conventional wiring as it leaves more copper. In any case, a large area of copper, called a pad, must be left at any point a soldered connection is to be made to assure that the copper does not delaminate (peel) when heat is applied. In Fig. 11-31 contacts have been laid out along the bottom edge so that the circuit built on this board will be a complete unit ready to be plugged into a commercial jack called an "edge connector."

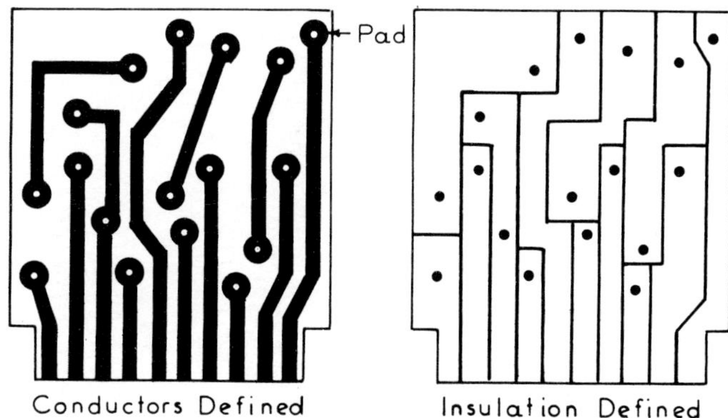

Fig. 11-31 Laying out conductors.

It is entirely feasible for a model railroader to design and etch printed circuits, but a description of the complete process is beyond the space limitations of this book. Complete information is available from Kodak and other concerns which make the necessary products. Kits for the purpose have been available from mail-order electronic parts supply houses. Also, for simple circuits such as the wiring on a car floor, the copper can be cut away using razor saws, sharp knives, or chisels. The remainder of this Section assumes the etching will be done by a commercial house.

Model railroad circuits are often simple and it normally would be possible to lay them out full size but better results are obtained by making the original, called the "art master" at a larger scale, at least 2:1 but there seems little advantage of more than 4:1. Always be as generous as is possible with the width of conductors and the size of soldering pads. If possible no conductor should be less than 1.6mm (1/16") wide and conductors carrying locomotive power should be at least 3.2mm (1/8") wide. The space between conductors should be at least 1.6mm (1/16") wide. These dimensions are suggested for reasons of reliability. 1980 commercial practice allowed conductors and spaces to be as narrow as .25mm (.01").

Before making an art master for use by a commercial etching house, check with the firm you are going to use for the process they find most economical. Art masters can be made by applying (as indicated at the left in Fig. 11-32) a black opaque tape made for the purpose by Brady (and others) to tracing paper or cloth although specially prepared Mylar sheets are better as they have greater dimensional stability. On the right, another method using a Mylar sheet laminated to a thin red film is shown. Appropriate lines are cut in the red film and the unwanted portion is stripped away. More accurate lines can be made this way as compared with tape. One supplier of such material is Keuffel and Esser.

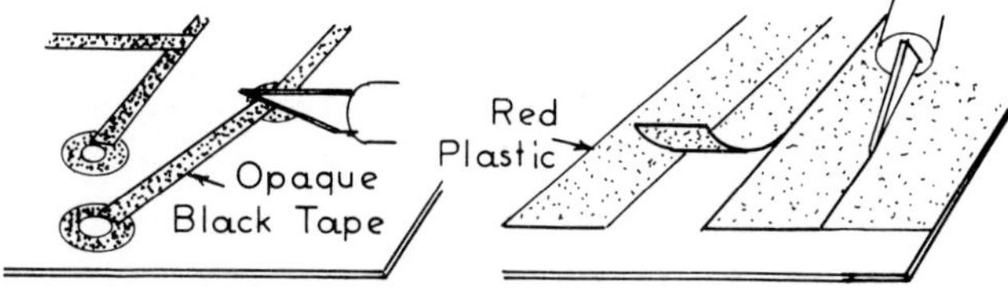

Fig. 11-32 Making art masters.

It is possible to make etched circuits by taping the conductor pattern directly on the copper. This is a one-at-a-time process and limited to simple circuits but it may save money if only one or two have to be made.

It is imperative that the art master be accurate. Making corrections on printed circuits, although it can be done, eliminates the advantages. A good way of checking for accuracy is to mount the devices on a board in the same relationship as they will be on the printed circuit, connect them using wires following the exact paths as on the art master, then test the circuit for proper operation.

The most common practice in connecting components such as

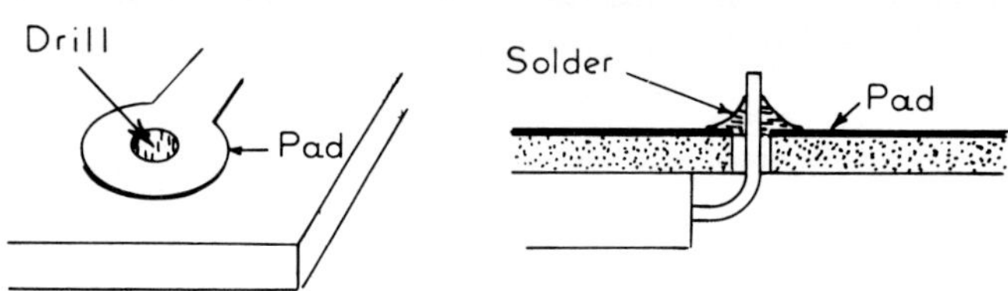

Fig. 11-33 Soldering to printed wiring.

resistors, transistors etc. to a circuit board is to drill holes at the center of the soldering pads as shown in Fig. 11-33, then insert the component leads into the holes from the opposite side of the board from the pads. Finally a fillet of solder is run in to connect the pad and the lead. Unless the circuit board was prepared using solder or gold plate as an etch resist, tin the soldering pads before inserting the leads to assure reliable connections. It is important not to overheat the pads to minimize the risk of delamination. If the lead is thick (as for a 2-watt resistor) apply the soldering iron to the lead first and run the solder from the lead to the pad. Apply only enough heat to the pad to assure that the solder wets all the way around the lead.

Commercial solder removers are available under names similar to solder gobbler which generate a sudden inrush of air at a nozzle. By the use of such a device the molten solder can be pulled up from a solder pad permitting the component to be removed easily. If plans call for several circuit boards, a solder remover is a good investment. Wick-like materials are also available which will remove molten solder.

11.7 TERMINALS

11.71 General

Wiring should always be from terminal to terminal. If two wires are to be connected, this connection should be made at a terminal. The use of terminals makes it possible to identify all wires easily and locate all connecting points. If connections are made at some ill-defined point by teeing two wires together, it may not be known that such a connection exists when it comes time to shoot trouble. An exception is the ground bus. Connecting to the bus at the nearest possible point reduces clutter, such connections are expected and will not be overlooked.

Many devices have terminals which are suitable wiring points but others have terminals which are mechanically weak or have no terminals at all. In the latter two cases external individual terminals or terminal strips should be provided. Separate terminal strips not part of devices have many uses including simplifying the installation and trouble shooting, a means of identification, a support to take strain, and a point to change from one type of wire to another.

11.72 Connection to Rail

For the connection to a rail a single terminal such as in Fig. 11-34 is recommended. It should be physically strong and well attached to take any pull on the feeder wire without transmitting pull to the rail. Because of its short length, the wire from the terminal to the rail can be of smaller size than the main feeder although it must always be large enough to avoid fire hazard in the event of a short circuit. No.

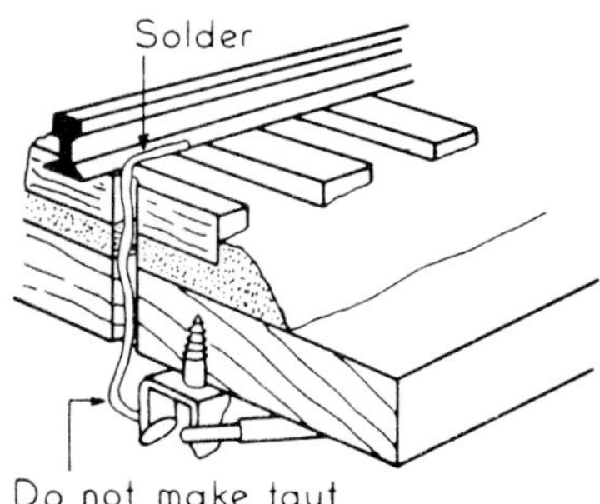

Fig. 11-34 Connection to rail.

18 is satisfactory for HO. Since the wire is totally enclosed, it may be bare for a bare wire is easier to slip down a small hole. To avoid strains due to the vibration of the track, do not make this wire taut. Very important: tin the rail before attempting to solder the feeder to it to assure that the solder completely fills in the space between the rail and the wire. For better appearance, the holes may be drilled directly under the final position of the rail before it is laid. These feeders are then inserted in the holes as the rail is laid.

Because rail is not made to be a soldering terminal, precautions should be taken to get a good connection. The rail should be brightened with a file or scraping tool at the point of connection and then should be well tinned. The tinned feeder wire then should be laid snugly against the rail and held firmly so that it will not move as the solder cools. With a small soldering iron, apply the heat mainly to the rail as it is much larger than the wire. Be sure that both the wire and the rail are well wet by the solder before removing the iron. Observe that no movement of the wire takes place while the solder is cooling. If there is any doubt, remelt the solder. Never use a large soldering iron or soldering gun to solder to rail. The mass of such tools prevents a sensitive touch on the rail thus greatly increasing the chance of kinking a rail. Hot rail is considerably weaker than rail at room temperature.

It is good practice to make a connection similar to Fig. 11-34 for every piece of rail on the layout thus no dependance is placed on rail joiners to carry the current. Even the best rail joiners will oxidize in time and add resistance to the circuit. If separate connections are not made to each piece of rail, bond the rail joints by bent wire by either method shown in Fig. 11-35. The wire is bent so that any movement, including vibration of the rail, will not place excess strain on the solder joint. For the utmost in reliability, The Model Railroad Club specifies that there will be an individual feeder to every piece of rail. As extra precaution for inaccessible track as in tunnels, they specify that all rail joints in such locations will be bonded (except at gaps).

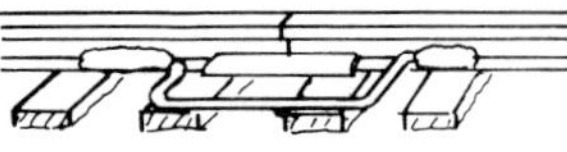

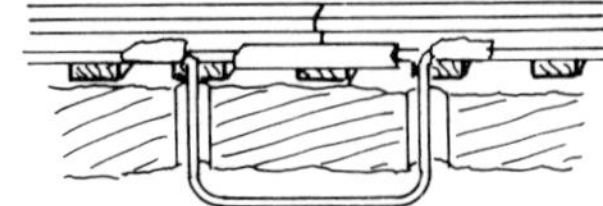

Fig. 11-35 Bonding rail joints.

The rail designations should be marked beside each terminal before any wiring is done. Regardless of how well the layout is known, it is difficult to recognize terminals by their position when looking up from under the benchwork. Once they have been designated, it is a simple matter to connect like-designated terminals as shown in Fig. 11-36. In that figure the common-rail terminals are connected directly to ground but, as explained in Chapter 15, there are advantages in sectionalizing the common rail into signal blocks which may not correspond to the sections of the control rail. In such cases the terminals for the common rail would be connected in groups just as are those from the control rail.

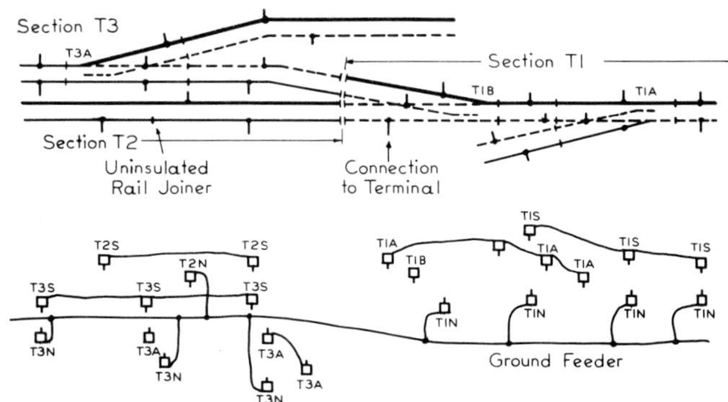

Fig. 11-36 Wiring terminals for rails.

11.73 Terminal Strips

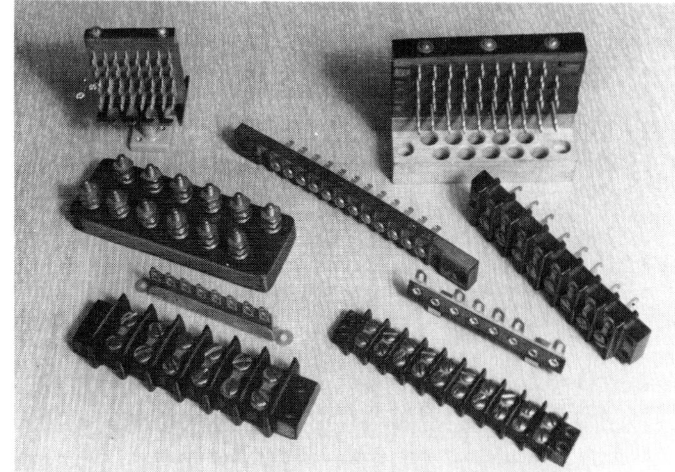

Fig. 11-37 Terminal strips.

When two or more terminals are mounted together the combination is called a terminal strip. Some of the various arrangements are shown in Fig. 11-37. The two at the bottom are called barrier-type strips and are the most useful type for model railroads. The screw terminals permit leads to be opened readily for tracing short circuits or for making changes and the barriers prevent the ends of the wires from shorting against the adjacent terminal The solder-type strips permit more connections in the same space but experience has shown that a heavy concentration of leads in a small area is not generally desirable for model railroads.

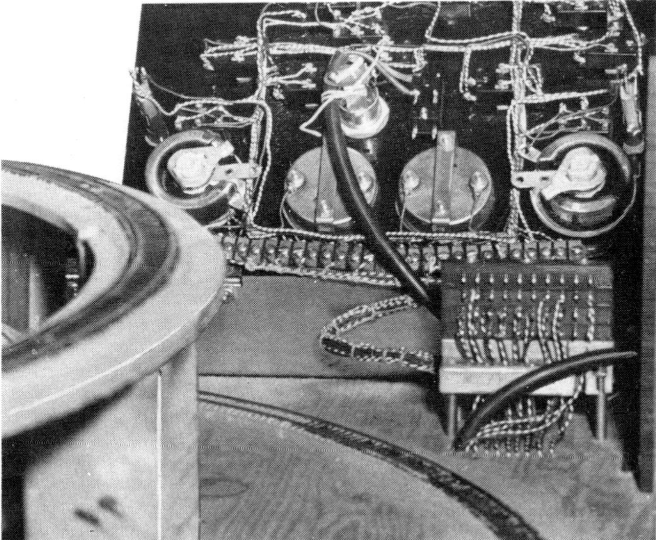

Fig. 11-38 Terminal strips on panel.

Among the more important uses of terminal strips is where leads enter or leave a unit such as a control panel. Terminal strips at such locations permit the unit to be built and tested at a bench then installed. They also permit ready identification for the large number of leads at such points. Fig. 11-38 shows two different types of terminal strips used to connect to the panel of the TT portable layout built by the Bell Laboratories Model Railroad Club in 1950.

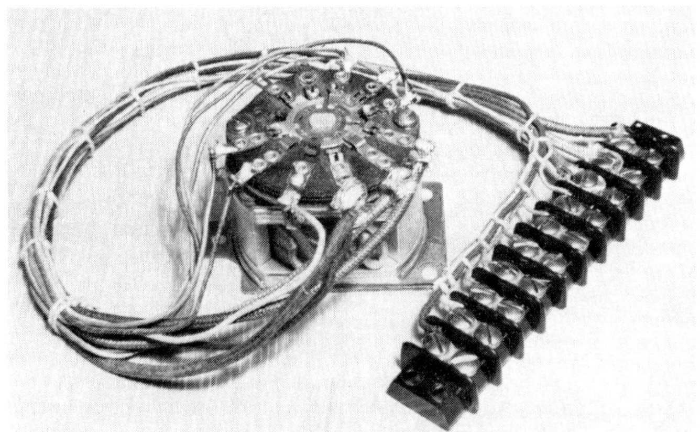

Fig. 11-39 Terminal strip for switch machine.

Terminal strips may be used to make difficult connections more accessible. Switch machines, for example, may be mounted at hard-to-reach positions and, unless all machines are identical, the connections may be different from machine to machine. By bench-wiring switch machines to a terminal strip with a short cable as shown in Fig. 11-39 not only can the strip be mounted at a convenient place for under-benchwork wiring regardless of the location of the machine but also the location of leads can be standardized on the terminal strips thus simplifying installation and maintenance.

11.8 IDENTIFYING LEADS

11.81 General

For trouble shooting or for making changes and additions, it is imperative that there be a means of identifying a particular wire. This involves designating the lead (see Section 8.6) and associating that designation with the physical location of the lead.

11.82 Tags

For small layouts or ones with simple wiring, tagging each lead may be satisfactory. The tags may be anything which can be attached to the wires but consideration should be given to the problems which arise if many tags are in a restricted area. One tag should be placed at each end of every wire where confusion may exist. The information on the tag must contain as a minimum the designation of the lead but might also give the other termination point.

A particularly neat form of wire tags are the adhesive wire markers such as made by the W.H. Brady Co. and available from many electronic parts mail-order houses. Fig. 11-40 shows how such wire markers are applied. They are available in letters and colors as well as numbers.

Fig. 11-40 Self-sticking wire markers.

The great disadvantages of tags is that, if more than a few leads must be tagged at any one point, looking for a specific wire becomes cumbersome and the likelihood of a tag being pulled off increases.

11.83 Identification by Terminals

Identification by terminals permits the exact location of a particular wire without regard to the other leads present. When possible the lead identification should be marked directly at the terminal as indicated in Fig. 11-36. Placing a piece of white card stock under a barrier strip before it is fastened down provides an excellent surface on which to note designations for each terminal. However if a standard arrangement of terminals exists, as is the case for the terminal strip of the switch machine in Fig. 11-39 there need be no designation markings at the strips as all such strips will be the same.

In all cases the terminals should be shown on the circuit schematic, their symbol being a small circle as indicated in Fig. 11-41. Both the designation of the terminal strip itself should be shown, for example in Fig. 11-41 there are two strips, TSA and TS1, and the number of the terminal. See also Section 21.5.

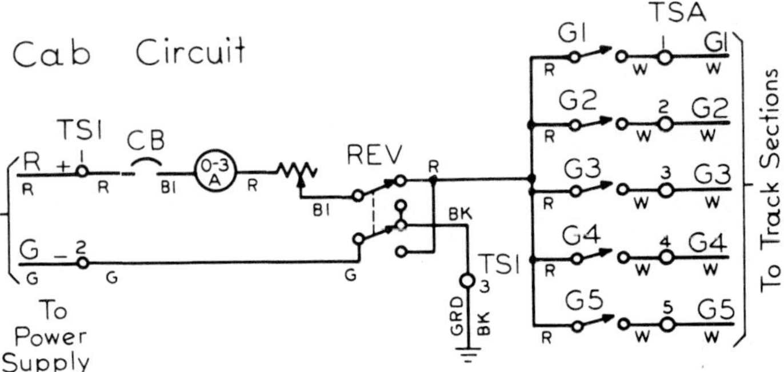

Fig. 11-41 Terminals designated on schematic.

The superb HO Virginian & Ohio Railroad of W. Allen McClelland is one of the best looking model railroads in the country. Extra thought and care in designing the electrical part of the pike also makes it one of the best operating layouts. The V&O is truly a real railroad, painstakingly reproduced in miniature.

Integrated circuit packages typically have their terminals (often called pins) on 2.5mm (.1″) centers. This is far too close to use any form of lead identification other than the terminal number. A detailed examination of pin numbers and functional designations for these circuits is given in Chapter 24. In general, integrated circuits are wired by the point-to-point method shown in Fig. 11-28. Thus identification by pin number is sufficient since the leads, not being cabled, can be traced individually. Nevertheless, it is desirable to follow a logical color code by classes of leads. The code used at The Model Railroad Club is as follows: ground = black; 5V = red; other voltages = yellow; clock = white; addresses = blue. All other leads are green.

12 CONTROL PANELS

12.1 GENERAL

Control panels mount the controls and indicators needed to operate model railroads. Proper design will greatly facilitate the ease of operation as well as contribute to reliability. For best results, each panel should be kept as simple and as logical as is possible. For ease in maintenance and in trouble shooting, all electrical devices should be firmly fixed to the panel and the wiring on the rear kept neat.

12.2 LOCATION

The location of a panel will depend upon its purpose. The main power panel, if provided, can be placed almost anywhere as long as it is accessible. A clear view of the railroad is unimportant from this panel. Panels for cabs, on the other hand, must be placed so the enginemen have the best possible view of their trains at all times. Towers should be near the track they control not only for visibility but also to permit the operator to give manual assistance when required. On small layouts with combined functions on the panels, these conflicting requirements must be compromised. Fortunately, as the layout gets smaller, the problems of accessibility and of visibility become less.

12.3 MATERIAL

There are many materials in sheet form suitable for panels. A list of the more popular materials and their relative merits follows.

Plywood: Inexpensive and readily available. Can be worked with ordinary tools but it is difficult to make holes without some splintering. Its grain presents a problem in finishing. Proper thickness, 6mm (1/4″).

Prestwood: Inexpensive, readily available and can be worked with ordinary tools. Does not splinter. It has a tendency to compress under mounting nuts, letting switches and other devices become loose in time. The hard-finish type (tempered) should be used. Even better are those types coated with a hard plastic finish for they are easy to clean and present an excellent appearance. Proper thickness, 3mm (1/8″).

Hard Rubber or Black Fiber: On the expensive side but excellent. Can be worked with ordinary tools. No finish required. Proper thickness, 3mm (1/8″) or 6mm (1/4″).

Aluminum: On the expensive side and more difficult to work than the materials listed above. Very durable but does not present a good appearance. Has the advantage that it can electrically ground all apparatus mounted on panel thus minimizing the possibility of shocks. Proper thickness, 3mm, (1/8″).

12.4 MOUNTING

Panels may be mounted at any angle from the vertical to the horizontal depending on location and purpose. Vertical panels are especially suited to power racks mounted under the benchwork as such panels are not often used during operation. Fig. 12-1 is a photograph of such a panel used at the summit-New Providence HO RR Club, 1950-1972. The meters are set at a slight angle so they can be read more easily from a standing position. This panel is made of aluminum.

A vertical panel is not convenient as an operating panel as it cannot be seen easily when the operator is in position to view the layout. Panels to be operated while sitting or standing should be either horizontal or slanted. For the same amount of floor space, a slanted panel offers more panel area and thus is generally preferred to a horizontal one. Slanted or horizontal panels should always be built on supports firm enough to sustain the weight of a person. It is better to build strongly once than lightly twice.

All panels should have some means of easy access to their rear for repairs or changes. The power panel of Fig. 12-1 is mounted on an open rack which rolls out from under the benchwork when desired. The heavy flexible cables connecting terminal strips mounted on the rack to terminal strips on the benchwork can be seen at the left in Fig. 12-1. A rear view of this rack can be seen in Fig. 19, Chapter 4.

More generally panels are hinged at one edge, examples being the cabs of the Summit-New Providence HO RR Club shown in Fig.

12-2. These panels were of aluminum and, in 1972 had been in heavy service for over 20 years. Note the strut which locks to hold the panel open. It can be released to let the panel swing out further. Experience has shown that panels should be able to swing to the horizontal position when open.

Fig. 12-1 Under benchwork power panel.

When a panel is hinged, it is vital that the wiring to it be installed so the panel can be opened and closed without damage to the wires. This is best accomplished by a cable running parallel to the hinge pins as explained in Section 11.53. Such a cable can be seen in Fig. 12-2.

Modern electronic devices are considerably more reliable than the older devices they have replaced; an LED compared to a lamp is a good example. As of 1982 there has been insufficient experience with panels with modern devices, and with reliable switches such as the rotary type, to state with certainty, but it seems likely that such a panel could be mounted without the great regard for access to its rear that was required before. The cab panel shown in Fig. 12-3 is an example of an effort to take advantage of the greater reliability of modern electronics by mounting the panel with screws with the expectation that the screws would be removed and the panel turned over for access to the wiring side if such access ever becomes required. Since the information carried by the 30-pair cable is multiplexed, this cable continues on to serve up to a total of eight cabs.

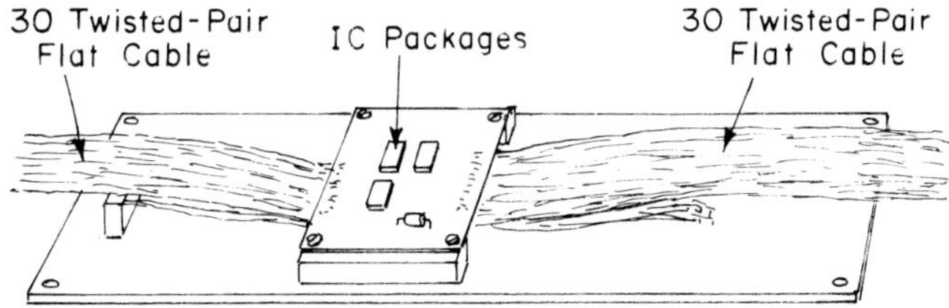

Fig. 12-3 Cab panel with time-division multiplex.

Fig. 12-2 Panels for cabs.

12.5 FINISHES

The finish on the surface of a panel not only affects the appearance but also can serve to make the diagrams stand out. Regardless of color, hard, smooth finishes of uniform color appear the best. Hard rubber, black fiber, and plastic-covered hard boards have an excellent finish as received. Plywood has a grain which services to conceal as well as to collect dirt. Commercial fillers for plywood, such as Firzite, are manufactured which kill the grain. They should be used before painting. Prestwood has a mottled appearance which serves to conceal complicated diagrams but is satisfactory for simple diagrams as can be seen on the tower panel in Fig. 12-4. Prestwood takes paint well but the plastic-covered types of prestwood are recommended as they are smooth and hard, thus much easier to clean than paint. Fig. 9, Chapter 2 shows a panel made of white plastic-coated prestwood, specifically Marlite.

Color is a matter of opinion but of all the colors the author has seen on panels, white seems to be the best, although black is the most common.

Fig. 12-4 Panel for tower.

12.6 ARRANGEMENT OF PANEL

The apparatus mounted on a panel should always be arranged so that its function is clear without reference to memory or written record. The power panel of Fig. 12-1 is an example. The meters at the top indicate the voltage and grouped under each set of meters are the circuit breakers and the on-off switches for that particular power source.

For operating panels there is no good substitute to placing the controls and indicators directly on the track diagram as shown in Fig. 12-4 for a tower. If the diagram is made so all parts are readily identifiable, the association of the controls to track switches and sections is obvious. For the diagrams, the pressure-sensitive tapes such as those sold for Christmas wrappings, are excellent. The tapes from tape labelers are also excellent and have the advantage that labels can be placed directly on the diagram lines. Color is important on the diagram. It can be used to distinguish the ends of the sections, also to associate sections, perhaps even parts of the layout. X Sections (see Section 8.7) should have a distinctive marking; the combined colors of the sections to which it connects is a possibility.

If controls must be mounted off the diagram, an example being the switch levers shown in Fig. 4, Chapter 9, some method must be adopted to associate a control with a specific point on the track diagram. This can be done with color or, as shown in Fig. 12-5 by labels or lines.

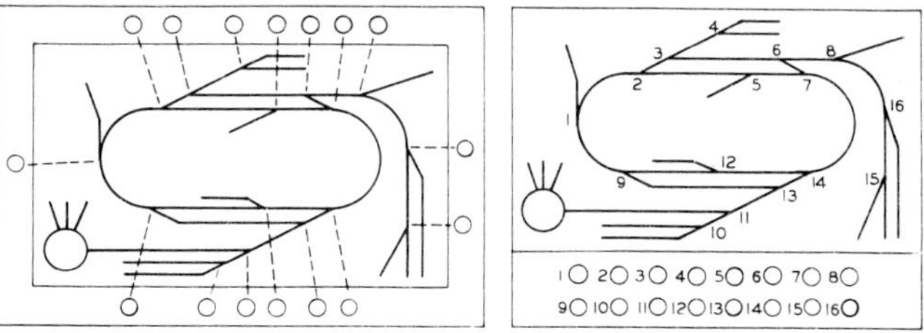

Fig. 12-5 Associating controls with diagram.

When the same type of panel (or even the same type of controls) is repeated, the different panels and controls should be duplicates of each other. This facilitates shifting from one to another during operation and also simplifies maintenance. The cabs shown in Fig. 12-2 are exact duplicates.

If the diagram is to be painted it may be found more convenient to paint the entire panel the color of one of the lines. Then with tape, mask the lines to be that color and paint the entire panel with yet another line color. When all line colors have been applied, and those lines masked, apply the background color. When the paint is dry removing the masking will expose the colored lines.

12.7 WIRING OF PANELS

Control panels are a concentration point for the wiring of a layout. This density of wiring, plus the fact that any modification or addition to the layout usually means a change in the wiring of the panel, places a great premium on orderly and reliable wiring on the backs of panels.

Panels should be connected to the rest of the layout wiring by terminal strips, see Section 11.73. This permits the panel to be wired on the work bench and installed as a unit. The terminals also serve as test points. Wires on the backs of panels should not run singly and unsupported, rather they should either be cables (Section 11.53) or as surface wiring against the back of the panel (Section 11.52). Solid, rather than stranded, wire should be used as it can be formed into place and will remain. Stranded wire will move around if not tightly confined. Also, with the many terminals on panels, loose strands from stranded wire present a major short-circuit hazard.

The preceding applies to conventional wiring. Integrated circuits have introduced the possibility of time-division multiplex to decrease the number of leads required, and have made possible systems such as computer cab control which do not require heavy leads to be brought to the panels. The use of LEDs instead of lamps has virtually eliminated the problem of mounting and replacing visual indicators. But, since integrated circuits have made possible far more sophisticated controls and panel displays, the actual number of leads which must be brought to a panel such as a cab may be considerably greater than before. At least a few integrated circuit packages will probably be mounted at the cab. One method is to mount a small circuit board on the back of the panel to hold the integrated circuits, the leads from the panel controls and indicators terminating on this circuit board. Also terminating on this board are flat cables connecting the panel to the group circuit which serves several of the panels and interconnecting panels of the same group. Fig. 12-3 shows this method applied to a cab panel at The Model RR Club. The circuit board mounts three IC packages for multiplexing displays and controls. A flat cable of 30 twisted pairs connects the panel to the cab group circuit which serves up to eight cabs. Another 30-pair flat cable extends those connections to the next cab. Since not all of the 60 leads in these cables were needed for signals, some are tied together to supply 5V power and others are tied together to carry ground.

Designate all electrical devices on the back of the panel, see Fig. 11-24. Also note the designation of each lead alongside its terminal on the terminal strips.

A schematic drawing should be prepared for every panel as, on many layouts, this is the most complex wiring on the railroad. A schematic diagram is invaluable in shooting trouble or in making changes.

13 SWITCHER MACHINE AND SPECIAL CONTROLS

13.1 GENERAL

The primary electrical control circuit is the one for the locomotive. On all but the smallest layouts, however there are others, those for switching machines, drawbridges, and turntables being examples. Only the electrical controls for such items are covered in this Handbook. Information on the installation of switch machines may be found in the "Trackwork Handbook for Model Railroads" and on the construction of all types of movable bridges in the "Bridge and Trestle Handbook for Model Railroads." Both are by the author of this Electrical Handbook and are available from their publisher, Boynton and Associates, Clifton, VA 22023.

13.2 SWITCH MACHINES

A switch machine is a device for setting the points of a track switch. Although available in many mechanical forms, electrically there are only two types in general use, the relay or single-coil type and the double-acting or two-coil type. In diagramatic form only, both are shown in Fig. 13-1. The relay type has an electromagnet or solenoid which pulls the points in one direction when its coil is energized and a spring to return the points to normal. The double-acting type has two solenoids (usually) which pull an armature into either of two positions. This movement throws the points and locks them in the new position. Double-acting switch machines typically have low resistance coils which will burn out if power is applied continuously.

The simplest control of a relay-type machine is a SPST toggle mounted directly on the control panel so its handle indicates the track for which the switch is set as shown in Fig. 13-2.

A relay-type machine can be held operated on less current than that required to operate it. Therefore some commercial machines operate on a high-current, low-resistance winding and switch in a high-resistance winding to reduce current demands after the relay operates as shown in Fig. 13-3. The rotary relay is of this type.

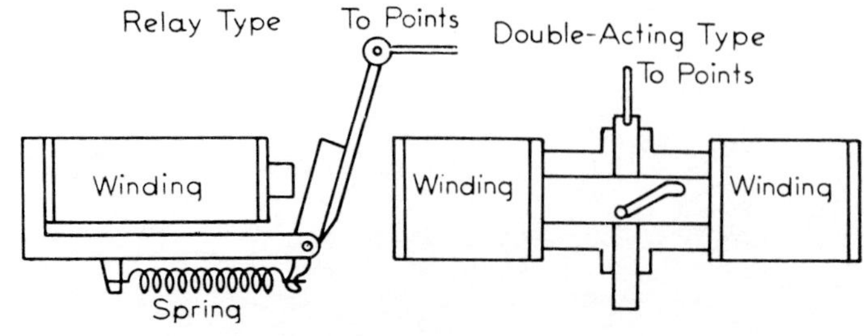

Fig. 13-1 Types of switch machines.

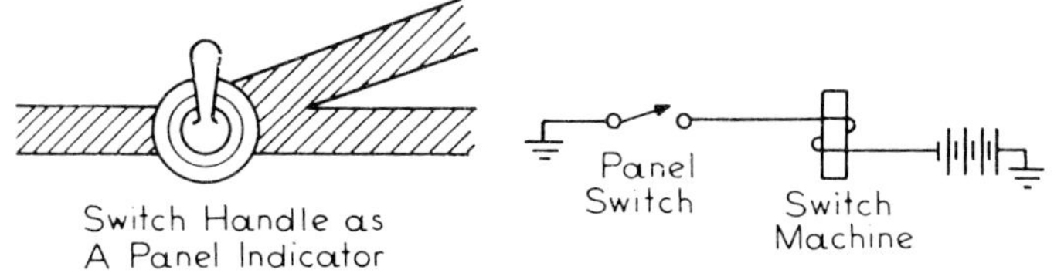

Fig. 13-2 Simple control for relay-type switch machine.

Power sources driving such high-current relays must be capable of driving them all simultaneously or have some form of protection which cuts off power if voltage drops below that which will operate the relays. Otherwise the switch machines cannot reduce their current and may burn out.

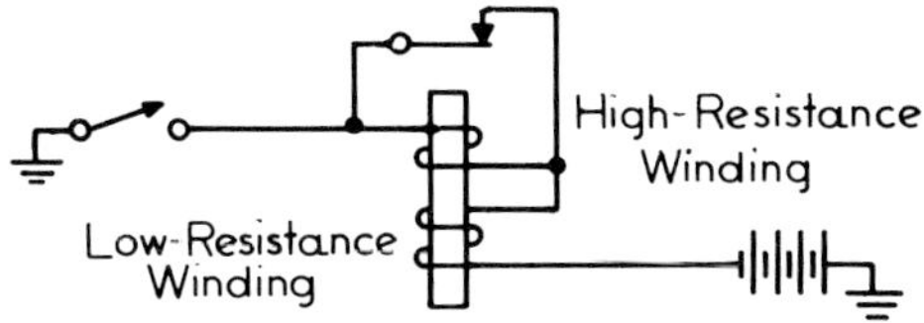

Fig. 13-3 Reducing hold-operated current.

The circuits of Figs. 13-1 and 13-2 permit the switch machine to be controlled only from one point. Often it is useful to set a switch from two or more separated locations, for example from a tower or at trackside. Multiple control is possible by using momentary switches such as the center-off switches of Fig. 13-4 or push buttons. The switch machine locks operated and is released by shunting. Since the panel switches cannot indicate the position of the track switch, indicator lamps have been added.

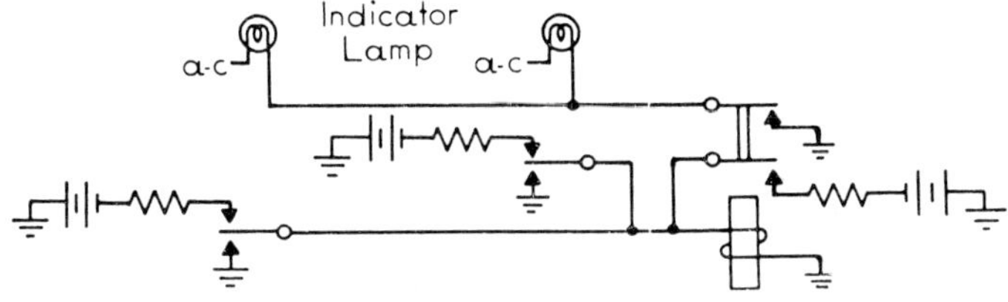

Fig. 13-4 Control from two points.

Double-acting machines are operated by momentary-closure switches such as the center-off switch of Fig. 13-5 or by push buttons. Indicator lamps, to show the position of the points, can be driven by contacts on the switch machine.

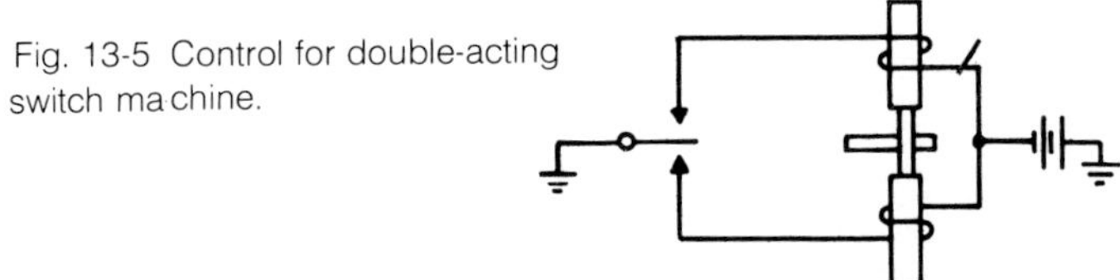
Fig. 13-5 Control for double-acting switch machine.

There is (1980) a commercial switch available designed specifically for double-acting switch machines, the Walthers E201 shown in Fig. 13-6. This switch is equipped with SPST momentary contacts to operate the switch machine. These contacts close and open as the handle is thrown from the center to either locking position so the handle indicates the direction in which the switch is thrown. In addition three-pole, double-throw locking contacts are provided.

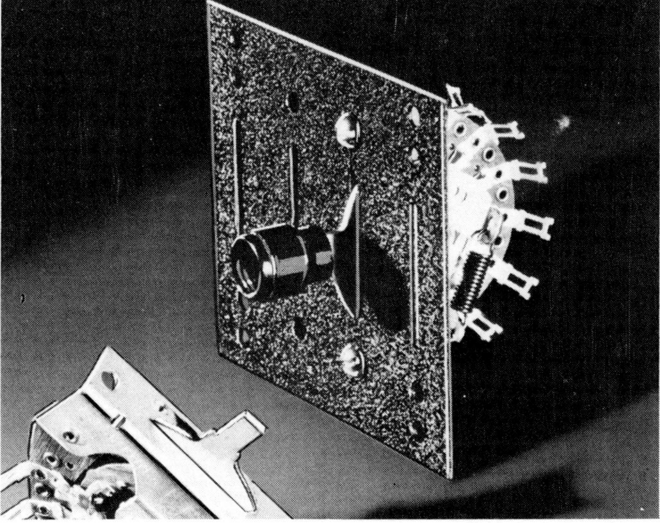
Fig. 13-6 Walthers E201 switch-machine control.

13.3 ROUTE CONTROL

For simple trackwork it may be best to control each turnout or crossover separately. Assuming double-acting machines and push buttons with indicator lamps on the panel, Fig. 13-7 illustrates one way of arranging individual controls on a panel.

In Fig. 13-7 setting the switch for the spur or the main track cannot choose the direction of the crossover, therefore these two must be controlled separately. On complex trackwork, however, many switches must often be set to establish a route. In such cases operations can be simplified and errors eliminated by operating all switch machines required for a route by the pressing of a single push button for that route. Fig. 13-8 is a simple example, a four-track stub yard leading from a single track. One push button is provided for each possible route as well as a lamp or LED which indicates the route selected. Pressing just one button will line up every switch required for the route, for example button 5 will set switches A, B, C, and D but pressing button 1 need only restore D to normal.

Fig. 13-7 Simple switch-machine control.

The operating paths for either the double-acting or the relay-type machines in Fig. 13-8 are identical. If push button 5 is pressed, ground will be connected through a chain of normally-made contacts to operate all switch machines as all are needed for that route. However if 4 is pressed, A will be disconnected before ground is applied to operate B, C, and D. Thus only the machines needed for the route are set.

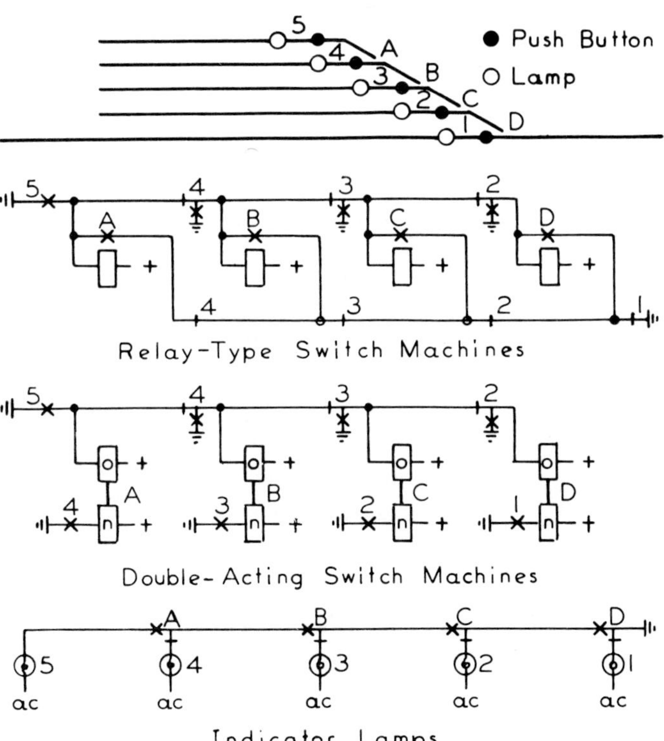

Fig. 13-8 Route control for stub yard.

When operated, the relay-type switch machines lock to a ground supplied through a chain of normally-closed contacts. Pressing button 1 will open the locking ground to all relays so all release. Even though only D had to be released for this route, releasing all reduces current drain. Pressing button 2 operates D but opens the lock path to A, B, and C.

Double-acting machines use power only when throwing so such machines are only thrown when their position must be changed. Thus, when button 1 is pressed, only D is restored to normal, the settings of the other three switches being immaterial.

The maximum number of contacts required on any one push button in Fig. 13-8 is one transfer and either one make or one break. Inexpensive push buttons of many types are available with up to two transfer contacts each. The author has never seen model trackwork so complex that a routing circuit could not be designed using only DPDT push buttons.

Route selection circuits using contacts on push buttons will work either for DC or AC powered machines. In designing such circuits with a limited number of contacts on the push buttons, the problem is to avoid building in a sneak path which will falsely operate or restore a switch. Some sort of chaining of the contacts is required. Use of contacts on the switch machines, sometimes called cascading, may help but requires the running of leads between the machines. Fortunately, if a DC power source is used to power the machines, all sneak paths can be blocked by diodes so circuit design is reduced to connecting the push buttons to the proper machines.

Using diodes for selection is not new. The author filed such a patent in 1948 (issued in 1953) but practical application to model railroads had to await develoment of low-cost, reliable diodes of suitable ratings. Such diodes are now available from many sources. Choose a silicon diode with a current rating above that of the switch machine and a voltage breakdown rating at least twice, preferably at least four times, the power-source voltage.

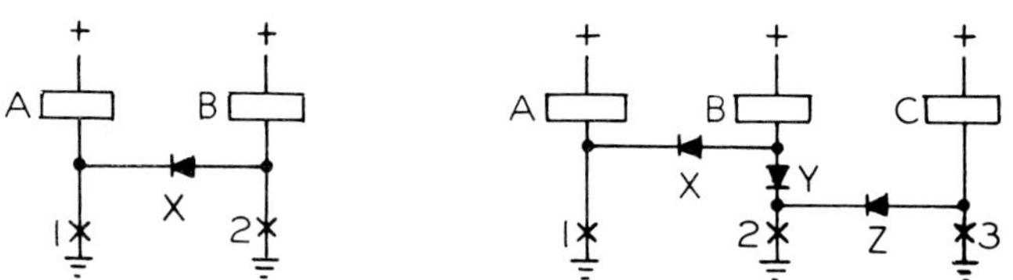

Fig. 13-9 Diode blocking of sneak paths.

Fig. 13-9 illustrates diode blocking of sneak paths. On the left pressing button 1 operates both A and B as diode X conducts. Pressing 2 operates only B as diode X blocks the path to the winding of A. On the right pressing button 1 still operates only A and B for diode Y bocks the path to C. 2 operates B and C with diode X blocking the operation of A. 3 operates only C with Z blocking. Note a diode must be placed in every lead between coils and push buttons except when a coil is energized by only one push button or a button energizes only one coil.

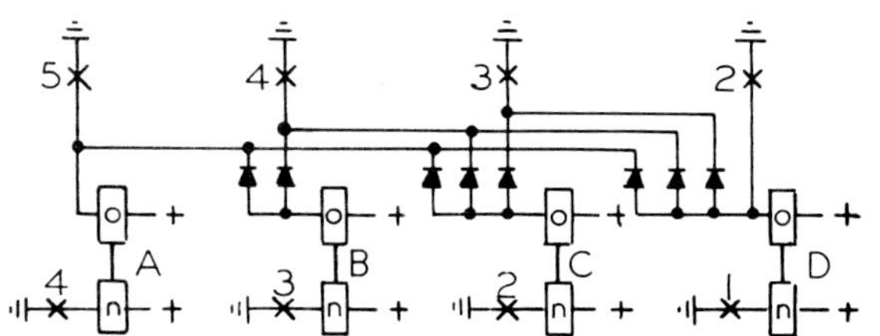

Fig. 13-10 Diode equivalent of Fig. 13-8.

The diode circuit for the double-coil switch machines of Fig. 13-8 is given in Fig. 13-10. This circuit is also directly applicable to relay-type switch machines provided they are released by shunt action.

This simple form of route control can be applied to any track configuration where pressing one button can define a route. Ladder tracks are an obvious application and, similarly, when a single-track line fans out to several tracks. Far more complex tracks can be handled in this manner. Fig. 13-11 shows a double-track main in which both the A and B sets of push buttons set up ladder-like routes independently but the two sets plus button 5 interact to control the crossover.

A straight-forward way of designing a diode route circuit for any trackage is first to make a diagram of the tracks showing the normal positions of the track switches and the push-button locations. Label

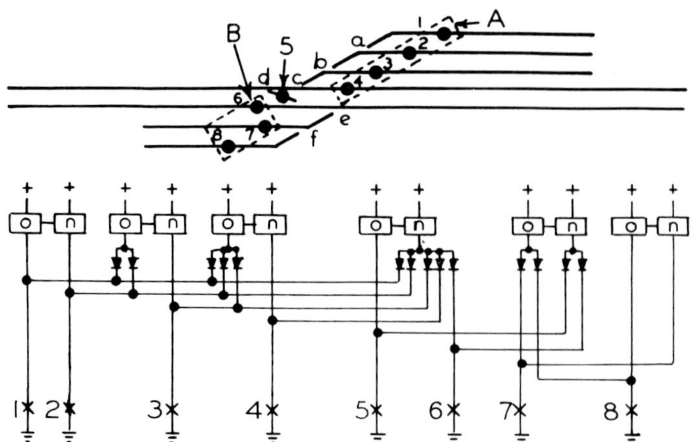

Fig. 13-11 Interacting routes.

every push button and switch. This has been done for a small stub terminal at the top of Fig. 13-12. This station was built and controlled by push buttons at the Summit-New Providence Club.

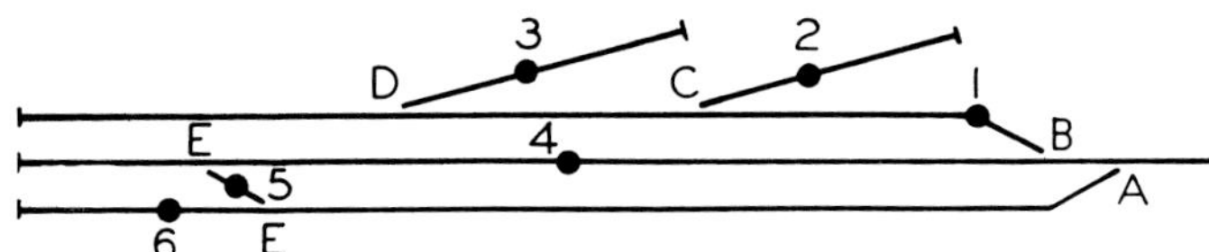

Button	Operate	Normal
1	B	ACD
2	C	D
3	D	
4		ABE
5	AE	
6	A	E

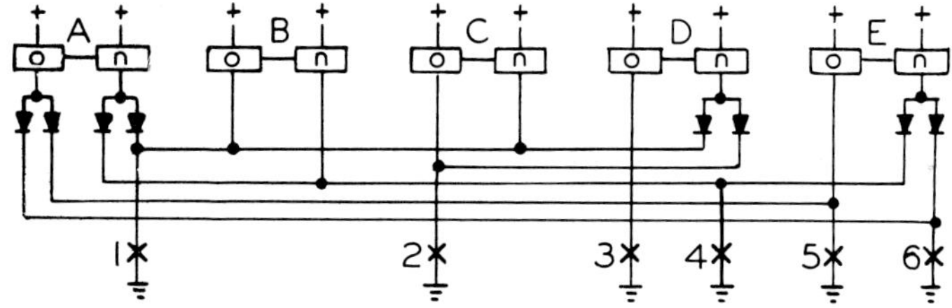

Fig. 13-12 Designing a route circuit.

Next make a listing showing all switch machines to be operated or released by each push button. Then draw a schematic diagram showing all push-button contacts and all switch-machine windings. Connect the contacts to the windings in accordance with the table. Finally draw a diode on every lead between a contact and a winding except those leads from a contact operating only one switch machine or from a coil connecting to only one contact. If in doubt, place a diode on all leads, they will do no harm other than adding expense and wiring effort.

On complex track, selecting a route by a single push button may be impractical. One solution is to place a push button on the track diagram at the ends of all possible routes as indicated at the top of Fig. 13-13. To set the switches for a route, it is necessary to press simultaneously the buttons at the entrance and the exit of that route. In addition to setting the necessary track switches, the push button circuit must leave undisturbed previously-set routes which are not involved with the new route.

First examine every switch to see which can be operated or restored by only one push button. In Fig. 13-13 pushing button 1 always restores B, 2 always restores A and C, 3 restores D, 4 restores A, 5 restores B and D, and 6 restores C. These windings and contacts can be immediately connected as in single-button routing.

The remaining switches require the pressing of two buttons. For example, to operate A, buttons 1 and either 5 or 6 must be depressed together. One side of the A operating coil is then connected to the grounding contact on 1 and the other side of the same coil to + contacts on 5 and 6. Thus A will only throw if 1 is supplying ground, and either 5 or 6 is supplying voltage. In a like manner the B operating coil gets ground from 4 and + from either 2 or 3. After all coils are connected, diodes are added in all sneak paths in accordance with Fig. 13-9.

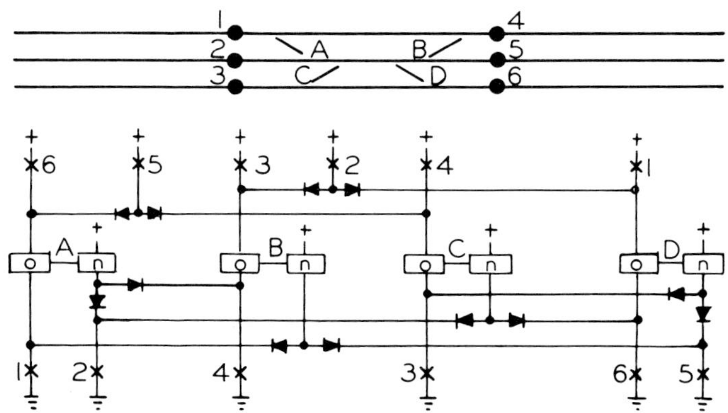

Fig. 13-13 Two push-button routing.

13.4 POWER SOURCES FOR SWITCH MACHINES

Switch machines should have power sources separate from those used by the locomotives. This prevents the sudden surges of current needed by the switch machines from affecting the operation of the locomotives. Although a transformer could serve as the power source for AC machines, for control reasons, improved performance, and protection, DC sources are recommended for all types of machines.

For relay-type machines, the power-source voltage must be great enough for reliable operation but below that which will overheat the coils. Double-acting machines, on the other hand, must be operated by a pulse regardless of the voltage and the higher the voltage, the better the operation but safety considerations limit the voltage to 50.

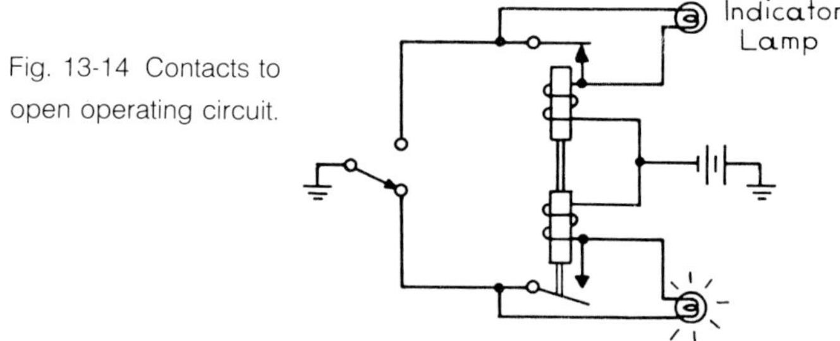

Fig. 13-14 Contacts to open operating circuit.

Double-acting switch machines should be protected against prolonged current flow to prevent burnout of their coils. Although contacts can be placed on such machines as shown in Fig. 13-14 to open the operating path once the machine throws, such contacts can lock closed or the machine may not be able to throw far enough to open the contacts. A safer solution is to provide a power source which can only deliver a pulse of current, the simplest and safest being the discharge of a capacitor as shown on the left in Fig. 13-15.

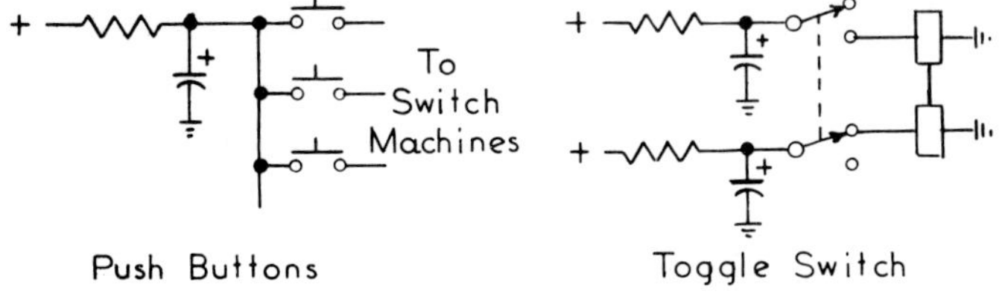

Fig. 13-15 Capicator-discharge operation of double-acting switch machines.

The resistor charges the capacitor to full DC supply voltage. When a push button is operated the entire charge of the capacitor is dumped into the switch machine then the resistor limits the steady current which can flow to a value which will not overheat the machine. As soon as the button is released the capacitor recharges ready for the next operation. The capacitor must be large enough to operate the switch machine or machines reliably. The resistance must be great enough to prevent overheating of the switch machines even if the button is held down continuously. The proper values depend upon the switch machine, the number to be operated in parallel, and the supply voltage available. They are best determined by trial.

A modification of the capacitor system permits a locking switch such as a toggle to operate a double-acting switch machine as shown on the right in Fig. 13-15. This has been found useful to permit a uniform panel control for both relay and double-acting switch machines. Both types of capacitor systems shown in the figure were used at the Summit-New Providence HO RR Club from 1954 to 1972 without a burnt out switch machine.

Capacitor discharge is simple and safe but if several switch machines are to be operated in parallel from one capacitor, that capacitor must be large and, since the minimum resistance is set on the basis of a single switch machine, recharging time may be long. One solution is to use two or more capacitors each with their own resistors so arranged to supply power to separate switch machines as shown in Fig. 13-16.

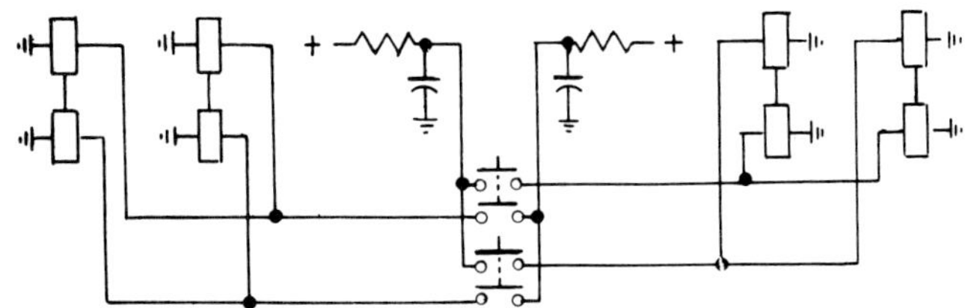

Fig. 13-16 Switch machines operated in parallel.

The control methods for operating the switch machines shown so far depend on handling the total current for the machine from the panel controls, and on the interconnecting wiring. When integrated circuits, including microprocessors, are used for CTC, interlockings, or other more advanced types of control, the integrated circuits may not be able to drive the switch machines directly due to lack of available power. Some sort of interface circuit capable of responding to the integrated circuit outputs, and of delivering the necessary power, is required. IC relay drivers exist in many of the families of integrated logic. These could be used to drive a relay, the contacts of which operate the switch machine. This type of an interface unfortunately inserts another electromechanical device into the circuit, thereby degrading reliability; it is better to provide a solid-state interface. Although SCRs are capable of switching the necessary current, experience has disclosed that they are too sensitive to noise to be practical in this application because just one short noise pulse can throw a switch at the wrong time. Some sort of a transitor interface, such as the one shown in Fig. 13-17, is more practical.

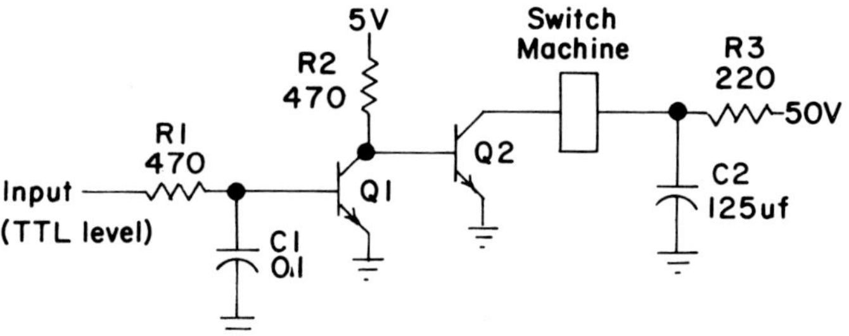

Fig. 13-17 TTL interface to switch machine.

In the circuit of Fig. 13-17, R1 and C1 serve as a filter to prevent Q1 from responding to noise. When the input TTL level is high, Q1 is turned on, holding Q2 off. To throw the switch machine, the TTL input is taken low, Q1 turns off and the 10ma previously flowing into its collector is diverted into the base of Q2 turning it on, and discharging C2 into the switch machine winding. Restoring the TTL input to high again turns Q2 off. The values of the resistors and C2 will depend upon the switch machine and the voltage used. The transistors are selected on the basis of the current they will handle and on the applied voltages. Q1 always can be a low-voltage transistor.

One of the ideas which made CTC (Centralized Traffic Control) practical on the prototype was that of controlling many switch motors over a single line by addressing the switch motor to be operated, and then sending it the proper command. This is done in the case of the microprocessor system described in Section 25.7. Any of the digital command-control systems described in Section 17.5 can be used to control switch machines either separately or together with locomotives. It would even be possible for an engineman to control the position of the switch his train was approaching. Do this by utilizing one of the commands available in the command-control system to send the appropriate signal to the switch machine via a contact mounted on the track on the point side of the switch.

13.5 CONTROL OF TURNTABLES

13.51 General

The significant electrical problems of a turntable are the selection of and precise alignment to a particular track. This can be done reliably only if the turntable is mechanically well made. Most successful automatically controlled turntables have an accurate, heavy central shaft turning in precise bearings mounted in a heavy frame, and a smooth, well geared-down drive. Since the construction of a turntable is outside the scope of this book, it is assumed that there is a precise shaft which is driven at scale speeds (approximately 1 rpm) by a conventional permanent-magnet motor (or by a stepping motor) through a speed reducer of some type.

13.52 Power to Track

It is common practice to connect power to the rails on the table by contacts sliding on the circle rail as shown in Fig. 13-18. The rail is divided into two semicircles, the insulated gaps being located between two approach tracks. This guarantees that the polarity of the rails on the table will agree with that of the approach tracks. Some tables have been built with a split ring and wipers mounted under

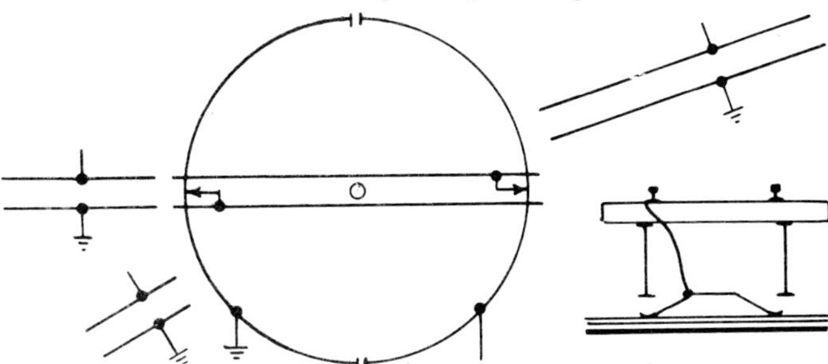

Fig. 13-18 Power to turntable rails.

the benchwork to perform the identical functions. In this case, connecting wires to the rails are led up through a tubular turning shaft. In either case, to assure reliable contact there should be at least two independently-sprung sliders at each end of the table.

Since there may be locomotives on every stall track, power must be connected only to the stall to which the turntable is aligned. One solution is to wire each stall track to its own push button as shown in Fig. 24, Chapter 8 but it is more convenient to connect to the proper stall automatically. One common method is to use a deck on the rotary switch which selects the position of the turntable as shown in Fig. 13-19. If a stall track is directly opposite another track, there must be a position on the rotary switch for each track for which automatic connection is required even though the turntable comes to the same position for both, otherwise the stall track will receive power when the other track is being used.

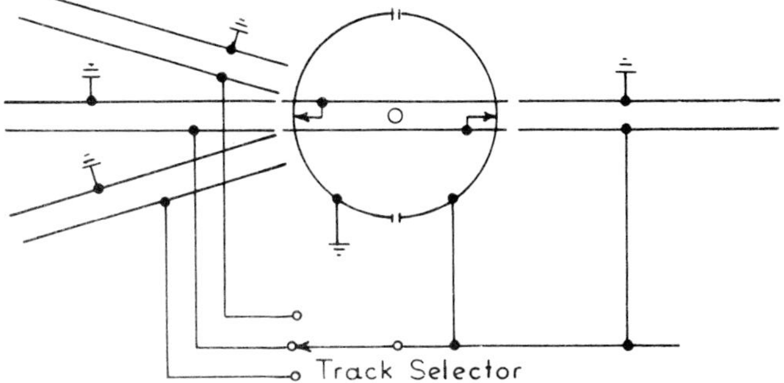

Fig. 13-19 Power to stall rails.

13.53 Turning and Alignment

The simplest turntables to control and align are those used only for turning locomotives. One accurate alignment method is to drive

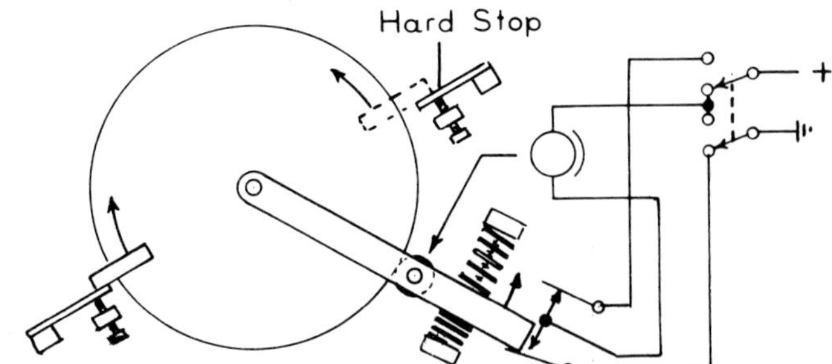

Fig. 13-20 180° rotation, two direction.

the table against an adjustable hard stop as shown in Fig. 13-20. The motor overdrives compressing the spring on its mounting until it strikes and opens a contact such as a snap-action switch often called Microswitch (although that is a trade name). Throwing the toggle switch to the opposite position reverses the motor and the table until it hits the opposite hard stop.

Another method is two adjustable projections on the turntable drive which strike and open a contact to stop the motor as shown in Fig. 13-21. To start the motor again, pressing a push button bridges the open contact. After the projection pushes by the contact, the contact closes and the push button may be released. The table continues to turn until the contact is struck and opened by the other projection. Since the table is always turning in the same direction at the same speed, coasting distance is uniform after the open contact so, if turning speed is kept low, the table indexes well.

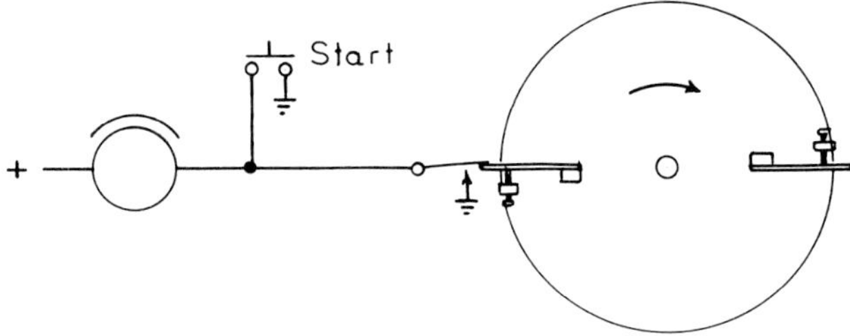

Fig. 13-21 180° rotation, single direction.

The continuous rotation method can be applied to tables with more than one stopping position. As shown in Fig. 13-22 separate, individually adjustable contacts are mounted at each stopping position. A non-adjustable projection turning with the table opens each contact in turn, a rotary switch selects which contact stops the motor. George Allen used this method on his Tuxedo Junction.

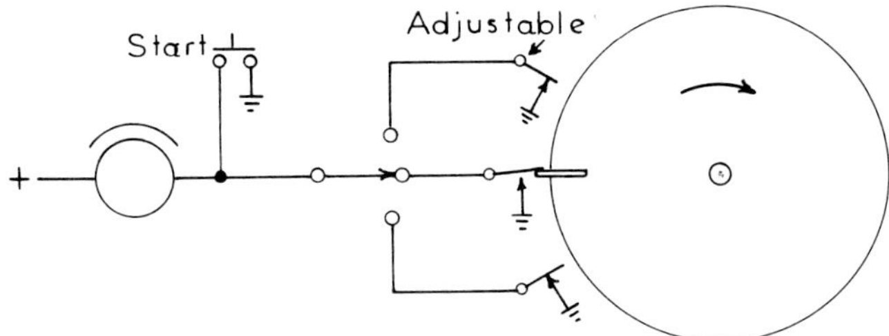

Fig. 13-22 Multiple stops, single direction.

Tables rotating in only one direction may require nearly a complete revolution to transfer a locomotive to an adjacent track. To turn by the shortest distance, the direction of rotation must be selected either manually or automatically by an indexing method which works equally well in either direction. For maximum accuracy, a coarse and fine index should be provided. The coarse index selects the track and slows the motor so the fine index can stop the motor with precision. Fig. 13-23 shows two methods which have been used.

At the top of Fig. 13-23 there is a contact for each stopping position which wipes on a grounded metal disk. The contact selected by the rotary switch connects ground to the solenoid which pulls the lock for the table and closes contacts to operate the motor in the direction set by the reversing switch. When the table approaches the selected track, an insulator in the disk opens the solenoid circuit dropping the plunger against the edge of the metal disk. This action opens one contact to place a resistor in series with the motor slowing the table to a creep. When the locking pin drops into the index, the remaining contact opens stopping the motor. Three methods have been used to align the tracks with positive latches such as this. One is to make the latch sockets on the disk adjustable. Another is to

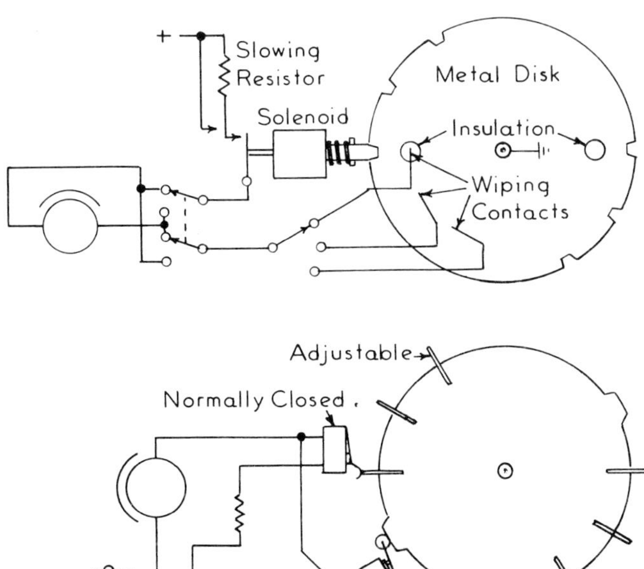

Fig. 13-23 Bidirectional turntable control.

build the turntable first and lay the tracks to the position it stops. Or, as was done by Dick Service, the table was lined up to the tracks and the notches then filed into the disk.

The lower half of Fig. 13-23 shows snap-action switches used for both fine and coarse indexing. The motor will continue to turn at full speed in the direction set by the reversing switch until the snap-action switch selected by the rotary switch is opened by a projection on the turntable. The motor now continues to run slowly through the resistor until the fine indexing switch is opened by an adjustable finger. Rudolph Wildermouth used a bendable projection for this purpose to permit adjustment for each track.

The methods shown so far do not permit a locomotive to be turned 180° without first selecting some intermediate track to start the table turning. Alternatively a push button could be added to run the motor until the coarse index switch closed.

Lamps or LEDs and phototransistors can be used in place of mechanical contacts.

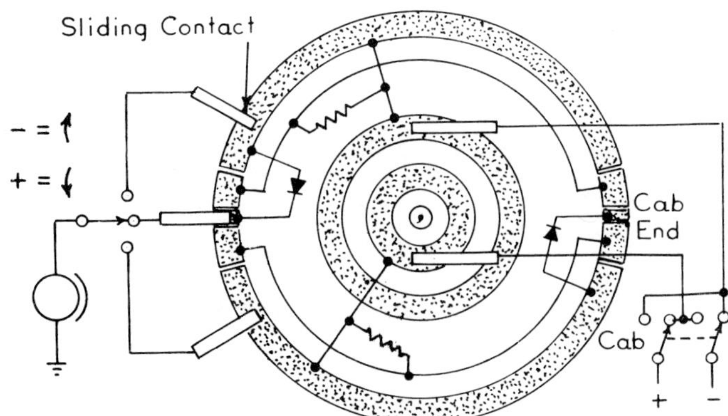

Fig. 13-24 Split ring indexing.

Fig. 13-24 shows a method of indexing whichever end of the table is desired. The toggle switch is set to select the desired end of the table, here identified by the operator cab on the table. This switch sets the polarity on the split rings which rotate with the turntable so that the selected end will move toward the wiping contact to which the rotary switch is connected. As the selected end approaches, the contact slides onto a short segment of the split ring which connects a resistor in series with the motor. The table continues to turn at reduced speed until the wiper slides entirely onto the indexing pad. If the table overshoots, it will reverse and regain the index pad. The wiping-contact must be just narrow enough that it does not contact either short slowing segment when it is on the indexing pad. If a locomotive is to be turned, the toggle switch is thrown to select the opposite end of the table and the diode conducts to start the table moving. The first known use of a split ring was in 1942 by Dick a'Merie, NYSME.

An accurate and simple way of making the split ring and the slip rings is to cut them into the copper of a single-sided printed circuit board (see Section 11.6). The only accurate cuts required are those on either side of the index pads. These are readily made using a razor saw. The use of a single-sheet permits an accurate layout around the centerline of the hole for the turning shaft. Building such rings up by rail on a plywood disk has also been done.

The turntable controls described so far depend upon mechanical contacts and are relatively difficult to construct and maintain. Also, it is not easy to include a feature such as gradually showing the table as it approaches the selected track. Sophisticated features require more logic. This is easily obtained through integrated circuits.

To permit a logic system to control a turntable, the first problem is to provide that system with information about the position of the table and the track selected. One method is to provide a binary-coded disk mounted on the turning shaft of the turntable. The binary code read from this disk then indicates the position of the table. This binary number then can be compared to the binary number corresponding to the track selected to determine which way the table is to turn and how fast. The particular system described here was developed by Bob Powell in 1976 for use at The Model RR Club.

The assumption was made that 256 stopping points were sufficient. Therefore 256 narrow indexing slots were provided at the periphery of the disk as shown in Fig. 13-25. The precise location of each slot is not important as the track will be laid to where the table stops. The eight inside rings have the binary code from all zeros to all ones. The position of the table is read by eight photodetectors. In Fig. 13-25 the disk position shows all of the photodetectors illuminated, table position 255.

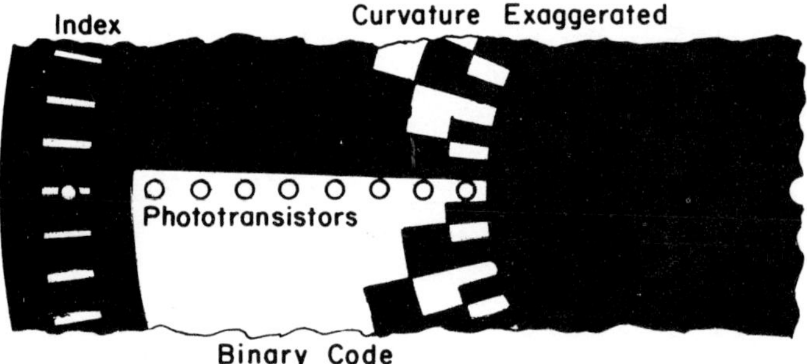

Fig. 13-25 Binary coded disk.

Each track to the turntable, including stall tracks, has a separate push button. To select a track, its push button is depressed which, as shown in Fig. 13-26, connects 5V to appropriate diodes to generate the 8-bit binary code corresponding to the selected track. The debounce timer delays the latching of the selected-track code until after the contact of the push button has finished bouncing. Virtually all mechanical contacts bounce, often for milliseconds, upon closure.

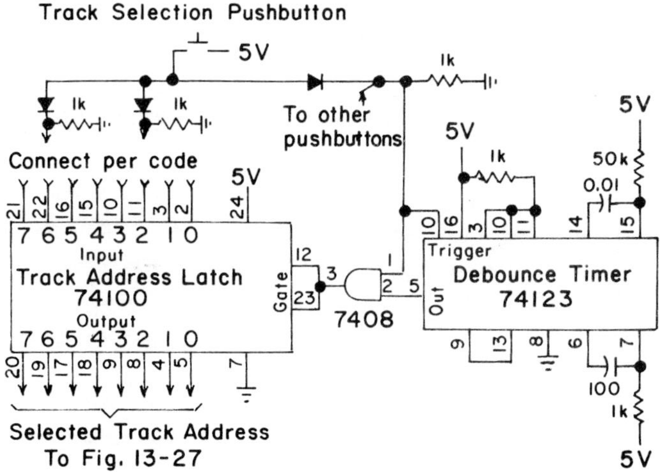

Fig. 13-26 Track select circuit.

To describe the action of this circuit, it is assumed that the turntable has been stopped for some time at a previously-selected track; its index phototransistor is detecting light through the indexing slot on the binary disk. A new track is selected and its binary code latched into the track address latch of Fig. 13-26. From the phototransistors the circuit knows where the table is and from the latch it knows where to go. These two binary numbers could be subtracted to determine in which direction and how far the table is to turn. However in the system being described, advantage has been taken of the high speed of ICs compared to the rotational speed of the turntable to make this determination by counting, thereby obtaining a simpler and less-expensive circuit.

The constantly-running clock of Fig. 13-27 will cause the table counter to count up until the comparator detects that the counter output matches the newly-selected track binary code. At that point the count gate is disabled, and if the turntable is at an indexing position, the position binary code will be loaded into the table counter and the process restarted. When the table is between indexing positions, the counter remains at the point where counting stopped. This count represents the distance clockwise the table must move to reach the selected track.

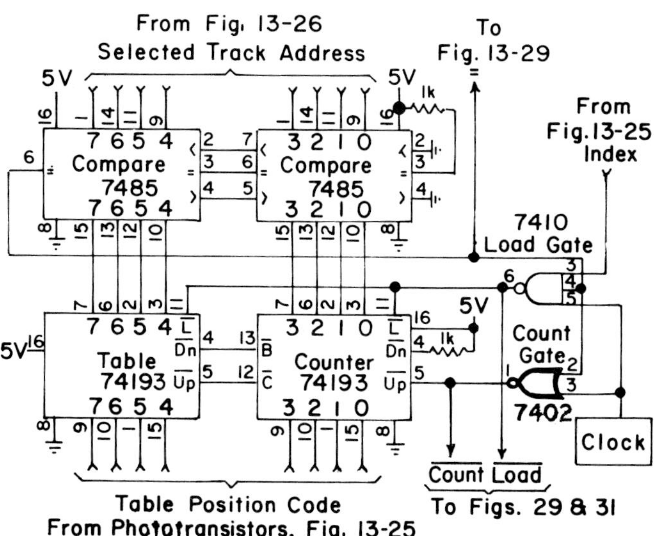

Fig. 13-27 Table counter.

The significance of the count is shown in Fig. 13-28. If there is no locomotive on the table, as in the left in the figure, the end of the table nearest the selected track should be moved directly to that track. For example, if 1 to 63 clock pulses have been counted to increment the table counter from the 8-bit code representing the position of the table to the 8-bit code representing the selected track, the closest end of the table to the selected track is the control-cab end, and the shortest turning direction is clockwise. On the other hand, if there is a locomotive on the table, we want to specify which end of the table is to move to the selected track so the circuit must determine which direction of rotation is the shortest. The proper directions are shown on the right in Fig. 13-28. For example, if the control-cab end of the table is selected and 1 to 127 clock pulses are counted between the position of the table and the selected track, rotation should be clockwise. Note in Fig. 13-28 that the proper direction of rotation is determined by the quadrant in which the counting stops.

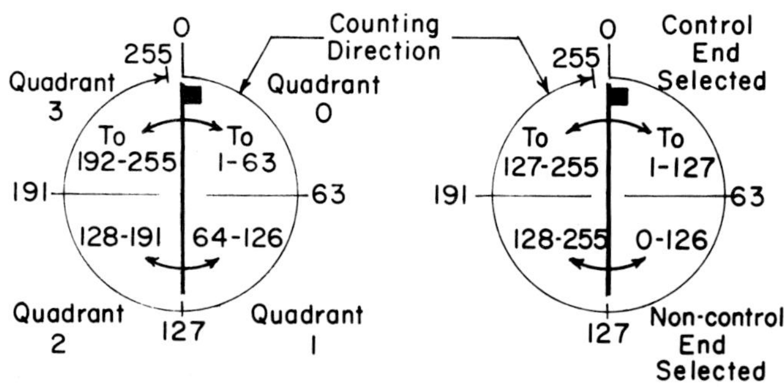

Fig. 13-28 Direction of table rotation.

To determine the quadrant we need an additional counter which starts at zero and counts the clock pulses until counting stops. Such a counter is shown in Fig. 13-29, the quadrant counter. Its most-significant bit (7) will be low if the counting stops in quadrant 0 or 1, or high if it stops in quadrant 2 or 3. The next most-significant bit (6) will be low if the counting stops in quadrant 0 or 2 or high if the count stops in quadrant 1 or 3. This counter is loaded to zero at the same time the table counter is loaded and counts in step with the table counter.

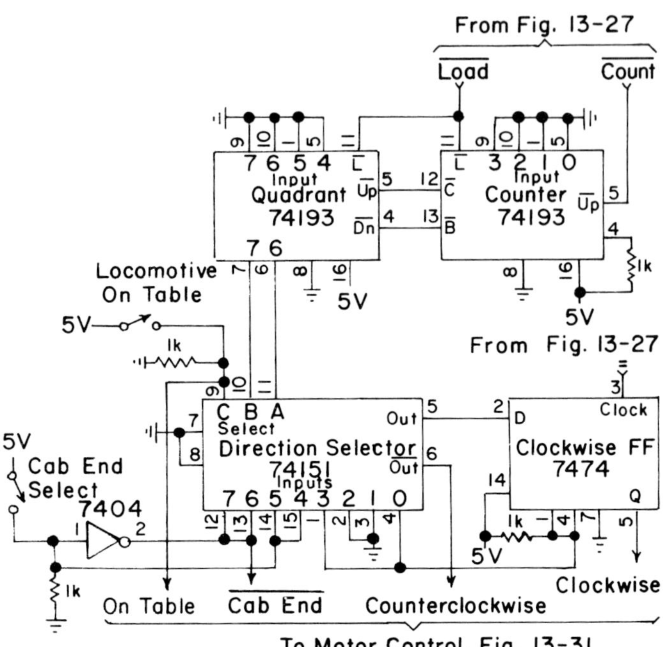

Fig. 13-29 .Direction control.

The direction the table is to turn depends not only on the quadrant selected, but also on whether or not there is a locomotive on the table. If there is a locomotive, rotation direction also depends upon the end of the table which is selected. The necessary inputs are brought to the direction selector as shown in Fig. 13-29. The locomotive-on-table input is shown as a panel switch, but it could be a track circuit. The correct direction is registered in the clockwise FF when the count is stopped. Therefore the direction of the motor driving the table will not change during the counting intervals.

Smooth starting of the table is simple because any capacitor momentum scheme will do. However to slow gradually and to stop precisely at the selected indexing point requires knowledge of the angle still to turn. Depending upon the direction of rotation, the count may either increase or decrease as the stopping point is approached. This is shown in Fig. 13-30. The counting direction is always clockwise as shown by the outside light line arrow. If the table is rotating clockwise to stop at track A, the count decreases as the track is approached. If it is rotating counterclockwise to approach track B, the count is increasing as the track is approached.

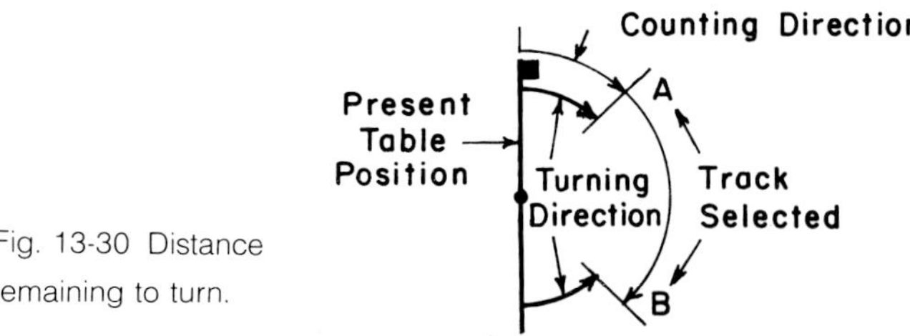

Fig. 13-30 Distance remaining to turn.

The speed counter in Fig. 13-31 determines the distance yet to turn. If there is no locomotive on the table, this counter is loaded with all zeros and proceeds to count up in step with the other counters until the counterclockwise input goes high for quadrant 1. Then the counter counts down, reaching zero at the end of that quadrant, counts up through quadrant 2, and down again in quadrant 3.

If there is a locomotive on the table and the cab end is selected, the speed counter is again loaded with all zeros but this time it counts up through both the 0 and 1 quadrants, and down in quadrants 2 and 3. If the non-cab end is selected, the speed counter is loaded with 127 (decimal) and will count down through the 0 and 1

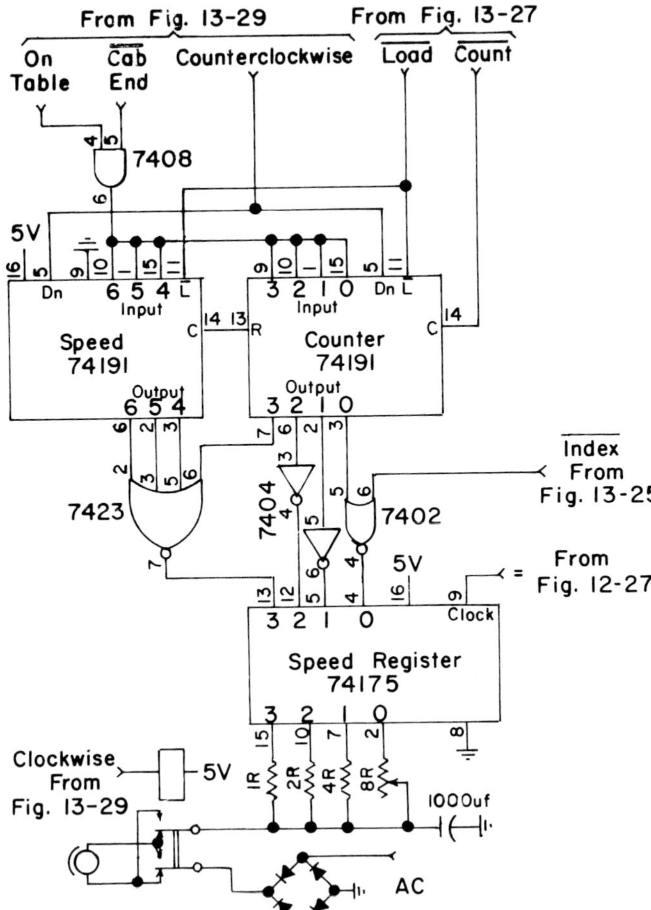
Fig. 13-31 Motor control circuit.

quadrants to zero, then back up through quadrants 2 and 3. In all cases the direction of count is determined by the direction selector of Fig. 13-29. When the counters stop, the speed count is latched into the speed register to prevent speed changes during counting. Since slowing need take place only during the last eight indexing positions before stopping, the most-significant bits of the speed counter are combined, any one high causing the table to turn at full speed. The output of the speed register and the clockwise FF then are available to drive any digital control suitable for the motor being used to drive the turntable.

It is always possible that the table may stop at some point other than an indexing position. If so, it must be made to move to the next indexing position so that the circuit action so far described can take place. Consequently the output of the index LED is also brought to the least-significant speed bit which guarantees that the table will rotate at not less than the minimum speed if it is between indexing locations.

The motor circuit shown at the bottom of Fig. 13-31 is illustrative only because, in the form shown, an instrument-grade motor and relay each capable of operating on the current which can be supplied by the ICs would be required. The 1R resistance is selected to operate the table at the highest desired speed. The other resistors are of increasing magnitude with 8R being the largest value which will reliably cause the motor to turn at low speed. It is shown as adjustable in the event that there are changes required with time. This is a pulse-power throttle of the type described in Section 5.32.

The coded-disk method described above to determine the position of the turntable is often used commercially to determine the position of a rotating shaft as on digitally-controlled machinery. But, for computer-controlled devices which require precise positioning, it is more common to drive those devices by a stepping motor; the computer keeping track of where the device is positioned and how far it is to be moved. It is required that the initial position of the device be made known to the controlling circuit. Although this type of control is directly applicable to the control of turntables and transfer tables, by 1982 there had been no known application of stepping motors for this purpose. Nevertheless, because of its potential value, the principle of a stepping motor is described below and a possible control circuit is shown in block form.

At A in Fig. 13-32 is shown the general construction of one type of stepping motor. There are two sets (X and Y) of magnetic cups with interlocking teeth. A separate winding around an axial sleeve is provided between each set of cups, the direction of current in the winding determining which cup is magnetic north and which magnetic south. The teeth of the cups are set exactly at the one-half position of the teeth of the Y cups. In the diagrams at B, C, and D, the teeth of the two sets of cups are drawn as if they were on the same cup for the purposes of description.

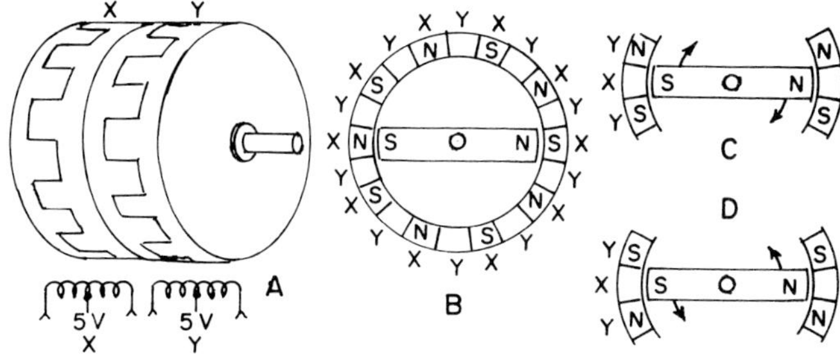
Fig. 13-32 Stepping motor.

At B in Fig. 13-32 current is flowing in one-half the winding creating the N and S magnetic poles shown. The Y coil is not energized. The permanent-magnet armature then will line up and lock magnetically with its south pole opposite a north-pole tooth as indicated. When power is first turned on, it is not known which tooth this will be, hence the necessity of initialization.

At C in Fig. 13-32 the current through the X winding has been discontinued. Therefore the X teeth no longer are polarized magnetically, but current is flowing in the Y winding creating the N and S poles shown. The attraction and repulsion of these poles will cause the armature to take one step clockwise and again lock magnetically. To rotate counterclockwise rather than clockwise, the current in the Y winding should be of the opposite direction, as shown at D.

If it knows the starting position, a control circuit can turn a table in the direction it has determined proper, move it a precise distance, control the speed of rotation by controlling the rate of pulsing of the motor and stop and lock the table at the desired track without any further information being supplied from the table of its position. Thus there is no need for a binary disk. If the table is blocked from moving, or moved by external forces, it must be reinitialized.

A possible turntable control circuit is shown in block form in Fig. 13-33. The clock is now a voltage-controlled oscillator because the speed of rotation is controlled by the oscillator frequency. This circuit assumes the table is initially moved manually to its zero location and that the counter is reset to all zeros. From this point the counter will count up for each step of the stepper motor clockwise, and count down for each step counter clockwise. Thus the content of the counter is always the position of the table. A 12-bit counter is shown providing 4,096 stopping places. This provides smooth motion and enables the stopping place to agree with the track location rather than requiring that tracks be laid to fixed indexing points.

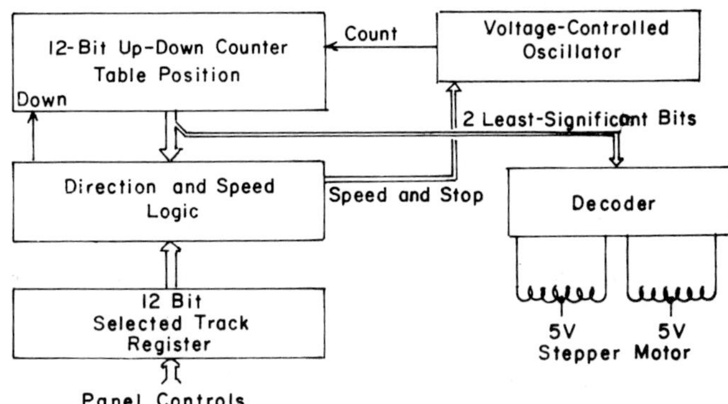

Fig. 13-33 Stepper-motor turntable control.

A method such as that of Fig. 13-26 must be supplied to generate a 12-bit code corresponding to the desired track. This number is compared to the contents of the counter. If they agree, the table is at the right track and the oscillator is stopped. If they do not agree, the oscillator is started and the counter either counts up or down depending upon the direction determined by the direction logic. A circuit similar to that of Fig. 13-29 could be used. The speed logic would determine the distance yet to go, and would adjust the frequency of the oscillator accordingly. The stepper motor itself is driven by decoding the two least-significant bits of the counter, its direction being determined by counting up or counting down and its speed by the rate of counting. Niel Carlson has demonstrated that small stepping motors can be driven directly by the outputs of an IC decoder such as the 74156. If a microprocessor is supplied for other purposes, it could also serve to control stepper motors for turntables.

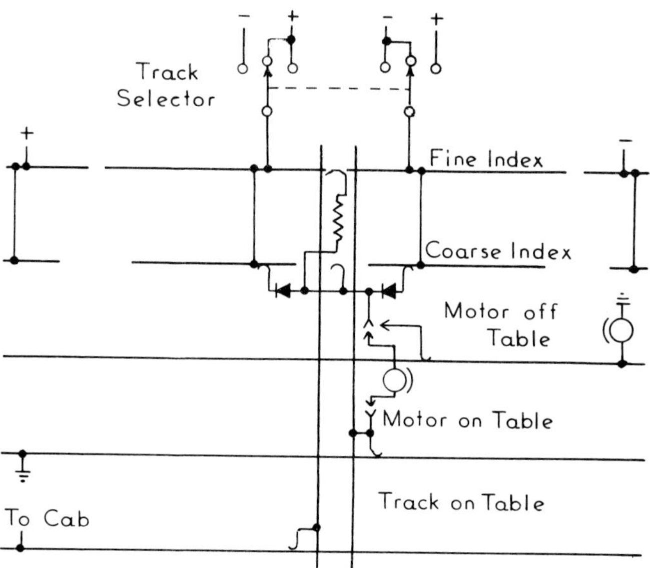

Fig. 13-34 Control for transfer table.

13.6 CONTROL OF TRANSFER TABLES

The primary mechanical problem in building transfer tables is to hold the table precisely at 90° to the rails on which it rolls. The construction of a transfer table is outside the scope of this Handbook. It is assumed the table is mechanically accurate and driven by a conventional permanent-magnet motor mounted either on the table or on the benchwork and that this motor is well geared down so table speeds are prototype , around 3Kph (2mph).

Unlike a turntable which can reach any track by turning in either direction, the indexing circuit for a transfer table must move it in the proper direction. The most practical method uses the rails under the table in the same manner as the split ring of Fig. 13-24. One rail is used for coarse indexing, another for fine. If the table only has approach tracks on one end, the fine index rail should be the end rail next to the tracks. If tracks are on both ends, the fine index rail should be at the center of the table.

The complete circuit to operate a transfer table is shown in Fig. 13-34. The only critical rail and sliding contacts are for the fine index. The insulated gaps in that rail must be accurately placed and be of equal widths. The wiper must be just narrower than the width of the insulated gaps.

The motor is connected so the table moves right if the index sliders are connected to + and left if connected to −. Thus the table will move to the indexing gaps which have + on the left and − on the right, in Fig. 13-34 this is at the center. As soon as the track selection switch is changed, one of the diodes will conduct and start the table moving toward the new track. These diodes also permit the table to cross unselected insulating gaps. As the selected track is approached, the coarse index slider breaks contact but the motor continues to run at a reduced speed by current supplied through a resistor by the fine index slider. This slider opens the motor circuit at the precise track location. If there is overshoot, the motor will reverse. Power to the track on the table is also supplied by sliders. There is no adjustment provided for each indexing position so the approach tracks will have to be laid to match the track on the table.

Although by 1982 there had been no known application of integrated circuits controlling transfer tables, they can be so operated. In particular, the use of stepper motors seems appropriate because a transfer table has a natural initializing position at each end of its travel. The motor can be required to drive until it stalls when the table hits the end stop. The table position counter is then initialized to zero. The logic for transfer tables is simpler than for turntables, direction is determined by whether the number for the table position or the number for selected track addresses is greater. The distance still to go is a simple subtraction of these two addresses. The drive from the stepper motor to the table would ideally be some positive device such as a lead screw or pinions in a rack. It is quite possible, however, considering how few times a transfer table moves, that a friction drive through the wheels would be accurate enough for practical purposes.

13.7 CONTROL OF MOVABLE BRIDGES

General

Swing, bascule, and vertical lift bridges move between two positions but only the closed position is critical. Construction of movable bridges is outside the scope of this Handbook, see Section 13.1 for a reference to construction information. Here it is assumed such bridges are well made and powered by conventional permanent-magnet motors.

Swing Bridges

Swing bridges are unlike turntables in that they usually have a much longer span which not only makes the angular alignment more critical but also the two end abutments may be supported on ordinary benchwork construction so, in time, some relative motion may take place in their position with respect to each other and the pivot of the bridge. Also trains move over swing bridges at much higher speeds than locomotives on a turntable.

The best alignment is achieved by lifting the ends of the bridge as it closes (prototype) and also driving both ends against a precision hard stop. The bridge should be attached to the turning shaft by some arrangement that allows it to be lifted, displaced to the side, and twisted slightly under spring pressure. This is shown in diagramatic form in Fig. 13-35.

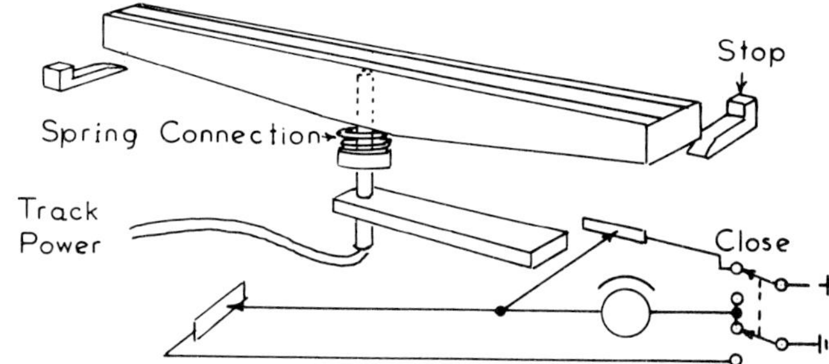

Fig. 13-35 Swing-bridge control.

When the bridge closes, both ends are driven up a slight ramp hard against fixed stops. This may force a slight displacement of the center of the bridge. The motor continues to turn building up spring pressure to hold the bridge firmly seated until the contact is opened stopping the motor. Power is connected to the rails on the bridge by flexible wire.

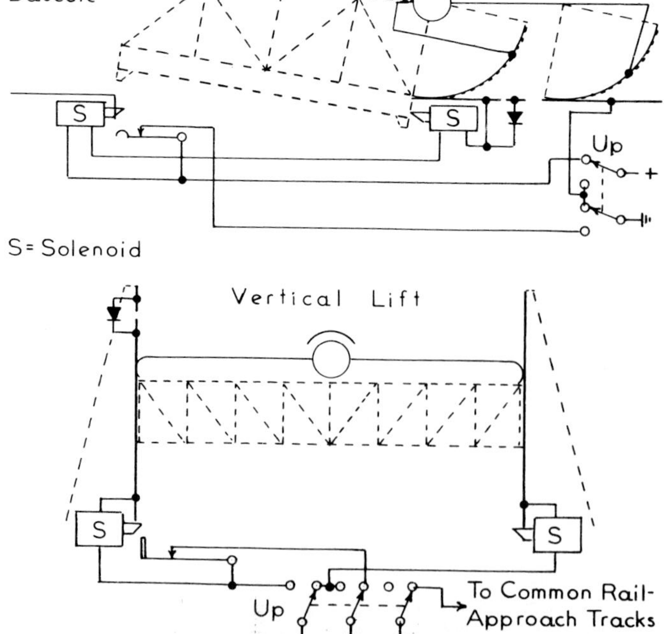

Fig. 13-36 Movable-bridge control.

Bascule and Vertical Lift Bridges

Some bascule bridges have trunions which effectively align the heel end of the leaf but the free end must still be brought into alignment and held down. Particularly on long spans where there may be some relative motion in time between the two abutments, alignment is more positive if the bridge is forced down with power. Rolling bascules and vertical lift bridges have no positive restraints at either end. If the bridge is operated by a motor on the bridge acting through scale operating members, it may be impractical to generate the forces required for positive alignment by using that motor. Train operation over the bridge can be made more reliable if solenoid or motor-driven latches are installed which both force the bridge into exact alignment and also clamp it down firmly. These clamps could take many mechanical forms, for example tapered pins driven into accurate holes on the bridge.

Fig. 13-36 shows a Scherzer rolling lift and a vertical lift bridge, both fitted with solenoid-operated latches at their ends. The electrical control is identical for the two bridges. The latches pull when power is applied to the motor and restore when the motor is stopped by either limit switch.

The wheel segments and the cogged tracks of the Scherzer rolling lift are of metal and serve as the electrical connections to the motor. The end of one track has been isolated and opens the motor circuit when the bridge rolls back onto it. A diode connects power to this isolated end piece to close the bridge. The same arrangement is used on the guides for the vertical lift, an isolated section of guide serves as a limit switch.

Power can be connected to the rails on the bridge by spring-wire contacts; phosphor bronze is a good material. For reliability there should be at least two such contacts for every rail. Do *not* use a suggestion which has appeared in the magazines, that of dipping wires into small pools of mercury. Mercury is too poisonous.

Safety Interlocking

To prevent running a locomotive into the river, it is best to disconnect power from the approach tracks. Although contacts on the control switch for the bridge could be used to open each control rail of the approach tracks but if there are multiple tracks, this may be several contacts. Alternatively the common rail to all tracks can be opened as shown at the bottom of Fig. 13-36. This will not provide absolute protection as trains in opposite directions could mutually supply each other with the common connection.

14 RELAYS AND THEIR CIRCUITS

14.1 GENERAL

Prior to the advent of integrated circuits, relays were the devices most-commonly used to perform logic functions, to operate block signals for example. Relays have been superseded by integrated circuits for virtually all logic functions. Nevertheless relays still retain a limited field of applications on model railroads. Examples are interfacing ICs with switch machines and motors, simple circuits requiring the handling of high voltages or high currents, and power connecting. The uses of relays in such specific applications are included in the sections describing those functions. In this chapter only basic relay functions are covered.

There are many reasons why relays have been superseded by ICs, among them the following: power consumption (a system requiring only 10 watts for ICs typically would require kilowatts for relays), size (an IC system which would fit into a shoebox might require a room of relays), simplicity (most of the complex wiring of IC systems has been done by the manufacturer but all connections to relays must be made individually), speed (ICs can operate millions of times per second, relays only a few times) and reliability (ICs do not wear out or get dirty contacts).

14.2 DIRECT AND SHUNT OPERATION

The normal method to operate a relay is by closing a current path by direct action to the relay winding as shown on the left in Fig. 14-1. Since greatest exposure to short circuits is at the contacts, generally they supply ground and the winding is connected directly to the power source. A short circuit to ground at the contacts then merely operates the relay and does not blow a fuse or breaker.

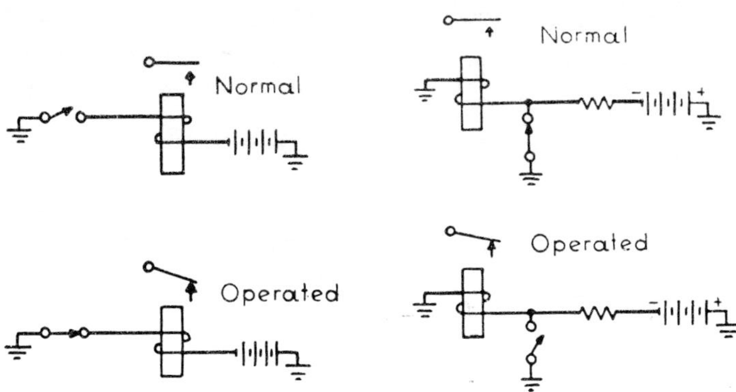

Fig. 14-1 Direct and shut replay operation.

Instead of closing the current path to the relay, the operating contact could shunt the relay thus diverting the current from the relay winding as on the right in Fig. 14-1. A resistor must be provided to prevent the contact from shorting the power source. The release of a relay by shunt action is considerably slower than by direct action as a path is established which permits the current in the winding to flow as its magnetic field decays.

14.3 SINGLE-RELAY FUNCTIONS

Connecting

The most elementary use of a relay is to connect one or more circuits. Some possible arrangements being shown in Fig. 14-2. On the left a relay is connecting just one circuit and so is doing nothing more than the switch which controls the relay could do unaided. There must be some particular reason to justify a one-contact relay, for example if the switch could not carry the current required.

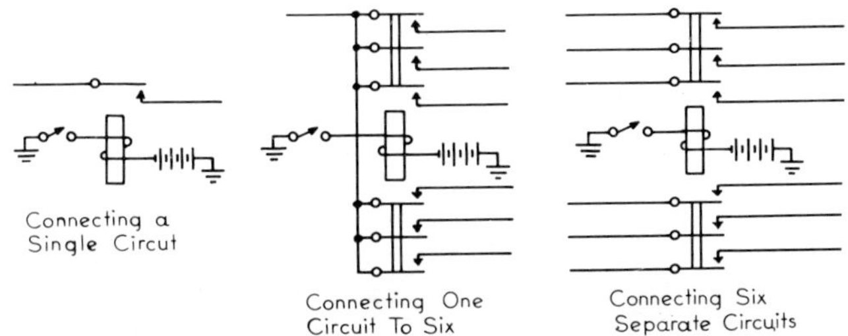

Fig. 14-2 Relays for connecting.

Although a relay is normally driven by other than a simple toggle switch, even used in this manner a relay is often more desirable than a multipole switch as it can eliminate the need to bring many leads to the back of a crowded control panel.

Splitting

Splitting is just the reverse of connecting. When the relay operates it splits the connections using break contacts as shown in Fig. 14-3. An important feature is that splitting inverts, that is closing the operating circuit opens the output circuits.

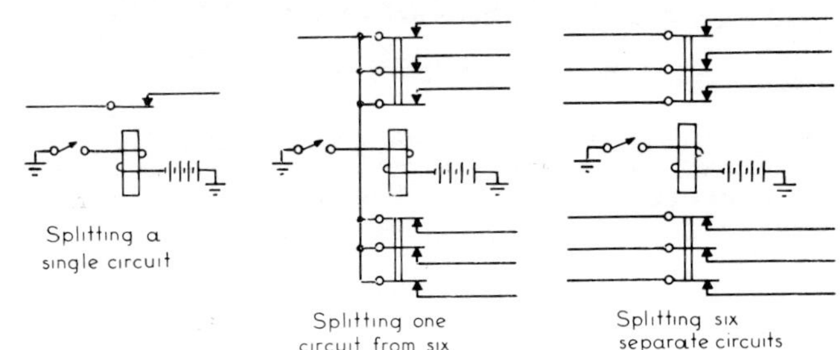

Fig. 14-3 Relays for splitting.

Transferring

Transferring is the combination of connecting and splitting so that one lead is disconnected from a second lead and reconnected to a third lead. Although separate make and break contacts can be used as on the left in Fig. 14-4, it is more economical and requires fewer connections to use transfer contacts as in the center. Transfer contacts can guarantee that the old connection is broken before the new connection is made (a break-make contact). Continuity contacts, as on the right, are the reverse, the old connection is held until the new connection is established (a make-break contact). Except for a continuity contact in the operating path of its own relay, as the top contact on the right in Fig. 14-4, circuit design can always eliminate the need for continuity contacts, see Fig. 14-11.

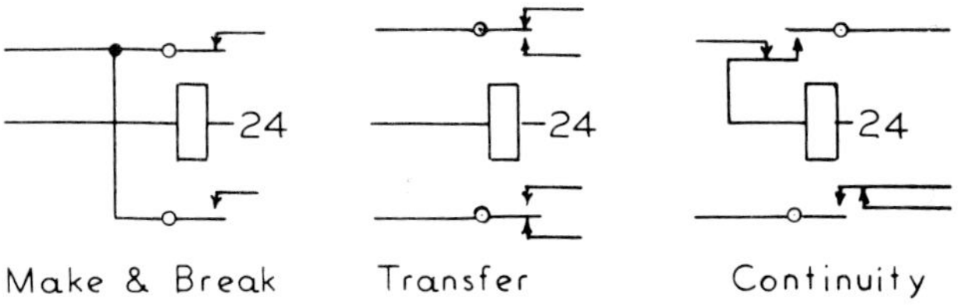

Fig. 14-4 Relays for transferring.

Memory

It is often necessary to remember that some event has taken place—that a locomotive has moved, a switch thrown, or that a train has passed. A relay can remember by operating (or releasing) then locking. By locking it is meant that once a relay operates (or releases), it remains in the new position regardless of further action until it is told to resume its former position. An older term for locking is "sticking" and this term is still used for prototype signal circuits.

The most common memory circuit is the lock-operated type. When the relay is to remember, it is operated and it then locks operated on its own make contact as shown on the left in Fig. 14-5. In this case the relay remembers the push button has been pressed. The relay could have been previously operated as on the right. In this case pressing the push button releases the relay. Once the relay contact opens, releasing the push button has no further effect.

Fig. 14-5 Direct action memory.

Shunt, rather than direct, action also is used for memory circuits. Fig. 14-6 shows a lock-up, shunt-action relay on the left. When the push button is pressed, the shunt ground is removed and the relay operates. Its contact opens the shunt path so release of the push button does not release the relay. Conversely the push button could apply a shunt ground to release a previously operated relay as on the right.

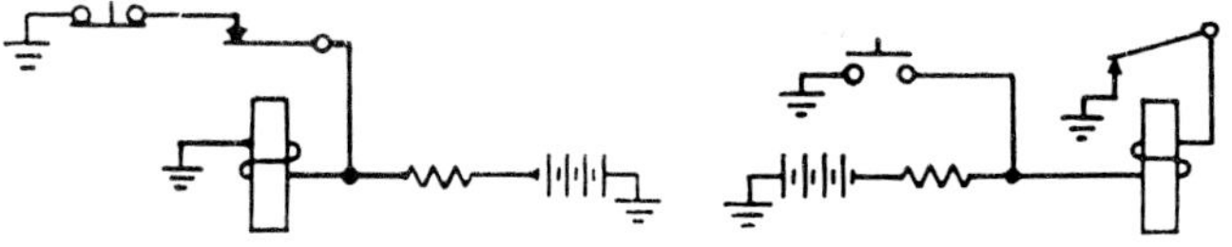

Fig. 14-6 Shunt action memory.

In Figs. 14-5 and 14-6, once a relay is operated or released, it will remain so. But in all applications a memory relay must forget as well as remember. Either shunt or direct action can be used to restore a relay to its original state. One possibility is shown in Fig. 14-7 where a relay is operated by direct action by push button A and released by shunt action by push button B. Resistor A prevents a short circuit if both buttons are pushed. This circuit is a way of controlling a relay-type switch machine over one wire.

Relays are useful as memory elements only when just a few bits of information are to be stored and the system is made up primarily of other relays, or when contacts of the memory relay are used to carry heavy currents. If there are many bits of information to be stored, IC memory is far superior. In 1982 a single IC memory package requiring the connection of only 16 leads, using less than one watt of power, and costing only $1.50 could do the work of about 2,000 relays.

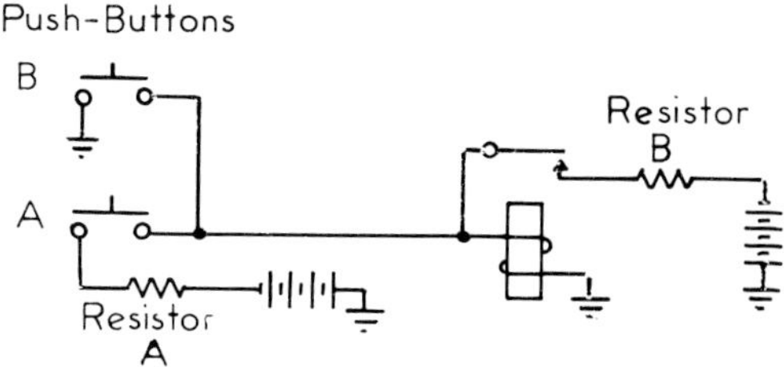

Fig. 14-7 Lock-up and lock-down memory.

14.4 TRANSLATION

Relays can translate one set of inputs into a different set of outputs. A very common use of this ability is to translate the occupancy of two blocks into the lighting of green, red, and yellow lamps on a signal.

A basic circuit used in translation is the relay tree, so called because of the appearance of its schematic. Fig. 14-8 shows a complete three-relay tree both straight forward on the left and folded on the right. Folding is used to even up the contacts on the relays. Note that for each possible combination of operated and released relays there is a specific output which will be grounded. A tree is the simplest possible circuit for this task. The IC for this task is called a decoder.

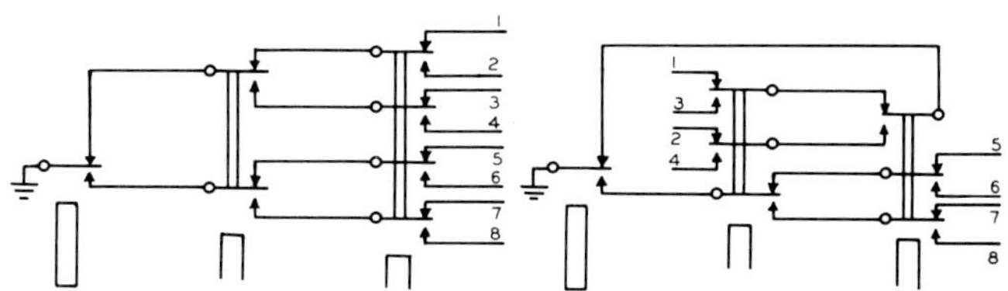

Fig. 14-8 Relay tree.

Generally it is not necessary to use a complete tree as either not all input combinations will be received or some outputs are not needed, perhaps some output combinations can be combined. Fig. 14-9 illustrates simplifying a tree when not all input combinations will appear. In this case only four possible input combinations exist, all relays released, 1 operated alone, 1 and 2 operated, or all operated. The first step is to eliminate all contacts and wires not associated with these inputs as on the left in Fig. 14-9. Then, as one the right, eliminate any contact which will never open a circuit. For example, since 1 is always operated if 2 or 3 is, there is no reason to have a break contact on either relay 2 or 3 for output 1. The same applies to the break contact on relay 3 for output 2.

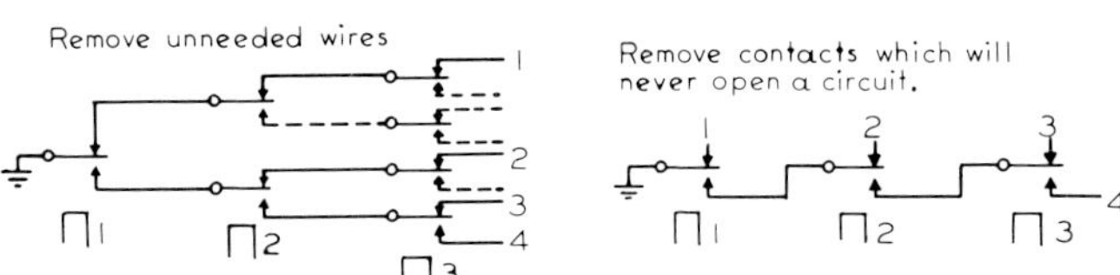

Fig. 14-9 Simplifying a relay tree.

When tree outputs are combined, it is usually possible to find contacts which have no effect on the outputs. For example on the left in Fig. 14-10 it makes no difference whether relay 2 is operated or released as far as outputs 1 and 2 are concerned, the same applies to relay 3 and outputs 3 and 4. The simplified circuit appears on the right. This figure uses the more modern symbol for contacts, symbols which are not only easier to draw but also easier to read, particularly for complex circuits.

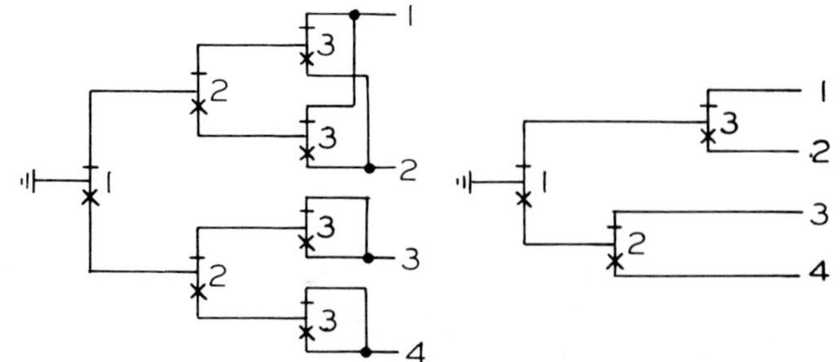

Fig. 14-10 Eliminating unnecessary contacts.

A simplification which is always possible is to eliminate continuity contacts which do not control the relay with the continuity contact. This simplification does not always save contacts but gives a greater choice of relays and enhances reliability. As an illustration Fig. 14-11 shows a circuit in which relay A operating operates D. Later relay B operates after which C operating will release D. On the left in the figure a continuity contact on B establishes the connection through the contact of C before it opens the original operating path. A rearrangement of the circuit as on the right permits a break contact to be substituted for the continuity.

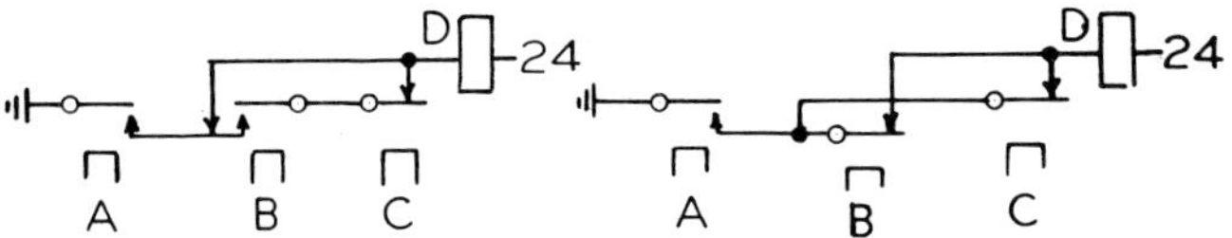

Fig. 14-11 Eliminating continuity contact.

When simplifying relay contact networks, usually it is not difficult to be sure the desired closures are maintained. The danger lies in introducing unexpected closures, the so-called "sneak" paths. Short of knowing how to use Boolian Algebra, the only recourse is to examine the simplified circuit critically for all possible combinations of inputs to assure that the circuit remains open when it must be open and closes when it must be closed. In particular, if the network has several outputs, as does a relay tree, it is possible when simplifying to connect two unselected outputs together, an elementary example of which is shown in Fig. 14-12. In this case W is to be connected to Z if A is normal or to X or Y or both if A is operated and either B or C or both. However when A is released and both B and C are operated, X and Y are connected together. This may cause no problem, for example if X and Y are lamps. However, if X, Y, and Z are track sections, it may cause all sorts of problems to other cabs if X and Y

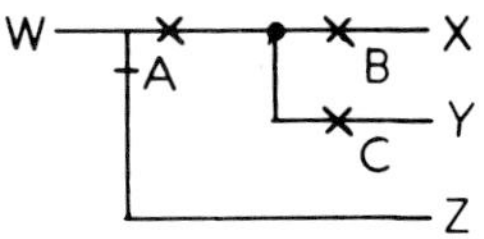

Fig. 14-12 Unselected outputs connected together.

are connected together by cab W when not needed by cab W.

Relay circuits can be designed for extremely complex circuits but most such complex circuits are combinations of simple circuits. For those interested in more information on the design of relay circuits, "The Design of Switching Circuits," by Keister, Ritchie, and Washburn, published by Van Nostrand, is recommended. But the decreasing cost and increasing availability of integrated circuits means that solid state circuits should be considered instead of relays, relays being used only when they are the best choice.

14.5 DETECTION

Relays may be used to detect that current is flowing in a circuit. This ability has been exploited for signal circuits (see Chapter 15). They can detect the polarity of a voltage (polar relays or relays in series with a diode). In this capacity they usually serve as amplifiers. For example the few milliamperes flowing into a resistor-equipped car can be detected and amplified to .1A to light a lamp. As detectors, relays, to a large extent, have been displaced by transistors and integrated circuits as the latter two are far more sensitive and do not introduce the dirty-contact problem. Relays, however, completely separate the input circuit from output circuits and their contacts can carry current equally well in either direction, both of which are significant advantages over semiconductor devices. Further a relay can simultaneously close or open many independent, completely isolated circuits.

15 TRACK CIRCUITS, SIGNALING AND INTERLOCKING

15.1 INTRODUCTION

This Chapter covers track circuits, signals, interlocking, and related subjects as they have been applied to model railroads. It is not a treatise on the prototype. Just as our throttles and motors are not like the operating parts of a steam locomotive, neither do our track circuits and signal circuits resemble those of the prototype. We desire only that our signals give the same aspects as similar signals on the prototype just as we want our locomotives to run in a realistic manner. On the model the emphasis is on the simplest and most practical way of reproducing the visible action of prototype signals. On two-rail layouts in particular we have the non-prototype requirement of supplying running power over the rails.

Prototype signal systems have been under continuous development for over a century and, as a result, detailed systems of circuit schematics and terminology have evolved which are confined to this narrow field. Unfortunately some prototype terms and practices are at variance with customary model railroad usage and if used, would confuse rather than assist. In such cases this Handbook uses terms and practices as understood by model railroaders.

The author acknowledges the assistance of Robert H. Haserodt, William Jambor, Jr. and Henry T. Wilhelm in gathering information for this Chapter.

15.2 TRACK CIRCUITS

15.21 General

A track circuit detects the presence of a locomotive or current-drawing car by detecting current being drawn by that car or locomotive. The output of a track circuit is the closure of a contact or semiconductor switch which in turn operates the signal or interlocking circuits. On the prototype the track circuit also detects broken rails and is designed to fail-safe, i.e. indicate occupancy, in the event of trouble. On the model simplicity, rather than safety, is the objective and, on two-rail layouts, running power must be transmitted over the rails. Therefore track circuits for model railroads are greatly different than those of the prototype. Only those for the model are described.

To avoid the problems of detecting on the same rails supplying the running power, other methods are sometimes used to detect that a train is at a given point, as for example track contacts operated by the wheels. In this Handbook such arrangements are called "presence detectors" and are covered in Section 15.4.

15.22 Model Series and Shunt Track Circuits

The detector of a track circuit can be placed in series with the running power source as on the left in Fig. 15-1 or, as on the right, the running power source can shunt the detector. A series track circuit must handle the heavy running currents yet be sensitive to small currents. A shunt detector is easily made sensitive but some means must be provided to block or interrupt signal current from flowing

through the running power source thereby giving a false indication. Such unwanted current paths are often called "sneak" paths. The essential differences among the various shunt-type track circuits is in how this sneak path is prevented from affecting operation. An additional problem of shunt-type circuits is that they must operate with either polarity of running voltage on the rails, a range of over 24V in most cases.

In Fig. 15-1 the common rail was shown as grounded and the track circuits connected to the control rail. This is the usual practice. If the track circuit is connected to the common rail, as shown in Fig. 15-2 for a series detector, it is possible to sectionalize the common rail into blocks for signal purposes which are independent of the sections for control purposes. This may be a significant advantage, particularly when modeling certain types of prototype signals for often signal blocks as used on the prototype do not correspond to the requirements of control sections on two-rail layouts. There is a slight chance that two cabs set for opposite directions could cancel into the detector. Placing transistor series detectors between the common rail and ground simplifies the circuits, see Section 15.23. Some types of shunt detectors can be connected between the common rail and ground.

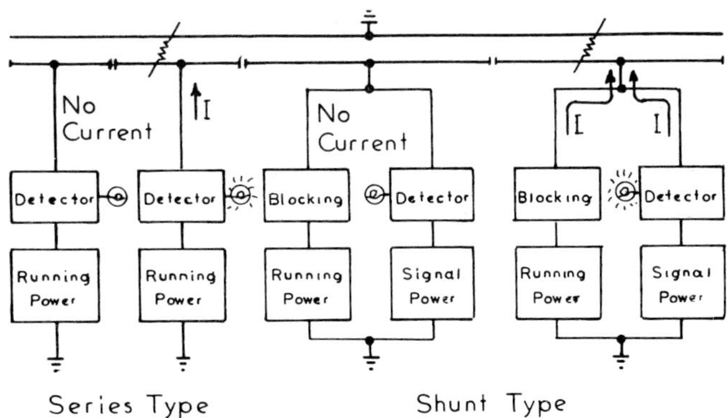

Fig. 15-1 Types of track circuits.

Although modelers tend to call any insulated rail joiner regardless of its purpose a "gap", on the prototype an insulated break for the purposes of signaling is called a "block joint" and one for dividing the line into sections for the independent control of power is called a "section break", both are indicated in Fig. 15-2. Part of the hobby is the correct use of prototype language. Because prototype nomenclature is more precise and less confusing than the model variation "gap", the prototype terms are used exclusively in this handbook where they apply. "Gap" is reserved for model-only applications such as insulated rail joints required because of two-rail.

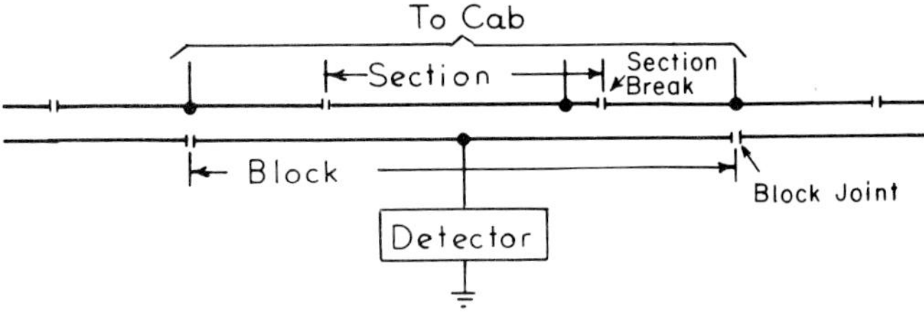

Fig. 15-2 Detector in ground lead.

15.23 Relay Track Circuits

Prototype track circuits typically use relays which are operated by current flowing through the rails and released when wheels and axles shunt the rails or the rails break; this arrangement, for all practical purposes, has never been used on model railroads. Nevertheless, until about 1958, relays were virtually the only occupancy detectors used on models. Due to their historical importance the basic relay track circuits which have been of widespread use are described briefly.

The first and simplest of model track circuits were those for three rail as shown in Fig. 15-3. Since the current to drive the motors did not have to flow through the relay, the winding could be of high resistance, making a relay sensitive enough to be operated reliably by a single pair of wheels shunting the rails.

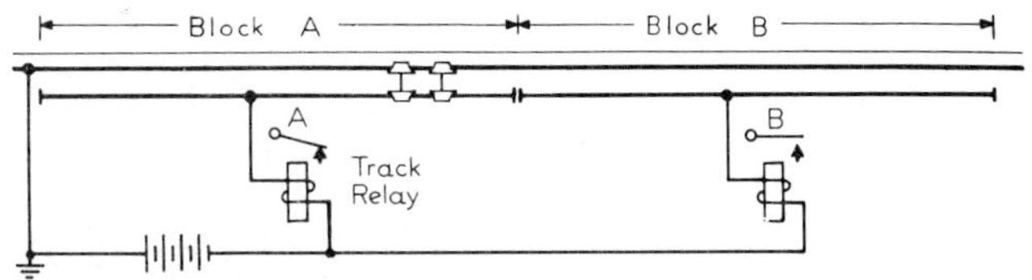

Fig. 15-3 Three-rail track circuit.

The first two-rail track circuit was a relay in series with the power to the track, Fig. 15-4. Because the high currents needed by the locomotives had to flow through the relay winding, that winding had to be of low resistance. Low resistance relays, unfortunately, are insensitive. In the early days this system was used for the lack of something better. The series relay track circuit was never considered satisfactory.

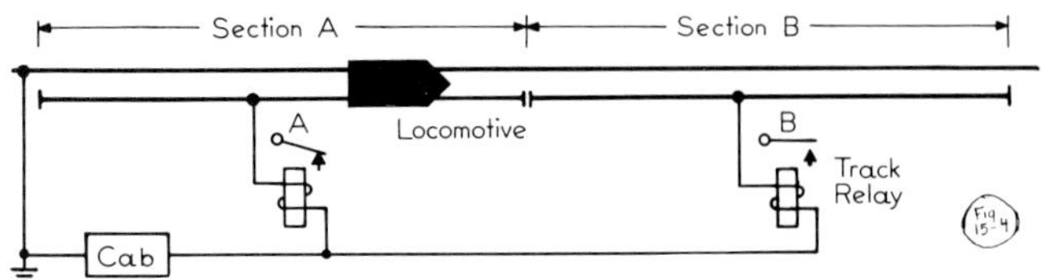

Fig. 15-4 Series relay track circuit.

The Coolidge Circuit, published by Albert Sprague Coolidge in 1935, and shown in its original form in Fig. 15-5, is of historical importance as it is the first of the shunt-type track circuits although the term "shunt" did not come into use until 1942.

In the early days DC power sources were expensive so Coolidge obtained his signal voltage by placing a 6V power source in series with the 12V running power source. This meant that both polarities had to be reversed when reversing direction. Later a separate signal power source, shown as 18V in Fig. 15-5, was used thus making the polarity of the running power independent of the signal circuit.

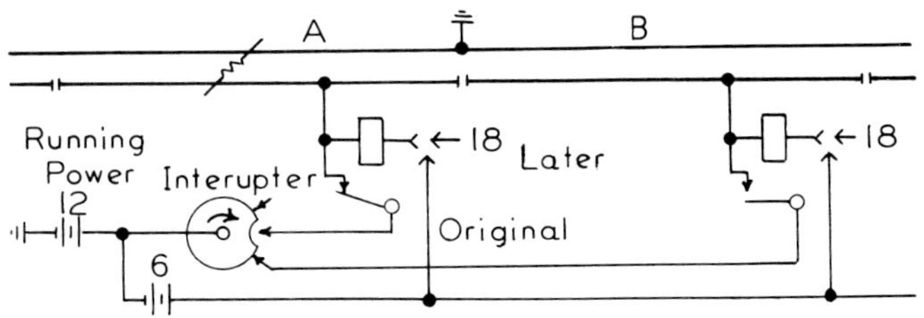

Fig. 15-5 Coolidge track circuit.

Since the relay does not have to carry the running current of the locomotive, it can be sensitive. A locomotive or resistor-equipped car in the section will draw enough current to operate the relay as at A in the figure. The contact on the relay connects running power to the section reducing the voltage across the relay to 6. The relay must hold operated on this lower voltage. The contact also closes the sneak path so the relay will not release even if the section were cleared. Coolidge solved this release problem by using a mechanical interrupter to open the track power circuit briefly at regular intervals. It is this periodic opening of the sneak locking path which identifies a Coolidge circuit.

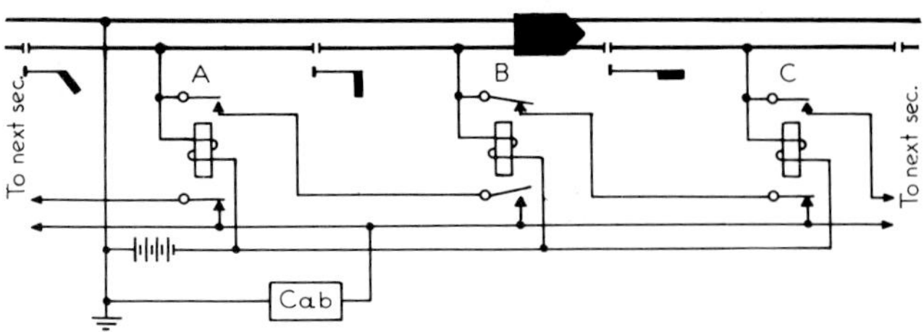

Fig. 15-6 ATC track circuit.

The early relay shunt-type track circuits used relatively low voltages and low-resistance relays. The original Coolidge Circuit, for example, had 80 ohm relays which required .1A to operate. Thus car resistances had to be low with a consequent heavy drain on the running power. In 1942 the author published a track circuit using 2,500 ohm relays and a 60V signal power source, later reduced to 50V. These relays required only a few milliamperes to operate. As in the Coolidge Circuit, a contact on the relay held the running-power path open until the relay was operated by a locomotive or resistor-equipped car. Once this sneak path was closed, it had to be opened by external means or the relay would remain locked. Obviously the high-impedance relay could be used directly in the Coolidge Circuit but in the 1942 article a contact on the next track relay was used to open this sneak path as shown in Fig. 15-6 thus forming an ATC (automatic train control) system as power is cut off to a following train.

If this track circuit is used on a layout equipped with a system of cab control which opens the connection to a section after it is no longer required, the cab-control system opens the sneak path so no other provision need by made. When so used, it is called a CC (Cab Control) track circuit. Apparently the first publication of a track circuit used in such a manner was in 1948 by Raymond Hein and Frank Arnaud of the Milwaukee, Wisconsin club. Fig. 15-7 shows their circuit.

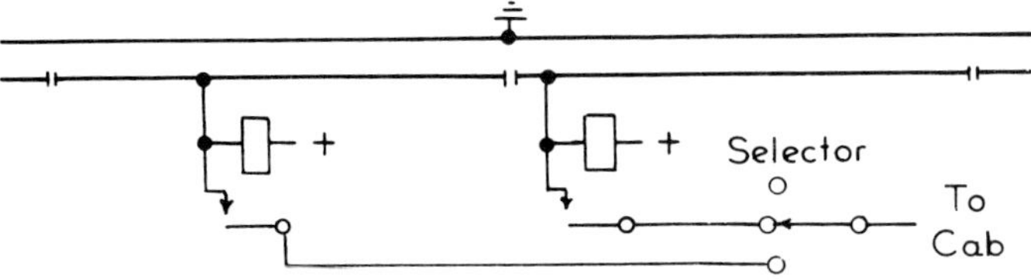

Fig. 15-7 Cab-control track circuit.

In 1947 the author published a variation of the high-impedance relay track circuit which used a diode to block the sneak path, the higher voltage of the signal power source holding the diode back-biased when the block was unoccupied. In 1949 this circuit was put out in kit form by the NMRA, hence its present name. The basic NMRA circuit is shown in Fig. 15-8.

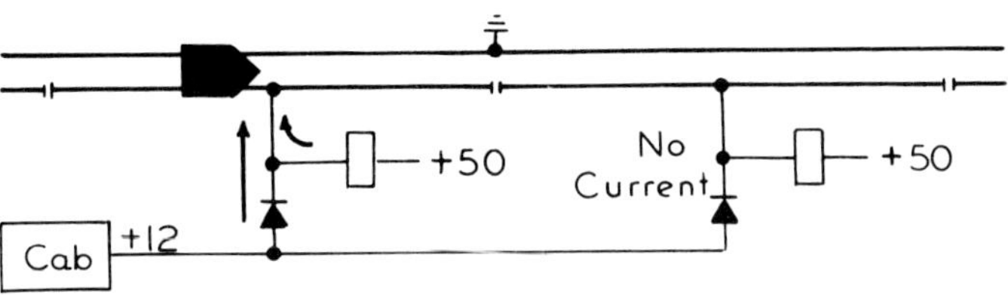

Fig. 15-8 NMRA track circuit.

15.23 Semiconductor Track Circuits

Although the NMRA track circuit used a diode to block the shunt path, it was not until the price of transistors had dropped to reasonable levels that semiconductor track circuits came into their own. There was, nevertheless, one intermediate step of importance. In 1953 John F. Brownlow disclosed a series relay circuit which used a sensitive relay rather than the usual low-resistance type and thus was able to detect much lower currents. To prevent the resistance of the relay from interfering with the large currents required for motor operation, diodes were used to bypass the relay once the voltage across the winding exceeded the threshold voltage of the diode paths. Thus the detector received all the current at low-voltage levels but the maximum voltage which could appear across this track circuit was determined by the diodes. See Section 2.57. In its simplest form this track circuit appears in Fig. 15-9. Sometimes such a circuit is called a 2-D track circuit.

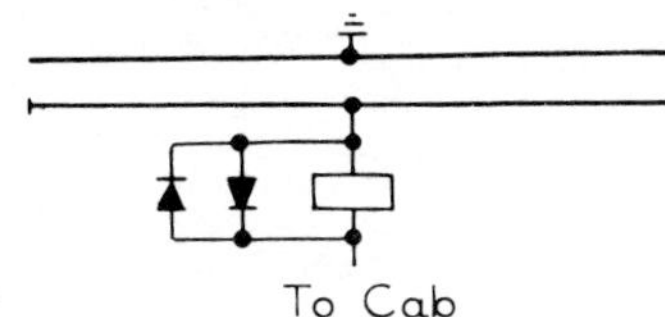

Fig. 15-9 Relay-diode track circuit.

Twin-T Track Circuit

A major breakthrough in track circuits came in 1958 when Linn Westcott published the Twin-T series track circuit shown in Fig. 15-10. This circuit passes the DC from the cab to the rails through the base-emitter diode of a power transistor (either npn or pnp). Two transistors are needed to permit bidirectional current flow, hence the name Twin-T.

The original Twin-T circuit passes the entire locomotive current through the base lead. Thus the base current rating had to equal at least the maximum current being supplied to the track. Even power transistors rated at 5A collector current and 75 watts virtually never have a maximum emitter-base rating of more than 1A. In HO and O, often in N, it is usually necessary to handle more than 1A track current, 3A being good for HO. For this reason the author never used the original Twin-T circuit but always added the two shunting diodes indicated in 15-10. These diodes are not critical, a 2A or 5A diode shunting a transistor with a 1A base current rating usually will operate well but too-large a diode may divert virtually all the current. Trial is the best selection method.

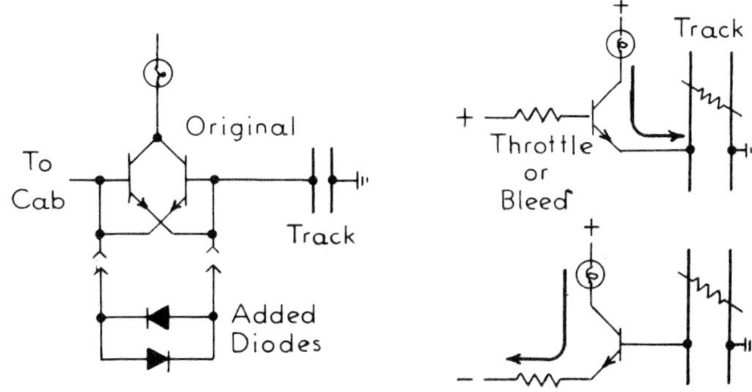

Fig. 15-10 Twin-T track circuit.

It is important to note that the output current of the Twin-T (the lamp current in Fig. 15-10 must flow either through the resistance bridging the rails or through the throttle (or bleed) resistor depending upon polarity as shown on the right. If either of these resistances are too great, the Twin-T will not deliver the necessary output current. As these two resistances probably are not equal, the sensitivity of the Twin-T will appear to be different for the two directions.

Germanium transistors, now almost obsolete, have leakage circuits which make them impractical for use in a Twin-T circuit; they tend to stay on. Always use silicon transistors for a Twin-T even if germanium transistors are free.

Transistor outputs are not isolated from their inputs. Therefore, if a Twin-T is placed in series with the control rail, its on output voltage will swing virtually as widely as the voltage applied by the cab, that is from +12 to −12, as shown at the top of Fig. 15-11. The voltage applied to the load must be higher than 12, 24 being shown in the figure. But if the Twin-T is placed between the common rail and ground, its on output voltage will never be much more than ± .5V from ground as indicated in the bottom half of Fig. 15-11. Also, when connected to the common rail, the blocks for signaling can be different than the sections for control. Because of these two advantages, the Twin-T circuits shown in this Handbook are generally connected to the common rail.

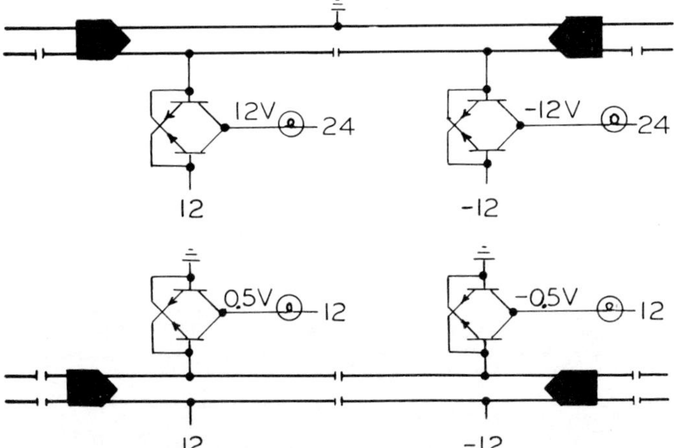

Fig. 15-11 Output voltage swings.

The voltages given in Fig. 15-11 assume that the resistances bridging the rail (locomotive motor) and those in series with the cab power are low enough that the transistor is turned fully on and lamp current is not limited by those resistances.

When a Twin-T is placed in the lead to the control rail, its load must be able to stand the wide swings of voltage indicated at the top of Fig. 15-11 or some sort of voltage shifter must be installed. A relay would serve, its contacts then being used to drive the signals and other lamps. Better than a relay is the transistor voltage shifter shown in Fig. 15-12. Either Q1 or Q2 will turn on Q3 so the output from Q3 is either 24V or ground regardless of the polarity of cab voltage. Equally important is that only a small current is required to turn on Q3 thus minimizing the resistance effects shown on the right

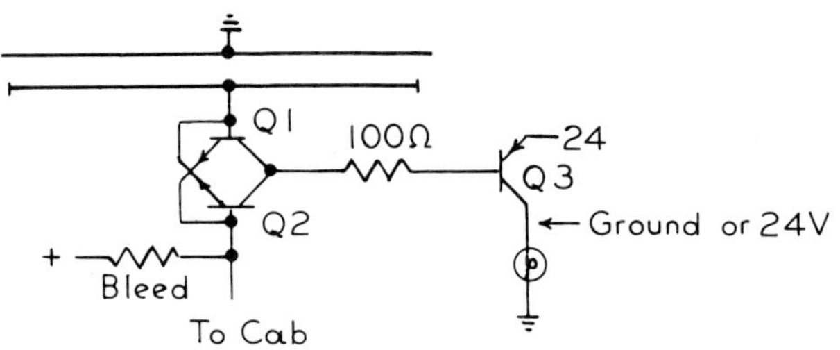

Fig. 15-12 Voltage shifter.

of Fig. 15-10. For this reason amplifiers are desirable on the outputs of Twin-T circuits even when they are connected to the common rail.

Also shown in Fig. 15-12 is the bleed resistor which supplies current to operate the Twin-T when the cab is not connected. This resistor should always drive current into a base so it is not in series with the collector current of the Twin-T. The bleed current should be the lowest which will operate the Twin-T for, if the cab is of the opposite polarity (minus in the case shown) and drawing approximately the same current, it will cancel the bleed. If the bleed current is low, the cab can always be made to draw a minimum current at least twice the bleed so cancellation is impossible.

Shunt-type Transistor Track Circuits

The shunt-type relay track circuit was developed and used extensively only because it could be far more sensitive than the series relay track circuits. Although it is a simple matter to design a shunt-type transistor track circuit, (indeed several such using both transistors and SCRs have been published) they will retain the problem of blocking the sneak path which plagued shunt-type relay circuits. Since the Twin-T circuit (with amplifiers if needed) and especially operational amplifier track circuits provide all the sensitivity required and they are series-type circuits, no advantage had yet been shown for any semiconductor shunt-type track circuit over that obtainable by the Twin-T or operation amplifier circuits.

Operational Amplifier Track Circuit

The major problems of the Twin-T track circuit are its lack of sensitivity and the need for large semiconductor devices to pass the train current. Integrated-circuit operational amplifiers (OpAmps) have voltage gains in the tens of thousands compared to the 20 or 50 of power transistors. OpAmps can, therefore, detect very small voltage changes such as those developed over a short piece of wire. OpAmp track circuits consequently do not have the problems of the Twin-T and, in addition, are smaller, easier to wire, and usually less expensive.

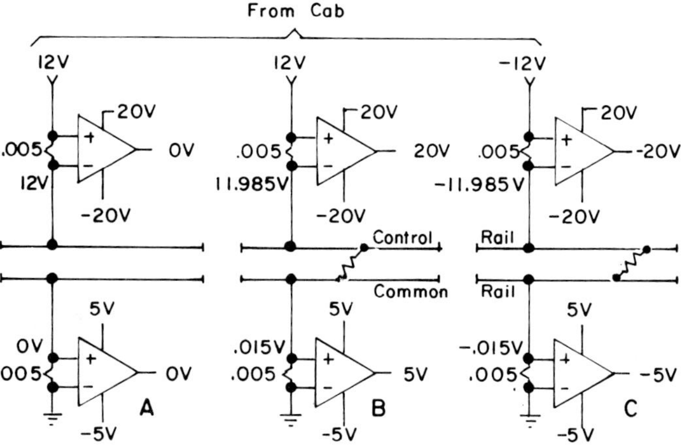

Fig. 15-13 Operational amplifier track circuits, bipolar outputs.

The output of an OpAmp depends upon the voltage applied between its two inputs, not on the voltage common from both inputs to the ground (see Fig. 24-51). The polarity of the output voltage depends on the polarity applied to the inputs. Fig. 15-13 shows three cases of inputs and outputs to OpAmp track circuits. In each case two track circuits are shown, one in the feeder to the control rail and the other in the series with the common rail. At A nothing is shunting the rails so no current is flowing through the feeders to the rails. In this case the output voltage of both amplifiers is approximately zero (ground). At B positive voltage is supplied to the control rail and current is being drawn. There is a 0.015V drop across the wires con- the same as the polarity marked inside the OpAmp symbol. This 0.015V is amplified and the output voltage of the OpAmp approaches that of the positive voltage supply. At C negative voltage is applied to the control rail so the voltage drop across each amplifier is reversed. The output voltage is applied to the control rail so the voltage drop across each amplifier is reversed. The output voltage now approaches that of the negative voltage supply.

Note that for the top three OpAmps of Fig. 15-13 both inputs of each OpAmp swing from approximately +12 (B) to −12V (C) as measured to ground. Although the voltage to ground is not amplified (only the voltage between the inputs is effective), for proper operation the common voltage to ground must be less than the power-supply voltages to the operational amplifier (±20V supplies are shown in Fig. 15-13). If the amplifier is in the lead to the common rail, one input is at ground and the other is never more than 0.1V from ground. Therefore the power-supply voltages can be much lower (±5V being shown). In 1982, the 741, an excellent, low-cost, widely available operational amplifier suitable for track circuits was available for about $0.44. Dual and quad units of essentially the same amplifier were also available.

The sensitivity of an operational-amplifier track circuit depends primarily upon the resistance of the wire between the input terminals. If we assume a gain of 10,000 and desire a minimum output of 5V when 0.01A is being drawn, we need a resistance of 0.005 ohms, about 150mm (6″) of No. 20 copper wire will serve. The voltage drop at 3A due to this track circuit would be 0.015V, a negligible amount as far as influencing the speed of a locomotive. The voltage drop across a Twin-T track circuit, in contrast, is about 0.8V.

In Fig. 15-13 (B and C) it can be seen that the polarity of the output of an operational amplifier track circuit depends upon the direction of the current being detected. If the amplifier is merely driving an occupancy indicator lamp on the panel, or if it is operating a relay, this bipolar output is quite satisfactory. But, if the output is to serve as an input to integrated-circuit logic, for most forms of logic the output must be unipolar and often must be limited in its maximum voltage. In the case of TTL logic, the output should be either near ground or not greatly in excess of 5V. One method of converting the bipolar output of the detecting operational amplifier into a unipolar output with limited swing is shown in Fig. 15-14. The output of the detecting operational amplifier is connected to the negative input of an inverting amplifier through a voltage divide. If the output of the detector goes negative, the output of the inverter will go positive. The selecting diodes will pass only the positive output and the limiting diode will hold the maximum voltage to about 5.6V. The voltage divider at the input of the inverting amplifier prevents a slight negative output from the detecting amplifier from being accepted as an occupied indication. Some ICs have internal limiting diodes so it is unnecessary to supply the separate diodes shown in Fig. 15-14. Check the circuit diagram on the manufacturer's specification sheet.

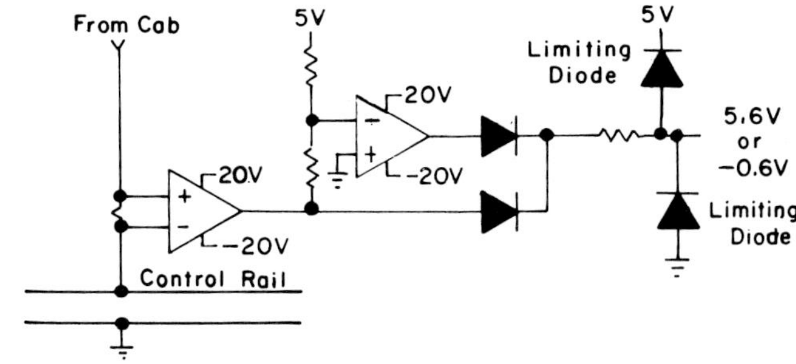

Fig. 15-14 Operational amplifier track circuits, unipolar output.

In Fig. 15-14 the track circuit is in the control lead and is powered by ±20V. If the track circuit were in the common-rail feeder, as at the bottom of Fig. 15-13, ±5V supplies could be used and the limiting diodes shown in Fig. 15-14 omitted as the output voltage could not exceed the +5V supply.

15.3 CAR DETECTION

DC track circuits detect the flow of current between the rails through a resistance path in the locomotives and cars. Motorized or lighted equipment have such paths built in but other cars, if they are to operate the track circuit, must be equipped with a resistor across the rails.

A conventional resistor can be connected between two trucks provided they have metal wheels as shown in Fig. 15-15. The resis-

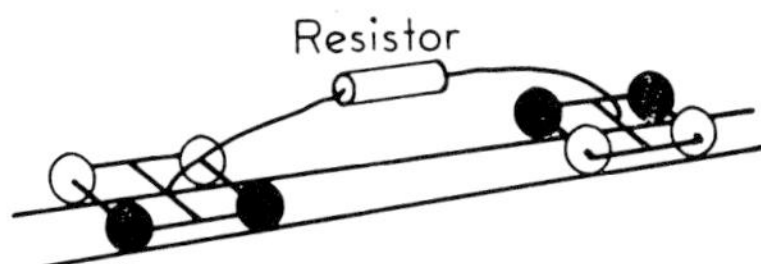

Fig. 15-15 Car resistor.

tance depends upon the current requirements of the track circuit. Cars which must operate the track circuit by themselves should have the highest resistance value which will reliably operate the track circuit. This is best determined by trial. The wattage rating of the resistor should be greater than 150 divided by the resistance if track voltage is 12.

Equipping many cars with resistors, particularly if they are already built, is a tedious job but one which can be simplified by applying resistance paint across the insulation between a metal wheel and the axle. Suitable resistance paints are available from several sources. Micro-Circuits Company, New Buffalo, Michigan, has marketed it in small quantities.

To apply the paint, first clean the wheel and axle on either side of the insulation and slightly roughen the insulation surface. Then, as shown in Fig. 15-16, draw a line over the insulation lapping both the wheel and the axle. A toothpick makes a convenient applicator. The resistance formed will depend upon the paint, the width and the length of the line. If the resistance of the paint is too low, the axle can be lacquered to provide a longer insulated path for the paint. For reliability there should be a painted resistor on each axle, each being four times the resistance desired for a single car. The use of resistance paint was reported by the author in 1951.

Fig. 15-16 Applying resistance paint.

The widespread use of plastic wheels by 1980 has made the installation of resistors in cars difficult unless the wheels are changed. Linn Westcott reported good success in painting the wheels with silver conducting paint from Micro-Circuits and connecting the silver with resistance paints but this method never gained wide acceptance.

When a track circuit is capable of responding to either AC or DC as is the case for the Twin-T and operational amplifier, cars can be equipped with capacitors rather than with resistors. To keep the capacitors physically small, the frequency impressed on the rails for the purpose of detection must be considerably higher than the 60Hz line frequency. Ultrasonic frequencies in the range of 25kHz to 100kHz are satisfactory. Cars equipped for ultrasonic-frequency lighting will, of course, operate such track circuits. One advantage of using capacitors is that, when many cars are equipped to operate signals, they do not load the DC throttles supplying power to locomotives.

One system of computer cab control existing in 1979 utilized detection of direct current to determine the location of powered units. Cars were detected either by presence detectors or by alternating current at ultrasonic frequencies.

15.4 PRESENCE DETECTORS

15.41 General

The problem of using the same rails for supplying running power and also for detection lead to an early interest in detecting the presence of a train by other than track circuits. The difficulty of installing resistors on cars with plastic wheels maintains that interest today. Presence detectors, as described in the Handbook, include all means of detecting a car or locomotive at a particular point except those depending on conducting current between the two rails.

Although presence detectors are usually associated with two rail, they were used in three-rail days, some taking the form of a short third rail contacting the free end of the third-rail shoe.

15.42 Track Contacts

Three forms of track contacts are shown on Fig. 15-17. On the left a guard rail is arranged to rub the inside of the flanges so metal wheels connect the guard rail to (usually) the common rail. R.W. Chaffee described such a system in 1934. At the center of the figure a short isolated piece of rail is connected to the adjacent rail by metal wheels. At the right a contact serving as part of the rail head is pressed down against the common rail to establish a connection.

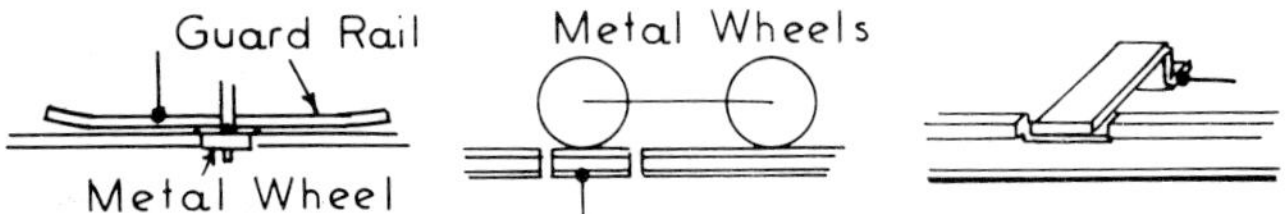

Fig. 15-17 Track contacts.

Systems which depend upon metal wheels to establish contact will not work with plastic wheels and so have fallen into disuse. Contact fingers which are forced down by the weight of a wheel of necessity must operate with very light pressure. The necessary contact flexibility is usually obtained by a long contact arm difficult to conceal. Further the contact normally is of base metal and unreliable. Best results are obtained if the contact drives a high-impedance detector. An integrated circuit gate, or as shown in Fig. 15-18, an inverter can be used. Care must be taken that voltages which will damage the detector are suitably blocked, diodes being used for the purpose in Fig. 15-18. Now, even if the contact to the rail is poor, perhaps hundreds of ohms, its closure will still be detected. Using an operational amplifier instead of a gate or inverter would make an even more sensitive detecting circuit.

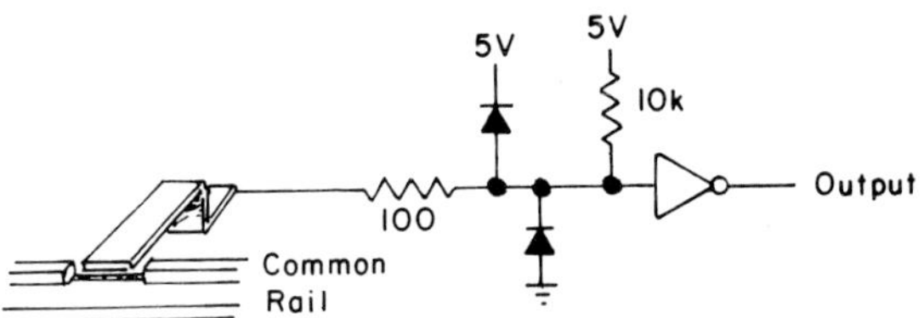

Fig. 15-18 Presence detector.

Another form of contact is one separate from the rail which is closed by a passing flange either by being forced down by the rim of the flange or sidewise by the back of the flange. Since these tend to lift wheels, they present a derailment hazard, especially in smaller gauges.

Contacts closed by the weight of a car on the rail have been used but introduce problems of track construction due to the flexibility required to permit the track to deflect sufficiently to close a contact reliably. Commercial track sections with such a switch have been available, one in HO being the Trigor by Walthers. Lionel and other of the toy-train makers have also extensively used such pressure sections in the past.

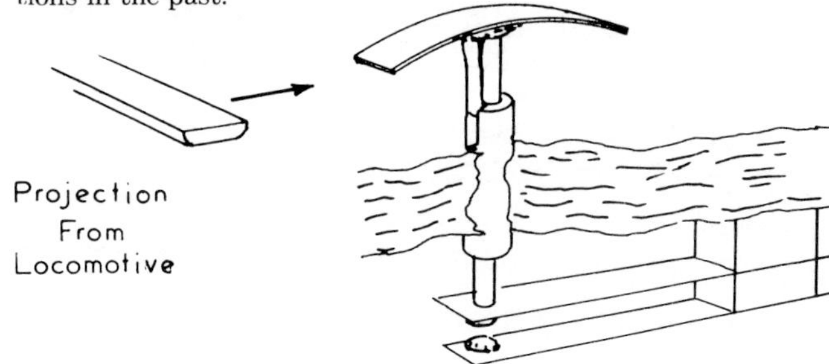

Fig. 15-19 Ramp-type contact.

Contacts which are operated by special shoes attached to locomotives and cars have been extensively used and have been commercially available. Generally, they are in the form of a short, double-ended ramp which is forced down and closes a contact. Fig. 15-19 shows a unit of this type. A variation is a dry-reed contact or some other switch which can be operated by a magnet-equipped locomotive or car.

15.43 Photodetectors

Due to the light weight of N scale cars and many HO cars, mechanical contact with them is not desirable. A more reliable presence detector than any contact is a photodetector such as a phototransistor which detects that a car or locomotive has interrupted the light from a lamp or light-emitting diode (LED). The advantage of using an infrared LED is that there will be no visible light. LED's have virtually infinite life in model railroad service.

Fig. 15-20 shows the angle of slant of the IR beam that is required to assure that the beam will be interrupted by any combination of cars or locomotives. This angle was determined by experiments on the HO layout of The Model RR Club. At that time (1979) the cost of the IR LED and the phototransistor was the controlling factor. The Club developed the circuit shown in the figure so that any of the available low-cost LEDs and phototransistors could be used. The circuit otherwise is standard, from detector to detector.

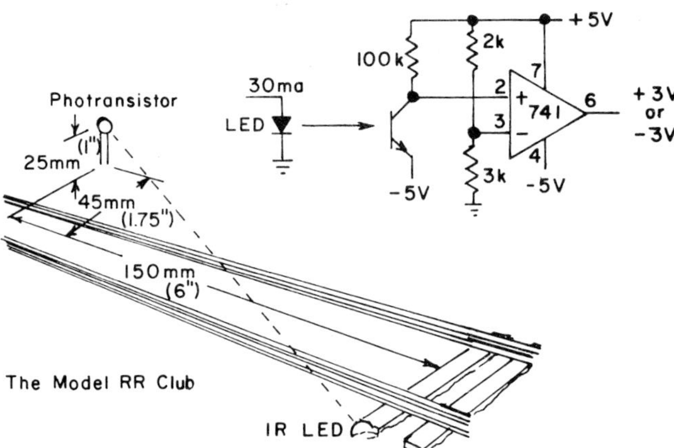

Fig. 15-20 Details of a photodetector presence detector.

Most model railroads never operate in the dark. Therefore the room lights can be used to activate the phototransistors. This is simpler because the phototransistors can then be mounted in the ties facing up, an inconspicuous position. Used in this way they will detect the openings between cars as the couplers do not block the ambient light sufficiently. If it is necessary to detect a train constantly from front to back, two phototransistors connected in series and spaced about 50mm (2″) apart along the center line of the track will serve. When one is exposed to light falling between cars, the other is shaded. See Fig. 15-55 for an example.

The beam of infrared light could be sent along the track using either a succession of LEDs and phototransistors or mirrors to follow curves. In this way a car anywhere in the block would interrupt the beam and the detector would serve as a track circuit. The tight and numerous curves on the average model railroad makes this method difficult. It is simpler to install a circuit which remembers the state of occupancy determined by the outputs of the presence detectors.

The circuits shown depend on an absolute difference, e.g. *shaded* yields a logical low and *not shaded* a logical high. If the photodetectors are serving as inputs to a microprocessor, the output of the non-shaded detector can be digitalized and stored in RAM. Any significant change from that value then can be recognized as a *shaded* indication. This not only would guarantee proper operation under changing conditions of the ambient lighting but also would reduce the number of photodetectors required as partial shading, as by couplers between cars, could be recognized as *shaded.*

15.5 SIGNALS

15.51 General

There are many types of signals on the prototype including hand and whistle signals but, in this Handbook, signal means only an electrically operated device such as a block signal or cab signal. To duplicate on a model the action and appearance of the prototype, a general knowledge of prototype signals is required. Section 15.52 covers the use of prototype block and interlocking signal systems and the signals themselves. Only typical applications of systems in general use after 1900 are included. Section 15.53 covers the construction of model signals, Section 15.54 the circuits necessary to operate model signals, Section 15.55, Interlocking, Section 15.56 Automatic Train Control (ATC), and Section 15.57 covers model cab signals.

15.52 Prototype Signal Practice

Block Signals

Block signals warn trains of the presence of other trains. The first attempts were based on time intervals, an early signal being a ball which was raised to the top of a mast when a train passed then slowly fell. A second train then would receive an indication of the time lapse between trains. Since time interval did not protect a slowly moving or stopped train, it rapidly gave way to space-interval systems based on blocks. The rule book definition of a block is a length of track within defined limits the use of which is governed by block signals: To avoid ambiguity in this Handbook the word "block" is used exclusively in this prototype sense. Many model railroaders apply this term also the electrically isolated track sections used for locomotive control.

Blocks can be manual or automatic. An example of a manual block is that portion of the railroad between two block stations. The operators at such stations have block signals which are normally at stop and cleared only when a train is to be admitted to the block. These signals are operated on the basis of records kept at the block station in accordance with the rules of the railroad. The block signal is restored to stop as soon as the train enters the block. In some cases this is done automatically by some sort of a presence detector operated by the passing train. The signal will not clear again without action by the operator.

Manual block is still extensively used as described above and in other forms. It is the stand-by system to automatic block on some railroads. It is also in use to control movements against the current of traffic in automatic block territory. Electrically it is trivial unless the signals restore to stop automatically. The operator merely needs some means of setting his block signals.

Automatic block uses electrical detection of a car or locomotive by track circuits both to set the signal at stop and also to clear the signal when the block is empty. Aspect is the appearance of the signal, e.g. red. Indication is the meaning of the aspect, e.g. stop.

The simplest automatic block system used two-position signals as shown in Fig. 15-21. For simplicity of diagrams this figure, and most others, indicate semaphores but any type of signal could be installed. In Fig. 15-21 the semaphore protecting an occupied block has a horizontal blade, the indication is stop. A lowered blade indicates a clear block, proceed. Two-direction track requires separate signals for each direction but they do not have to be of the same type, e.g. semaphore one way, color light the other.

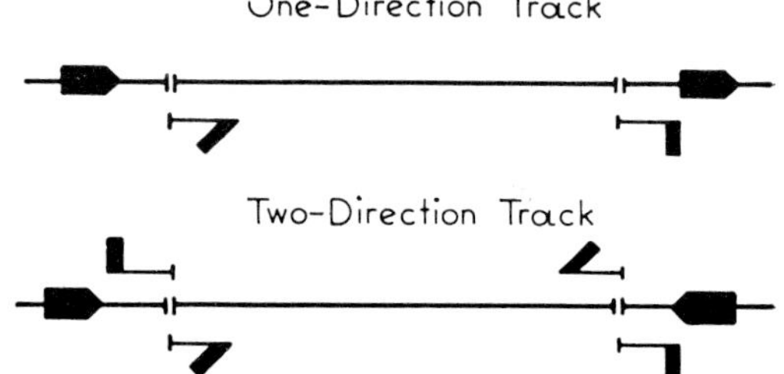

Fig. 15-21 Two position signals.

Two-position signals provide no warning of approach to a red aspect. It is conceivable on two-direction track that opposing trains could cross into the same block simultaneously, both on green signals. This was the apparent cause of the disastrous head-on wreck between two fan-trip trains at the 1950 NMRA National Convention.

An early solution to warn of an approach to a signal indicating stop was to provide a distant signal which repeated the aspect of the home signal which governed entrance to the block. Such distant signals could be mounted on a separate mast as shown on the top in Fig. 15-22 (used when blocks were long and for manual block) or on the mast of the preceding home signal as at the bottom. To distinguish a distant signal from a home, distant semaphores typically had yellow fish-tail blades and displayed a yellow or green light and home signals had square or pointed red blades, the light being red or green. The yellow aspect of a distant signal is "approach prepared to stop at the next signal," usually just called "approach."

Although 3-position lower-quadrant semaphores were used, it was not until the upper-quadrant semaphore was introduced about 1903 that 3-position signals came into common usage. Fig. 15-23 shows three-position semaphores. A 45° blade with a yellow light indicates approach.

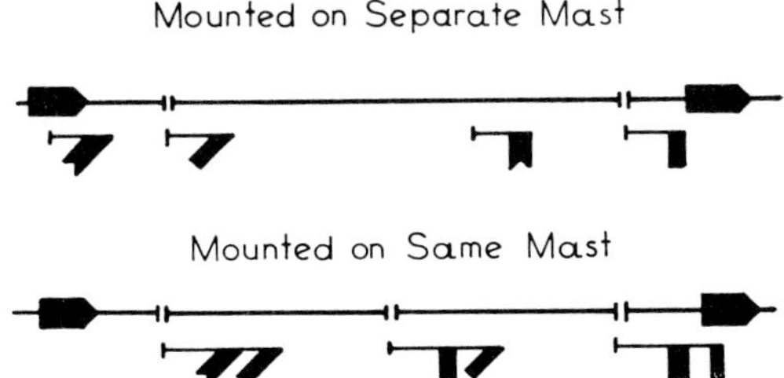

Fig. 15-22 Distant signals.

Three-position signals do not guarantee that opposing trains will see a stop indication before they enter the same block. To prevent such a meet, traffic can be established by setting all signals of the opposing direction to stop as at the top of Fig. 15-24. The signal governing the entrance to the single track is sometimes called the "headblock" signal. It is set to stop when traffic is established in the opposite direction by a block operator, CTC operator, or automatically by the first train entering the single track. An automatic system of this type is called APB (absolute permissive block) as the headblock signal is absolute, the others permissive.

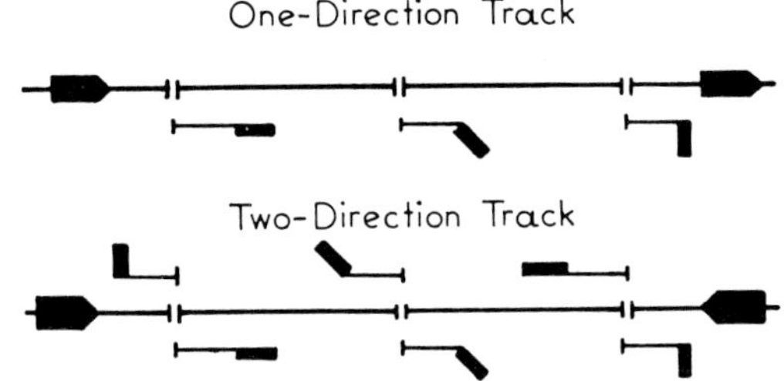

Fig. 15-23 Upper quadrant signals.

For ABS (automatic block system) a system called "overlap" is installed. As shown at the bottom of Fig. 15-24, a train approaching a clear block sets the signal protecting the opposite end of that block to stop as soon as the overlap track circuit is reached. An opposing train would have done the same for the opposite direction. Thus it is impossible for two trains to enter the same block without either of them seeing a stop indication.

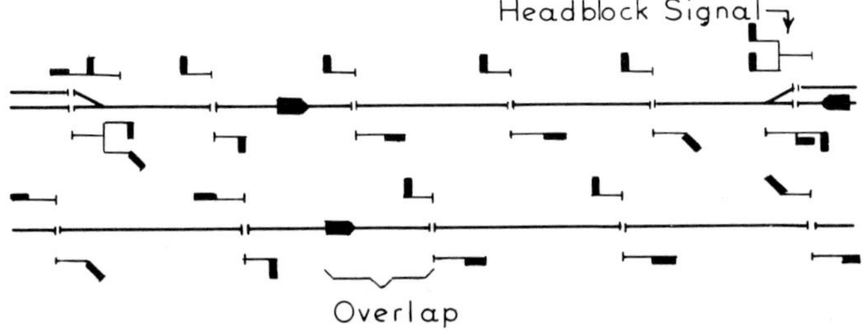

Fig. 15-24 Protection against opposing trains.

For heavy traffic, short blocks are installed. This makes it desirable to indicate track conditions for more than two blocks ahead. A common solution is to add another signal head as shown in Fig. 15-25. The extra indication, yellow over green is approach medium, meaning approach the next signal at medium speed.

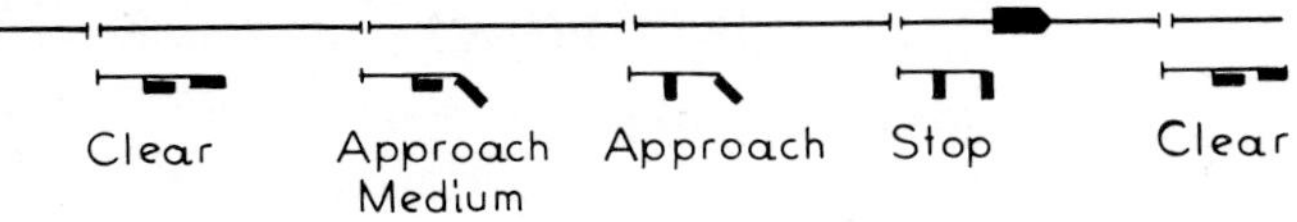

Fig. 15-25 Signals for short blocks.

The most restrictive indication of automatic block signals generally is "stop and proceed," a permissive signal. This permits a train to proceed past a red signal in such a manner that it can stop short of any obstruction including a broken rail. The purpose is to avoid tying up the line in the event of a signal failure or other cause which does not prevent the safe passage of trains. A number of means are used to indicate that a signal is permissive, the most common being a number plate on the mast as shown in Fig. 15-26. Semaphores often use a pointed blade and they, as well as light signals, may display a red marker lamp or another signal head diagonally below the top signal head.

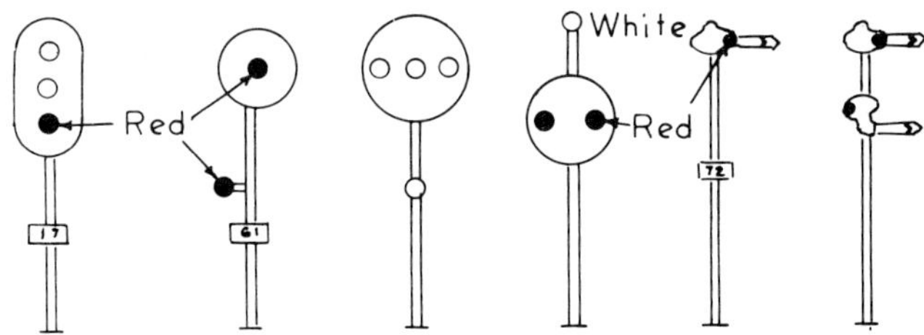

Fig. 15-26 Aspects indicating stop and proceed.

When the indication is stop and stay, the signal is called absolute. These usually are interlocking signals although they may also serve as block signals. Such signals commonly do not have a number plate although the Missouri Pacific numbered all signals and displayed a plaque with an A on the mast of absolute signals. As shown in Fig. 15-26 absolute signals may display a red marker on the mast. On absolute signals, markers or multiple heads are in a vertical line with the top signal head. On permissive signals they are at an angle across the mast. Semaphores usually have a square-ended blade on absolute signals.

To lengthen lamp life and conserve power, approach lighting is used by some railroads on block signals. The signals are illuminated only when a train is approaching that signal. On multiple track, all signals are illuminated together, not just the one controlling the approaching train. On model railroads, approach lighting tends to reduce the effectiveness of block signals.

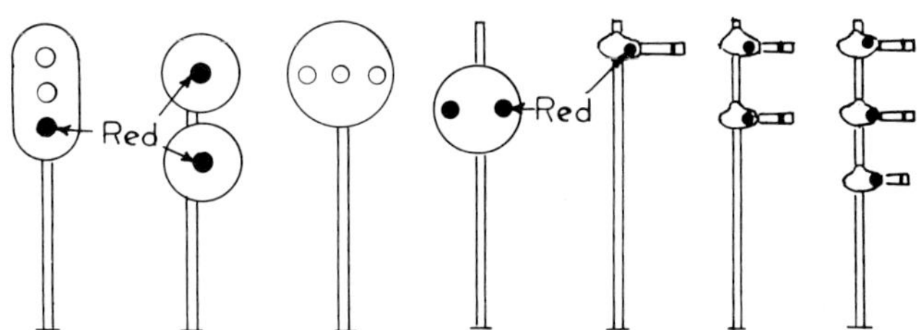

Fig. 15-27 Aspects indicating absolute stop.

Interlocking Signals

Interlocking signals govern the movement of trains over switches, crossings, drawbridges and similar track configurations. The signals which govern the entrance into an interlocking plant are called home signals, the same as those at the entrance of a block, and are always absolute. Distant signals are used with interlocking home signals in much the same manner as distant signals in automatic block except there are usually more aspects for interlocking service.

There are many variations of interlocking practice among railroads and, often, even between two interlocking plants on the same railroad, especially on a railroad formed by a merger of two or more large railroads, such as Conrail. If modeling a particular prototype, it is necessary to obtain precise information about that railroad and for that particular location. This Handbook covers typical interlocking practices for various types of signals rather than specifics for any particular system.

To a modeler an important distinction is whether all signals are normally red or if they normally show a clear route. Some railroads hold all interlocking home signals at stop, even if a route is clear, and clear them only for a movement. These cleared signals automatically return to stop in block-signal fashion as the train passes the signal. In some plants the signal will "stick": remain red even after the train clears the block unless restored to clear by the operator. In other plants the signal will change to approach, then to clear in normal block-signal fashion as the train moves on. The normally set-to-stop system is shown for a grade crossing on the top of Fig. 15-28.

Other railroads display clear signals for a route which has been cleared through the interlocking plant, e.g. NYC, NYNH&H, and rapid transit lines. This is shown at the bottom of Fig. 15-28. Railroads which use the stick system often are able to convert a plant to non-stick (normal clear) for the preferred route at towers which are closed part time. Model railroaders generally prefer the normally-clear system as the signals then provide an indication of which route is established and, in most cases, the circuits and operation are simpler.

For automatic interlocking, the signals are normally set to stop but the first train on the approach will cause its route to clear.

Signals at early interlockings indicated the cleared route. For example red over green would indicate a clear diverging route. However indicating each specific route in complex trackage requires many signal heads and possibly many signal bridges. About the time light signals started to displace semaphores, speed indications rather than route indications came to the fore, e.g. red over green would indicate medium speed clear, called medium clear. Thus enginemen were informed at what speed they should pass through the interlocking but not the route they would follow. For example the final

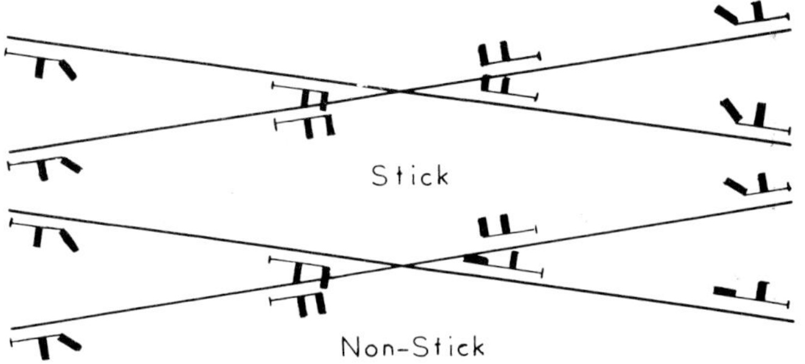

Fig. 15-28 Grade-crossing interlocking.

interlocking signals at the DL&W Hoboken terminal had only two aspects, red (stop), red over yellow (proceed at restricted speed). The engineman did not know to which of the many platform tracks he was being sent.

As a practical matter on small interlockings there is no difference between these two types but, for model railroad operational purposes, route interlocking signals are generally preferred as a visual indication of the route cleared and has more value than a speed indication.

Once a train is in the interlocking, it is detected by track circuits which then lock the machine preventing any changes which affect the occupied route. Complex trackwork may require several short sections of track called "cut sections" within an interlocking, each with its own track circuit. Such sections are similar to the X Sections described in Section 8.7. If track exists within the interlocking which cannot be protected by a track circuit (a crossing with no insulated joints in the crossing itself is the most common example), "trap circuits" are used. The trap is set by a track circuit as a train approaches the unprotected track and cannot be released until the train enters and clears the track circuit on the exit side of the unprotected track. If a trap is set by a movement which does not continue, it must be released manually by the tower operator or by a signal maintainer depending upon the particular interlocking. Trap circuits are important to a model railroader primarily because they are the nearest prototype for "check-out" systems used for two-rail signaling.

Interlocking plants typically use two or three heads on each signal although one or two of the heads may be replaced by red markers. Older interlockings, particularly with lower-quadrant semaphores, often used one-head interlocking signals as did the SP, UP, WP, and NYC among others. In recent years, for economy, some roads have changed to single-headed interlocking signals where

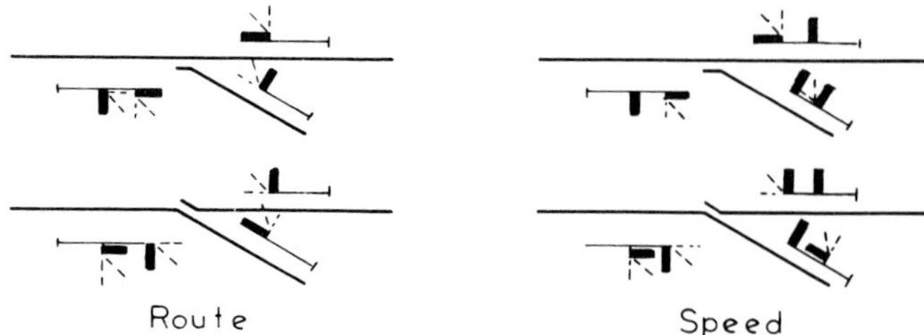

Fig. 15-29 Interlockings for a diverging route.

there is only a high-speed route. The CRRNJ normally used three-headed interlocking signals on that road, and single-headed signals, both high and dwarf were assumed to be the lowest head with the upper two displaying red.

Early route interlocking systems used only as many heads as were necessary to indicate the available routes. This simplification is another reason why route indications are preferred by model railroaders. Fig. 15-29 shows a simple diverging route, route indications on the left and speed on the right. These signals would also show block signal aspects. In this simple example the speed signals show the route as clearly as do the route signals.

Dwarf signals are extensively used within interlockings to govern low-speed and reverse movements. These signals may have the same force as the lowest head on the interlocking high signals or they may replace a single-headed high signal depending upon the railroad. Fig. 15-30 shows dwarf signals controlling movements over crossovers. In general dwarf signals are physically small and mounted at track level but some roads also mount them on bridges. Dwarf signals are absolute.

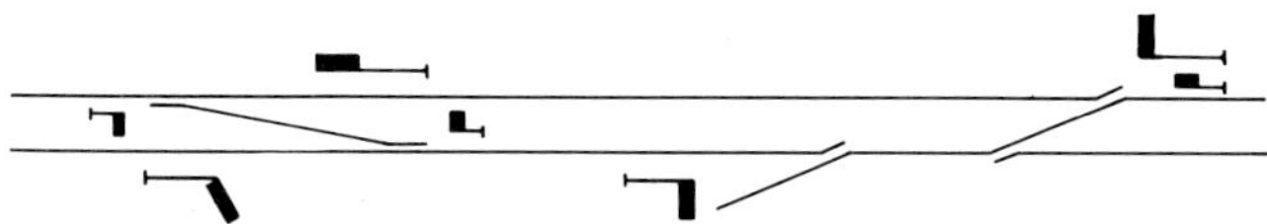
Fig. 15-30 Dwarf signals.

Although speed-type interlockings are the most common today, Fig. 15-31 shows the Reading -CRRNJ junction, tower RK, as it existed in 1971. Semaphores are diagrammed but the signals were actually color light. Although nominally a speed-type tower, the signals actually displayed routes. The Model Railroad Club included a scale model of this interlocking in their plans.

In Fig. 15-31 note that the westbound signals for both tracks 2 and 4 display medium clear, R over G over R, for the diverging route to Reading 1, but the speeds authorized by the timetable for these two routes are different. For a speed-type tower, medium clear

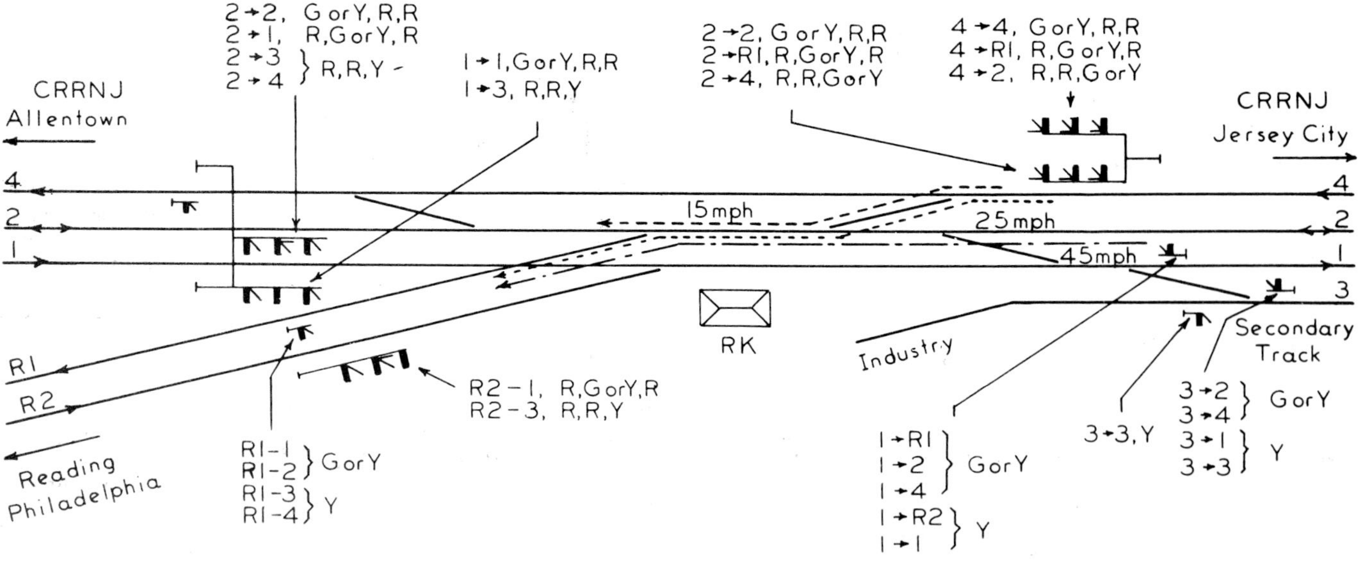

Fig. 15-31 Interlockings for a diverging route. main lines.

should indicate the same speed on all signals within the interlocking. This figure also shows that not all heads, high or dwarf, are equipped for all colors.

When a route has been lined but is occupied, the home signal will indicate stop, e.g. R over R over R in Fig. 15-31. The tower operator can "call on" a locomotive into such a route by pressing a button on his interlocking machine to change the aspect to R over R over Y. The exact signal will depend upon the interlocking and the type of signals in use. When three-arm semaphore signals, as on the right in Fig. 15-27, are in service, in most cases the lowest arm is shorter than the other two and it is customary to call such a blade the "call-on" although it may serve other functions as well.

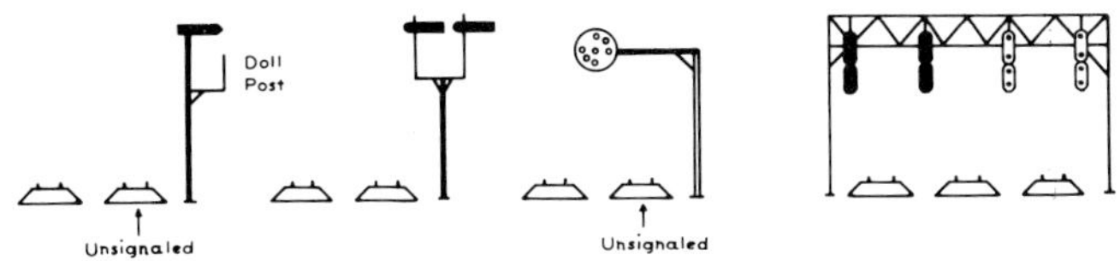

Fig. 15-32 Signaling parallel tracks.

If possible, signals are set directly to the right of the track they govern looking in the direction of movement, although in the seventies it became common practice to put signals on the left if more convenient. In the past, when signal masts could not be directly to the right, one of the means shown in Fig. 15-32 was used. Dummy masts, called doll posts, can be bracketed to the signal to show unsignaled tracks between the mast and the track governed. Doll posts display a blue or purple marker lamp. A single mast may carry two signals on separate short masts to govern parallel tracks. A bracket mast or a bridge may be used to support the signal in its proper location with respect to the governed track. Bridges often carry signals for both directions of travel.

Prototype Signals

Early in the 20th century the common types of signals in use were the Hall disk signal (commonly called a banjo signal), lower-quadrant semaphore, and, after 1903, upper-quadrant semaphores. Examples of these three types are given in Fig. 15-33.

The Hall disk signal was a totally-enclosed two-position signal. For a clear indication the white background of the large aperture of the case was unobstructed and the light was white. For a stop indication at a home signal a red disk was swung into the opening and the light was red. After 1900 most railroads changed from white to green as the clear aspect and modified their disk signals to conform. At a distant signal clear was as for a home signal but approach was originally a green disk and light, changed to a yellow disk and light after 1900.

Lower-quadrant semaphores usually had only two positions but three roundels were provided so the light would not be extinguished as the blade moved. Some lower-quadrant signals had two elongated roundels for the same purpose. The heavy frame for the roundels (the spectacle) also served as a counterweight to assure that the signal returned to stop by gravity. Lower-quadrant semaphores were still in service in 1981.

Upper quadrant semaphores were introduced in 1903 to minimize false-clear failures due to ice forming on the semaphore arm. With the counterweighting problem eliminated, a vertical position could be obtained thus making three distinctly different positions possible. Fig. 15-34 shows the 1930 ARA designs for upper-quadrant semaphore spectacles and blades. Two types of spectacles were provided to allow the use of staggered lamps on signals other than interlocking home signals.

In general semaphore blades pointed away from the tracks, exceptions being on interurban electric lines where they pointed toward the tracks so as to be visible inside the overhead wire poles, and on the New Haven.

Representative types of light signals are shown in Fig. 15-35. All the signals shown have sheet-metal backgrounds to bring out the effect of the lamps, also each lamp is equipped with a hood to prevent the sun from obscuring the light. Signals located in dark locations such as in tunnels do not require either. Dwarf light signals do not have the background sheet.

Color-light signals have one lamp per color. The three lamps may be arranged in a horizontal line (C&NW) as well as in a vertical or triangle as shown. The signal on left shows DL&W practice, red on top. Generally red is on the bottom. A difficulty with color lights is that a locomotive headlight might be reflected back through a roundel and give a false indication. A searchlight signal has a single clear lens and so eliminates the problem of reflecting a false color. A minia-

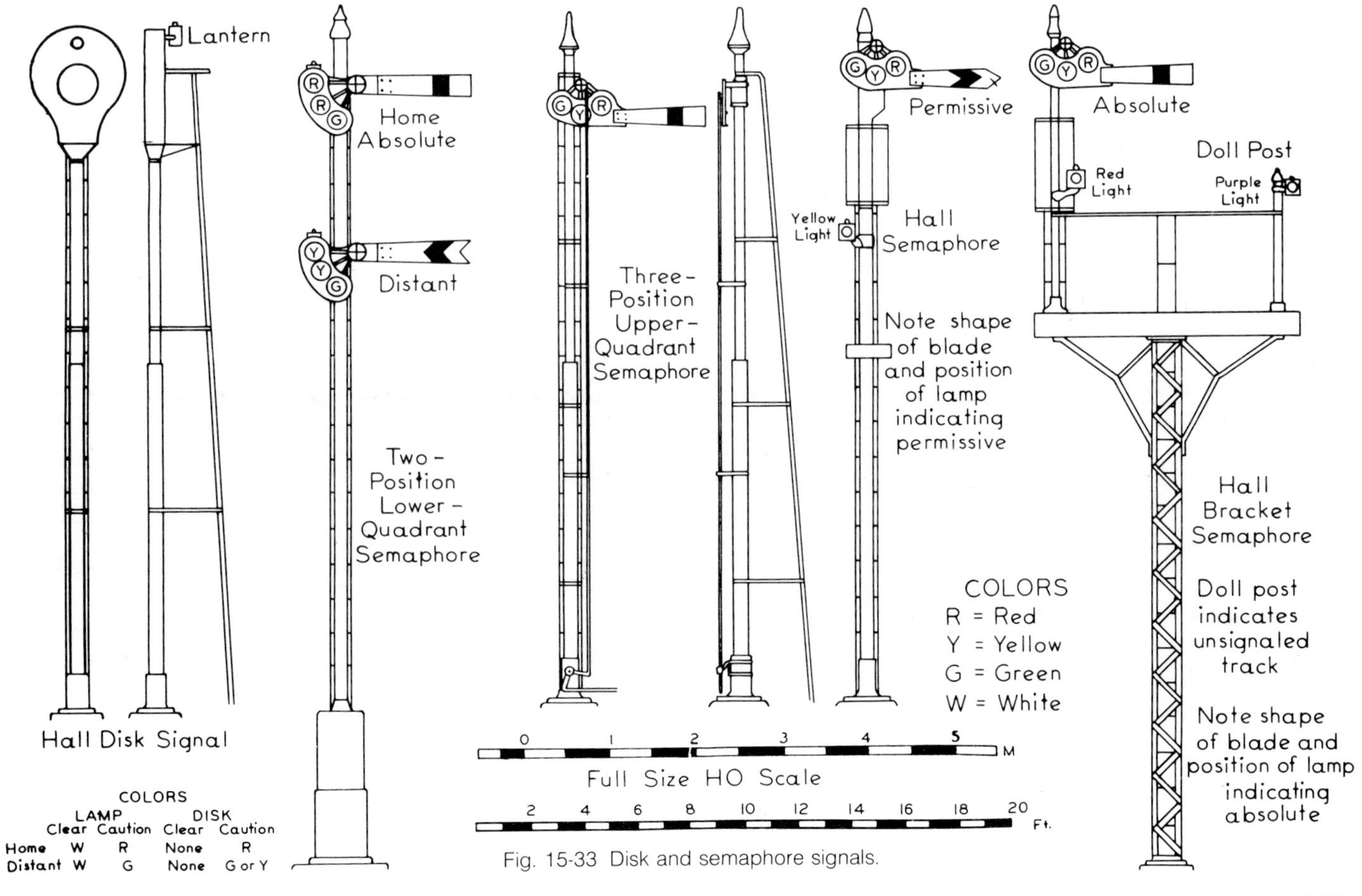

Fig. 15-33 Disk and semaphore signals.

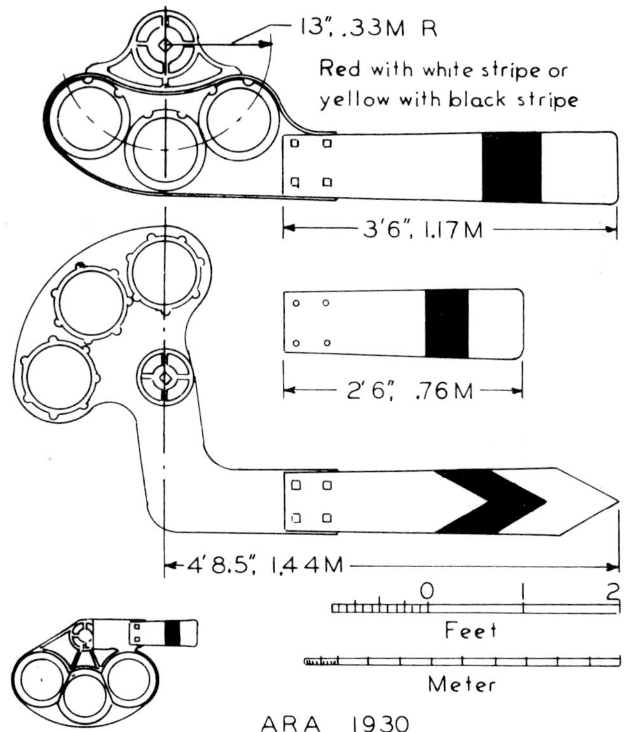

Fig. 15-34 Upper quadrant semaphore signals.

ture semaphore-like spectacle with color roundels behind the lens changes the color aspect of a searchlight signal. Another advantage of the searchlight signal over the color light is that the relative positions of the lights on multihead signals do not change with aspect. Many railroads continue to use color light signals for reason of economy.

To avoid dependence on color, in 1913 the Pennsylvania introduced the position-light signal using four white lamps in a row to simulate a semaphore blade. Later the number of lamps was reduced to three in a row and the color changed to a light lemon yellow for better fog visibility. A position-light signal has more aspects than a color light, e.g. the reverse 45° (permissive or slow speed) and two special aspects: a circle (lower pantographs) and an X (take siding). On the PRR a single lemon-yellow marker lamp below the upper head changed an absolute stop to a stop-and-proceed indication. This lamp had other uses also.

The aspects of positon-light signals were not exactly the same on the several railraods which were equipped with this type of signal. Even on a single railroad in 1971, the Penn-Central, absolute stop at some interlockings had been changed to two horizontal red lamps but remained three horizontal lemon-yellow lamps at other interlockings. The N&W had changed some position-light signals to show two vertical greens, two diagonal yellows, or two horizontal reds.

Also shown in Fig. 15-35 a color-position light signal as introduced by the B&O about 1920 and used by at least three other railroads. It combines color with semaphore-like positions of lights in pairs. The reverse 45° displays lunar white (bluish white) and is used as a permissive or slow-speed signal.

Only one head is used on either block or interlocking signals but its indication depends upon which marker light (usually white) is illuminated. A lighted upper marker denotes the high-speed route, a lower marker denotes the medium-speed route, and absence of markers indicates the slow-speed route. An offset marker on a bracket makes the signal more restricting than a centered marker. Some special aspects use an offset yellow marker. A color-position light could show 15 different aspects. Only those markers required for a particular signal were provided.

15.53 Model Signals

General

This Section covers only those aspects of modeling which are unique to signals, specifically illumination and operation of the semaphore arm. The construction of signals otherwise is identical to any other model.

Illumination

Even for O gauge, the small size of scale signal heads presents a problem of illumination. The smallest available lamps force a deviation from scale if mounted directly in the head. Nevertheless this has been the most common way of building working signals. In 1971 light-emitting diodes (LED) became available at reasonable prices.

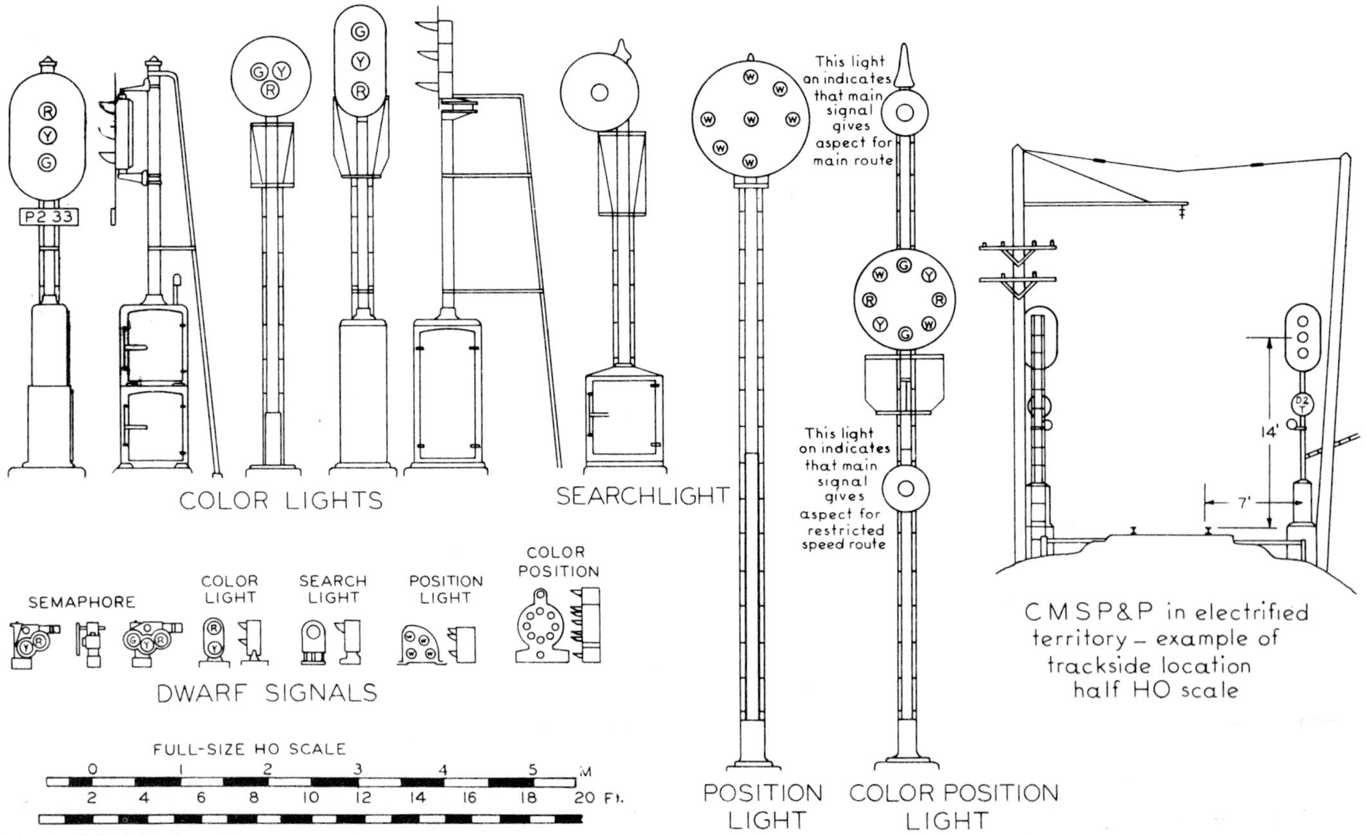

Fig. 15-35 Light signals.

These can be small enough to build scale signals even in N and have the additional advantages of extremely long life and low-current operation. White LEDs were not available in 1983 so yellow had to be used for position-light signals and similar applications.

The chief problem when lamps or LEDs are used in the head is bringing up the necessary electrical connections. Often a brass tube is used for the mast and it serves as the common connection to all lamps as shown on the left in Fig. 15-36. The ladder, if of metal, can serve as a second conductor. If more wires are needed, they are often brought up inside the tube. An alternate method used by the author is to twist insulated wires together, each wire being brought out at the point required as shown on the right in Fig. 15-36. The wires are then covered with epoxy cement which, after curing, is brought to the correct shape using abrasive paper while the mast is being turned in a chuck. A 150mm (6″) mast in HO scale can contain 14 No. 28 wires. If fewer leads are needed, they can be wrapped around a steel rod before applying the epoxy to create a stiffer mast.

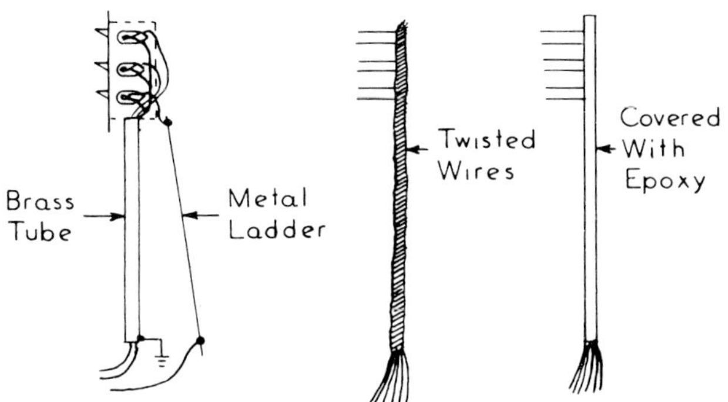

Fig. 15-36 Connections to signal masts.

Searchlight signals require that all colors appear in the same opening. LEDs which have oppositely poled red and green diodes in the same package have been available. Red or green can be shown by causing the current to flow in the correct direction. Some of these LEDs produce a very presentable yellow if the red and green diodes are illuminated alternately. A circuit to drive such an LED is shown in Fig. 15-37. The two resistors limit the current into the diode which is turned on. Their value should be selected to obtain the desired brightness. Remember that prototype signals cannot be seen unless viewed almost directly from their rear. There is a tendency for modelers to light up the landscape with their signals. In Fig. 15-37 both the resistors are shown to be of the same value. It may be necessary to select the values separately to obtain apparent equal brightness of the two colors.

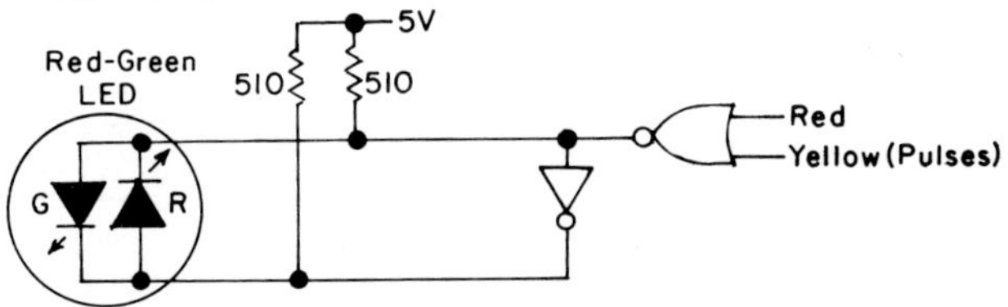

Fig. 15-37 Three-color searchlight signals.

If both the red and the yellow inputs are low, the output of the NOR gate will be high and that of the inverter low, turning on the green LED. When the red input is high, the output of the NOR gate will be low and that of the inverter high, turning on the red LED. When present the yellow input pulses, turning on the red LED when high and the green when low. The ratio of high to low should be adjusted to obtain the best yellow for the particular LED being used. Note that if red is high it will hold the signal red whether or not yellow is pulsing. Thus this signal arrangement is directly usable for a three-color block signal without further logic. The red lead is controlled by the track circuit of the block in advance; the yellow is controlled by the track circuit of the distant block. See Fig. 15-44.

Rather than mounting the lamps in the head, larger, easily replaced lamps can be mounted under the benchwork and the light brought to the head through some sort of light pipe as described by William K. Walthers in 1932. He specified glass rod but a clear plastic will do as well and is more easily worked. This method is particularly applicable to searchlight signals as at A in Fig. 15-38. In the figure the plastic is flared out so three colors of lamps can be placed under the mast but it is obvious that a semaphore-like spectacle and a single lamp would do as well. Fiber optic strands also offer options for small size installations.

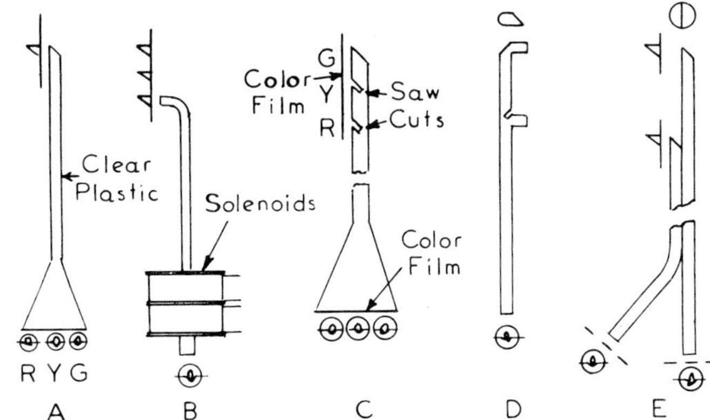

Fig. 15-38 Light pipes.

About 1950 Midlin produced a commercial color-light signal in HO in which the light pipe was raised by solenoids to direct the light through the proper one of three colored roundels as shown at B. Another way of building a three-color signal is shown at C where the red, yellow, or green light being sent up the mast is filtered by the roundels, only the roundel which is the same color as the light will glow brightly. How dark the two other roundels will be depends on the purity of the colors both of the lamp filter and the roundels. One method of obtaining good color filters and also having one piece for all three colors for ease in handling is to take a color slide of a suitable color diagram.

Since semaphores need only a white light, multi-blade signals can be served by a single channel with suitable take-offs as shown at D. Obviously commercial flexible light pipes also can be used but they do not form a suitable mechanical structure in themselves.

As these light channels are efficient, two half-round channels can be used for a mast to serve two heads as shown at E. For light guides, all surfaces should be polished. An easy way of getting a polished surface on plastic is to wet it with its solvent, MEK for polystyrene for example, and let the surface tension pull the dissolved surface into a smooth layer.

Semaphores

Most model semaphores operate by a wire connecting blade to an electrically operated power unit mounted under the benchwork. If a mechanical semaphore, such as the one shown at the center of Fig. 15-33 is being modeled, the operating wire can be attached to the semaphore spectacle in prototype fashion and run down outside of the mast. However most models of electrically operated semaphores have the operating wire inside the mast. Once the wire is brought below the benchwork it can be driven by any convenient means including a switch machine. Solenoid operation, unfortunately, is rapid unless coupled with a suitable dash pot, and so moves the blade rapidly in contrast to the slow movement of the prototype semaphore. Vince Caselli, in 1961, used a geared-down motor drive and controls identical to those shown in Fig. 13-35 for a movable bridge to provide the desired slow operation.

About 1952 Kurtz-Kraft marketed an HO semaphore using the expansion of a nichrome wire when current is passing through the wire as the source of movement. This results in an excellent reproduction of prototype action. Edward Ravenscroft incorporated the nichrome wire operator into a signal unit which could be plugged into position and thus it could be checked and adjusted in a test station on the workbench rather than in place on the layout. The basics of his semaphore drive is shown on the left in Fig. 15-39. An adjustable resistor permits the current to be reduced to provide a 45° aspect.

The author has used nichrome wire mounted on the mast as shown at the center of Fig. 15-39 to drive the semaphore arm directly. This is possible since the sidewise movement of the center of the wire when it expands is far greater than its length elongation. This method permits multihead signals and bridge-mounted semaphores. So as to be nearly invisible and also to hold down current requirements, the nichrome wire must be fine; the author using 40 gauge. The chief problem is attaching the nichrome wire to the conductors extending from the mast, as nichrome cannot be soldered. The author wrapped the nichrome wire around the copper leads, crimping over the end of the copper. Adjustment is made by bending the copper wire extensions from the mast.

To avoid a mechanical connection for driving the semaphore arm, the author in 1946 used an iron mast with an electromagnet at the bottom. A shaped armature as shown on the right in Fig. 15-39

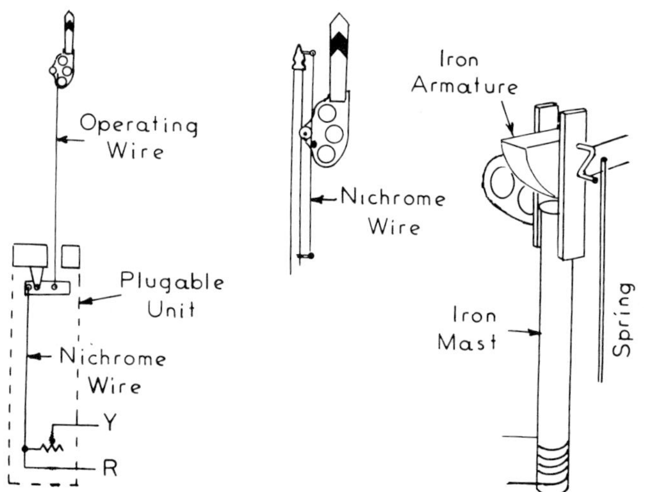

Fig. 15-39 Semaphore operations.

was mounted on the semaphore spindle. Energizing the magnet raised the blade. At the 45° aspect, a crank on the spindle contacted a wire spring attached to the ladder stopping the blade unless the magnet was on full. This method can be used only for one-head signals.

Illumination of a semaphore head can be made by mounting a white miniature lamp directly behind the spectacle in the manner of the prototype or by a light pipe as shown in Fig. 15-38D. White LED's were not available in 1983.

The color roundels are most easily obtained by making a color slide of a suitable drawing. In this way all three roundels are on one piece of film thus making for ease of handling and assembly to the blade. Even the correct diameter black roundel frames can appear on the film.

15.54 Signal Circuits

General

A vast number of signal circuits have been published in model railroad literature. Only typical examples are included in this Handbook. Both relay and integrated circuits are shown, in some cases for the same signals so a comparison can be made.

On both the prototype and model there may be more than one track circuit per block. In such cases the circuits shown in this Section assume that any track circuit operated will operate the relay or IC which is controlling the block signals.

Block-Signal Circuits

Two-position signals, even if distant signals are provided, depend only on the track circuit of their home block as shown in Fig. 15-40. The semaphores shown are of the normal-clear type operated by either a solenoid or a nichrome wire.

For three aspects it is necessary to interconnect two track circuits. A popular circuit for three-color signals is given in Fig. 15-41. It permits all lamps to have a common connection to the mast of the

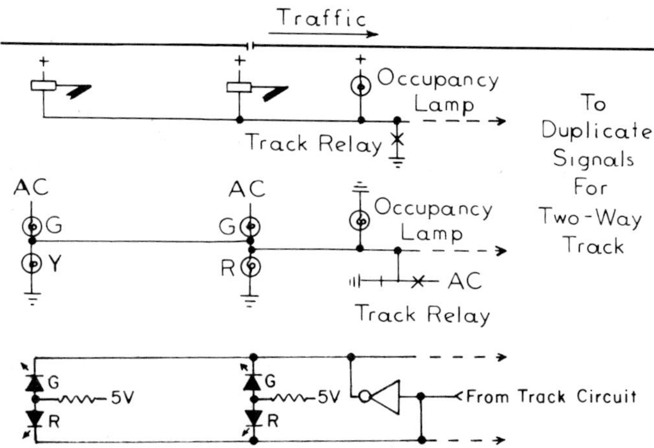

Fig. 15-40 Two-aspect signals.

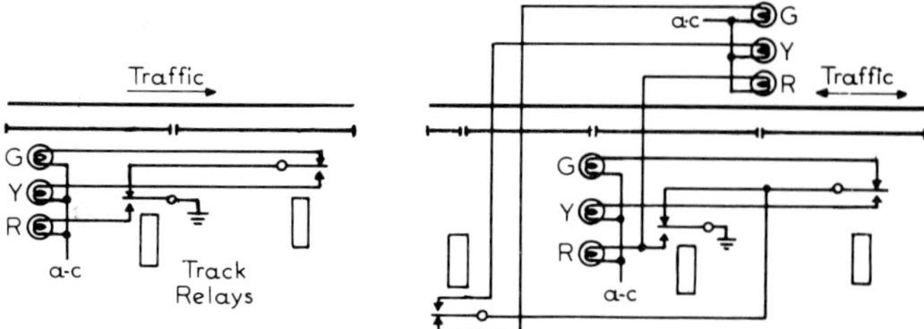

Fig. 15-41 Three-color signals.

signal, the usual wiring scheme of commercial signals. This circuit requires three transfers per relay plus six wires interconnecting relays for two-direction track.

To simplify interconnection wiring between blocks, as early as 1932 circuits based on connecting the three lamps in series were in use. The one shown in Fig. 15-42 was published by Robert H. Haserodt in 1955.

Only two wires connect track relays in adjacent blocks but, in addition, two wires must be run from each signal to the track relay of their block.

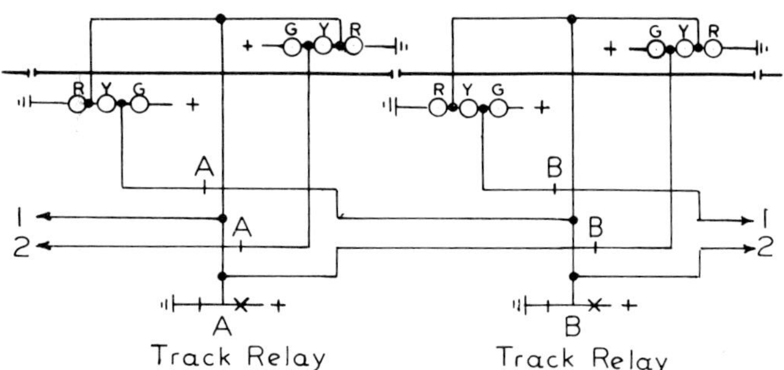

Fig. 15-42 Series lamps for three-color signals.

In Fig. 15-42 when all track relays are normal, their contacts connect ground to the green lamps turning them on. All yellow and red lamps have ground on both sides and so do not light. If a track relay is operated, its transfer contact connects + to the red lamps of its home signals lighting them and its two break contacts open the connections between the green and yellow lamps of its home signal thus no green or yellow lamp is lit, and they have + on both sides. The transfer contact also connects + between the green and yellow lamps on the approach signals which turns off the green lamps and lights the yellow lamps (assuming that the approach block is unoccupied).

Integrated circuits started to displace relays and discrete transistors for model signaling around 1972. Since ICs are smaller, less costly, easier to mount, easier to wire, consume less power and are far more reliable than relays, there seems little reason to use relays today for this purpose. A circuit for a three color ABS with detection by track circuits is shown in Fig. 15-43. The four NAND gates shown can be the four gates contained in a single 7400 (TTL) package. The CLEAR output of the track circuit is high for clear and low for occupied. When low, the track circuit must have the capability of sinking enough current to illuminate the red LED of both signals protecting its block (a 7400 will sink 16 ma, most LEDs will light on 3ma). This low also inhibits the yellow and green LEDs of the two signals. When the labeled block is unoccupied as well as the block in advance, the NAND gate for the signal of the corresponding direc-

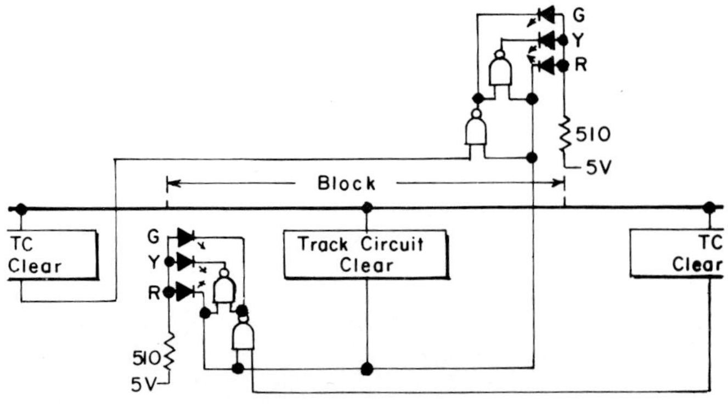

Fig. 15-43 Three-color automatic block signals.

tion is enabled and it illuminates the green LED. If the labeled block is clear but the block in advance is occupied, neither the red nor the green LED will illuminate, but the NAND gate for the yellow LED will illuminate the yellow LED. This circuit is replicated for each block to be equipped with signals, the clear output of each track circuit being used for its own signals as well as for the distant indications of the adjacent blocks.

The circuit of Fig. 15-44 is for ABS with searchlight signals using the red-green LEDs shown in Fig. 15-37. The occupied output of each track circuit is held high for occupied and low for clear. The yellow flasher is an oscillator of the proper timing to produce the best-possible yellow color. It is common to all blocks. The NOR gate of each distant block is used for the signals protecting the blocks on both sides of that distant block.

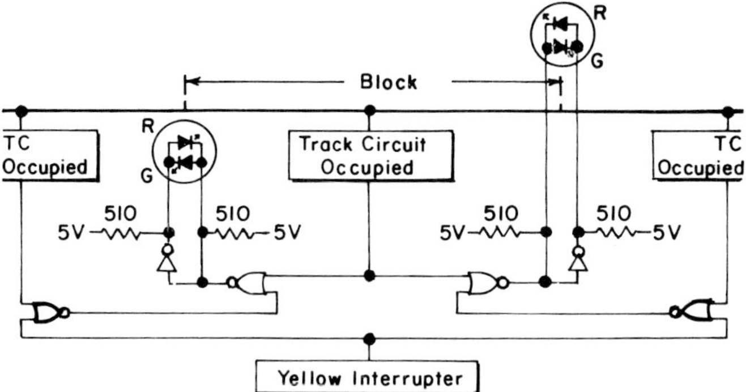

Fig. 15-44 Tricolor searchlight signal automatic block system.

The circuits of Figs. 15-43 and 15-44 depend on detecting the current drawn by motors or car resistors by a track circuit. Instead of track circuits, described in Section 15.2, it is possible to detect a train passing a given point by a contact which is closed by the train, or by interrupting the light falling on a phototransistor. So-called "check-out" block signal systems operate by detecting a train entering a block, setting a memory element indicating that the block is occupied, and restoring that memory element to the unoccupied state when the train is detected at the exit end of the block. Such systems will not protect a car accidentally dropped from a train but, since no lives are at stake, there is no reason why model block signal systems must be fail-safe.

The presence detectors of a check-out system, if providing inputs to a powerful logical system (such as the microprocessor described in Section 25.7), can realistically operate any form of block signal system, interlocking, or CTC. They also can be used to operate the simple, earlier systems.

A simple system which has been used as early as 1934 employs a double-acting relay as the memory element for a block on track with currents of traffic (one-direction traffic). As shown in Fig. 15-45, metal flanges on a train entering the block will short-circuit the contact rail to the common rail and operate the switch machine indicating that the block is occupied. When the train exits the block, the metal flanges provide the operating path to restore the switch machine to normal, clearing the block. The contacts on the switch machine can be used to drive any desired signal circuit.

Since it is possible for a standing wheel to hold power on one of the windings, some means such as the capacitor-resistor shown in Fig. 15-45 must be provided to prevent burnout of the switch machine.

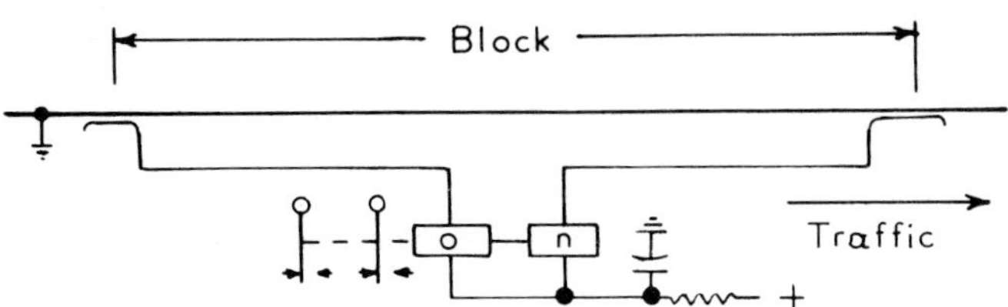

Fig. 15-45 Switch-machine type block circuit.

The check-out circuit of Fig. 15-45 operates for only one direction of traffic and uses a high-current memory element. A much better method is to use a solid-state flip-flop such as the integrated circuit shown in Fig. 15-46. The track contact is connected to a Twin-T detector so that direction of travel is sensed when the track contact is connected to the control rail by a passing wheel. Positive on the control rail will turn on Q1 of the Twin-T bringing its collector to near ground. This will set the flip-flop (F/F) to the east to indicate occupancy of the block and reset the F/F to the west. The output of the flip-flops can be used to drive any desired signal circuit.

For westward traffic, the control rail will be negative which will operate Q2 of the Twin-T circuits. Q2 on will set the F/F to the west and restore the F/F to the east so this circuit works equally well in both directions. Since the track contacts need drive only a small current into transistor bases, operation is far more reliable than circuits requiring heavy currents.

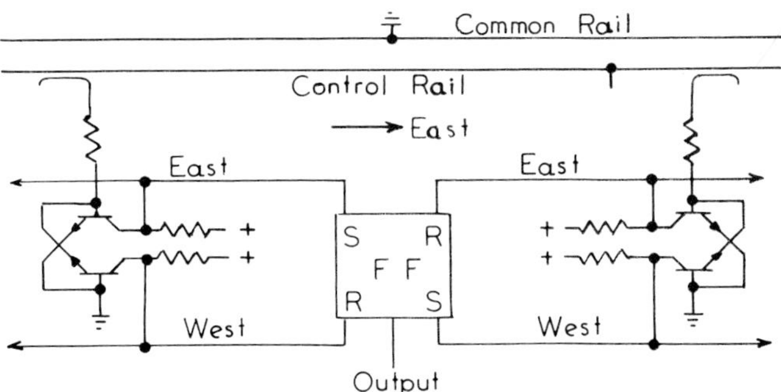

Fig. 15-46 Flip-flop check-out circuit.

The two previous check-out systems clear as soon as the leading end of the train reaches the exit end of the protected block. In contrast, prototype signals clear only when the last car clears the block. To duplicate prototype action, the clearing signal must be generated only by the rear end of the train. One method is to follow those prototype systems which counted cars into a block and did not clear until the same number of cars were counted out of that same block (Nachod, United States, Kinsman); this gives protection against dropped cars. Much simpler but quite satisfactory for model-railroad use is to clear when the end of the train has been detected in the adjacent block.

Read-End Detection

A practical end-of-train detector can be constructed of two photodetectors, each arranged so that it will indicate shade for the full length of the train, i.e., not detecting light falling between cars. Either the slanted-beam arrangement of Fig. 15-20 or the two phototransistors in series method of Fig. 15-55 will suffice. For the purpose of further description, it is assumed that when a photodetector is shaded, its output is low.

As shown in Fig. 15-47, when a train enters the protected block, the photodetector at that entrance to the block is shaded and sets the occupied flip-flop (FF). It does not matter whether the photodetector at the leaving end of the other block is shaded or not, the occupied output will be high. When the train proceeds into the block, all photodetectors will be illuminated but the occupied FF will remember the block is occupied. When the train in the protected block starts to exit that block (in either direction), the photodetector within that block at the exit end will be shaded and hold the occupied output of the FF high. As soon as the rear end of the train clears the protected block, only the photodetector on the outside of the protected block will be shaded and its low output will reset the occupied FF. The output of the FF then can be used to drive any desired signal system. Note that this circuit is bidirectional and therefore completely suited to single-track operation.

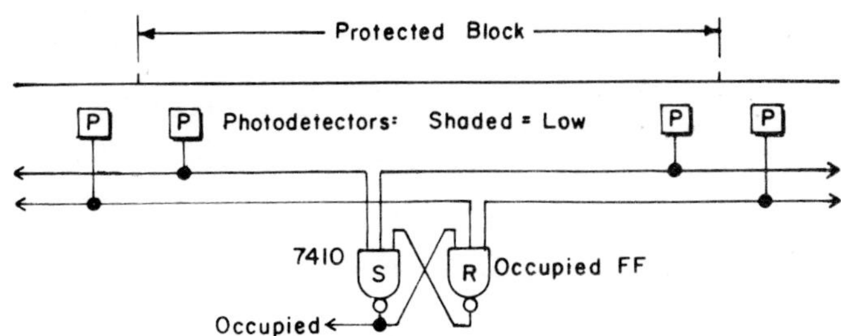

Fig. 15-47 End-detection occupancy circuit.

Count-In, Count-Out

If trains always pass completely through the block, their cars can be counted into the block by a single photodetector which, while shaded by the cars, is exposed to light between cars. As shown in Fig. 15-48, an up-down counter is used. It is necessary to initialize

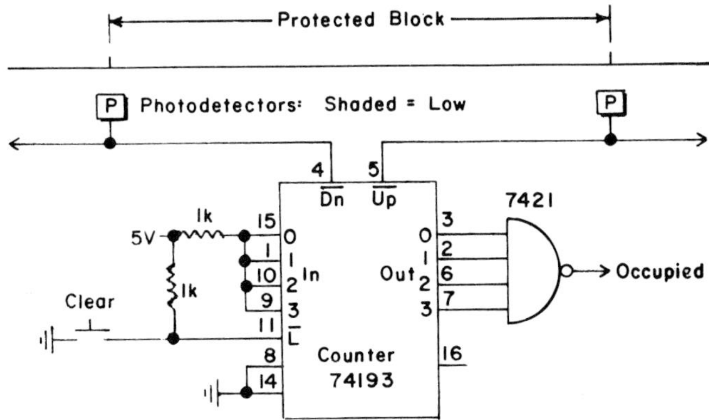

Fig. 15-48 Count-in, count-out occupancy circuit.

this counter to its normal (unoccupied) state of all ones, and that function is performed by the clear push button. Each car of an eastward train entering the protected block will cause the counter to decrement, and will increment the counter on clearing the block. Therefore the counter will return to its normal (unoccupied) state after the last car clears. The circuit operation for westward trains is just the reverse as far as incrementing or decrementing is concerned.

As shown, the circuit will operate properly for any length train except for one of multiples of 16 cars because 16 cars will bring the counter back to its normal state. Adding an additional counter package and changing to an 8-input NAND gate will cause the circuit to operate correctly except for a 256-car train. If the block is shorter than the train there may be a problem due to simultaneous count in and count out.

So that the signal system will work properly if cars are moved into the protected block but are removed from the same end (by a switching movement for example), and to decrease the probability of false operation if the block is shorter than the train, short counting pulses depending on the direction of movement can be generated as indicated in Fig. 15-49. The two photodetectors at the block end are mounted closely enough together that both will be illuminated between cars, but they are far enough apart so that one will be shaded before the other as the cars move.

Whichever photodetector is shaded last will cause a short pulse to be developed by delay-line action (see Fig. 24-49). If this pulse represents a car moving into the protected block from either end, the counter will be incremented, if representing a car moving out, decremented. Thus, when the same number of cars leave the block as entered, regardless of direction, the counter will be restored to its normal (unoccupied) state. The rest of the counter circuit is as shown in Fig. 15-48.

Although the possibility of simultaneous attempts to count both up and down by a train longer than the block still exists, the probability of such an event has been greatly reduced from that of Fig. 15-48 as the counting pulses are only about 30ns long.

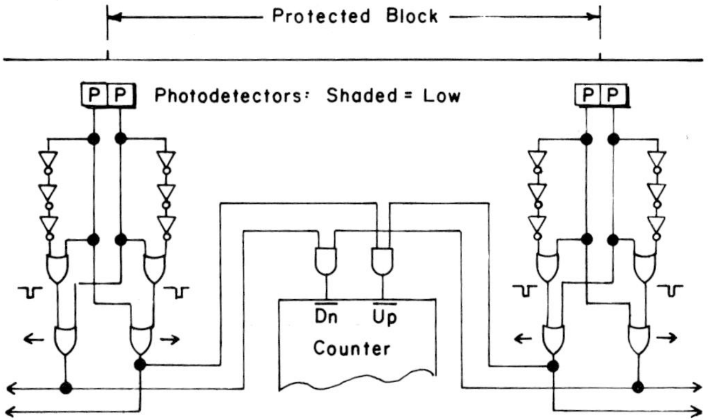

Fig. 15-49 Reversible count-in, count-out occupancy circuit.

Combined Detector and Track Circuit

In building a CTC machine in 1982 for the Trenton Northern, the interurban line at The Model RR Club, Steven Mallery combined photodetection at the ends of each block with an OpAmp track circuit. Several phototransistors were wired in series at both ends of each block to detect cars being shoved or pulled by a motor so an occupied indication was developed as soon as the block was entered. The track circuit maintained this indication as the train past beyond the photodetectors into the block, the indication only clearing when the last car left the block. This circuit works equally well in either direction.

Signal Operation

After occupancy of a block has been determined (track circuit or memory), that information can be used to operate any type of signals either by ICs (Chapter 24) or by a microprocessor (Chapter 25). Already described are gate circuits for operating three-color signals (Fig. 15-43) and for operating searchlight signals (Fig. 15-44). If it is desired to set traffic manually on these signals (as at the top of Fig. 15-24), it is necessary to add gates to control the red LED from the traffic-control lever as well as from the occupancy circuit. A modification of the three-color signal circuit to include traffic is shown in Fig. 15-50. As before a low from the occupancy detector will turn on the red LED at both ends of the block. If traffic has been established westward, the traffic west input will be high and will turn the eastward signal red regardless of occupancy. Traffic west low will turn the westward signal red.

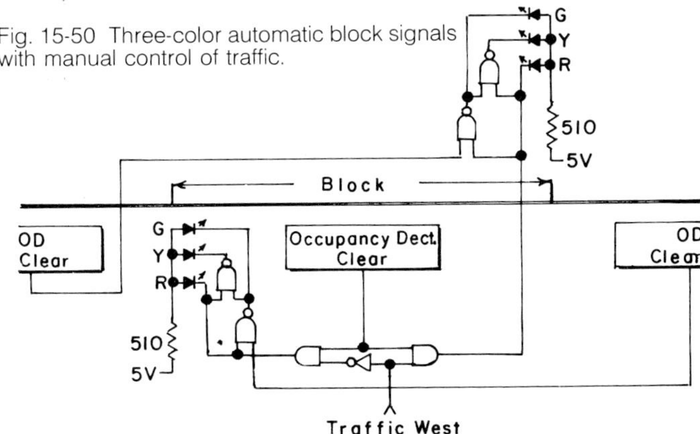

Fig. 15-50 Three-color automatic block signals with manual control of traffic.

The circuit just described can be carried one step further to create an APB system (absolute-permissive block) by automatically determining the direction of the first train to enter the single track and establishing traffic in that direction. For APB three states are required: no traffic established (all signals green as at the top of Fig. 15-51), traffic east and traffic west. Since it takes two bits to remember three things, two flip-flops (FFs) are shown in Fig. 15-51. If all single-track blocks are clear (clear high), the clear gate is able to reset both FFs. If a train enters the single track from the west, a low on the clear lead from that block will set the traffic east FF and will remove the reset input to both FFs. The output of the traffic east FF going high will prevent the traffic west FF from being set, so traffic will remain eastward until the eastward train has passed beyond the headblock signal at the western end of the single track. At this time all the blocks on the single track will again be clear (unless another eastward train is following) and the clear gate enables the resetting

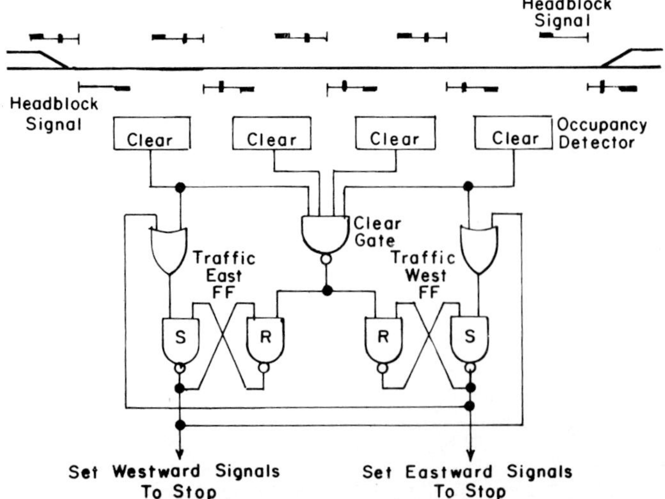

Fig. 15-51 Automatic setting of traffic for absolute permissive block.

of the traffic east FF. During the time the traffic east FF is set, its high output is used to set to stop all westward signals governing the single track. Identical actions for the traffic west FF will occur if a westward train is the first to enter the single track.

In the circuits shown thus far, at least one of the LEDs is always illuminated. Some prototypes use approach lighting, that is, the signal is not illuminated until a train is detected in the block to the rear of the signal. The ABS system shown in Fig. 15-43 is readily modified as shown in Fig. 15-52. If the block to the rear of the signal is unoccupied, the clear output of the high occupancy detector will cause the inverter to sink the current from the 510 ohm resistor, thus extinguishing all three LEDs of the signal. When the block to the rear of the signal is occupied, the output of the inverter will be high and the signal will operate as described for Fig. 15-43.

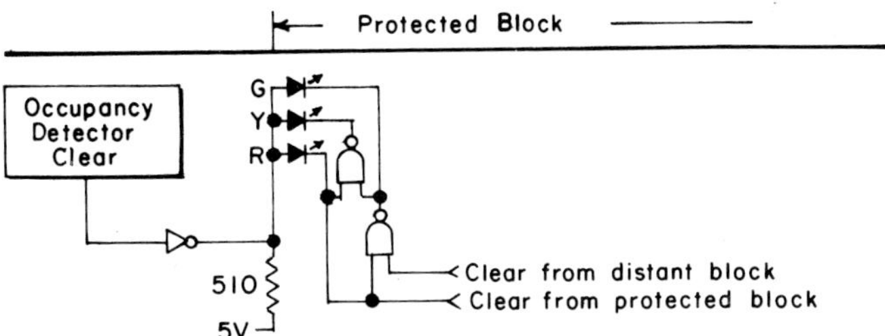

Fig. 15-52 Approach-lighted signal.

Multiplexed Block Signals

The IC block-signal circuits so far described essentially duplicate the logic of the earlier relay circuits. Therefore the interconnecting wiring required by the relays has been retained. It is necessary to design relay systems in this manner since relays are slow and, in terms of number of operations, short-life devices. By comparison, ICs are fast and can operate continuously without wearing out. These two factors make possible an entirely different concept of block signal systems, one based on a high-speed central processor which contains only enough logic to determine the aspect for one signal at a time. Once the aspect of a signal has been determined, that signal is flashed on for a brief moment, the central processor

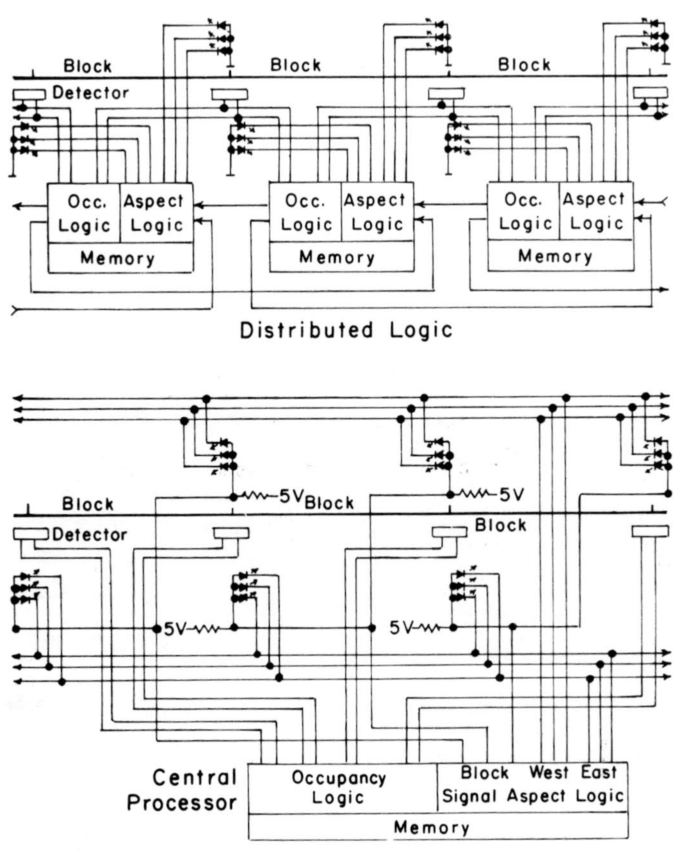

Fig. 15-53 Three-color ABS, comparison of distributed logic with a central processor operating with time division multiplex.

then goes on to the next signal. If each signal is flashed on at a rapid enough rate, at least 24 times per second, the eye will see it as continuously illuminated. This process is called time-division multiplexing, hereafter called multiplexing. Among other things this is also used for pocket calculators as it simplifies the circuits and reduces power drain, see Section 24.84. The primary advantage of multiplexing in model-railroad applications is that intervals of time are substituted for wires. If time is available, for block-signal systems it is, time costs nothing and is maintenance free.

A comparison of distributed wiring and multiplexing is shown in Fig. 15-53. For clarity only three blocks are shown so the savings by multiplexing do not stand out. These savings, however, become obvious when it is recognized that there must be one logic unit per block for distributed logic, but only one central processor is needed regardless of the number of blocks. The distributed-logic system requires the following number of interconnecting wires per block: between blocks, 2; to detectors, 4; to signals, 6. The total is 12 per block. For a system of 16 blocks 192 interconnecting wires are required. For the multiplexed system the following number of wires are required: per block, 3; per direction, 6. For a 16-block system, a total of 54 wires is needed. This is a saving of 138 wires although it must be considered that the signal wires run between all signals of the same direction.

A microprocessor, inherently a multiplexed device, is well suited to serve as the central processor. A block-signal system based on a microprocessor is described in Section 25.7. For a simple system, however, it may be easier and less expensive to build the central processor of standard LSI. The description of such a system follows.

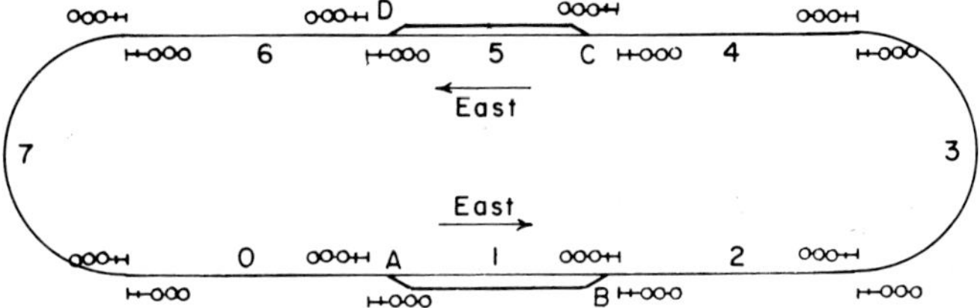

Fig. 15-54 ABS on an 8-block loop.

The design described is specifically for the 8-block loop shown in Fig. 15-54. The signals are standard 3-color ABS with only the main track signaled. Reversing any switch sets the home signals protecting the block in which that switch is located to red. The assumption is made that the system is to operate with unmodified standard cars, i.e., cars drawing no current. A block is to be determined as occupied as soon as the leading end of a train enters the block. A block will be cleared only when the last car of a train leaves the block but it is not required that the system protect against cars left in the block.

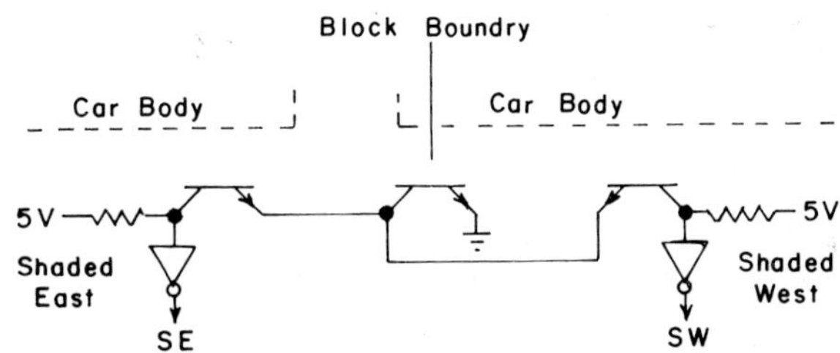

Fig. 15-55 Optical presence detectors.

To detect leading and rear ends of trains, the 3-phototransistor presence detector shown in Fig. 15-55 is assumed. A car on the block boundry will shade the center transistor to develop both a shaded-east and a shaded-west indication. If light falling between two cars turns on the center transistor, the other two transistors will remain shaded. Therefore a continuous shaded indication is given to both blocks as the train passes the block boundry. The last (or first) car or locomotive will shade only an end transistor, giving a shaded indication only to the block on that side.

For time-division multiplex it is necessary to divide time into specific, identifiable intervals here called time slots. In this system eight time slots are required to serve each block and there must be eight cycles of these eight (0 to 7) time slots. In Fig. 15-56 a square-wave oscillator of 1.5kHz or greater drives a 6-bit counter. The least-significant three bits are decoded for time slots, the most-significant bits for blocks. In addition a strobe pulse is developed at the center of each clock pulse.

As this is a multiplexed system, only those inputs that are required for the operation being performed at a particular time are received by the central processor. As shown at the top left of Fig. 15-

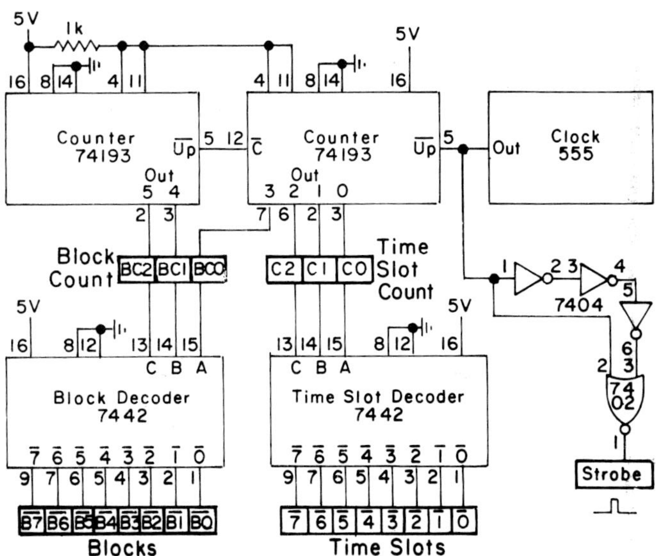

Fig. 15-56 Clock for multiplexed ABS.

57, the switch multiplexer (Mux) will connect a low signal from the contacts of any reversed switch in the current block (the block being served), and write "occupied" in the memory bit for that block.

Determination of "occupied" by the photodetectors is identical to the system shown in Fig. 15-47. If either of the two photodetectors within the current block are shaded, the block is occupied. If neither of the two photodetectors within the block are shaded, but either of the pair just outside the block are shaded, the block is to be cleared. If no photodetector is shaded, the state of the bit in memory for that block is to be left undisturbed. The block count bits by themselves cause the detector Mux to select the SE photodetector output within the current block. The adder, however, changes this selection so that the two photodetectors just outside the current block are selected during time slots 0 and 2. Either found shaded will set the shaded FF when the strobe pulse appears at the center of the time slot. During time slots 1 and 3 the outputs of the photodetectors within the current block are connected both the data input and to the write pulse gate of the memory. Therefore, if any photodetector is

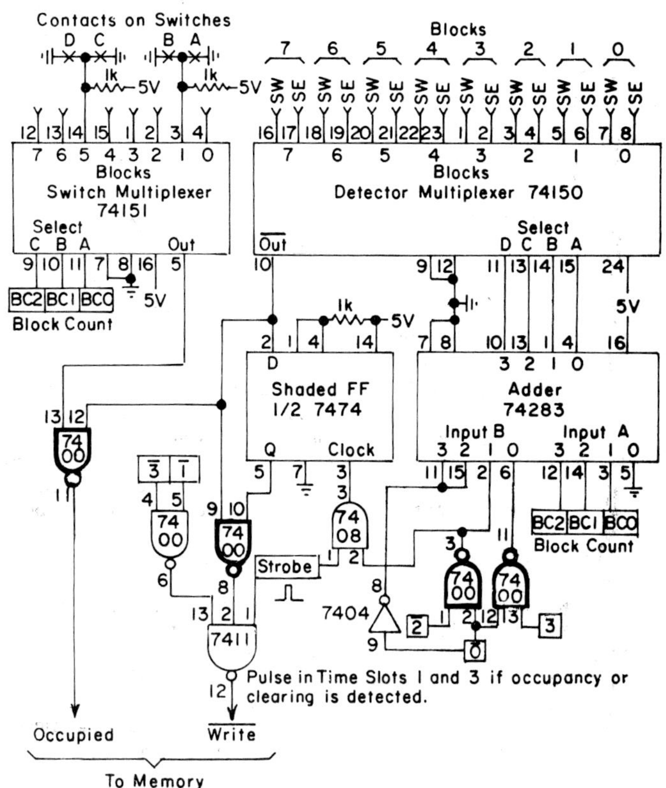

Fig. 15-57 Occupancy logic for multiplexed ABS.

shaded, a write pulse will be applied to the memory during the strobe pulse in time slots 1 or 3. The bit in memory will be written as "occupied" or "clear" as required. A further minor refinement would be to set another FF if "occupied" was determined during time slot 1 so "occupied" would also be written during time slot 3 regardless of the state of the photodetectors at the west end of the block. Fig. 15-57 completes the box labeled "occupancy logic" inside the central processor of Fig. 15-53.

The status information of block occupancy is stored in the memory shown at the bottom left of Fig. 15-58. For only eight blocks, this memory is very small; one inexpensive package could easily handle up to 1024 blocks. Indeed, for eight blocks, a simple redesign could utilize the occupancy shift register as the memory. Nevertheless, a separate memory is shown to make it apparent that the system is readily expandable to far more than eight blocks.

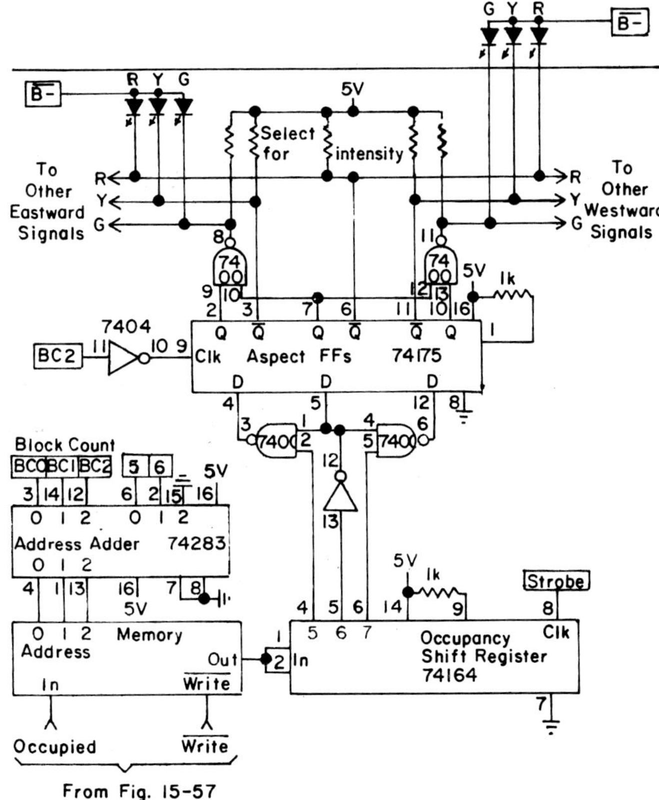

Fig. 15-58 Aspect logic for mutliplexed ABS.

When the memory is being written (time slots 1 and 3), it is being addressed by the block count for the current block as the address adder is adding zero during those time slots. To obtain the information to determine signal indications, it is necessary to make available the status bits not only of the block being protected but also of the adjacent two blocks. This is accomplished by shifting the status of the current section during all time slots except 5 and 6 into the occupancy shift register. During those time slots the address adder causes the new two higher-numbered blocks to be addressed. After the strobe pulse during time slot 7, the three bits in question will be in positions 5, 6, and 7. Note that the center bit corresponds to the next current block. The gates determine whether or not a LED, either red or yellow, is to be illuminated for the next block. This determination is clocked into the aspect FFs at the end of the serving of the old current block. Therefore, the necessary aspect outputs are available to the signals of the new current block during the entire time that block is being served. It is important when multiplexing LEDs that they be switched on for the maximum available time to avoid requiring high-current pulses.

Fig. 15-58 completes the boxes labeled "block signal aspect logic" and "memory" in the central processor of Fig. 15-53. It is not obvious whether or not it is less expensive and easier to install a multiplexed block signal system compared to a distributed-logic system when only eight blocks are to be installed. The multiplexed system becomes only slightly more complex (primarily adding bits for decoding the current block) when the number of blocks is doubled or quadrupled. With distributed logic, such enlargement doubles or quadruples the circuit and wires required.

Highway Crossing Signals

Highway grade-crossing signals should operate as the train approaches the crossing and restore as soon as the crossing is cleared. If operated by track circuits, there must be one on each side of the crossing as shown in Fig. 15-59. Should signal blocks end at the crossing, the track relays for the blocks could be used to operate the crossing flasher but, in most cases, the crossing is within a block as indicated so the block must be divided into two cut sections (prototype terminology), each with its own relay. The track relay on the side of the approaching traffic turns on the flasher but both track relays operate the block-signal relay which controls the block signals.

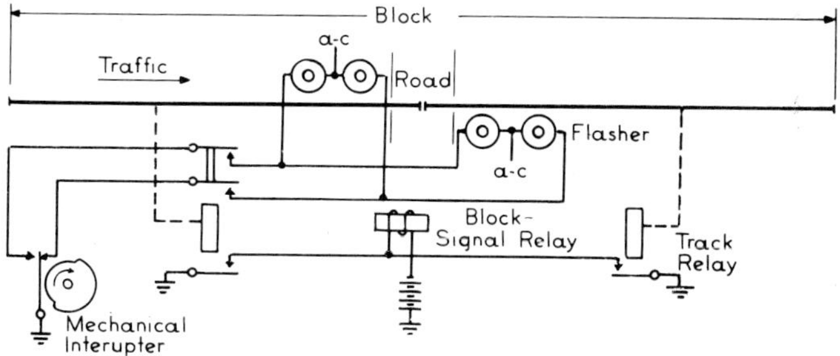

Fig. 15-59 Mechanically-operated highway crossing flasher.

Fig. 15-60 shows a crossing flasher operated by transistor track circuits. A train approaching from either direction will turn on its detector transistor (one of the transistors of a Twin-T) and apply ground to the multivibrator. One of the multivibrator transistors will turn on and draw current through its flasher lamps. The voltage of the on collector coupled through the capacitor will hold the other multivibrator transistor off. However the capacitor will charge through the resistor and soon will be positive enough to turn on the other transistor. As this second collector turns on, its voltage swing is coupled through the other capacitor to the base of the first transistor turning it off. This pumping action between the two transistors will continue at a rate determined by the values of the capacitors and resistors. Raising either lengthens the flashing periods of the lamps.

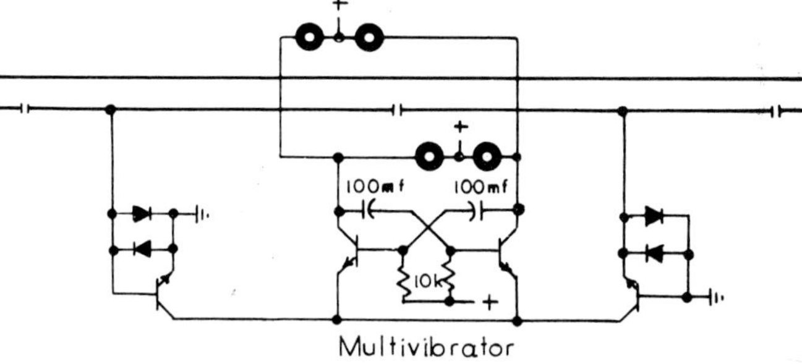

Fig. 15-60 Transistor crossing flasher.

The circuit shown in Fig. 15-60 is for two-way track as which detection transistor turns on the flasher depends upon the polarity of the control rail. This is difficult to do directly with track relays but Fig. 15-61 shows two methods which will work. At the top a direction relay operated by the cab or perhaps through a diode from the control rail, selects which track relay controls the crossing gates. At the bottom the first track relay operated operates its auxiliary relay to close the gates. Either auxiliary relay operated will prevent the operation of the other auxiliary relay when the second track relay operates. These auxiliary relays are really traffic relays.

The relay circuit functions of Fig. 15-61 are best accomplished today using semiconductors. A combination of the occupancy detection of Fig. 15-47 and of the automatic determination of traffic of Fig. 15-51 is shown in Fig. 15-62. If neither block is occupied, all FFs are reset. A train entering either of the two blocks sets the FF of that block which, in turn, sets its corresponding traffic FF. When either traffic FF is set, it inhibits the setting of the other traffic FF. The occupied FF which established the traffic will cause the crossing flashers to flash until the last car clears. When the train clears both blocks, the traffic FFs are reset in preparation for the next train.

If a multiplexed signal system (Fig. 15-53) or a microprocessor signal system is installed, that system can be made to operate crossing flashers.

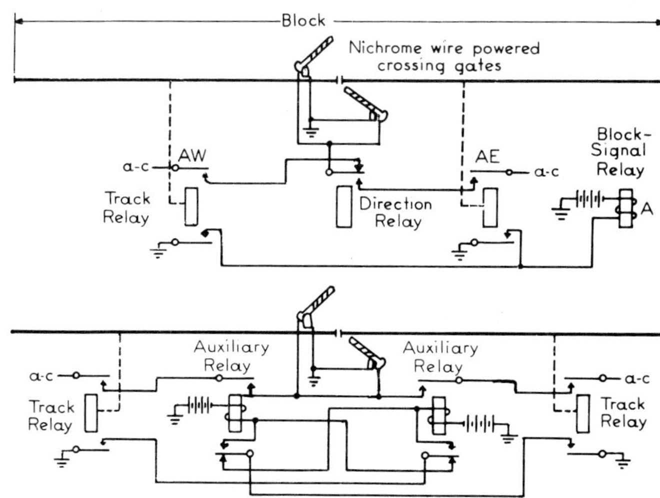

Fig. 15-61 Crossing gates on bidirectional track.

15.55 Interlocking Circuits

General

Since safety is not of great importance on a model railroad, true interlockings are seldom built as they add complications both to circuits and to operation. Most model railroaders want to establish a route by the quickest, most convenient means possible, as for example by pressing a single push button (see Section 13.3). For scenic reasons and to provide information of the route set, many would like interlocking signals operating essentially in the prototype fashion but they are willing to depend on observation and operator skill to prevent throwing of switches under a train. In this Handbook such systems are called "simulated interlockings."

An interlocking plant is an interesting model in itself and a few true interlockings have been built for service on model railroads.

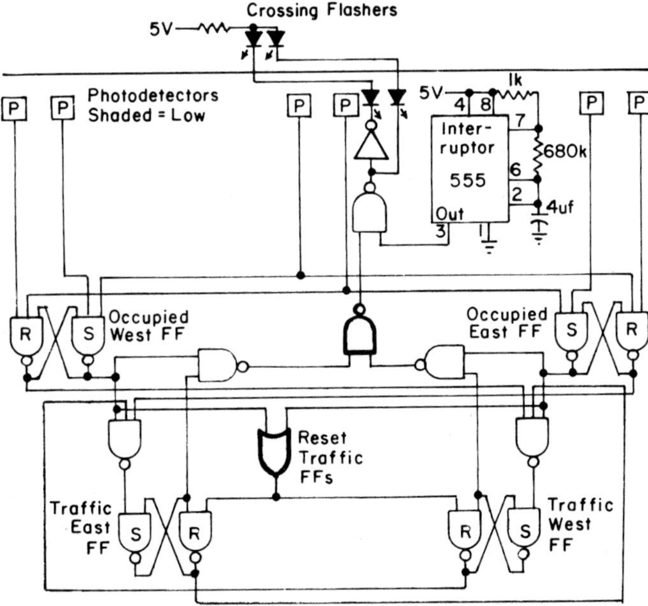

Fig. 15-62 Crossing-flasher control using ICs.

Simulated Interlocking

Simulated interlockings use any convenient method of aligning a route but operate the signals in accordance with the chosen prototype practice. In the most usual form the signals are operated in accordance with the route set and, if automatic block is in service, display the block signal aspects for the cleared route. Even this simple system results in considerable circuit complexity as is shown by the single diverging route and the six signals affected in Fig. 15-63. For maximum clarity the track circuits (or check-out circuits) are not shown but are merely indicated by T0 through T6. Contacts on the switch machine are designated S.

Fig. 15-63 shows the signal lamps operated by contacts on the track relays and switch machine. Diodes, as described in Fig. 13-9, are used to reduce the number of contacts required. Actually these diodes are one form of semiconductor OR gates.

The circuit of Fig. 15-63 has been designed to minimize the number of contacts required, the usual practice in designing relay circuits. The cost paid is many wires interconnecting the various track relays and switch machine.

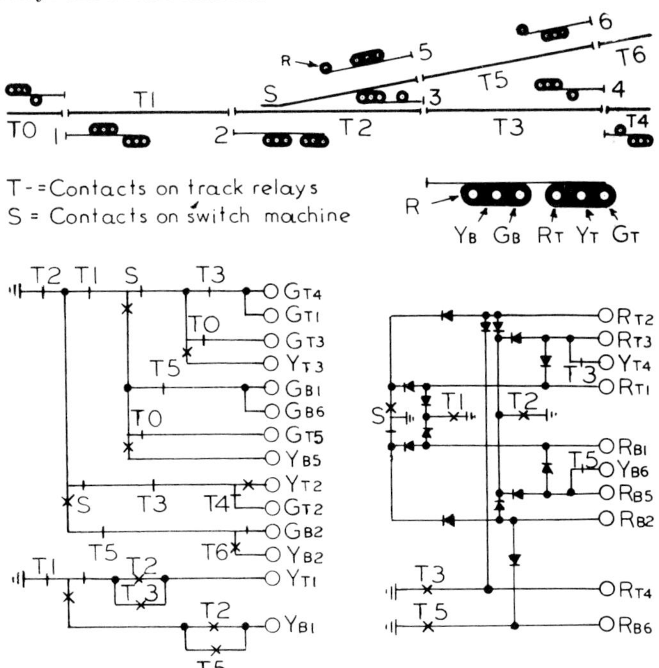

Fig. 15-63 Simulated interlocking circuit.

Fig. 15-64 shows just the No. 2 signal of Fig. 15-63 operated by integrated circuit gates. The interconnecting leads have been reduced to just one wire from each track circuit and two from the switch machine.

In designing a circuit such as this, it is easiest to start with the red LEDs. Looking at Fig. 15-63 it can be seen that if section T2 is occupied, both the top and bottom reds will be on. Therefore the output from track circuit T2 can immediately be connected to an input of the noninverting OR gates driving the red LEDs. The top red will be on if T3 is occupied or the switch is thrown so those two inputs can be connected to the OR gate for the top red. Similarly the bottom red will be on if the switch is normal or T5 is occupied so those inputs are connected to the OR gate for the bottom red. If red is on, then the other two LEDs in the head must be off so the output of the OR gates is used to inhibit the NAND gates for the green and yellow. This completes the wiring for the red indicators.

If a red is not on, and the next block is unoccupied, the green will be on. So the T4 circuit is connected to the upper green NAND gate and the T6 to the lower green NAND gate. If those blocks are occupied, their track circuits will inhibit the NAND gates for the greens. They will also, through the inverters, enable the NAND gates for the yellows.

With either circuit, assuming the blocks are not occupied, the signals will transfer from one clear route to the other when the switch is thrown. On an actual interlocking all signals would go red first, the switch would be thrown, and finally the new route cleared. This action can be simulated by causing track circuit T2 to operate, say by a bleed resistance to the track, before the switch is thrown, then releasing T2 after the switch is thrown.

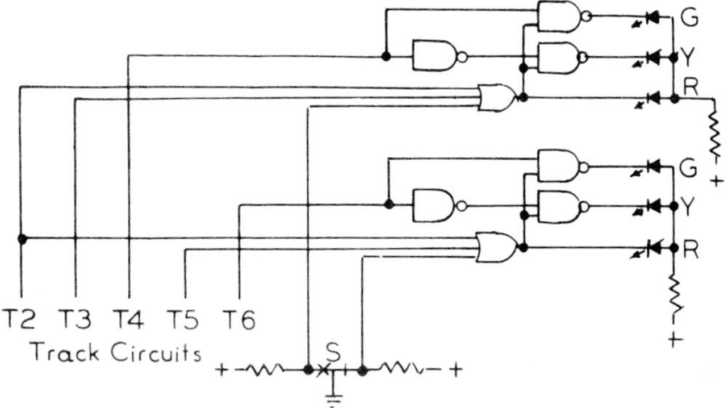

Fig. 15-64 Integrated-circuit signal operation.

Both of the circuits shown in Figs. 15-63 and 15-64 are logic circuits. This means the outputs are determined logically based on the states of the input, in one case by contacts, in the other by gates. To hold the number of gates or contacts to a minimum, it is necessary to use design techniques which have been developed for this purpose (Boolean algebra is one such technique). An alternative to logic which requires no design effort and may reduce the number of packages and the number of interconnecting wires is to use memory, specifically ROMs. For this technique each possible combination of inputs is written on a separate line of a truth table, as shown in Fig. 15-65. In the case of the interlocking of Fig. 15-63, there are eight inputs (the switch and seven track circuits), 256 possible combinations of inputs. For each combination, the desired signal aspects are shown on the output side of the truth table. Once completed, the truth table is used to program the necessary number of PROMs. Programming can be done by the modeler using the information supplied by the manufacturer or, in some cases, the manufacturer may have a service to program the PROMs to the customer's specifications. Once programmed, the only wiring required, as shown in the lower part of Fig. 15-65, is to connect the inputs to the address inputs of all the ROMs and to connect the outputs of the ROMs to the corresponding signals.

Inputs								1						2						3			4			5			6		
S	Track Circuits							T			B			T			B			T			T			B			B		
	0	1	2	3	4	5	6	R	Y	G	R	Y	G	R	Y	G	R	Y	G	R	Y	G	R	Y	G	R	Y	G	R	Y	G
0	0	0	0	0	0	0	0	0	0	1	1	0	0	0	0	1	1	0	0	0	0	1	0	0	1	1	0	0	0	1	0
1	0	0	0	0	0	0	0	1	0	0	0	0	1	1	0	0	0	0	1	1	0	0	0	1	0	0	0	1	0	0	1
0	1	0	0	0	0	0	0	0	0	1	1	0	0	0	0	1	1	0	1	0	1	0	0	0	1	1	0	0	1	0	0
1	1	0	0	0	0	0	0	1	0	0	0	0	1	1	0	0	0	0	1	1	0	0	0	1	0	0	1	0	0	0	1

Truth Table: Aspect of each signal for each possible input combination

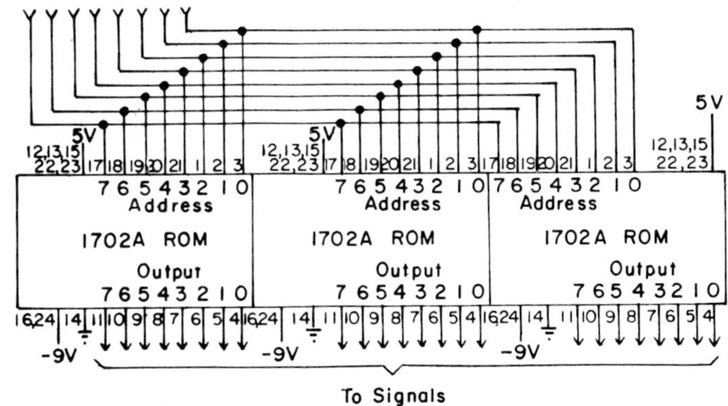

Fig. 15-65 ROMs to control signals.

For a more-complex interlocking, many inputs may be involved. To hold down the number of ROM packages needed, advantage can be taken of the fact that no signal depends on all the inputs. For example, signal 3 of Fig. 15-63 is set to stop whenever the switch is normal, regardless of the state of any track circuit. The state of T3 and T5 is of no importance to signal 3. These inputs can be eliminated from the ROM operating signal 3. Similar observations can be made for other signals. See Fig. 15-66 for examples of ways to reduce the number of inputs required for the ROMs.

It is obvious that even a simple diverging route requires a complex circuit if a full set of interlocking and block-signal aspects are to be displayed. Therefore most model railroaders simplify the signals. One way is to eliminate the distant aspects for the interlocking and substitute a single green if either route is clear and a single yellow as an approach.

True Interlockings

A true interlocking, as defined in this Handbook, is one which follows prototype interlocking practices. A switch can be thrown only if the route over the switch is clear and if all signals protecting routes over that switch (and any conflicting routes) are set to stop (dropped). The original prototype interlocking machines were built using sliding bars and dogs. A few of this type were constructed for models. Relay-type interlockers, including those of the entrance-exit type, also have been installed on models. Unfortunately, both types

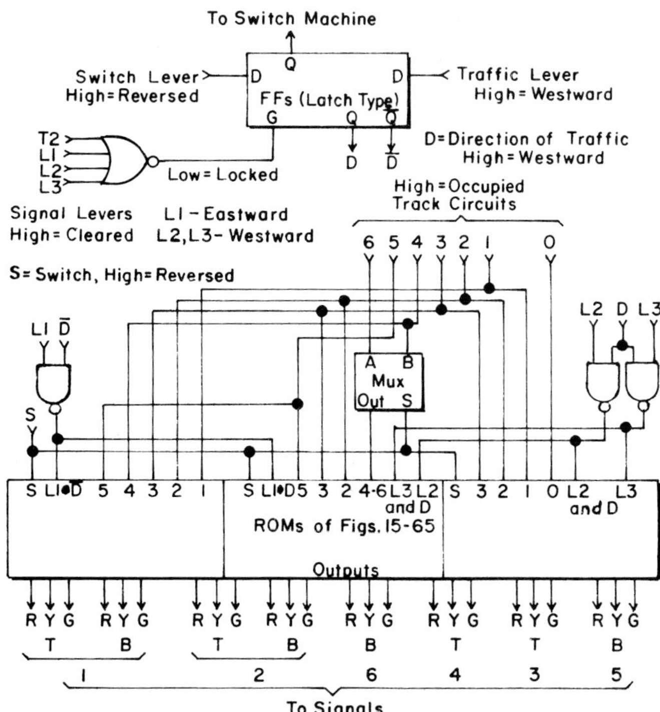

Fig. 15-66 True interlocking for plant of Fig. 15-63.

are difficult to design and to construct. Today integrated circuits have made interlockings (and CTC) practical. For a large layout with several interlockings, or even with one rather complex interlocking, the use of a microprocessor as described in Section 25.7 is the simplest and least-expensive choice. With a suitable algorithm, one program can handle any simple or complex track configuration. Despite this, it is practical to design a separate IC circuit for each interlocking. A true interlocking circuit for the switch and signals of Fig. 15-63 is given in Fig. 15-66.

Three signal levers have been provided. L1 controls signal 2, L2 signal 3, and L3 signal 5. If any signal lever is pulled up to clear the signal, or if track circuit T2 detects occupancy, the output of the NOR gate top left of Fig. 15-66 will be L, that L disables the inputs to the two latch-type FFs. Therefore no change can be made in the setting of the switch or in the direction of traffic (the machine is locked). Dropping all the home signals when the plant is unoccupied will unlock the machine (enable the FFs). Switch position then will follow the setting of the switch lever, and traffic direction the setting of the traffic lever. As soon as one of the home signals is pulled up to clear a route, the machine is again locked. The figure does not show approach locking (a train approaching a cleared home signal will lock its route). A route locked by an approaching train may, nevertheless, be changed if the home signal protecting that route is dropped and a time interval (called winding down) expires. This interval is to assure that a moving train will either have time to stop in the rear of the dropped signal, or will lock the plant by entering the interlocked block. For Fig. 15-66, approach locking could be accomplished by a timer which would be triggered by dropping a signal. During the timing interval the plant will be locked by an additional input on the NOR gate unless the approach block is unoccupied.

The signal aspects for the true interlocking of Fig. 15-66, once a route is cleared, remain the same as those of the simulated interlocking of Fig. 15-65 for the cleared route. There are, however, four more inputs to the ROMs, the three signal levers and the direction of traffic. This is a total of 12 address bits if the straightforward ROM design of Fig. 15-65 is used. Fortunately, it is usually simple to avoid increasing the size of the memory by combining inputs, or by using only those inputs needed for the signals which are being controlled by a particular ROM package as the address for that ROM. For example, a ROM controlling only eastward signals (leftmost ROM in Fig. 15-66) has no need of inputs from westward signal levers, and a ROM controlling westward signals only (rightmost in Fig. 15-66) needs only the westward signal levers. Signal levers and the direction of traffic can be combined since a home signal cannot be cleared unless both inputs are in the appropriate state. The home block track circuit output (T2) also can be combined with the signal lever and direction of traffic but this simplification is unneeded in Fig. 15-66. Occupancy inputs which are not involved in the aspects of the signals controlled by a particular ROM may be omitted from that ROM's address. All three ROMs of Fig. 15-66 have such omissions. Even another way of reducing address bits is to select (using a multiplexer) occupancy inputs required by route (T4 or T6 selected based on switch position in Fig. 15-66). In the case illustrated, the need for the Mux could have been avoided by combining the occupancy of the home block with the signal levers and direction of traffic thereby freeing one of the address inputs to the ROM.

15.56 ATC

General

On the prototype there are several systems in use which permit the signal system to have automatic control to some degree of the operation of the locomotive. The simplest types merely set the brakes if a train passes a red signal. This is called automatic train stop (ATS) and is very common on rapid-transit lines where the signal system raises an arm to operate a lever on the train. Railroads have long used automatic train control (ATC) which will stop the train if the engineer fails to take appropriate action at signals. Such systems usually depend upon detection at the locomotive of a signal impressed on the rails or by a shoe on the locomotive contacting what amounts to short sections of third rail at appropriate locations. In recent years systems have been developed, primarily for rapid transit, which control the train completely. This is called automatic train operation (ATO). On the model only the term ATC has been in common use. In this Handbook, therefore, all automatic systems of this nature are called ATC.

Simple ATC

Block signals are seldom installed on street-car lines. Nevertheless some form of automatic control is particularly useful as then several cars could follow each other around to create scenic interest. Because they are single cars, it is possible to adjust the cars by placing resistors either in series with the motors or shunting the motors so all run at approximately the same speed for the same applied current and voltage. This permits the use of the simple circuit developed by Mac Emshwiller in 1965 and shown in Fig. 15-67.

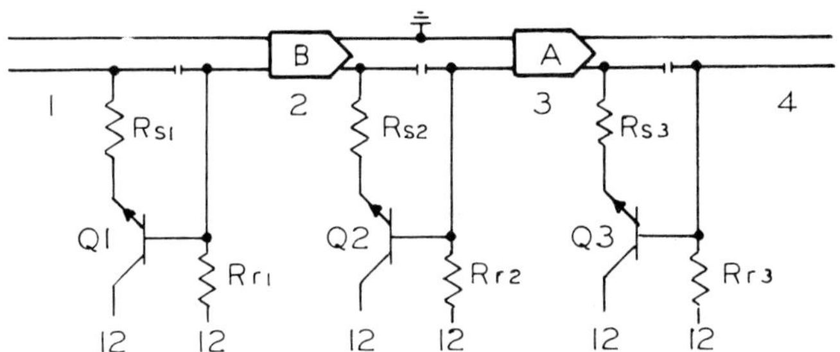

Fig. 15-67 Simple ATC.

Normal operating speed is set by resistor Rs for each section. When there is no car in front, as for car A in Fig. 15-67 the transistor for that section is turned on since the base is connected to 12V through Rr. The resistance of Rr should be high enough that cars cannot run on current supplied by it, 150 ohms is enough. Car A therefore is being supplied by 12V through resistor Rs3. Assume the track voltage for section 3 is 9. This 9V is connected to the base of Q2 reducing the voltage applied to Rs2 to less than 9V and resistor Rs2 further drops the voltage so car B runs only slowly if at all. If a third car entered section 1 it would see even a lower voltage and would definitely stop. To stop the lead car a low resistance is shunted across the section to reduce the voltage across the rails. This preserves ATC action for following cars.

These transistors are operating as emitter followers and so will generate heat when slowing or stopping cars. They should be mounted on a heat sink. If transistors with the case connected to the collector are used, one heat sink for all transistors can serve as the common + connection.

Control in Locomotive

In the thirties methods were proposed for ATC which mounted relays in the locomotive. Those relays were controlled either by trackside contacts or by superimposed signals on the rails. Such systems never gained a following. The advent of command control (Chapter 17) has introduced possibilities for this type of ATC. For systems without on-board memory, it would only be necessary to block the speed signals to the locomotive; the selective equipment already on board would then stop that locomotive. Systems with on-board memory require that the ATC system somehow control the memory; as of 1981 there had been no known attempts to accomplish ATC in this fasion.

Dead Sections

Most ATC systems used in model railroading disconnect power from a stopping section. Fig. 15-6 shows a simple circuit of this type. However if two locomotives or perhaps a train of powered cars (MU) are in service, only the first powered unit will be stopped, stalling and perhaps burning out the motors of following units. It is better to disconnect power from the entire block when the stopping section is reached thus stopping all motors together. Fig. 15-68 shows one method using relay track circuits. If block B is occupied, operation of relay AS disconnects power to both sections of block A. To permit both locomotives to move into block B, a special transfer section is provided at the entrance of block B which serves as part of block A until the locomotives have advanced far enough to operate relay B. This transfer section must be long enough to accept all powered units before relay B disconnects power from block A.

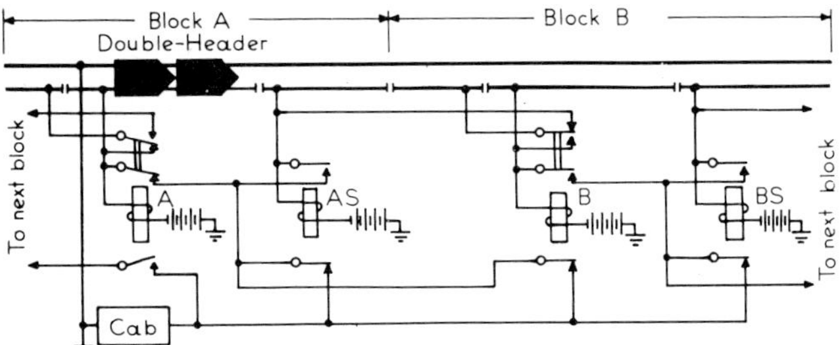

Fig. 15-68 ATC circuit for double headers.

ATC of the simple on-off type has not found general favor because of the rapid starts and stops. Slowing resistors are not practical unless all powered units draw about the same current for the same speed and voltage. Integrated circuits, however, make it economical to install a small transitor throttle at each stopping section. If the train were not to be stopped, this throttle would hold the same voltage on the rails as set by the cab. If the train were to be stopped, as soon as it was detected entering the stopping section, the voltage on the rails would be smoothly decreased to near zero. Then, when the train was to proceed, the voltage would be increased smoothly to that set by the cab.

15.57 Cab Signals

On the prototype, cab signals repeat inside the locomotive cab a limited number of the aspects of wayside signals. Such signals are useful at a model railroad cab not only because the engineer often cannot see the signal in front of his train but also, even on unsignaled track, he must not enter a section not connected to his cab. Only cab signals for model railroads are covered.

Essentially all of the cab signal circuits developed by 1971 depended upon a connection established by the cab control system to the location of the locomotive. In 1951 the Summit-New Providence HO RR Club demonstrated an automatic cab control system which used relays with 12 contacts to connect a cab to a section. This enabled a four-indication cab signal plus position-in-section lamps to be operated from the track relays. The various forms of route and progressive cab control also establish connections to the location of the locomotive. Fig. 15-69 shows a simple system in which a relay detects occupancy of the section ahead of the locomotive. It cannot distinguish between a section occupied by a current-drawing car or locomotive and a section connected to another cab.

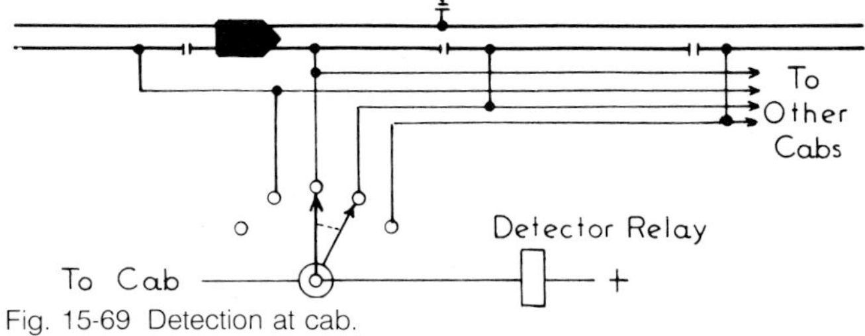

Fig. 15-69 Detection at cab.

An extra lead or leads can be carried through the cab-section rotary switch to sense the state of the wayside signals. But, to a model railroader, the most important information is whether or not the next section can be entered. Fig. 15-70 shows a simple method of indicating that the next section is connected to another cab. The rotary switch is connecting + to terminals A and B to indicate that the cab shown is connected to sections A and B. It is also sensing on terminal C. If any other cab is connected to section C, the + being supplied by that other cab will turn on Q3 lighting the absolute stop cab signal. As long as the locomotive is in section A, it can continue to advance into section B at which time it will be detected by Q1 turning on the "In Last Section" which, combined with the absolute stop signal informs the engineer that he must stop before leaving section B.

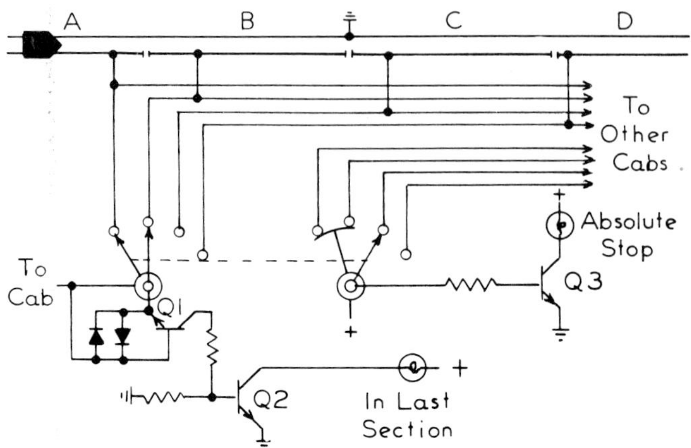

Fig. 15-70 Detection of occupied section.

On large layouts the running of additional wires for cab signals is undesirable. For cab-control systems which have metallic connections (wires) between the cabs and the sections, there are several possibilities of using the same wire which is sending power to the track to carry signal information in the reverse direction. Such possibilities include superimposing an AC signal or, when track power is full-wave rectified AC, using the node of the power wave to send back a signal pulse.

Computer cab control systems inherently must have occupancy information about all the sections available to the central processor in order to seize and release sections required by the movement of the locomotives. This information then can be processed and signal aspects sent to the cabs without any additional wiring to the sections. It should be noted that cab control systems are concerned only with sections for independent control of power to locomotives. If based on the prototype, blocks for signaling do not typically correspond to sections. If cab signals are based on sections, the information needed to operate them is already developed. If they are based on blocks, additional information is needed. For example, during the period 1972 to 1979 The Model RR Club designed and constructed an exploratory computer cab control system. The initial proposal was to have a cab signal based on blocks (including interlocking) which operated in the manner of the prototype, and a simple section signal which showed the availability of the next section. As the system design progressed, it was found easy to make more and more information available on the section signals. Eventually it was obvious that the prototype-type cab signal based on blocks added no useful information. This signal was eliminated when the system was built for testing. If command-control signals which provide the capability of information transmitted from the locomotive are adopted (see Fig. 17-9), it would be possible for the locomotive to pick up signal information and relay it to the cab much like the way prototype cab signals operate.

16 TRANSISTOR THROTTLES

16.1 HISTORICAL NOTES

The transistor was invented in 1947 at the Bell Telephone Laboratories. The first commercial circuit to use transistors was the Card Translator Circuit of the 4A Toll Switching System designed by the author in 1950. Early transistors had current capabilities of less than .02A but by 1957 they had progressed to the point where they could handle over 1A. At that time George Rupprecht and the author built a series of throttles including some with gradual response and a separate speed control and brake. (Patent filed 1959, granted 1963). Performance was excellent but the germanium power transistors then available were judged too costly and too critical for practical use by the average model railroader. Motorola published some advertising literature about 1959 which included a transistor throttle. The first transistor throttle to appear in a model railroad publication apparently was by Jim Haning in the Nov. 1960 Model Railroader. Until about 1972 a major effort was placed on holding the number of transistors in a throttle to a minimum. Most designs contained three or four transistors. The increasing availability of integrated circuits since that date has completely changed the picture. Now even thousands of neatly packaged and wired transistors can be purchased inexpensively.

16.2 GENERAL

Transistor Throttle has become the generic name for all types of solid-state throttles regardless of whether the device actually used to control the current is a transistor or some other device such as an SCR. Therefore all types are covered in this Chapter.

To avoid ambiguity in this Handbook, the device which actually controls the current to the locomotive is called the throttle. The control on the panel is called the speed control.

The details of transistor throttles have constantly been in a state of change. Transistor types leave the market to be replaced by other types. This chapter covers the principles involved rather than specific designs. The chapter also compares the different basic types of throttle by performance. In most cases specific devices, such as a particular transistor type, are not specified. A suitable transistor can always be selected from among the types available at the time by considering voltage, current, and power ratings.

16.3 TYPES OF THROTTLES

16.31 Dissipative or Switching Throttles

To control the speed of a motor the throttle must be able to adjust the power supplied to the motor. There are two basic ways of doing this by semiconductor devices. One is to switch the power on and off, the percentage of the time the power is on determines the average power supplied. The other is to dissipate some of the power to the throttle, leaving the remainer to be supplied to the motor. A distinct disadvantage of the dissipative throttles compared to switching throttles is that they can get quite hot. This requires a heat sink to avoid overheating.

Several of the output wave forms which have been used by model railroad throttles are given in Fig. 16-1. These waveforms can represent voltage, current, or power. At A is one of the first waveforms used by model railroad transistor throttles (1957). Power is turned on for a variable interval centered on each half-wave of the full-wave rectified AC source. At starting and low speeds, the pulse is very narrow with steeply-rising leading and trailing edges of virtually the maximum supplied voltage. This is an extremely effective waveform for precise control of starting and low-speed running. Therefore it is an excellent choice for operating a turntable by circuits such as that of Fig. 13-31. When widely-spaced, steep, and high pulses are applied to a motor, the resulting vibration which makes for good control unfortunately produces noise often judged unacceptable for locomotive use.

The waveform at B is just the opposite of that at A, the power is switched off for a variable interval about the center of each half wave. This waveform was introduced in 1963 for voltage regulation, but apparently was not applied to model railroads until 1978. It has steeply-rising edges of the pulse but at starting and low speeds these are of low amplitude, thereby reducing locomotive motor noise to

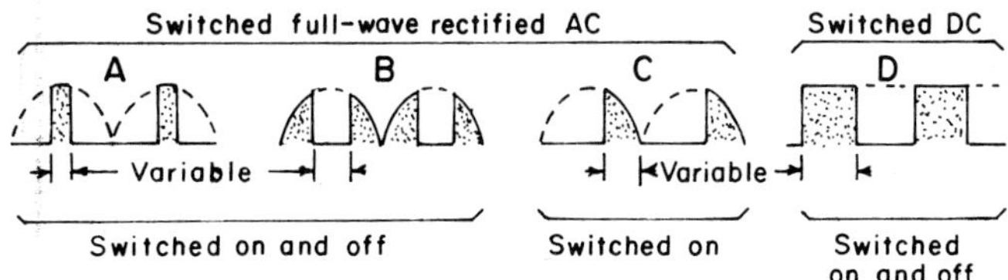

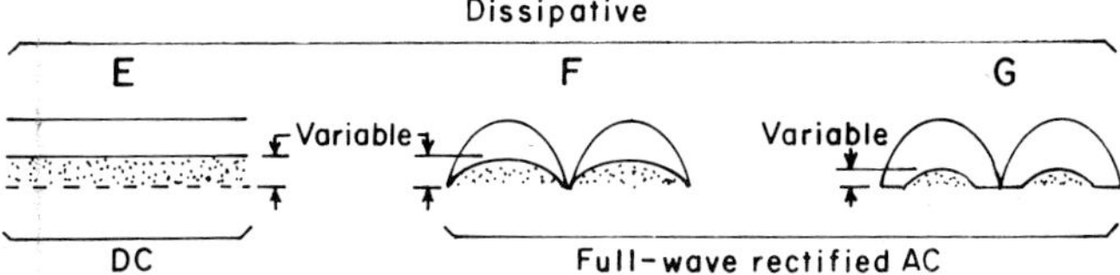

Fig. 16-1 Throttle output wave forms.

acceptable levels. This waveform has 240 pulses per second, making it more suitable for driving small motors such as those used in N scale than switching throttles generating 120 pulses per second such as those of A and C.

At C is the output waveform developed by devices such as an SCR. These can have a controlled turn on but are turned off when the current is reduced to zero. This waveform also is noisy since, for many motors, the steeply-rising edge is near full amplitude at starting and low speeds.

At D is the output waveform of a throttle switching a smooth DC source off and on; speed is being controlled by the ratio of on to off. This has the same noise problems at those of A and C but there is an advantage because the pulsing rate can be adjusted to meet the needs of a particular motor. The major application of this waveform today is in command control.

In most applications dissipative throttles merely reduce the amplitude of the DC supply. At E in Fig. 16-1, the throttle is dissipating a variable portion of the power supplied by a smooth DC source. This is the most common type of throttle for use when sound-effect tones are sent over the rails to speakers mounted in the locomotives. It also is the poorest type of throttle from the standpoint of smooth starting and slow-speed running.

At F a dissipative throttle is adjusting the amplitude of a full-wave rectified AC power source. The amplitude is changed but the wave shape is not. Although they are better than smooth DC for smooth starting and low-speed running, throttles of this type are poorer than those with pulses for such control.

Dissipative throttles can produce the output wave form at G in which a variable portion of the full-wave rectified AC appears on the rails. When starting and when at low speeds short, well spaced and rounded pulses are applied, giving much superior control compared to the waveform at F but, because these pulses are rounded, without additional motor noise.

A stated above, when sound signals are superimposed on motor power, it is necessary to apply smooth DC to the rails for the motors. As indicated in Fig. 16-2, this can be done either by a dissipative throttle and a DC power source or by a switching throttle whose output charges a large capacitor. The advantages of the switching throttle are lower power dissipation. Because of this, there is no need for a heat sink.

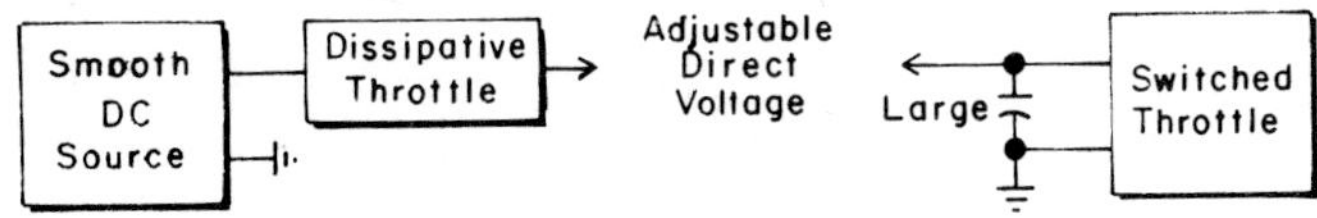

Fig. 16-2 Throttles for use with sound tones over rails.

Most throttles approximate a constant-voltage source, that is they tend to maintain the same output voltage regardless of current changes. Thus, under short circuit conditions, excessive current can flow which could damage the throttle, the DC source, or a stalled motor. Classical answers to the problem of protection are to provide a circuit breaker (this opens the output when the current rises above safe levels) or to connect a lamp in series with the output, the lamp limiting the current to a safe value (Section 2.41). Such arrangements are difficult to make adjustable so that currents can be limited to values safe for motors. In contrast, it is relatively simple to limit the maximum current output of a transistor throttle to any desired value.

A simple method of limiting the maximum output current is to limit the maximum base current which can flow in the output power stage. One method is shown in Fig. 16-3. The 68 ohm resistor limits the current flowing into the base to approximately 0.18A. This limits the maximum output current which can flow, even into a direct short circuit, to about 3A for a typical power transistor. The entire 13V of the power source appears across the transistor, so the latter is dissipating 13V × 3A = 39 Watts. To handle this much heat the transistor must be mounted on a heat sink which will hold the transistor case temperature at or below about 100°C (200°F). For 40 watts a piece of 3mm (1/8") thick aluminum 300mm (1') square will do. Commercial heat sinks with fins are available. These may be more convenient due to reduced over-all dimensions.

The power transistor can be selected based on the values given in Fig. 16-3. To avoid breakdown by the voltage spikes generated by the motor, the reverse voltage rating of the collector should be 5 to 6 times the applied voltage. A 60V transistor would do, but an 80V rating is safer. The emitter and collector must handle 3A so a 5A or better transistor should be selected. It must dissipate 40 watts, so it would be advisable to select a unit rated at about 75 watts. Only silicon transistors should be used in an application such as this, indeed it is well to avoid germanium transistors for any application in model railroading even if the germanium types are free.

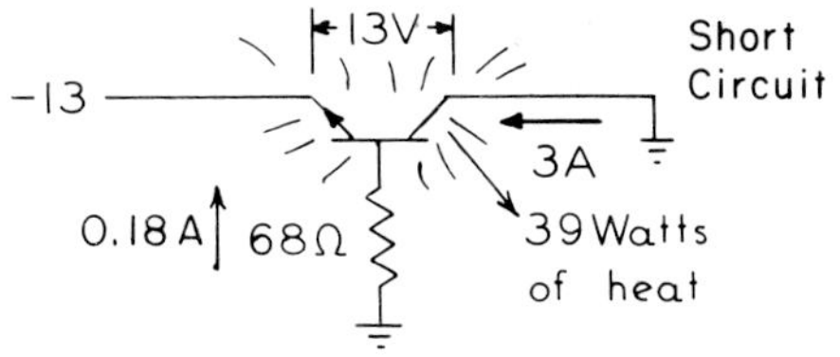

Fig. 16-3 Limiting maximum current.

To change the maximum current value, the 68 ohm resistor is changed to suit. If a rheostat of 500 ohms were placed in series with the 68 ohm resistor, the maximum current could be adjusted downward to protect the particular motor being controlled. It is better, however, to include this maximum-current adjustment control in the driving circuit for the power stage. The control then handles a smaller current than that required to drive the base of the power stage.

The dissipative method of limiting maximum output current shown in Fig. 16-3 is best suited to dissipative throttles since they require the heat sink for normal operation. A switching throttle can use the same method of protection but it will require the same size heatsink as a dissipative throttle. Switching throttles need only a small heatsink for normal operation. A large heatsink for protection can be avoided by causing the switching throttle to switch off when the current exceeds the maximum selected value. A shut-down circuit can be seen in Fig. 16-13.

16.33 Simple Throttles

When a throttle does not require sophisticated controls, one of the simple designs may be adequate. Fig. 16-4 shows a one-transistor dissipative throttle. The Max I resistor limits the maximum current

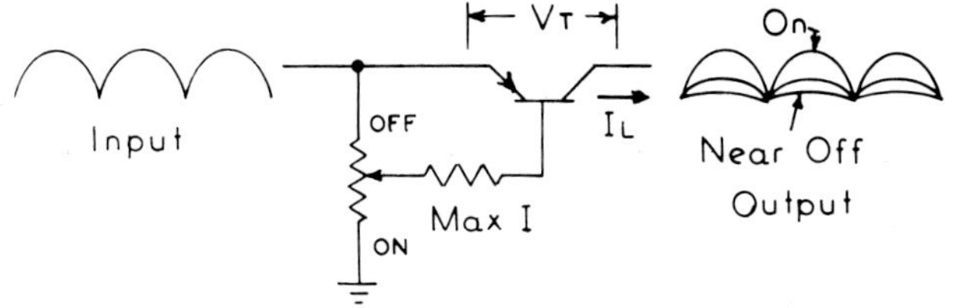

Fig. 16-4 Simple dissipative-type throttle.

which can be delivered, as described in Section 16.32 The potentiometer is the speed control. Its value will depend upon the maximum current to be delivered by the throttle (a 100-ohm, 2-watt potentiometer is satisfactory for a 3A throttle). This resistance can be increased if less maximum current is required. As a replacement for a rheostat, a throttle of this type has advantages because it is self-protecting, and because the panel control is a considerably smaller size than a rheostat of equivalent current-handling capability.

The above throttle can be improved significantly with respect to smooth starting and low-speed running by placing a capacitor across the transistor, and by adding two low-current diodes to the bridge rectifier as shown in Fig. 16-5. These extra diodes are to generate a constant voltage since the two power diodes connecting to the nega-

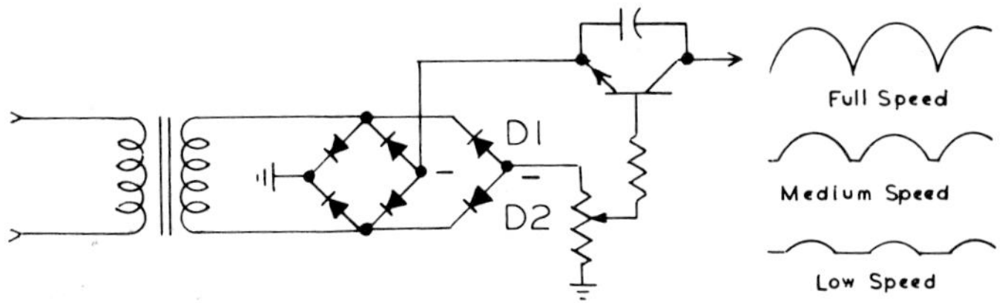

Fig. 16-5 Capacitor-type pulse power.

tive output of the bridge are back-biased by the voltage across the 100uf capacitor as a means of generating the pulse-power output. The capacitor can be of any value greater than 100uf. This type of throttle will operate virtually any locomotive at a steady speed of 2KMh (lMph) or less.

Switching throttles also can be simple. Fig 16-6 shows a throttle which develops the output waveform shown at A in Fig. 16-1.The capacitor charges to near the peak voltage of the full-wave rectified AC. The potentiometer speed control sets a voltage on the base of the transitor. Only when the half-wave voltage exceeds this base voltage does the transistor conduct, so the output is a pulse centered around the midpoint of the half wave as indicated on the right. The Max I resistor limits the maximum current which can be delivered but, when it begins to control the current, the throttle becomes a dissipative throttle. Therefore the transistor must be mounted on an adequate heat sink as described for dissipative throttles in Section 16.32.

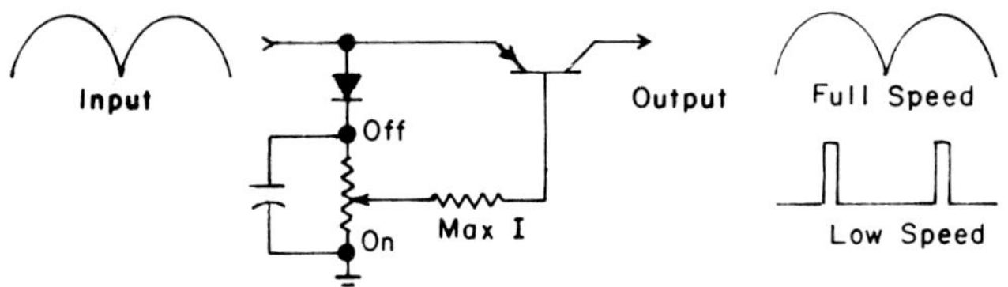

Fig. 16-6 Simple switching throttle.

So far transistors have been shown both for switching and dissipative type throttles. The silicon controlled rectifier, SCR (see Section 2.10) has also been used for switching-type throttles. The simplest SCR throttles are more complex than basic transistor throttles as it is necessary to generate a trigger pulse synchronized with the full-wave input and whose position in the cycle can be controlled. One arrangement is shown in Fig. 16-7. Capacitor C1 charges each half cycle at a rate determined by the setting of the speed controller, R2. When the voltage across C1 becomes high enough to turn on the unijunction transistor, the capacitor is discharged through the unijunction transistor and R2 generating a positive pulse to turn on the SCR at that point in the cycle. The output of the throttle is a steeply rising pulse followed by the rest of the normal half-wave.

Unijunction transistors should not be confused with the more customary bi-polar transistors described in Section 2.92. They are useful only in special applications such as drivers for SCR's.

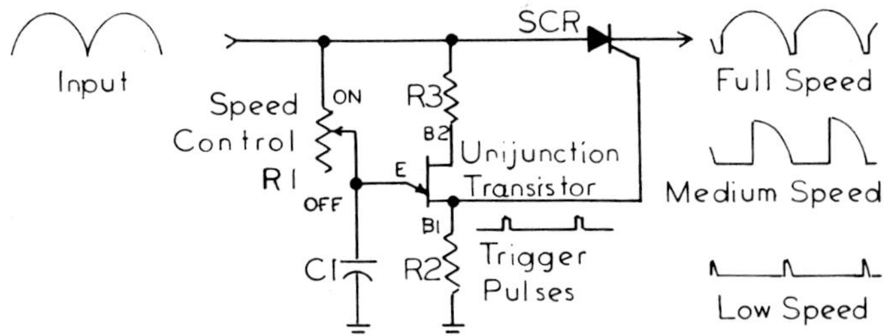

Fig. 16-7 SCR throttle.

The steeply rising output pulse of an SCR throttle adds motor noise and, particularly for N gauge, may cause erratic operation of motors although for HO generally their starting and low-speed running control is excellent. One commercial throttle used the SCR to drive a transistor equipped with a smoothing capacitor but that is really a transistor throttle. This approach is covered in Section 16.6

Once an SCR is turned on, its input gate loses control. Therefore an SCR throttle in itself cannot be made current limiting for protecting itself or the motors.

As an SCR is a rectifier, it can substitute for the diodes of the rectifier as well as serve as a throttle. Fig. 16-8 shows two SCR's serving as a full-wave rectifier. Used this way each SCR conducts

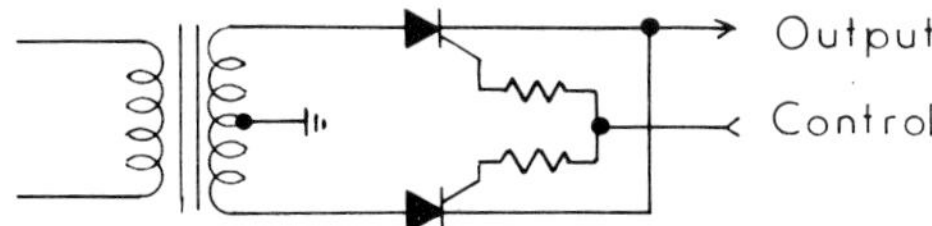

Fig. 16-8 Combined rectifier and throttle.

only every alternate half cycle which makes it possible to turn them on at any point in the half wave (180° phase control). If used to control the output of a separate rectifer, the range of control is reduced although not enough to make it unsatisfactory for model railroad throttles. Most SCR throttles have used a single SCR and a separate bridge rectifier but Hugh R. Wahlin, (1967) described a throttle with two SCR's as part of a full-wave bridge rectifier. For more information about SCR's, the General Electric SCR Manual is recommended.

16.4 TRANSISTOR THROTTLE DRIVERS

A transistor throttle can be driven directly from a speed controller as in Figs. 16-4 and 16.6. If so, the control current required by the throttle is roughly 5% of the output current, e.g., a 3A throttle requires 0.15A from the control. This current is too high to be convemient, so a throttle driver is customarily provided. In many published throttles this driver has taken one of the two forms shown in Fig. 16-9.

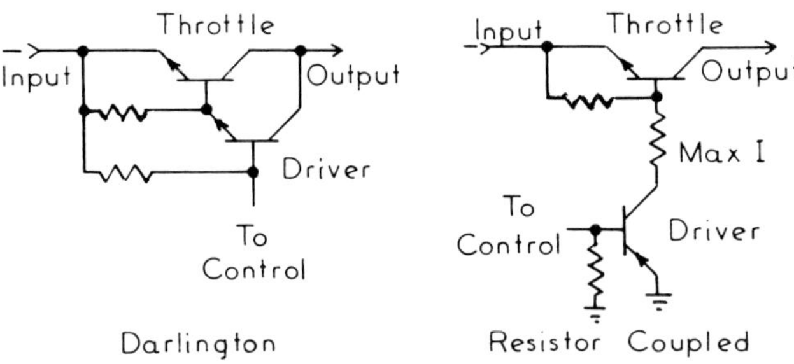

Fig. 16-9 Throttle drivers.

The Darlington connection on the left in Fig. 16-9 is a direct connection and, as such, has disadvantages. For several reasons such a connection tends to be unstable and the transistors should be matched for this type of operation. Further a failure of either transistor is likely to destroy the other. Although this connection will work most of the time, it must be regarded as living dangerously. Integrated Darlington pairs have been available. Because the pairs are matched and operating at nearly the same temperature, operation with such devices is more reliable than if separate transistors are used. In contrast the resistor-coupled driver on the right in the figure is stable and the failure of one transistor will not damage the other. The coupling resistor can be chosen to limit the maximum current which the throttle is to deliver and thus make the throttle self-protecting.

A complete throttle using a resistor-coupled driver is shown in Fig. 16-10. Although specific device types are given, only the ratings shown are important. Any device meeting those ratings may be substituted.

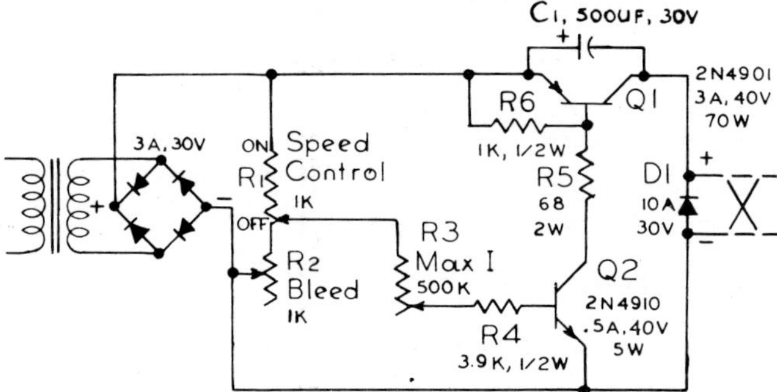

Fig. 16-10 Complete simple throttle.

In Fig. 16-10 the throttle is the same as that in Fig. 16-5 and the driver that of Fig. 16-9. R4 was selected to limit the maximum base current of Q2 so that even if R5 was shorted, the throttle output current would still be limited to 3A. The Maximum I rheostat R3 permits the maximum current to be set at any value between about 0.1A and 3A to protect a motor. In actual use it is customarily set to limit maximum speed as that current is usually lower than maximum permissible motor circuit. R2 sets a minimum resistance for the speed control to bleed current into the track when the controller is off. R2 is adjusted so the locomotive will start to move as soon as the speed controller is advanced. Thus the full range of the speed controller is available for any locomotive. D1 protects the throttle against reversed voltages from the track.

16.5 GRADUAL-RESPONSE THROTTLES

It is a simple matter to make a transistor throttle respond slowly to rapid changes of the speed control and to require the use of a brake to slow or stop the locomotive, in short, to add inertia to the system. The NMRA Glossary defines this as gradual response. Published throttles have accomplished this gradual response by a controlled increase or decrease of the charge on a large capacitor, a method included in the patent mentioned in Section 16.1

Fig. 16-11 shows the basics of gradual response. If the speed control is suddenly turned full on, the inertia (sometimes called momentum) capacitor will charge at a rate determined by its capacity and the acceleration resistance. Thus the locomotive speed increases at a rate determined by the capacitor, not by the speed control.

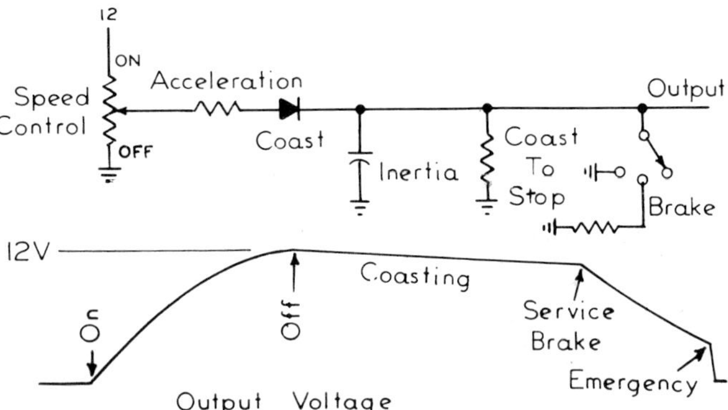

Fig. 16-11 Gradual response.

When the speed control is turned off (or to a lower speed), the coast diode blocks the discharge of the capacitor through the speed control but the capacitor discharges slowly through the coast-to-stop resistor so the locomotive will coast a long way then drift to a stop. For more rapid stops, the brake can apply added discharge paths. Generally, as shown, an emergency position is provided to give a virtually instant stop.

To suit various locomotives and enginemen, some of the controls are usually made adjustable. Fig. 16-12 shows a gradual-response unit. It can be connected directly to R3 of the throttle shown in Fig. 16-10 replacing resistors R1 and R2 to make a complete throttle.

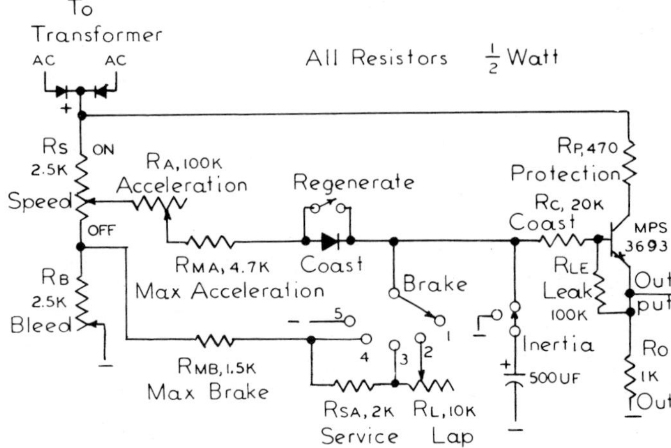

Fig. 16-12 Gradual response unit.

R_A Acceleration, permits the rate of acceleration to be adjusted as a Metroliner should accelerate much faster than a heavy freight drag. However R_{MA} sets a maximum acceleration rate even if the adjustable resistor is full on. The regenerate switch around the coast diode permits the speed control to reduce as well as increase speed. The brake has five positions. 1 is release, 2 is called lap, really a light application. (On the prototype the lap position holds the brake application already made so the train continues to slow. To duplicate this action would take more complex circuits). Lap is made adjustable although it is questionable that such an adjustment is worth the panel space. Positions 3 and 4 are more rapid applications with 5 being the emergency. Position 5 is connected directly to − rather than bleed so there will be a brief delay after an emergency application before the train again can be started, simulating the time required to recharge the train line.

The inertia switch can remove the capacitor from the circuit eliminating the gradual response feature as many model railroaders including the author prefer to operate without, and it is inconvenient when performing operations such as uncouping at a ramp. The transistor has been added to provide an additional stage of gain as the cost of the transistor is less than that of the much larger capacitor which would be required if the throttle driver was controlled directly from the capacitor. This transistor is operating in the common-collector mode (emitter follower), see Fig. 50, Chapter 2. R_P protects the transistor against burnout if the output lead is shorted to −. Although a specific Motorola code is given, any silicon NPN transistor with a voltage breakdown of at least 20, a current rating of 0.01A, and a dissipation rating of 120 milliwatts will do.

IC OpAmps can be used to improve the operation as well as to simplify the construction of throttles with gradual response. In Fig. 16-13 an OpAmp integrator is used not only to provide gradual response, but also as a memory to make a throttle suitable for walkaround control. When the throttle is off, the output of the integrator OpAmp will be ground, the turn-off OpAmp is then holding the power transistor off virtually all the time. Pressing the faster pushbutton will cause the output of the integrator to move positive. The turn-off OpAmp now will turn off the transistor for a decreasing interval around the center of the half-wave until full speed is reached. Pressing slower reverses the processes, turning off more and more of the half-wave. The emergency stop pushbutton returns the output of the integrator quickly to zero. The shut-down OpAmp also discharges the integrator capacitor rapidly if the set maximum current is exceeded. All four OpAmps can be in a single package, for example, the 747.

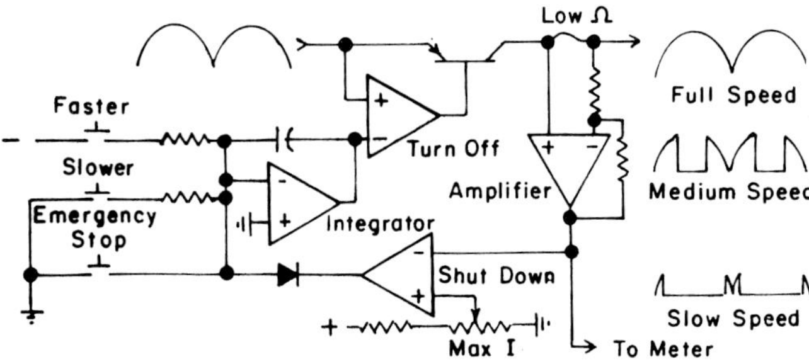

Fig. 16-13 Walkaround-control unit.

16.6 DIGITAL THROTTLES

The throttles described so far in this chapter are analog (linear) in nature. A variable voltage from the speed control commands the application of the desired variable voltage on the track. Modern electronics, however, have a strong trend toward digital and away from analog for the reasons described in Section 24.3 This trend already has had great impact on command control, see Section 17.5 Digital throttles, as compared to analog, offer the following established benefits: greater precision; more-readily integrated; less costly for complex functions; more reliable; and easier to design. Digital throttles are the obvious choice in the following applications. When speed and direction are determined by some sort of a digital processor, including microprocessors (see Fig. 13-31 for a turntable control example). When the speed commands from enginemen are to be processed before voltage is applied to the rails (e.g., block-signal systems with ATC). When memory is required (e.g., walkaround control). When speed commands are sent as "increase speed" or "decrease speed" (advantageous for walkaround control, command control, and computer cab control). When the command system is otherwise digital (e.g., when a microprocessor is used).

As of 1981 little definite information had been published with regard to digital throttles but all known digital throttles were of the switching type.

The simplest digital throttles are represented by the turntable motor control of Fig. 13-31. The only function performed by these simple throttles is to convert a binary-coded speed signal into an appropriate voltage applied to the motor. To illustrate the power of digital throttles to meet more complex requirements, the essentials of the throttle designed and tested in 1978 by Ken Stiefel for the exploratory computer cab control will be described.

This sytem placed three requirements on the throttle; these all had been difficult to implement with the previously-investigated analog throttles.

1. Only speed-change information was transmitted from the cabs (three rates each of acceleration, braking, and emergency stops).
2. As there was to be one throttle per section, the voltage applied to the rails had to be independent of the current supplied, and precisely that commanded by the speed code. This was to prevent noticeable changes of speed as locomotives crossed section breaks.
3. Because hundreds of throttles would be required, the cost per throttle had to be low. This implied centralized processing for all the throttles in the same general area.

The above requirements also bear on systems other than computer cab control; 1 and 3 are equally important for command control, for example.

The essence of Ken Stiefel's digital control is shown in Fig. 16-14. A binary-coded ramp (8 bits=256 ramp steps) is generated centered in every half-wave of the full-wave rectified AC. The ramp clock to drive the ramp counter is supplied from the central processor. Therefore any variations in the ramp will affect all sections alike. When the ramp count is less than the speed code, the throttle transistor of the proper direction is turned on. When the ramp count exceeds the speed code, the throttle transistor is turned off, generating the track-voltage wave shape shown at the bottom of the figure. Thus the differences in outputs between two throttles receiving the same speed code can easily be held to a few millivolts.

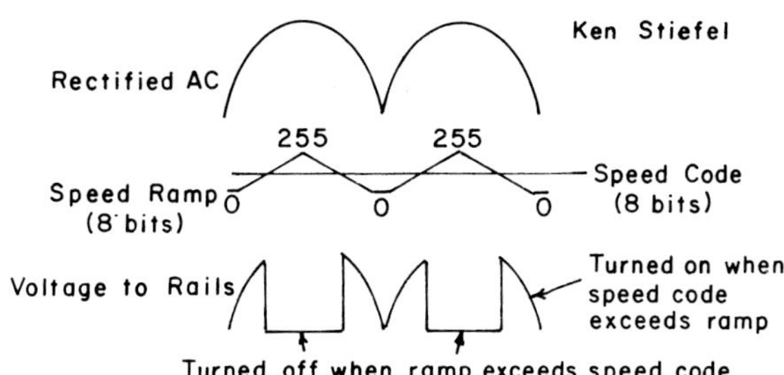

Fig. 16-14 Digital control of pulse.

For the purposes of economy, the central processor did not deal with each equipped section individually, rather it exchanged commands and information with section group circuits, each such circuit serving up to 16 sections located in the same general area. Fig. 16-15 shows in block-diagram form that part of the section group circuit necessary to control speed.

At the top left of Fig. 16-15 is the address decoder, which recognizes when a section in this group is being addressed. At center left is the system clock decoder. These two circuits are needed for all functions, not just for speed control. The speed shift register receives the two direction bits (one is for checking) and the eight speed bits. Converting speed change or emergency stop commands from the cabs into the proper speed code was done by the central processor. After the speed command had been received in the speed shift register, if the section addressed were in this group, the speed code would be written into the speed RAM at the address of the section concerned. Any section not under control of a cab would be periodically addressed by the central processor and its speed code would be set to zero. This action prevents an error from causing false energization of a section.

The 12-bit ramp counter is driven by the ramp clock. This clock is synchronized with the 60Hz line rather than with the system clock. Therefore, the ramp will be as shown in Fig. 16-14 regardless of the system clock rate. The least-significant four bits of this counter address the speed RAM, so all 16 sections are addressed for each step of the ramp. The ramp counter counts up to 255 and then back to zero.

Each time the speed RAM is addressed for a particular section, the speed code in the RAM is compared with the ramp count. If the speed code is higher than the ramp count, the speed FF for that section is set, causing the throttle to turn on. When the ramp count is higher than the speed code, the speed FF for that section is reset, turning the throttle off, the action required as shown in Fig. 16-14. If the current being drawn by the section exceeds the maximum permitted, the speed FF for that section will be reset, thus shutting down the throttle when overcurrent is detected.

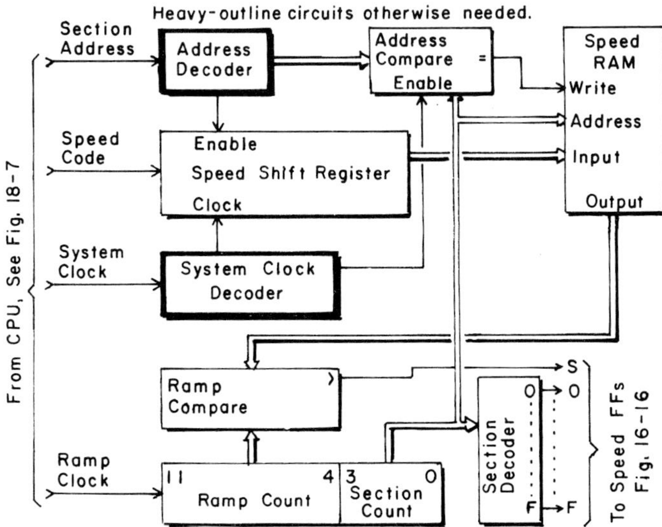

Fig. 16-15 Receiving digital speed commands for 16 sections.

The digital throttle circuit tested by Ken Stiefel is shown in Fig. 16-16. The state of the direction FF determined which throttle transistor was to be turned on during the period that the speed FF was set. The central processor would not change the state of the direction bits sent to the section group circuits unless the speed code, as stored in the central processor, was zero. The direction bit was sent in time slot 0 and its complement, as a check, in time slot 1. This check prevented an error of transmission causing a reversal of direction.

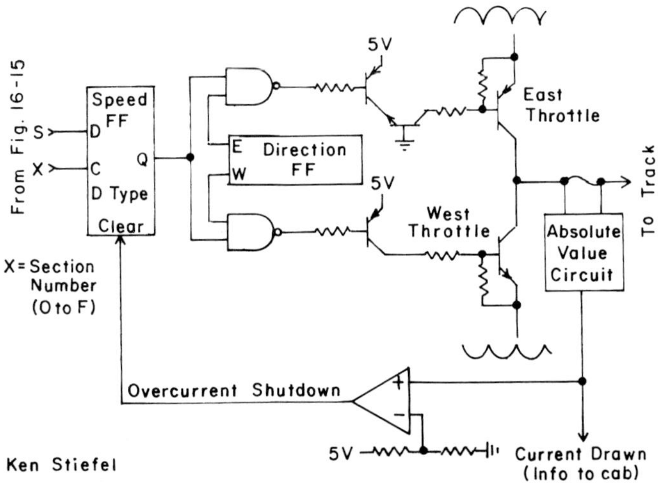

Fig. 16-16 Digital throttle.

16.7 FEEDBACK

For the best control of speed, the output of the throttle must adjust to any change in the power demand of the motor. The demand may change slowly, as when a train starts up a hill, or rapidly, as when there is a bind in the gears.

Any form of compensation to eliminate changes of speed depends upon feedback, that is the change of speed causes a reaction either to increase or decrease the applied power as required to maintain the set speed. The simplest illustration is when an engineman sees his locomotive slow down, he opens the speed control a bit more. But human response time is long and cannot compensate for rapid changes of speed, therefore electrical feedback is used.

Ideally a feedback system should be based on an accurate measurement of motor speed but some improvement of control is possible by monitoring the current being supplied by the throttle. A motor slowing down draws more current and one speeding up draws less.

If increase of current will increase throttle output and a decrease of current will decrease the output, motor will tend to run at a constant speed. This type of feedback was used in Linn Westcott's TAT throttles. Fig. 16-17 shows a simple application. Q3 detects (with a sensitivity adjusted by R4) the current of the throttle. The greater the current of the throttle, the larger the current Q3 supplies to the summing point SP. The output of the throttle then is function of the current being supplied by the control plus the feedback. The summing point, in one form or another, is characteristic of feedback control, often called servo control. To permit rapid response, the summing point must not be affected by the smoothing effect of the inertia capacitor if one is provided. The ratio of resistors R2 and R5 determines the degree of control by the feedback as compared to the control circuit.

Feedback in Fig. 16-17 is positive, that is an increase of current increases output voltage which in turn increases current and so on until some external means stops the cycle of increase. Positive feedback is inherently unstable, in fact it is the operating principle of oscillators. Careful adjustment is imperative. Nevertheless this method can improve the control of locomotives but its limitations should be recognized. For example, if a motor slows due to increased resistance, output current will drop and the feedback will then decrease throttle voltage leading to a further slowing of the motor.

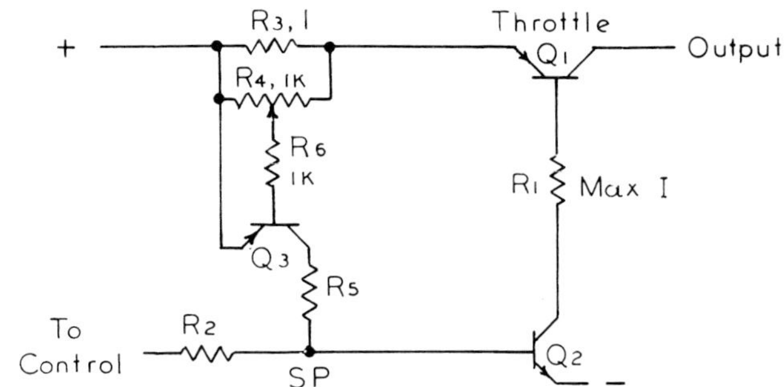

Fig. 16-17 Current monitor feedback.

A better source of feedback signal than the current supplied by the throttle is the counter emf of the motor. Counter emf of a permanent-magnet motor depends only on the speed of the motor (see Sections 3.3 and 16.8) and can be used directly to control the firing angle of an SCR throttle. Circuits of this type are widely used for the control of fractional horsepower motors and examples can be found in all manuals and books covering SCR's.

Published SCR motor controls with feedback were for 110V motors. Although the principles remain the same, exact values of resistors and capacitors depend upon the output voltage and current as well as the SCR type. In particular the unijunction transistor must be selected on the basis of the SCR type. Proper selection of values and types is more critical for an SCR throttle than for a transistor throttle.

The steeply rising output pulses of an SCR throttle may be a problem for some locomotives, particularly in N gauge. One method of rounding these pulses is to use the output of the SCR throttle to drive an emitter follower as shown in Fig. 16-18. The counter emf will still be fed back to the SCR but the capacitor will smooth the pulses. Actually the SCR is now a driver for a transistor throttle.

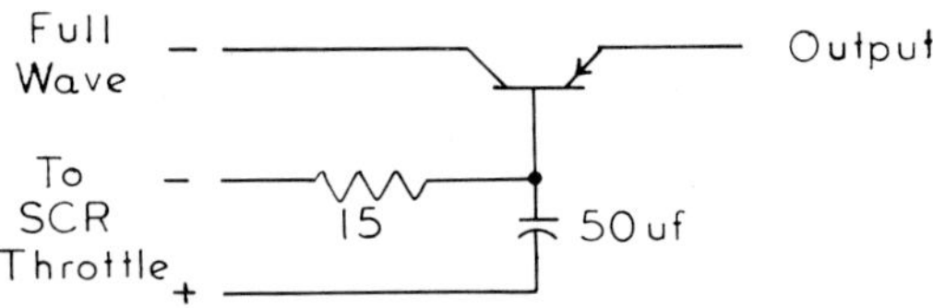

Fig. 16-18 Smoothing circuit for SCR throttle.

The most precise method of motor control is to measure speed and compare the voltage representing actual speed with that of the speed control to generate an error signal which then corrects any deviation from the speed desired by the engineer. The essential elements of such a control circuit are shown in block form in Fig. 16-19. This is a true servo control and requires careful design.

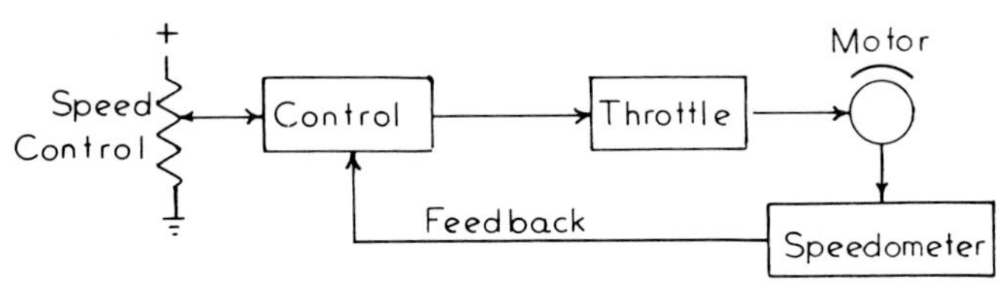

Fig. 16-19 Servo-type feedback throttle.

16.8 SPEEDOMETERS

A speedometer indicating the actual speed of a locomotive is a useful addition to a cab, particularly when the locomotive is out of sight or when it is important to know that a locomotive has just started to move. It also makes more meaningful speed restrictions.

For accuracy, a speedometer must be operated by a signal generated by the locomotive. Fortunately all permanent-magnet motors generate two signals which are directly proportional to speed and not affected by direction, grades, length of train, or the current and voltage being supplied by the cab. These are commutator ripple and counter emf.

As illustrated in Fig. 16-20, as the commutator segments make and break contact with the brushes, they generate spikes of voltage on the rails. These spikes can be separated from the throttle power by a high-pass filter (a small capacitor will do) amplified, integrated, and the output displayed on a meter. About 1960 Bill Nordahl developed such a speedometer which produced accurate speed measurements. Unfortunately the commutator spikes have high-frequency components, indeed they are the chief source of radio and TV interference generated by a model railroad. Since model railroad wiring is not designed to isolate high-frequency signals, the commutator ripple developed by one locomotive can operate the speedometers of all cabs.

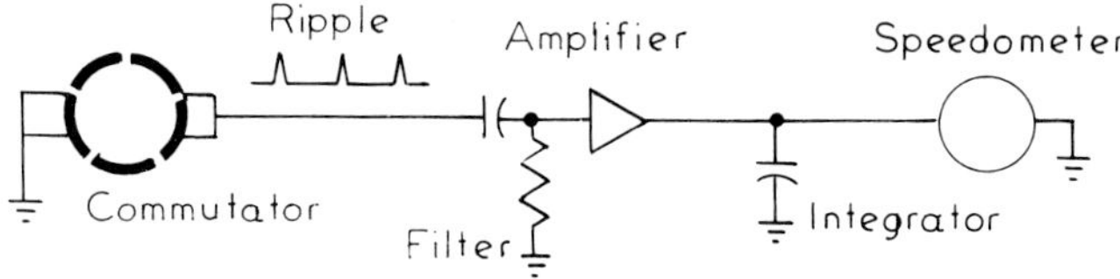

Fig. 16-20 Commutator ripple speedometer.

In contrast to commutator ripple, counter emf is DC and therefore is easily isolated to the wiring between the locomotive and its cab. Linn Westcott, in 1954, published a bridge-type circuit to measure the counter emf of a motor. It is shown in Fig. 16-21.

To operate this speedometer, the bridge is first balanced (with the motor stopped) by R2 so that the meter reads zero (voltages at A and B are equal). As soon as the motor turns, its counter emf raises the voltage at B so the meter reads up scale proportional to speed. The calibrate control permits the meter to be adjusted so that .6ma = 60 mph scale for direct reading in scale speed. In general changing from one locomotive to another requires the adjustments of both R2 and R3. A change in resistance of the wiring as the locomotive moves is interpreted as a change in speed.

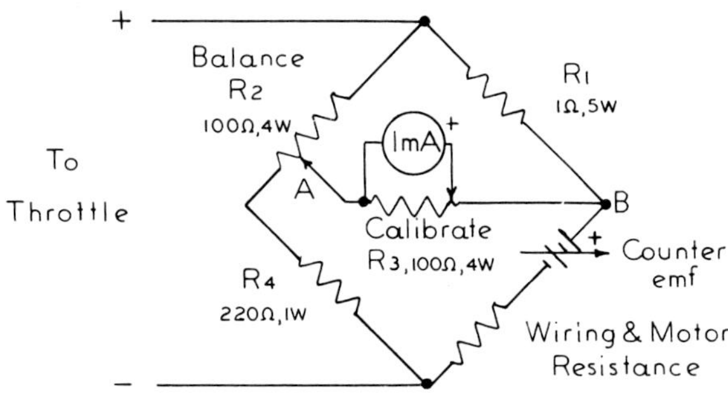

Fig. 16-21 Bridge-type speedometer.

Note in Fig. 16-21 that if the motor does not start (no counter emf), current and voltage to the motor increase and decrease proportionally. The meter actually is reading the differential between the change in current and voltage when the motor turns. Using two operational amplifers, as shown in Fig. 16-22, to develop and measure that differential voltage makes the circuit much more sensitive than the bridge of Fig. 16-21, permitting the resistance in series with the track power to be greatly reduced. The gain of the current amplifier is set by the rheostat "Balance" to adjust for the resistance of the locomotive motor. The rheostat "Calibrate" adjusts the gain of the differential amplifier to adjust for differences among motors as far as generating counter emf for a given track speed is concerned.

In the event of an open circuit to the locomotive, the meter will be driven off scale upwards and a short circuit will drive it off scale downwards. This characteristic of the above two circuits can be used to operate short circuit and open circuit lamps at each cab. Thus the engineman will know, even before attempting to start, that the locomotive will work or, if not, why not. Also, if the locomotive stops, he

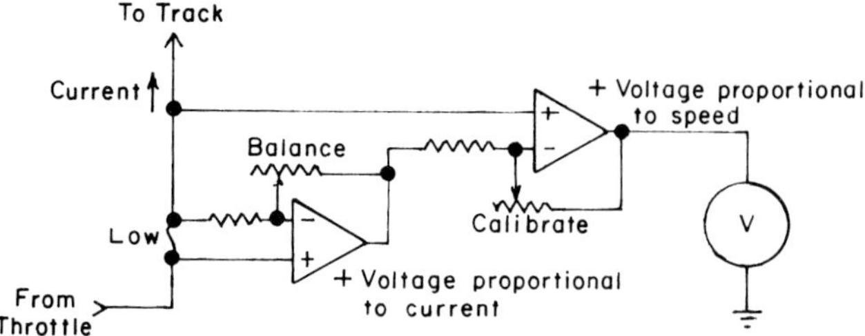

Fig. 16-22 OpAmp speedometer.

does not have to interpret meters to determine the cause. The circuit is shown in Fig. 16-23.

For the purpose of detection, a short circuit is defined as any resistance across the track of two ohms or less. Such a short circuit will make point C more positive than point A. The high-gain integrated-circuit operational amplifier will detect that polarity on its inputs and turn on the short lamp. An open circuit of 200 ohms or more will make point C more negative than point B and the other operational amplifier in the 747 integrated circuit will turn on the open lamp. The 747 integrated circuit is actually two 741 operational amplifiers. Any other operational amplifier capable of operating at model railroad voltages would do as well. As used in this circuit an operational amplifier is simply a sensitive amplifier, see Section 24.94.

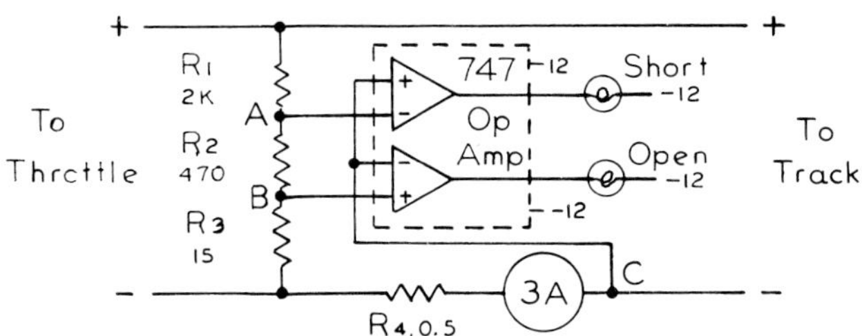

Fig. 16-23 Short and open amps.

In 1968 the author developed a speedometer which measured counter emf directly thus eliminating any dependance on wiring or motor resistance changes. It reads zero when the motor stops regardless of whether there is a short or open circuit. This speedometer is shown in Fig. 16-24 and may be attached to any full-wave throttle.

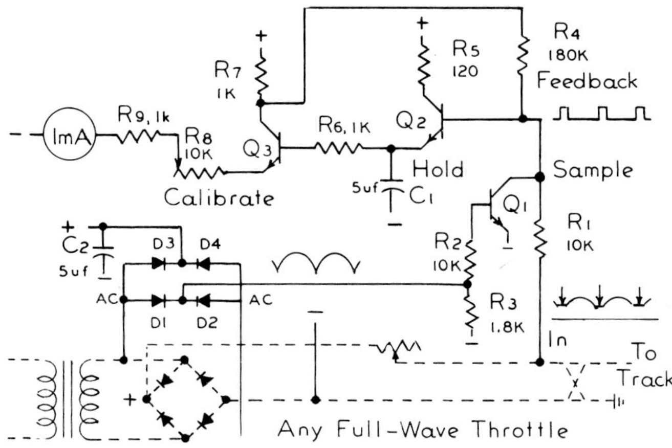

Fig. 16-24 Sampling-type speedometer.

As indicated at the lower right, the voltage wave shape at the track shows the counter emf of the motor whenever the output voltage of the throttle is lower than the counter emf. Thus if the voltage on the track is measured only at the points indicated by the arrows, the measurement will be the counter emf. This type of repetitive measurements is called sampling. To generate the precise timing points for sampling, diodes D1 and D2 loaded by R3 generate a clean full-wave rectified voltage, the zero points of which are the sampling points. This full-wave voltage is applied to transistor Q1 turning it on except for the short interval around the zero point of the wave. Therefore Q1 holds the base of Q2 at − except during the sample intervals when the counter emf is allowed to reach Q2 in the form of pulses. Q2 is an emitter follower which changes the hold capacitor to approximately .6V less than the pulses applied to its base so the voltage on the capacitor is equivalent to the counter emf of the motor. Since an additional transistor is less expensive than a sensitive meter, Q3, an emitter follower is added to drive the 0-1mA meter. A calibrate adjustment is provided so the meter will read .6 for 60 mph scale for all locomotives. The feedback resistor R4 compensates for the voltage drop through the emitter followers so the meter will register for the slightest movement of the motor and also adds negative feedback for stability. D3, D4, and C2 are a source of smooth 12V DC and can be eliminated if this voltage is otherwise available. Any silicon low-power npn transistors can be used.

Fig. 16-25 is a photograph of this speedometer showing the circuit built on a piece of plastic mounted on the terminals of the meter to make a self-contained unit.

16.9 SPECIAL FEATURES

Although in use as early as 1957, transistor throttles, particularly those exploiting IC's, continue to be developed. For analog throttles, integrated OpAmps offer the availability of high gain at low cost, and with minimal wiring effort. As such, they can be used directly to replace the low-gain one or two transistor drivers in the early transistor-throttle circuits. More important is the summing connection for OpAmps (see Fig. 24-51 I). This makes simple the introduction of a signal to provide any form of pulse power desired.

A feature desired by some is a method by which the speed control is advanced from zero as soon as the locomotive will start to move. In the past this has been accomplished by a manually-set bleed control such as those shown in Figs. 16-10 and 16-12. Integrated circuits offer the possibility of making this type of adjustment automatic.

16.10 CONSTRUCTION OF THROTTLES

The greatest single error made in building transistor throttles is inadequate cooling. All too often model railroaders judge heating effects under normal operating conditions. If the throttle is to have a long, trouble-free life, it must not overheat under trouble conditions. For example the temperature at the case of the main power transistor of a 3A, 12V throttle will reach 175°C (350°F) under a sustained short circuit even when mounted on an aluminum heat sink measuring 3 × 300 × 300 mm (1/8″ × 1′ × 1′) and open to free movement of air. Therefore the first rule in building a transistor throttle is to use a heat sink which will handle the maximum wattage to be dissipated under the most adverse trouble conditions and to mount the heat sink in the vertical plane so air can flow freely over its surface by natural convection.

Except for self-contained portable units, it is best to divide throttles into two units, one containing all bulky and all heat-producing parts such as the transformer, rectifier, and main throttle transistor and other part the controls and indicators. This permits the bulky items to be mounted remote from the panel which not only saves panel space but also places the heat sources at a location where cooling can be more easily accomplished.

When making a heat sink from a metal sheet, remember that it must be thick enough to conduct the heat rapidly away from the transistor as well as large enough to transfer the heat into the air. 3mm (1/8″) aluminum is about as thin as can be used for the main throttle transistor.

Fig. 16-25 Self-contained speedometer.

Jim Boyd at the portable control handles a westbound passenger train on the Virginian & Ohio layout of W. Allen McClelland. Such flexible controls give the engineer a remarkable degree of freedom in train following.

The transistor can be mounted to a heat sink so that it is electrically isolated but a much better thermal connection is made by bolting the transistor metal to metal. It is easy to mount the heat sink itself so that it is insulated from the rest of the throttle circuit.

Drivers for the throttle do not dissipate much power but, as they must be mounted in any event, it is safer to place them on a small heat sink. An approximately 50mm (2″) length of 20mm (3/4″) aluminum angle is both convenient and an excellent heat sink.

If the output protective diode is connected to the collector of the throttle as is D1 in Fig. 16-10 the diode can have its mounting stud driven into a tapped hole in the heat sink of the transistor. The heat sink then will serve as the electrical connection. Choose a diode with the mounting stud attached to the proper terminal, they are available both ways. Mount the diode as far away from the transistor as is practical.

A transistor throttle lends itself well to placing all controls in a miniature, hand-held control box connected to the throttle by a flexible cable and thus give the engineer considerable freedom of movement. To avoid heavy track-power leads in the cable, a reversing relay can be provided at the throttle and controlled by a miniature switch on the control box as shown in Fig. 16-26. Even an ammeter can be installed without heavy leads. Mount a miniature 0-3 or 0-5mA meter in the box and connect it with light wires to a shunting resistor mounted at the throttle, also shown in the figure. The shunt resistor is easily made from a piece of nichrome wire from a replacement heater element. Adjust the amount of nichrome wire length between the meter terminals so that the milliammeter reads directly in amperes as measured by an ammeter in series with the shunt resistor. Note that the nichrome wire terminates on its connections to the throttle and output but only passes under the terminals for the meter. This prevents any damage to the milliammeter if any terminal becomes loose.

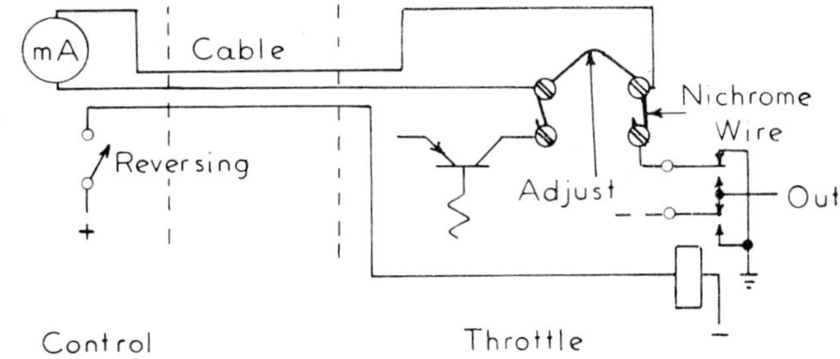

Fig. 16-26 Remote reverse and ammeter.

16.11 TROUBLE SHOOTING TRANSISTOR THROTTLES

The general trouble-shooting principles of Chapter 22 apply to transistor throttles. In particular a multimeter is an almost indispensable tool. Choose one with a low-resistance ohms scale, often labeled Rx1. Some of the low-cost multimeters have as their lowest resistance scale Rx1000. Low resistance scales are useful in checking transistors and diodes.

If possible, record the voltage measurements made on a working throttle. Take these measurements at all convenient points, in particular at the terminals of transistors and other semiconductors, and under various conditions such as speed control off, on, no load, and shorted output. Record these voltages directly on the circuit diagram for easy reference.

With all power off, measure and record the resistance between each pair of terminals on transistors and diodes. Use both polarity of leads from the meter. When a throttle fails, these normally are the first measurements to check. As described in Section 2.92, resistance measurements of the diodes of a transistor usually will disclose a bad unit. In some circuits it may be necessary to disconnect one or two leads to prevent a low-resistance shunt path from obscuring the measurements on the transistor.

If a transistor is blown, do not merely replace it. Try to determine the cause first. In throttles without self-protection it could be a high current overload; circuit breakers and fuses may not react quickly enough to protect a transistor. An inadequate heat sink might lead to overheating even for currents below the designed maximum. Perhaps the transistor type used had too low a voltage breakdown rating. Whatever the cause, it should be corrected before replacing the transistor.

If a newly built throttle does not operate, check it out one step at a time. First make sure the power-source voltage is correct and present at all the proper points. Then connect a voltage which will turn on the power transistor of the throttle. For example, in Fig. 16-10 short the collector of Q2 to −. This should turn Q1 full on. If it does not, the trouble is isolated to the circuit of Q1 or Q1 itself. If the power transistor turns on, try the same thing for its driver. Again using Fig. 16-10 as an example, connect the junction of R3 and R4 to + which also should turn the throttle full on. The key is to examine the circuit and determine what connection is the maximum and what is minimum and then use these. In Fig. 16-12, for example, checking out the controls will show that the output voltage from the transistor will be highest when the voltage connected to Rc is highest. Therefore connect Rc to + and observe that the output voltage follows.

Whenever a voltage is applied to a point within the throttle to check operation as described above, make certain there is a resistor in the circuit which will limit currents to safe values. In the examples given, the voltage was connected to a resistor in the circuit which would provide the necessary protection, in Fig. 16-10 it was the Max I resistor. If there is no such resistor in the circuit, then place one in the test lead being used.

SCR throttles are more difficult to trouble shoot than transistor throttles as, in most cases, their operation is dependent upon a short pulse generated at the proper time. This can readily be checked only by the use of an oscilloscope. With only a multimeter it is possible to check for voltages and also make resistance measurements which might pinpoint the source of trouble but final determination must be made by substitution of parts.

17 COMMAND CONTROL

17.1 GENERAL

Conventionally, when more than one standard DC locomotives are operating on a layout the way to control each one independently has been to divide the tracks into sections. After this, apply the voltage and polarity required by a particular locomotive to the sections which are being used by that locomotive (Chapters 9 and 18). The task of connecting cabs to the proper sections, and of releasing no longer needed sections for use by other cabs, is not trivial. Even when this is done successfully, locomotives are forced to remain some distance apart so as to be in separate sections (if independent control is to be maintained). Both of these problems would be eliminated if the cab controlling a particular locomotive could command the speed and direction of its locomotive, regardless of the location of the latter on the layout. The command controlling each locomotive's speed and direction must in no way affect the speed and direction of any other locomotive, even though all locomotives receive the same command.

Since the middle forties, many systems have been demonstrated which successfully selectively controlled the locomotive assigned to a particular cab. All such systems depended on placing some sort of selective equipment in all, or in all but one, of the locomotives. As described later in this chapter, this selective equipment can be as simple as a diode, or it can be every complex. Many different names have been used over the years for this type of control but, by 1980, "command control" seemed to be well on its way to becoming the generic name for these types of systems.

Commands to the locomotive are only part of the story. In conventional DC control, the wire connecting the cab to the locomotive can not only transmit commands to the motor, but also can return information from the motor to the cab. The most-commonly displayed information from the motor is the current it is drawing, but scale speed is also transmitted by the motor in the form of counter e.m.f. No command-control system demonstrated by 1980 transmitted such information back to the cab but, as explained in Section 17.5, this is possible.

17.2 HISTORICAL NOTES

Prior to World War II, selective control of two locomotives had been accomplished on three-rail layouts. Those with overhead wire

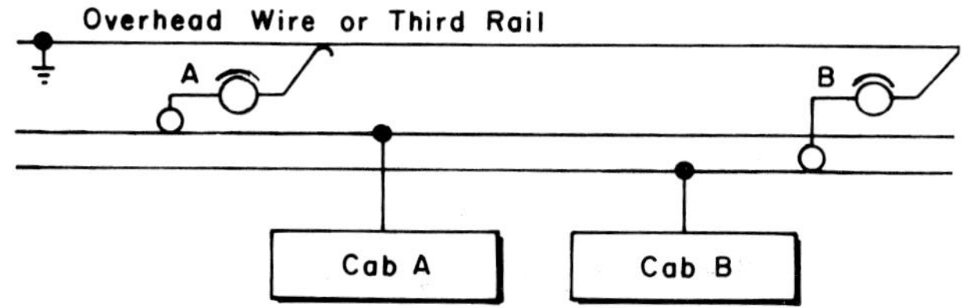

Fig. 17-1 Three conductor control.

were done by making one of the three available conductors common, and by using the other two independently to control separate motors as shown in Fig. 17-1. Such a system is not command control as the term is used here, because neither locomotive receives the commands sent to the other. The first true command control system, one using selective equipment in the locomotive, was the alternate half wave system shown in Fig. 17-2. Each of the two cabs were connected to the rails by a diode so that the cab could control the amplitude of its half wave without affecting the other half wave. The selective equipment mounted in each locomotive was a similar diode, each poled so that it would respond only to the half wave of its cab, i.e., cab A controls only locomotive A. The amplitude of the selected half wave controlled only speed.

Direction had to be controlled either by a manual reversing switch on the locomotive or by a sequence switch operated by turning the half wave on and off. This system originated right after World War II and found its greatest application on toy-train layouts, and for model traction. In the latter case, when two such systems were installed in the manner of the two cabs of Fig. 17-1, using the three conductors, it is called the Detroit System.

The first commercial system of command control was a 10-channel frequency control system introduced by Lionel about 1946. It was used for remote uncoupling as well as controlling locomotives,

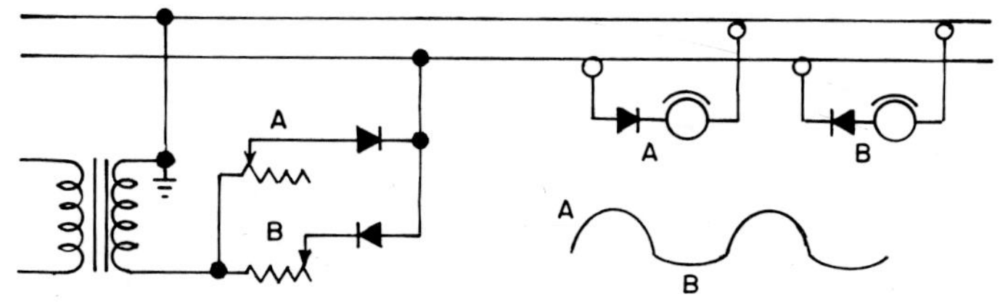

Fig. 17-2 Half-wave control.

but the latter could only be controlled for direction (when running) or stopped. There was no variable speed control. In the early sixties Earl G. Hallman used the Lionel system to control a locomotive-mounted motor-driven rheostat and thereby obtained speed control.

The next development was to place 60Hz on the rails and control direction by turning on an electronic switch in the locomotive during either the positive or negative half cycles, and to control speed by the duration the switch was closed. The first system of this type publically demonstrated was by David Friedman of the Summit-New Providence HO RR Club in 1962. His electronic switch was a single power transistor. About a year later General Electric introduced ASTRAC, a very similar system but using two SCRs as the electronic switch. Although soon discontinued by GE, this system was later revived using a triac as the switch by Alphatronics. This was still available in 1980.

Due to problems of operating with motors designed for full-wave rectified AC power, no half-wave system achieved acceptance. One solution to the half-wave problem was to use the technology that was developed for radio-controlled model airplanes to operate a servo motor controlling an on-board transistor throttle. Like the earlier Hallman system, this method required a bulky receiver in the locomotive. In 1980 a commercial system (RFPT) of this type was available.

Of significance to small layouts was the development of two-locomotive systems in which only one locomotive required a receiver, the other running on conventional DC control. In 1980 two such commercial systems were available, EMS and MRC.

All frequency-selective systems are basically analog in nature but the overwhelming trend in electronics is to move from analog to digital. A major reason for this trend is that digital circuits are far easier to integrate than analog. In 1972 the first partially digital system (Digitrack) was introduced; this system was marketed until 1976. It was not an IC system and therefore it was bulky and expensive, a system idea ahead of the technology of the time. Its basic ideas were revived in 1979 by Keith Gutierrez, using integrated circuits. About the same time an even-more integrated system, the Zero 1, was introduced based on a different system of selection.

17.3 STATUS OF COMMAND CONTROL

In 1981 the technology of building command-control receivers which would fit into N-scale locomotives had arrived. The digital systems had very good control but general acceptance was held back due to incompatability of the various sytems offered. The status of command control in 1981 was similar to that of television just before it became popular, and to that of HO motive power in the late thirties. In the latter case locomotives were marketed for both AC and for DC and for various voltages. It is to the NMRA's everlasting credit that in the thirties it standardized on DC and on voltage. The electronic industry also recognized that TV would never be inexpensive or popular unless the signals transmitted by all TV stations were standardized. Note that standardization of transmitted signals does not imply standardization of devices. The integrated-circuit color TV set of 1980 is vastly different than the vacuum-tube black-and-white set of 1950 but both can receive a program broadcast either in 1950 or in 1980. With today's digital technology, standardization of command signals to locomotives would be far simpler than the analog standardization required for TV.

As explained in Section 17.5, by 1981 there seemed no technical reason why a standard set of pulses could not be adopted which would be suitable for the immediate needs of speed and direction control, as well as providing for future requirements. Specifically such standard pulses should be suitable for a low-cost, bare-bones speed and directional control system for the smaller layouts, thus creating a large demand for an IC reciever. Additional pulses beyond those needed for a bare-bones system would expand the capabilities of control to meet the needs of the largest layouts; these pulses could be used for special features such as controlling on-board sound generators and remote uncoupling. The latter are particularly valuable for switching locomotives. Even pulses sent from the locomotive back to its cab could be provided to operate a speedometer on an ammeter. Such standardization of command signals to the locomotives and of information signals back from the locomotives would create vast new markets because the demand for the equipment would be high. In addition, the opportunity of developing and marketing many different types of controllers, etc. would exist, since each could be applied to existing layouts just as a newly-developed DC power pack can be connected directly to the layouts of today. A market for add-on systems such as sound and speedometers would be created. Development-minded modelers would have a field day working up microprocessor systems of all types, simple ATC and CTC systems, on-board sound, headlight controls, remote uncoupling, etc.

17.4 FREQUENCY CONTROL

With the exception of the special two-cab systems described in Section 17.6, the frequency-control systems up to 1981 applied a constant voltage to the rails, either AC or DC. For controlling speed and direction, these systems sent signals of a specified frequency over the rails. Mounted on the locomotive was a receiver tuned to the frequency assigned to that locomotive. In some cases a memory device was carried on board the locomotive. In such systems a signal needs to be sent by the control only when speed is to be changed. If no signal is sent, speed remains the same. Systems with memory are particularly well-adapted to walkaround control. In the early Hallman system and in systems based on model-airplane radio control, the memory device is an on-board motor driving the speed control. The physical size of motor-driven systems makes them unsuitable for use in small locomotives.

On-board rheostats and dissipative transistor throttles are not only bulky, they also generate heat. In contrast, an electronic switch is small and remains cool. Such switches control speed by being turned on and off for definite intervals thus controlling the power to the motor. Fig. 17-3 represents in simplified form the first practical switching-type systems. In all cases approximately 15V 60Hz are connected directly to the rails. A transmitter superimposes a burst of the frequency assigned to the locomotive which is being controlled on the 60Hz. As shown by the waveforms at the right in Fig. 17-3, these bursts occur only in the half-cycles corresponding to the polarity on the rails which is required for the direction selected. The location of the burst within the half-cycle determines when the switch is closed and thus how much of that half-cycle is applied to the motor. In this way only one frequency is required for each locomotive, speed and direction are controlled by the position of the transmitted pulse with reference to the 60Hz waveform.

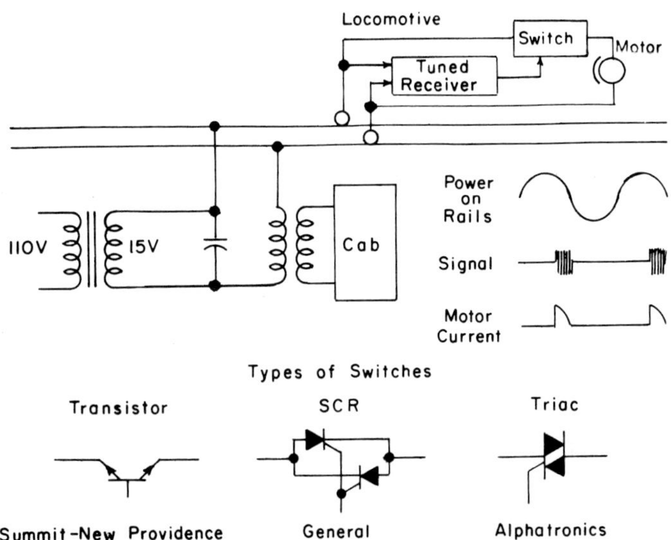

Fig. 17-3 Half-wave frequency control.

The bottom of Fig. 17-3 shows the three types of switches which have been used in this type of system. At the left is a single transistor (shown with two emitters since the direction of current flow depends on the polarity of the 60Hz when the switch is on). With this type of switch, the control pulse is applied during the entire period the motor is to receive current. At the center are two SCRs in parallel. The one in the conducting direction will turn on when an input is applied, and will remain on until the motor current drops to zero. Thus only a short pulse need be sent for this type of switch. The triac on the right is essentially two SCRs in one package and operates as such.

Since direction is controlled by conduction only during the selected half wave, as shown by the motor-current waveform in Fig. 17-3, these are inherently half wave systems. The motors at the time these systems were developed did not respond well to half-wave power. Some motors would overheat and others would run too slowly or fail to generate sufficient drawbar pull. Nevertheless, this system found some success on layouts where its disadvantages could be minimized, in particular in light service on traction lines (because the motors did not have to deliver high performance).

It is possible to use the same principle as above but to apply full wave current to the motor by the use of a pulse controlled full wave rectifier. Any system based on frequency control must have tuned circuits. In 1981 such circuits were not integratable to the extent possible with digital circuits. As a result, they remained both expensive and bulky. In additionl, the poor selectivity of low-cost tuned circuits limited the maximum number of locomotives which could be controlled independently to less than the number that was needed on the largest layouts. Phase-locked loops (PLL), available in integrated form and used in one commercial command control system (Dynatrol by Power Systems) provide a major improvement in selectivity. In 1981 frequency control was in a poor competitive position compared to digital control.

17.5 DIGITAL CONTROL

Because digital circuits are far more readily integrated than the analog circuits required for frequency control, it would be surprising if the swing to digital methods which was sweeping the electronics field in 1981 did not offer the greatest opportunity for command control. By 1980 such systems were only beginning to be demonstrated and reasonably rapid developments were to be expected. Unfortunately, several incompatible methods of selecting a locomotive and controlling its speed and direction are possible. As explained in Section 17.3, whether digital command control becomes widely installed or not seems to depend primarily on whether there can be an agreement on the signals which are sent between the control and its locomotive. Descriptions of the principles of the two types of digital control available in 1980 follow. Particular attention is given to their capabilities for adding new features in the future.

Fundamental to any system of command control is the transmission of a signal which can be recognized by the controlled locomotive as its unique signal. In the case of frequency control, it is a signal of a specified frequency. In the case of digital control two different selection methods have been demonstrated. In one method each pulse which controls a particular locomotive is determined by the position of that pulse in the train of pulses. In the second method, a set of "address" pulses are sent which cause the locomotive addressed to respond to the command pulses which follow, and to return information to the cab. All other locomotives are not addressed at this time, they ignore the command pulses and send no information. The address system offers greater possibilities than the pulse-position system, including control of couplers and the offerings of the capabilities of on-board sound generation. A restriction is that only one cab at a time can send or receive information.

Synchronization

Regardless of the pulse system adopted, it is necessary for the receiver in the locomotive to identify the first pulse of a string of pulses, a process called "synchronization". Although many methods of synchronization have been developed for commercial applications, such as in the telephone system, the two shown in Fig. 17-4 appear to be the simplest and lowest in cost for model railroad application. At the top of the figure successive strings of 16 pulses are being sent. The strings can be of different lengths than 16. At the end of each string there is an appreciable interval with no pulses. This interval provides the information necessary for the receiver to identify the next pulse received as the first pulse of the next string. A familiar use of this type of synchronization is the rotary telephone dial. The central office equipment distinguishes the end of the pulses for one digit from the start of the pulses for the next by the much greater interval between digits compared to the individual pulses of a digit.

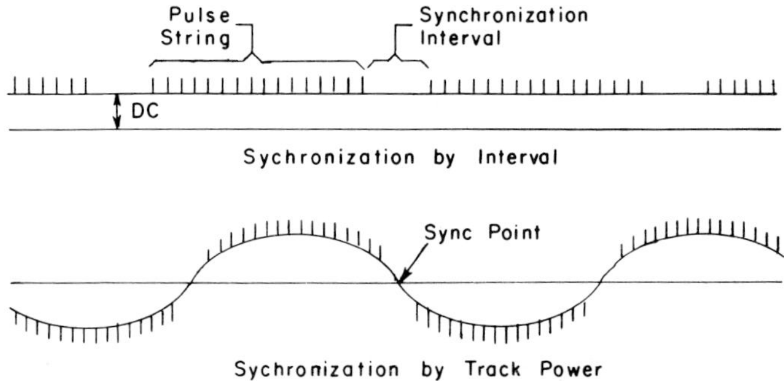

Fig. 17-4 Synchronization.

Although, in Fig. 17-4, the interval synchronization method is shown for DC running power on the rails; AC running power is equally suitable.

With AC, the AC itself can be used for synchronization, as shown at the bottom of Fig. 17-4. The first pulse after reversal of polarity is recognized as the first pulse of the string. Obviously, if there is to be compatibility, a decision must be made whether running power is to be DC or AC, and on the type of synchronization. Further discussion will assume that the pulse string has been synchronized so that the receiver can identify the first pulse of each string.

Locomotive Identification

The next step is to identify the command signals for the particular locomotive. One way is to assign each pulse to a particular locomotive as shown in Fig. 17-5, (Digitrack, Gutierrez). In that figure, 16 pulses are in the string. Each is unique to a particular one of 16 receivers. Since there is only one pulse for each locomotive, speed and direction commands must be sent by suitably modifying the width or amplitude (or both) of the pulse, as described under the speed and direction commands below. Such modulation, unfortunately, is not digital but analog and analog is not well adapted to integration. More pulses could be added to the string to control more than 16 locomotives. If fewer locomotives are required than the number of pulses, two pulses could be assigned to each locomotive, the second pulse being used to control on-board sound or uncoupling.

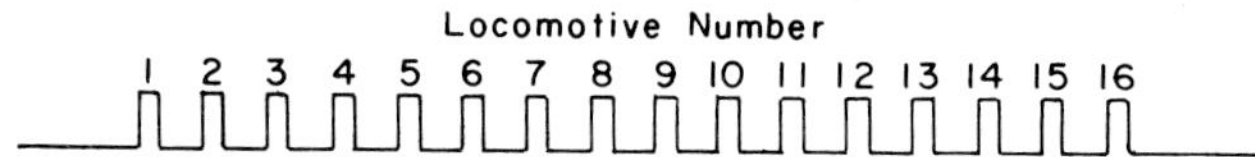

Fig. 17-5 Separate pulse for each locomotive.

The receiver for this type of system must be able to be forced to an initial state when pulses are not being sent. Once the pulse train starts, it must count each pulse and develop an output corresponding to the pulse assigned to its locomotive. The selective equipment for the receiver, published by Keith Gutierrez in 1980, is shown in Fig. 17-6. The bridge rectifier assures that the receiver will be supplied with the proper polarity of voltage and pulses, regardless of the polarity of the DC on the rails. The zener diode reduces the output voltage of the rectifier by 10V so the two inverters can respond to the command pulses.

When no command pulses are being received, the synchronization interval, the transistor shown in Fig. 17-6 is turned off. The load bar input of the counter is taken low, which loads the binary number for that locomotive into the counter. When the string of pulses again starts, the transistor is turned on, removing the load signal. The capacitor serves to hold the load input high between pulses of the string. Each pulse detected decrements the counter (Dn bar input). When the pulse corresponding to the number loaded into the counter is received, a pulse appears on the borrow bar output of the counter, this pulse corresponds in width to the pulse received. The borrow output is used to control the analog circuit which drives the motor.

From the standpoint of the use of pulses, a far more efficient method of selecting is to address each locomotive by the binary code

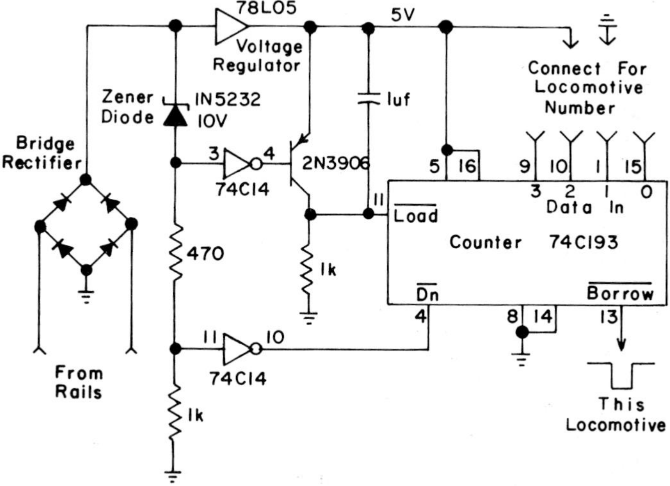

Fig. 17-6 Selective section of the Gutierrez receiver.

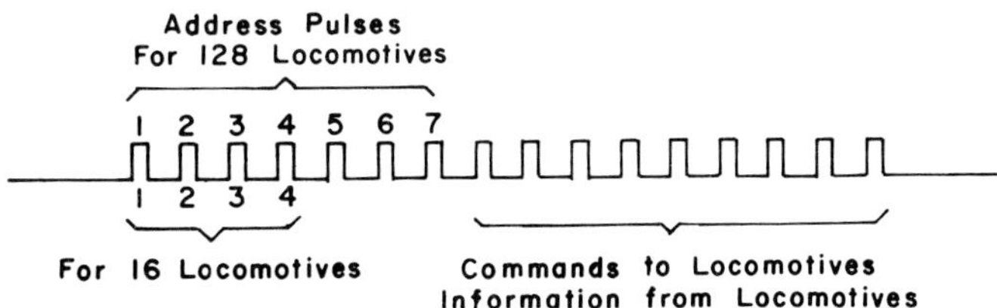

Fig. 17-7 Addressing locomotive.

of the first pulses sent, as shown in Fig. 17-7. The Zero 1 system uses this approach. Only four pulses are required to address 16 locomotives. This is sufficient for a bare-bones sytem. As indicated in the figure, assigning seven bits would provide for a maximum of 128 locomotives. This is an adequate number. In 1981 the Model RR Club, building the largest model railroad attempted to that date, estimated it would probably run a maximum of 64 engines simultaneously on its HO layout. The capability of an extra 64 locomotives would provide for multiple-unit engines and for locomotives at engine terminals. Even with seven pulses assigned for addressing, nine remain in a string of 16. These are for use as commands to locomotives or for information back to the cab. Any addresses not needed for locomotives could be used to control track switches, signals, and operating equipment on cars.

Speed and Direction Commands

When only one pulse is available to send commands to a particular locomotive, as in the system shown in Fig. 17-5, that pulse must contain both the speed and the direction commands. This is possible by making the width or the amplitude of the pulse variable, or by a combination of both. Two of the possibilities are shown in Fig. 17-8. At the left a low-level pulse commands forward, a high-level commands reverse. A narrow pulse commands stop, and widening the pulse increases the speed. At the right of the figure is the method used by both Digitrack and Gutierrez, a method using width modulation only. A pulse width which is approximately half way between minimum and maximum, commands stop. To increase speed forward, the pulse is made narrower. To increase speed in reverse, the pulse is made wider.

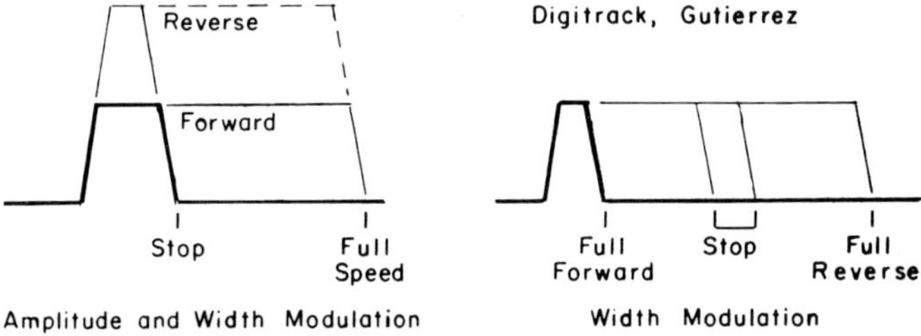

Fig. 17-8 Speed and direction from one pulse.

In a system addressing the locomotive that is to respond to the commands, see Fig. 17-7, the choice of speed and direction commands is much greater. From the standpoint of the number of pulses transmitted, an efficient method would be to send the direction command as one bit and speed commands as two bits, the latter sent only when speed is to be increased or decreased. Indeed two bits could be made to suffice for both speed and direction commands. In Fig. 17-9 the three command bits are shown as being transmitted directly after four address bits, so a bare-bones system need only receive seven bits. To extend the addresses available beyond the 16 of the bare-bones system, three additional address bits are sent following the commands.

Sending commands only to increase or decrease speed requires that the speed control be an on-board memory, probably a counter. Such a system would be well adapted to walkaround control. If the

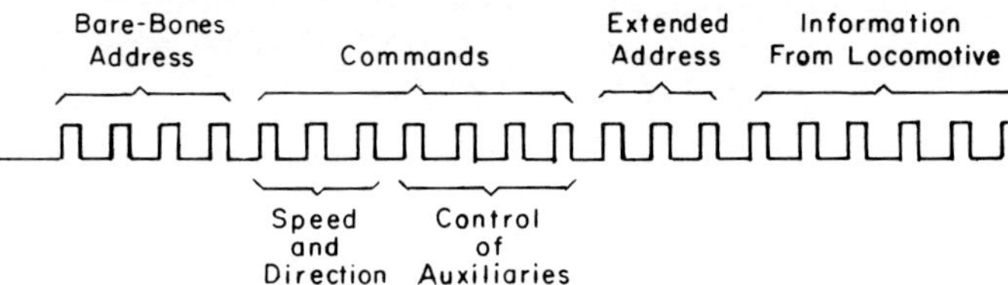

Fig. 17-9 Possible complete digital code.

direction memory in the receiver can change state only when the speed memory is at zero, there is no danger that a transmission error would suddenly reverse a running locomotive. In addition, unrealistic reversing when the locomotive is moving would be prevented. Sending commands to increase or decrease speed builds in momentum.

Auxiliary Commands and Information

In Fig. 17-9, four command pulses are shown as assigned to auxiliary devices such as an on-board sound generator, a unit to turn on, off or dim the headlight and control of uncoupling. The latter would be an enormous benefit on a switching locomotive. Also, as indicated at the right in Fig. 17-9, spaces can be reserved for pulses generated on the locomotive to send information back to the cab. Among the best uses of such information are the current being drawn, scale speed, an excessive temperature alarm, and cab signals.

Note that unused locomotive addresses can be employed to send commands to other devices, switch machines for example. It would even be possible to utilize one of the auxiliary commands to set the switch that the train is approaching to the desired position by an appropriate signal to a contact on the track.

Standardization

For reasons stated in Section 17.3, if command control is to become low in cost, specifically low enough that most if not all locomotives will be so equipped, it appears vital that the track power be standardized (AC or DC and voltage), as well as the command and information pulses (method of synchronization, order of pulses, etc.). Such standardization has two important considerations, short run and long run. For the short run, the possibility of rapid acceptance would be enhanced if the standard were compatible with available integrated circuits. For the long run, the standards should allow expansion of the number of locomotives which can be controlled, provide for control of other than the locomotive motor, and provide information to be sent from the locomotive to the cab.

For the purposes of illustration, a theoretical digital receiver is shown in Fig. 17-10. The pulsing is for clarity only; no consideration has been given to compatibility to existing ICs. The circuit diagrammed could be integrated on a single chip but it might be more economical to use a separate chip or even discrete devices for the full-wave rectifier and the full-wave switch.

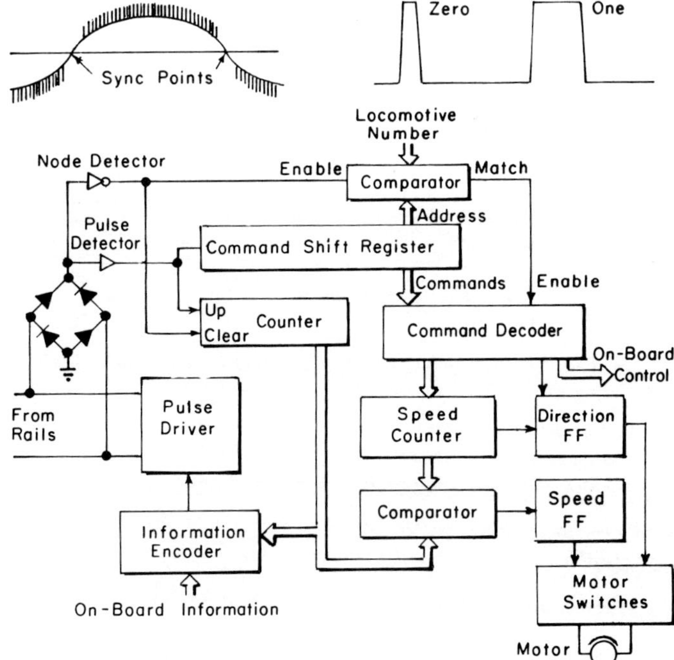

Fig. 17-10 Theoretical digital receiver.

Track power is AC to obtain synchronization. The cab always transmits 32 pulses per half wave. A narrow pulse has the binary value of "zero". To transmit a "one" the pulse is widened as indicated at the top right of Fig. 17-10. This widening is accomplished at the cab for a command to the locomotive. For information from the locomotive, the receiver widens the narrow pulse sent by the cab.

Since there is always a full complement of pulses sent by the cab, these pulses are used as the clock by the receiver, eliminating the need of an on-board clock.

The bridge rectifier delivers positive pulses and full-wave rectified AC to the receiver. The node detector clears the pulse counter and resets the speed FF at the start of each half wave. The pulse detector clocks the commands received into the command shift register and also increments the pulse counter. If the address bits correspond to the locomotive number (upper right) applied to this receiver, the match output will latch the commands received into the command register. Note that the address bits can be anywhere in the pulse train. Thus this receiver is totally compatible with a bare-bones system, yet it can utilize additional pulses to increase addressing capability.

The command bits, as registered in the command shift register, are decoded. The outputs corresponding to added features such as on-board sound are made available on terminals. Internally in the receiver the speed and direction bits, after decoding, will increment or decrement the speed counter and, if the speed counter is at zero, will allow changing of the direction FF. Niceties such as the capability of a panic stop, or clearing the speed counter when power is first turned on or when the locomotive is placed on the track, are not included in the figure.

The content of the speed counter is compared with the content of the pulse counter during each half cycle. When they match, the full-wave switch is turned on for the proper direction. This is a digital-throttle technique developed by Ken Stiefel in 1978. (See Section 16.6).

Information generated on board the locomotive, e.g., scale speed, is applied to the on-board information inputs shown at the bottom left in Fig. 17-10. This information is decoded and sent back to the cab in the assigned intervals. Here we have a fine example of the advantages of a compatible system of pulses. It would be possible to market a separate on-board speedometer unit which could be mounted in the locomotive together with a bare-bones or any other level of command receiver, and also a separate speedometer unit to be mounted at the cab. Cabs not equipped with a speedometer unit would simply ignore the information pulses sent by the locomotive. The same would be true for any other information desired from the locomotive.

For even greater flexibility and ease of operation, command control can be combined with computer cab control, see Section 18.7. Instead of transmitting commands from the cabs directly to the locomotive and receiving information in return also directly, each cab and each locomotive could be considered to be a separate I/O device for a microprocessor (uP), probably one data bus to all cabs and another to the track. Since, with an addressing scheme, there must be means for sending only one address at a time, the uP could take care of that. Any cab could be initialized to any one unit or any group of locomotives to operate multiple-unit. If it proved impossible for a standard pulsing set to be adopted, the uP could make the necessary code changes to suit the particular cab or locomotive. Furthermore, it could adjust the speed commands to permit several locomotives with distinctly-different characteristics to be lashed together as a multiple-unit engine. If more than one unit of an engine sends back signal indications to the cab, the uP could select only the signals sent by the lead unit. If more than one benchwork-mounted large speaker is installed to provide the low tones to make sound effects more realistic, the uP could generate the necessary tones for the particular case and direct them to the speaker nearest the location of the locomotive.

17.6 DC-AC SYSTEMS

Since permanent-magnet motors respond only to DC and ignore AC, as early as 1947 command-control systems of the type shown in Fig. 17-11 were proposed. The DC cab places a controlled direct voltage on the rails. The standard DC locomotive responds to that voltage and polarity in the usual manner. The AC cab superimposes an alternating voltage centered on the DC level, applied by the DC cab. This alternating voltage is ignored by the DC locomotive but the receiver in the AC locomotive, while ignoring the DC, rectifies the AC and applies the rectified voltage to the permanent-magnet motor in the locomotive. For straight command-control, this system is limited to just two independently-controlled engines (rule-book definition of engines) but has the distinct advantage that any standard DC locomotive can be operated as one of the locomotives.

Until the advent of modern electronics, a system such as that shown in Fig. 17-11 was not practical; permanent-magnet motors of the type used in model railroading do not have enough inductance to prevent overheating if 60Hz power is applied to them. Note that the

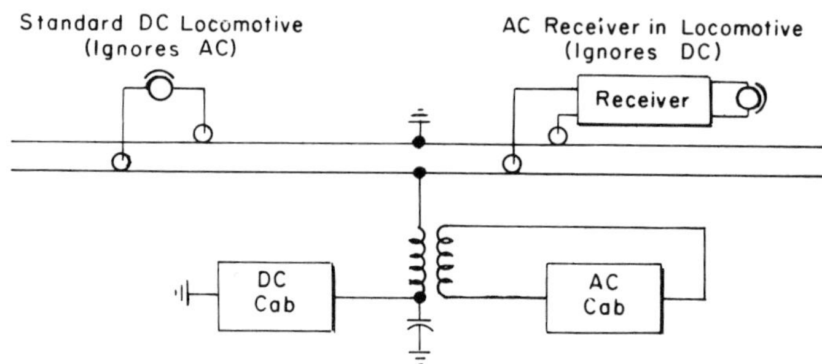

Fig. 17-11 Two-cab AC-DC system.

AC in DC-AC systems supplies the running power unlike the frequency-control systems described in Section 17.4 in which the AC was low-power signal easily generated. Only in recent years the generation of power at frequencies in excess of 60Hz has become practical from a cost point of view for model railroading. Since this is not a frequency-selective system, the exact frequency does not matter as long as it is high enough to avoid overheating the DC motor. The 1980 MRC system used 8kHz.

There is the problem of controlling direction with conventional AC motors. Toy trains typically used a sequence reverser but this never was a truly satisfactory solution. In the MRC system, control of direction has been solved by using AC consisting of assymetrical short pulses of high amplitude, and longer pulses of low amplitude of the opposite polarity. The MRC receiver is capable of distinguishing between the short and long pulses and is therefore able to control direction by the polarity of the pulses.

DC-AC systems are best suited for layouts which have only two cabs. They are also well-adapted to starting operations on large layouts to postpone the need for sectionalization for control until it is necessary to operate with three or more cabs. The Baton Rouge Model RR Club used an MRC system for just that reason. Although it is obvious that one AC locomotive could be operated in conjunction with several DC locomotives if the latter were served by some sectionalization method for independent control, the problem of superimposing the AC separately on each of several direct voltages is important.

Operating position light signals are important to successful operation on the HO Durham & Southern Railroad of Jim Paine. Signalling is overlooked by many modelers as too difficult. Many excellent commercial signals are available and the actual wiring, taken step by step, is relatively easy to plan and do.

17.7 ADVANTAGES AND DISADVANTAGES OF COMMAND CONTROL

The advantages of command control are obvious. Locomotives retain independent control at all times even if close together. There is no need to establish and release cab-section connections. Constant lighting is simple and signaling is easier. As of 1981 there were three obvious disadvantages of command control with respect to conventional DC systems: receivers must be mounted in all locomotives except for DC-AC systems, cost, incompatibility among systems. There are other subtle disadvantages which only become apparent when an attempt is made to use such a system. One very important aspect is that if an attempt is made to operate a layout without sectionalization, the power source must be capable of delivering the maximum current required by all locomotives operating at one time. This could be several to many amperes, depending upon the layout. A derailment then may cause very heavy arcing, even the destruction of wheels and trucks. Also, a derailment may stop every train. Sectionalization is therefore required for safety as well as to avoid interference among operating trains. The above reasons are exactly those which led the prototype railroads to sectionalize. The prototype has always had a form of command control.

In addition to sectionalization to limit current and to prevent interference, section breaks are needed to help find shorts. Wiring and track are exposed and subject to many problems. It is far easier to find such troubles if they can be isolated by disconnecting sections. The aforementioned Baton Rouge Club found it had to divide up its one-section layout for just this reason.

With the exception of DC-AC systems, if standard DC locomotives such as those of visitors are to be operated from time to time, it is necessary to have conventional sectionalization in addition to command control. Sections are needed in any event for reversing loops, wyes, and to turn off lights (unless light control is one of the commands).

In summary, as of 1983, command control offers many important advantages over conventional control. Whether these advantages offset the costs is a matter of personal decision. As more features become available (on-board sound, control of uncoupling and speedometer are examples), the relative position of command control versus standard DC control will improve, even if compatibility among systems is not achieved. The single most-important step in maximizing the advantages of command control and minimizing its disadvantages is the adoption of a compatible set of signals for transmitting the necessary information.

18 ADVANCED CAB CONTROL

18.1 GENERAL

The principles of cab control and its basic terms are discussed in Chapter 9. Independent control of locomotives by command control is covered in Chapter 17. This Chapter is devoted to methods of simplifying cab control operation on both small and large layouts and to cab control for multicab systems.

All methods included in this chapter are based on dividing the layout into electrically isolated sections, each such section being for the exclusive use of one locomotive at a time. For clarity, in this Handbook, such isolated pieces of track used for control are called sections, the correct prototype term for an independently powered rail or overhead wire. The word block is reserved for use only in its prototype signal sense. Some model railroaders use the word block ambiguously for either a control section or a signal block.

18.2 X-SECTION SIMPLIFICATION

On layouts with considerable track per locomotive, it is possible to simplify operation greatly by liberal use of the X section described in Section 8.7. An example is given in Fig. 18-1.

It is obvious that an engineman could run completely through both stations merely by connecting his cab to sections A2.0 and B2.0 for all other sections are X sections and receive their power through contacts on the switch machines. In contrast, the simple two-cab system described in Section 9.3 would require making connection to six sections, three times as many.

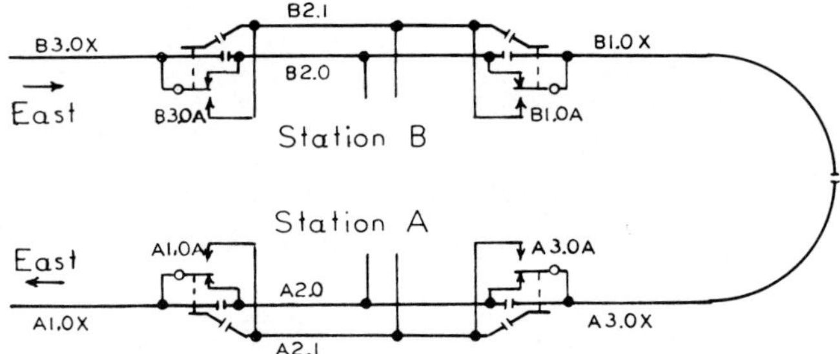

Fig. 18-1 X-section control.

The contacts on the switch machines automatically take care of power routing for most types of movements. For example two trains are to meet at station B. Track switch B3.0A is set for the siding and section B2.1 is connected to the eastward cab. The eastward train now can be run into the siding and the westward train onto the main track at station B. Then reversing the track switches at both ends of the siding not only provides the routes for the trains but also automatically connects the cabs to the proper main-line sections.

This technique can be extended to virtually any type of trackwork including reversing loops and wyes. The cabs need only be connected to those sections where parallel routes exist. But using X sections in this manner violates the normal rule that X sections should be short and so located that a locomotive would not be held on the X section. The penalty paid for this violation is lack of flexibility and a greater requirement of care in setting track switches. For example, with a conventional application of an X section, a track switch can be set for a new route nearly as soon as it is physically cleared by the preceding movement. But in Fig. 18-1 a track switch cannot be thrown until the locomotive has run the length of an X section, possibly a considerable distance. Also restrictions are placed on train movements. In Fig. 18-1 two trains following each other down the main track through both stations must never get into the same station. These restrictions may present no difficulties on a large layout with light traffic.

X sections as described in Section 8.7, that is for short sections which form part of several routes, are one of the great simplifiers of most cab-control systems. Every layout should be studied to find all possible applications of X sections.

18.3 AUTOMATIC CAB CONTROL

In 1951 the Summit-New Providence Club demonstrated a fully automatic cab control system which operated a relay with 12 make contacts to connect the cab to the next section needed just before the locomotive entered the new section. Many features were provided such as cab signals, even three lamps which told the enginemen where he was in the section. Although the system operated well, it was obvious that the complexity made an impossible maintenance problem as the layout grew in size. Therefore it was abandoned and the all-manual Delaware cab control system installed. Nevertheless automatic cab control may well be the best solution to a specific problem such as for independent control of a pusher locomotive in a helper district. See Section 18.7 for automatic control using computer techniques.

A pusher locomotive should remain under independent control of the head-end locomotive not only to permit it to couple onto the train and uncouple later but also to permit the use of a pusher not speed-matched with the road locomotive. Since a helper engine operates over a very restricted route, the locomotive itself can be used to operate its own cab control relays by a magnet or by a projection on the locomotive (or a special car) striking trackside contacts. The projection system is described.

One possible circuit is shown in Fig. 18-2. The helper grade is divided into sections shorter than the shortest train which needs a pusher. As the helper approaches the next section, its projection opens a trackside contact which does nothing at this time. Then it closes a contact to operate the relay of the next section transferring control from the road cab to the helper cab. The relay locks operated. As the helper advances into the next section it first closes a contact which does nothing at this time then opens a contact to release the relay of the section behind. In this manner the helper can run up and down its route automatically connecting itself to its own cab and restoring unneeded sections to the normal cab control system.

Since helper sections must be shorter than the trains, there probably will be too many sections for practical use by the normal cab-control system. The helper sections, however, can easily be made into sub-sections of the normal sections. In Fig. 18-2 helper sections A7.0-1 to A7.0-3 are combined into A7.0 for the normal cab control when all three relays are released (relay A7.0-3 not shown).

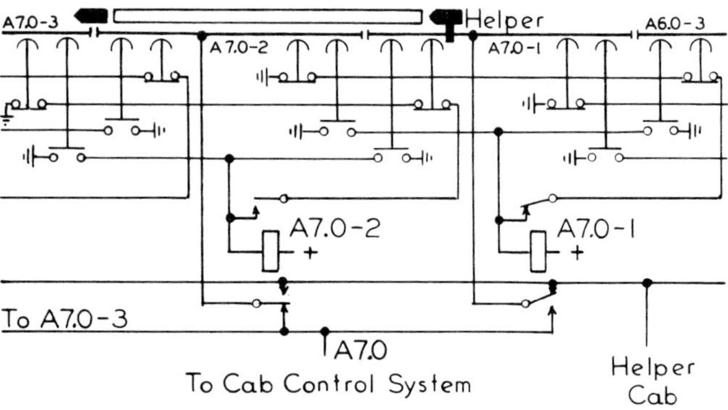

Fig. 18-2 Automatic cab control for helper.

18.4 ROUTE CAB CONTROL

Route cab control, introduced by Linn Westcott in 1949, takes advantage of the fact that a locomotive can move only into an adjacent section as explained in Section 9.4. The connection to the next section must be made before the locomotive enters the new section to assure continuity of power. Normally the new connection is made by advancing a rotary switch.

When alternate routes are available, say a main track and a siding, means must be provided so that the selector switch connects to the proper alternate route. One method is to provide a route switch per cab at points where alternate routes exist as shown in Fig. 18-3. There will be as many route switches connected to a given section as there are cabs. These route switches do not interfere with each other as they connect nothing unless their sequence switches are advanced to that position. Therefore the route switches can be set at any convenient time, even before the train leaves its terminal.

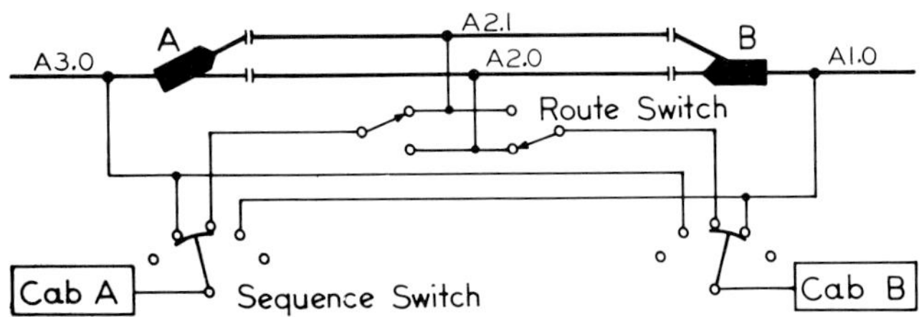

Fig. 18-3 Route switches.

Note the designation system used for sections. The main track is always designated .0, parallel sections to the north by odd decimals, .1, .3, etc. and parallel sections to the south by even decimals, .2, .4, etc. This permits the base number of all parallel sections, e.g. A2, to be the same for the same terminal on the rotary switch.

A simple system with a rotary switch which can connect to either one or two terminals as indicated in Fig. 18-3 can operate with equal ease in either direction merely by reversing the direction of rotation of the sequence switch. More often, however, commercial rotary switches are used so staggered connections are made to individual contacts on multiple decks. Fig. 18-4 shows one method for wiring a two-direction system. The east-west switch connects the cab to the proper decks of the switch.

Also included in Fig. 18-4 is a "One Section Only" switch which permits an engineer to disconnect from the rear section. This allows him to take a siding and disconnect from all but the siding or, when he is waiting for a track to clear, to disconnect from the section behind so that another train can use it.

Route Cab Control establishes connection from the cab only to that part of the layout in which its locomotive is operating thus it can carry the information to operate cab signals as described in Section 15.56. For example it is simple to add an indicator that the locomotive is in the advanced section and it is necessary to advance the selector switch if operation is to continue. A lamp indicating that the

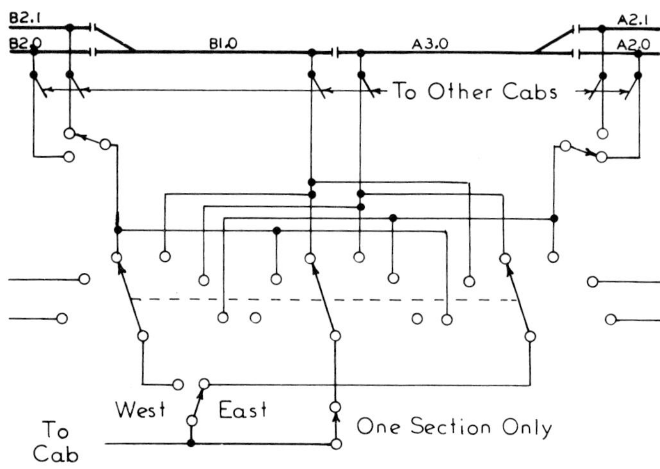

Fig. 18-4 Multi-deck sequence stitches.

next section is connected to another cab is a helpful operational aid.

If the above cab signals are provided, they can be used to advance a stepper-type selector switch automatically. Such systems are called Progressive Cab Control and are covered in Section 18.6.

Route cab control is well suited to layouts featuring train running. If the emphasis is on switching, Delaware Cab control (Fig. 9, Chapter 9), in the opinion of the author, is the best all-manual cab-control systems.

18.5 WALKAROUND CAB CONTROL

Some modelers prefer to follow their train as it moves around the layout. This permits precise control by the engineman, for example at uncoupling ramps, and also allows him to operate groundthrows for track switches or to uncouple manually. Even if the main-line cabs are operated from a fixed position, walkaround cabs could be useful for switchers.

For main-line use, the layout must be designed so that an engineer can physically follow his train. In addition the constant walking alongside a train is tiring and, if there are several enginemen, there is a lot of traffic in the aisles.

Walkaround cab control has been implemented in many forms. One is similar to the old divisional or pass-the-buck system (see Section 9.1) in that separate speed and directional controls are supplied for all sections. The engineer then merely walks ahead of his train to the next controls and sets them to agree in speed and direction with the controls he has just left. Ed Ravenscroft, in 1952, developed a system he called Autostat in which the rheostats were mounted at the sectionalization points and lock-out relays were provided to prevent a control from being seized from both directions. At sidings the track to be controlled was determined by the setting of the track switch.

Another variation of pass-the-buck control is to equip each station for cab control within the limits of that station only. A train is run from one station to a transfer section. The engineer then walks to the next station panel and brings his train in from the transfer section.

The above methods involve transferring control from cab to cab although the engineer moves with the train. If control is passed between cabs while the train is in motion, the problem of setting both controls for the same speed exists. To solve this problem some of the walkaround cab control systems in service use cabs located at a fixed point which can be remotely controlled by the engineer as he follows his train.

Fig. 18-5 shows some remote control methods. At A the speed control and reversing switch are in a small, handheld control unit connected to the cab by a flexible cable. With a transistor throttle it is unnecessary to have heavy wires in this cable.

At B a motor-driven speed control is at the cab and push buttons located at strategic points along the tracks are used by the engineer to increase or decrease speed, also to reverse. At C the inertia capacitor sets the speed and the push buttons charge or discharge the capacitor. Fig. 16-13 shows a throttle designed for this purpose. If the capacitor is large, speed will remain essentially constant over long periods of time between pressings of the push buttons. Instead of a capacitor, an IC counter can be installed to serve as the speed memory. A counter will not suffer changes of speed with time.

At D a portable radio transmitter, citizen's band, is used to control a motor-driven speed control and reversing relay at the cab. The

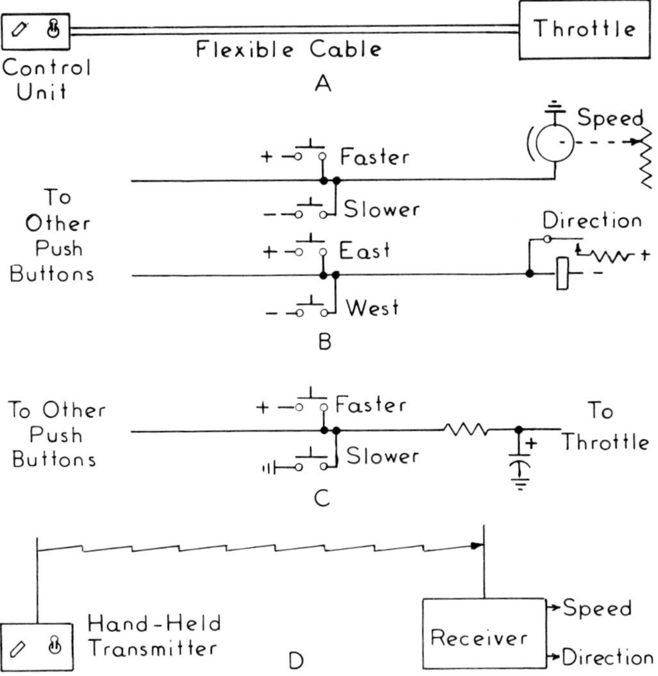

Fig. 18-5 Remote control of cabs.

commercial equipment available for radio-controlled model airplanes and boats is directly applicable.

With the throttles in a fixed location, the same cab-section connections must be made for walkaround control as for the conventional type of cab control. Any cab control system may be used, for example the rotary switches of the elementary tower-type cab-control system shown in Fig. 6, Chapter 9 can be mounted near the sections they control. The engineer sets these switches as he walks ahead of this train. Bruce Robinson, 1969, substitutes two relays for each rotary switch as shown in Fig. 18-6. By pressing the 0 button first as he approaches, the engineer releases both relays thereby connecting cab 0 to that section. If he is operating on another cab, he then presses the 1 or 2 button for cab 1 or 2, or both 1 and 2 for cab 3. The advantage of this system is that push buttons can be located at both ends of each section which could be important if the sections are long. This system substitutes two relays and four push buttons for one rotary switch of the basic tower-type cab control.

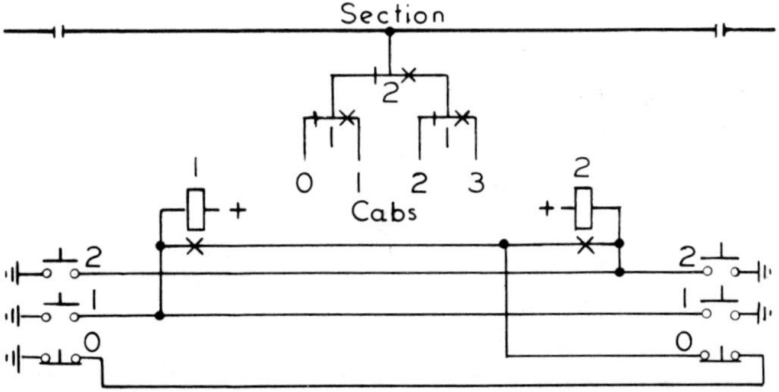

Fig. 18-6 Push-button control of cab connection.

Computer techniques such as those described in Section 18.7 can be used to keep the engineman in control of his locomotive without human attention to changing the cab-section connection as the locomotive moves. The central processor of such a computer can readily supply the speed memory required for walkaround control. Command control systems with memory (see Chapter 17) are ideally suited to walkaround control as they eliminate completely the need for changing the cab-section connection.

18.6 PROGRESSIVE CAB CONTROL

When route cab control is installed, it is possible to include lamps showing when the selector switch can be advanced and when it must not be (see Fig. 15-70). Instead of informing the engineer to move the selector switch, these signals could advance a power-operated switch automatically. About 1950 Linn Westcott coined the name progressive cab control for such automatic route cab systems. Although well adapted for continuous running of trains on a large layout, only a few such systems have been installed; a good example is at the Columbus (Ohio) Model RR Club.

The heart of a progressive cab control system is its automatic switch. Since virtually all commercial multipoint stepper switches (see Section 2.12) step only in one direction, for two-direction traffic special provisions must be made. The following three methods have been used: 1. Separate stepper switches for each direction. 2. Multiple banks on a single switch, one bank wired for each direction. 3. Transfer the contacts of a single bank from one sequence to the other by a relay. The most common solution, however, has been to avoid commercial stepper switches and build bi-directional switches. Although it would be possible to construct an electronic progressive cab control system using ICs, computer cab control is far more powerful, and would seem a better choice.

18.7 COMPUTER CAB CONTROL

As the term is used in this handbook, "computer cab control" (CCC), means a cab control system in which an electronic central processing unit (CPU) maintains the control of each engine by its assigned cab without manual attention. By 1981 several systems based on using a general-purpose minicomputer or microcomputer had been demonstrated. Most of the early versions used CPUs for setting up some sort of metallic connection (relays or electromechanical switches) between the section in which the engine was located, and the cab in control of that engine. Control of the engine and information from the engine, current drawn for example, were exchanged between cab and section over this metallic connection, just as in all-manual cab control system. In contrast, systems based on modern computer practices process all commands to the engines and all information from the section in the CPU. In short, the engineman tells the CPU what the engine should do (speed, direction, whistle, etc.). Note, execution can be via command control or by connection to the proper section. Also, information generated either at the section in terms of binary bits or returned as information in a command-control system is processed by the CPU for display at the cab in human-readable form. Although the automatic cab control system of 1951 mentioned in Section 18.3 essentially performed the same functions, there was no CPU; every cab and every section added greatly increased the number of relays. A CPU, in contrast, handles one cab at a time, regardless of the number of cabs or sections being served. As of 1981 the documentation of only one CCC system had been made public, the exploratory system developed by The Model RR Club during the period 1972-1979. That sytem, therefore, is used to illustrate the essentials of CCC.

Although one of the driving forces toward the development of CCC was the elimination of any requirements of manual attention to maintaining the control of the engine by its engineman, the great power of computer technology makes possible many other desirable features, most of which are equally applicable to command control. Therefore, even if standardization of the command and other information signals for command control mentioned in Section 17.3 takes place and is successful to the point of replacing control of DC locomotives by sectionalization, the other features of CCC such as cab signals and position-on-layout indicators would still retain significant advantages. In addition, CCC would solve some of the problems inherent in a straight command control system. Specifically CCC combined with command control could simplify the cab circuits, particularly those for walkaround control. This combination could assign the addressing of the units controlled so any cab could control any locomotive or combination of units to be operated MU. By processing the commands of the cabs this combination could economically provide sophisticated momentum and braking effects, as well as synchronizing locomotives operating multiple units. The descriptions which follow, however, are based on DC control by sectionalization.

The need which caused The Model RR Club to start its exploratory work with CCC in 1972 was not the elimination of manual attention to the cab-section connection, desirable as that may be. A combination route Delaware cab control system was judged to be adequate from that standpoint. The need was to eliminate the cost and the maintenance associated with the amount of under-benchwork wiring required by any then-known system for their proposed extremely large HO layout. As described in Section 24.84, time-division multiplexing is a well-established way of substituting intervals called time slots for wires. Since computers are essentially time-division machines, computer technology offered the savings required.

The exploratory system built and tested had the capability of addressing 1024 sections, section 0000 being unusable as it was the section addressed by all cabs not controlling a locomotive; sections 0001, 0002, and 0003 were test sections. This system could serve 128 cabs of which one was the housekeeping cab for use by the CPU, one a test cab, and one a cab position used for system synchronization. The block diagram of this sytem is given in Fig. 18-7.

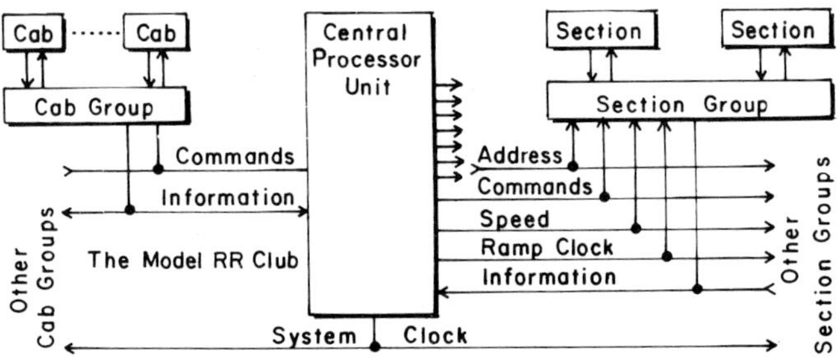

Fig. 18-7 Block diagram fo a computer cab control system.

Although it might be possible to transmit all information over one transmission line, it was judged easier to design and to maintain if only one-way lines were used and the information was kept separate. The most-significant three bits of the 10-bit section address were decoded and 1-out-of-8 section addressing lines were used to confine section addresses to 8 time slots. Initially multiplexing was contemplated only between the CPU and the section group and cab group circuits located at strategic points under the layout; the wiring from those circuits to the cabs, rails, etc. was to be conventional DC. As the system was built it was found possible to reduce underbenchwork wiring even more by multiplexing those leads, see Fig. 12-3. For this it was found necessary to include a memory package in all group circuits so information could be exchanged with the CPU at a high rate, but used locally at a much lower rate. The transmission lines between the CPU and the group circuits were quality twisted-pair lines (Fig. 24-50) to permit high-speed pulsing (16us Time Slots). The lower speed mutiplexing was over conventional wiring.

The memory on which operation was based was concentrated in the CPU. The cab RAM, Fig. 24-38, contained the 48 bits of information necessary for each cab, and the section RAM, of 1024 words of 6 bits each, contained the status information of each section,

The address of the next section required by the cab was determined by adding the route code received from the section group circuit to the lowest-numbered of the possible next sections as stored in the next section ROM, see Fig. 24-40.

When a cab was to be connected to a locomotive, it was turned on and a 4-digit octal code representing the section number in which the locomotive was located was dialed from the cab using a thumbwheel switch. This switch then was used to identify the type of locomotive for purposes such as sound effects. Once a cab was initialized to a locomotive the seizure and release of sections was automatic until the cab was again turned off. The cab would not release from the section under the leading end of the train, even if the locomotive was lifted from the rails. Further, it would not release a section until seven successive attempts to find the locomotive still in that section had failed.

In addition to the strictly cab-control functions, this system displayed a very complete set of cab signals providing information such as whether a stop signal was displayed because no route was available through switches, the next section was occupied by another cab, by a locomotive not under control of another cab, by cars only, or by an approach to a bumping post. There was even a warning if the cab was approaching a section which an opposing train was about to enter from the opposite end. Originally both block and interlocking signals were to be displayed together with a simple section signal but, as sections and blocks do not coincide, providing signals based on blocks proved to be difficult. Also the section signals grew to include so much information (27 aspects) that the block signals, if provided, would have added little. Other information provided at the cab was a 4-character digital readout giving the station and the section in the station occupied by the leading end of the train, a digital scale speed readout, a digital current drawn readout, and two LED indicators. One indicator giving the number of sections under control of the cab, the other whether an open or short circuit had been detected.

Included in the design, but not implemented for the tests, were automatic connection of the engineman's telephone to the tower of concern, and sound effects directed to the fixed speaker nearest to the locomotive.

A test panel was included which provided all the critical information of circuit operation for any selected cab. This panel was also equipped with a test cab and three test sections. A working cab could be exercised on the test sections, but the test cab did not have speed control facilities.

19 LIGHTING AND SOUND EFFECTS

19.1 LIGHTING

19.11 General

The primary requirements for lighting on model railroads are for work on the railroad, viewing the railroad in operation, scenery lighting, train lighting, and for indicators on control panels.

19.12 Room Illumination

Room lights provide the illumination for work and also for display of the railroad. It does not necessarily follow that both of these objectives can be satisfactorily met by the same lamps, particularly if the lighting is to simulate day and night operation.

Normally work lighting is supplied by conventional fixtures, fluorescent are best, and portable lights commonly called trouble lights. Convenience outlets for the use of such lamps and powered tools should be installed at intervals of not more than 3m (9′) under the benchwork. All wiring of this type should be in accordance with the National Electrical Code, copies of which can be obtained at a fee from the National Board of Fire Underwriters. Better, the code with explanations is given in the National Electrical Code Handbook, by Arthur L. Abbot and published by McGraw-Hill.

Lighting for display can be compared to stage lighting. Fig. 19-1 shows a method practiced by the Bayridge Society of Model Engineers. The curtain prevents the lights from direct view by the spectators, particularly important if some are of the ultraviolet type for use with fluorescent paint on the scenery. If the lamps are to be dimmed to simulate the change from day to night, commercial lamp dimmers of the variable-voltage transformer or electronic-switch type are recommended rather than building a dimmer, thus all 110V wiring will be accomplished with Underwriter Laboratories inspected equipment. If fluorescent lamps are to be controlled in brightness, make sure that the type selected is suitable for such service.

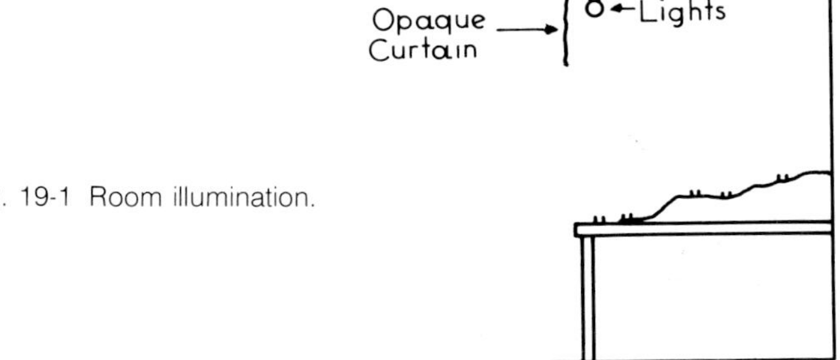

Fig. 19-1 Room illumination.

19.13 Control Panel Indicators

Lights on the control panel are one of the most effective ways of showing occupancy of track, positions of switches, and almost anything which needs an indicator. The operation of such lamps are described in other chapters, here the lamps and their mountings are covered.

Traditionally panel lights used incandescent lamps mounted in special panel sockets, see Fig. 20, Chapt. 2. Front-changeable mountings are preferable, particularly if there are many lamps, to facilitate replacement of the lamps and also to permit close spacing of the mountings.

LED panel indicators are now available at reasonable prices. Their advantages are extremely long life (virtually infinite in model railroad service), small size, and compatibility with transistor and integrated circuits. Remember that an LED is a diode, not a lamp. Its current must be limited by external means, such as a series resistor.

If lamps operated by contacts are used exclusively, they can be operated on AC to avoid loading the DC rectifiers. So that smaller wire can be used, it is best to choose lamps which operate on 24V rather than 6 or 12. However lamps operated by transistors or integrated circuits must be powered by DC. LEDs are operated best by DC.

19.14 Scenery Lamps

Perhaps the greatest single error made in scenery lighting is overbright lamps. Prototype signals are not normally visible unless the observer is reasonably close to viewing them head on. The light from house windows is a soft-glow at night yet on the model signals often can be seen from almost any angle and house lights illuminate the landscape. One answer is to run the lamps at less than rated voltage, about one-half is usually satisfactory. In addition to making appearance more realistic (not only in brightness but in color, as real lights viewed from a distance are not white), reduced voltage increases the life of lamps to where, in model railroad service, they should never burn out as explained in Section 2.42. This is particularly important for the small lamps mounted in difficult locations such as in signals.

Lamps may be run on reduced voltage by any of the three methods shown in Fig. 19-2. The easiest way is to use a lamp rated at a higher voltage than the supply as on the left. At the center two lamps are run in series. To divide the voltage equally, they must both be of the same type. On the right a series resistor has been used to drop part of the voltage.

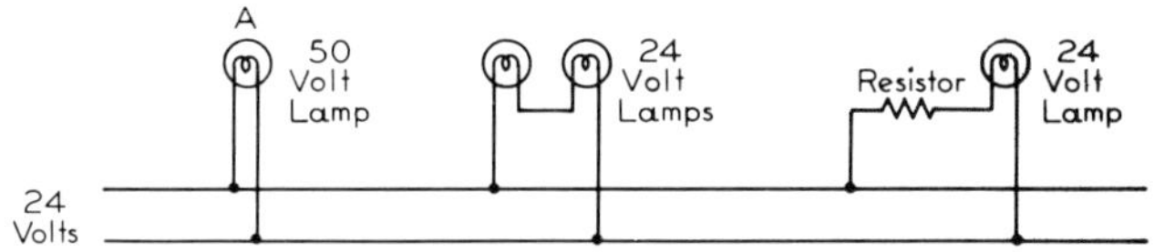

Fig. 19-2 Methods of increasing life of lamps.

For scenery items such as traffic lights and any other places where red, yellow, or green lights are required, consideration should be given to LEDs instead of lamps due to their long (infinite in model railroading) life and their small size. For white light, lamps will have to be used but the light itself can be conducted to the proper location by fiber optics which are flexible light guides. It is also possible to use plastic rods to make street lights and similar items with the light being conducted by the lamp pole. (Fig. 15-38).

The location and number of scenery lamps is not an electrical problem, but their control is. Do not operate a number of lamps in the same area from one switch. Arrange it so that when a switch is turned off, a lamp goes off here and there rather than plunging an entire section into darkness. This makes for greater realism when changing from a day scene to night and back again. Note that most real buildings do not have every window blazing with light. Compartment your structures to confine the light to a reasonable number of rooms, maybe even just the kitchen of a home.

19.15 Train Lighting

The most common way of lighting cars and locomotives is to connect the lamp across the rails as shown in Fig. 19-3. If command control (Chapter 17) is in use, a constant voltage is maintained on the rails so the lamps will maintain an even level of brightness. The problem then reduces itself to one of turning the lamps off when they should be off; this includes times when passenger cars and cabooses are standing in the yard, or locomotive headlights when a train is standing in the clear on a siding. An answer is to sectionalize so power can be turned on and off on a given track. More convenient would be to provide additional command capabilities in the system to control the lights from the cab (Fig. 17-9).

Fig. 19-3 Lamp operated by track power.

When conventional DC locomotives are controlled by varying the voltage applied to the rails, and the car and locomotive lights are operated directly from track power, the lamps change their intensity when speed is changed; often these lamps go out completely if the locomotive is stopped. To provide constant illumination under these conditions, some model railroaders have mounted batteries in the cars although this is normally done only on special cars. A concealed switch then is necessary to turn the lights on and off. Probably the easiest solution is a miniature toggle switch. Another possibility is a switch operable by a magnet held outside of the car as this avoids a mechanical projection to operate the switch. Linn Westcott described a magnetically-biased dry-reed contact for this purpose in 1963. His method is shown in Fig. 19-4. A commercial dry-reed switch is mounted in the car and a small magnet placed near it, the exact position of the magnet depends on its strength as it must be capable of holding the contacts closed after they have been operated by an external magnet but not strong enough to close the contacts after the external magnet has been used to release the contacts.

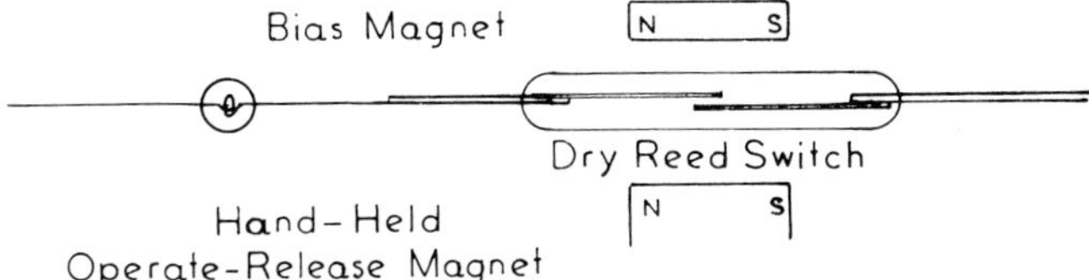

Fig. 19-4 Magnetically operated switch.

Switches such as that of Fig. 19-4 can be installed to turn lights on and off even when they are operated by track power. Selective lighting of lamps based on direction is possible by connecting diodes in series with the lamps as indicated in Fig. 19-5 for headlights of a switcher.

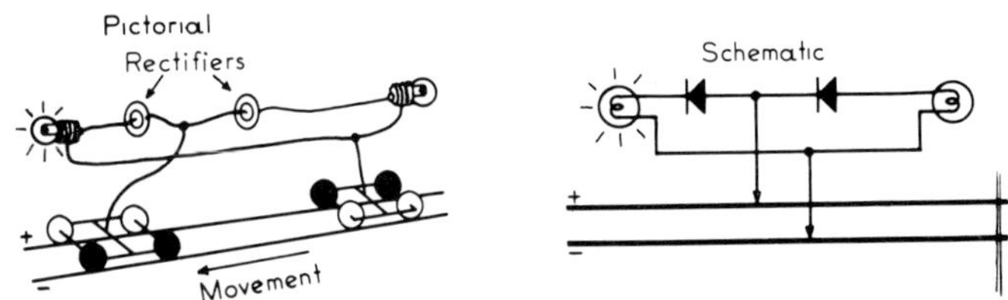

Fig. 19-5 Selective lighting of lamps.

The variation of lamp brightness due to changes of voltage on the track can be reduced by operating them from the voltage drop of diodes in series with the motor as indicated in Fig. 19-6. Silicon diodes have a voltage drop of about 0.8 V, (Section 2.57) so two in series as shown will operate a 2 to 3 V lamp.

Fig. 19-6 Brightness stabilization.

It is possible to reduce light variations even more by using a transistor voltage regulator. If pulse power is used at low speeds, simple voltage regulation on the lamps will not produce uniform brightness as the average power from the pulses is reduced as shown in Fig. 19-7 even though the peak voltage of the pulses is held precisely. It is necessary to provide energy storage in the form of a capacitor or even a nicad battery to provide uniform DC to the lamps. These methods are applicable to cars as well as locomotives but in cars a dissipative element such as a resistor or transistor must be used to drop the voltage difference between that of the lamp and that on the rails, a function performed by the motor in a locomotive. Thus such stabilization of lamps in cars requires a considerable increase of the power supplied to the track.

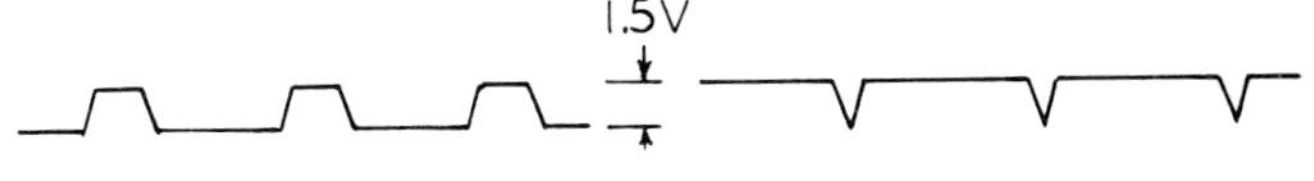

Fig. 19-7 Pulse power changes average voltage.

19.6 ULTRASONIC LIGHTING

For constant lighting on layouts operating conventional DC locomotives, perhaps the best solution is to operate the lamps on AC of a constant voltage. As shown at the center of Fig. 19-8, a capacitor in series with the lamp blocks the DC running power to the motor from the lamp. Only when AC is applied, as on the right and left in the figure, will the lamp light. To prevent heating of the motor by the

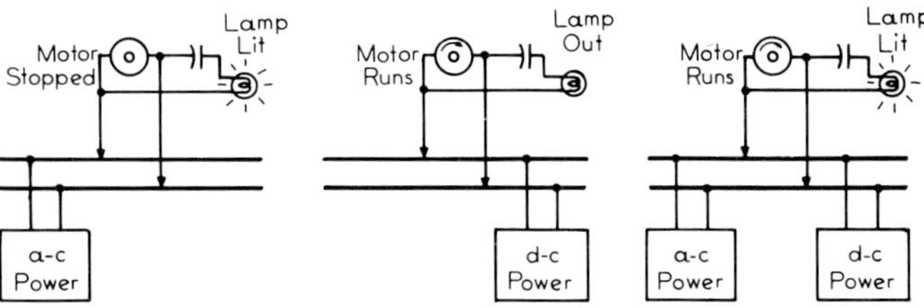

Fig. 19-8 Ultrasonic lighting.

AC, the lighting frequency must be high enough that the inductance of the motor effectively blocks the AC from flowing through the armature, 8kHz is high enough. Even higher frequencies are desirable to reduce the physical size of the capacitors. A commonly-used frequency for lighting has been 25kHz. This frequency is just above the audible range, and is usually termed ultrasonic. If it is a reasonable sine wave, there is no possibility that such a frequency will cause radio or TV interference. A problem has been the lack of published circuits to generate frequencies and powers suitable for ultrasonic lighting. When first introduced in 1950 by Mel English and Bob Gilliand, Pacific Seaboard Club, electron-tube oscillators were used leading to a high-impedance source. With such a source, adding more lamps changed the intensity of all lamps. The source of AC should have a low impedance to give a reasonably-constant output voltage of about 24V over a wide range of currents. One possibility is a sine-wave oscillator driving a power amplifier, as shown in Fig. 19-9. The circuits published for high-fidelity amplifiers are probably satisfactory. These circuits can be simplified by eliminating the components which were included to provide a flat response at lower frequencies.

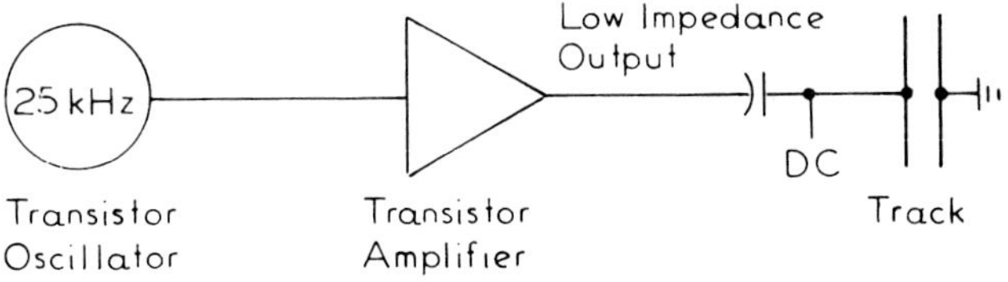

Fig. 19-9 Ultrasonic power source.

Much simpler, less costly, and without the heating problems of sine-wave amplifiers are square-wave generators such as the one shown in Fig. 19-10. Provided the output transistors are driven hard enough to stay turned on at the maximum currents required by the lamps, the output voltage will be approximately as stable as the DC supply voltage. The steeply rising and falling wave will, unlike a sine wave, have high-frequency components but experience with the switching-type throttles would indicate that trouble in terms of radio and TV interference is unlikely. The methods described in Chapter 16 to make throttles self-protecting against external short circuits or overloads can be applied to AC generators of this type.

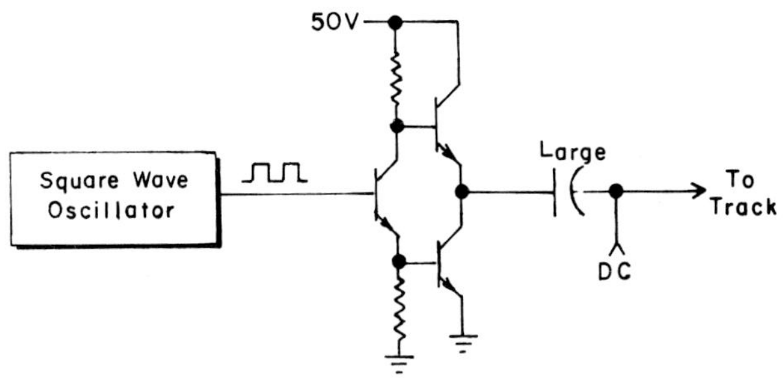

Fig. 19-10 Switching transistor driving stage.

The ultrasonic power must be distributed to all track sections. This can be done using the same leads which supply track power but more often it is distributed over a separate bus and connected to each section by capacitors as shown in Fig. 19-11. The parallel capacitors and coils are tuned blocking filters to prevent the flow of ultrasonic current in those paths. They are one reason frequency should remain constant.

It is has been reported that if the ultrasonic frequency power is of sufficient voltage amplitude, it serves to reduce the dirty-track problem for the motors.

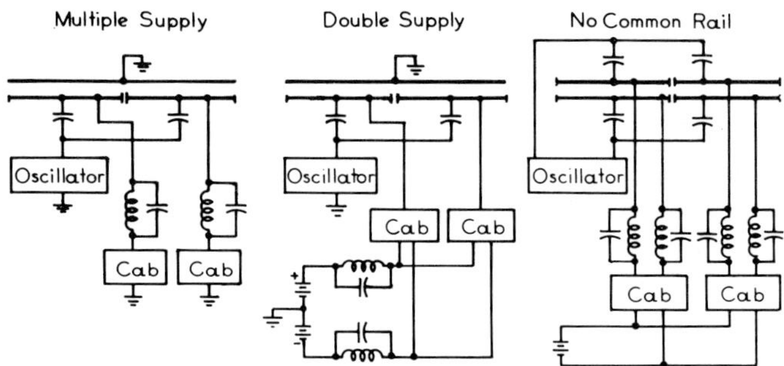

Fig. 19-11 Ultrasonic power distribution.

19.2 SOUND EFFECTS

19.21 General

Three approaches have been used to provide sound effects for model railroads. One is to generate the appropriate sounds at fixed locations on the layout. This is the obvious solution for sounds such as crossing bells. As the ear is not sensitive to exact direction of sounds, fixed sound generators can also be used effectively for locomotive sound effects. For moving locomotive sounds, the second approach is to mount remotely-controlled sound generators on the locomotive. At one time such on-board sound generators were motor driven and commercially available for toy trains. Modern IC sound generators and command control make this a viable method today even for scales which are too small for motor-driven whistles and other mechanical sound generators. The third approach is to generate the sounds at the cab and transmit them over the rails to a speaker in the locomotive. Commercial systems for this type of sound were readily available in 1981.

19.22 Speakers in Locomotives

Minature speakers were mounted in O scale locomotives as early as 1936 and more recently have been mounted in the smaller scales. The chief problem is the small size of the speakers. Small speakers cannot faithfully reproduce any sound with low tones. Fortunately the sense of direction of the human ear depends primarily on the high tones. Therefore it is possible to install a centrally-located speaker which reproduces the low tones of any sound generated for any locomotive, while the speakers in the locomotives provide the high tones and the sense of location of the source of the sounds.

The speaker in the locomotive should be as large as possible with as large a sound chamber as is possible. Although its use had not been reported by 1981, a logrithmic horn with a mouth of the maximum dimensions permitted by the tender or locomotive body, and driven by a crystal ear piece, appears to offer the maximum fidelity possible in the limited dimensions available.

The usual system of driving a speaker in a locomotive is shown in Fig. 19-12. A fixed sound generator is arranged to transmit its output over the rails to drive the speaker. Capacitors are used to block DC from the audio-frequency circuits. If a fixed speaker were also installed to reproduce the low-frequency tones, the speaker would be driven through a low-pass filter from the same sound generator.

Smooth DC must be used with this sytem because pulse power or full-wave rectified AC will cause the speaker to hum. The small solid-state radios which are available raise the possibility of using them to receive an audio signal on some low-frequency carrier. They

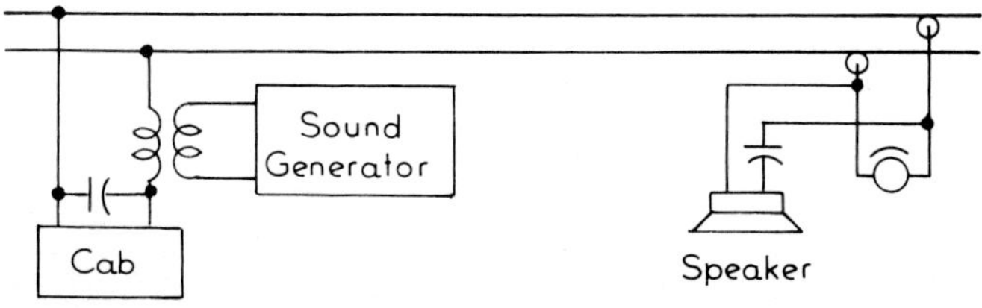

Fig. 19-12 Locomotive-mounted speaker.

would eliminate the need for smooth DC for locomotive power while improving speed control.

Modern IC sound generators and command control make possible the installment of sound generators on the locomotives, also eliminating the requirement of smooth DC for locomotive power. If a fixed speaker were used to add the low tones, it would have to be driven by a separate sound generator under the same command as the one sent to the sound generator in the locomotive.

19.23 Speakers on Layout

Although there is a problem of concealment, speakers on the layout can be made large enough for effective reproduction of all sounds. For a small layout, a single, centrally-located speaker can give excellent effects for sounds presumably coming from a moving locomotive. For larger layout two or more speakers may be required. The speaker nearest the locomotive can be selected either by the cab-control system or by a rotary switch operated by the engineman. Computer cab control is particularly well adapted to handling sound effects by fixed speakers. As mentioned earlier, a fixed speaker can be used in conjunction with speakers mounted on the locomotives, the fixed speaker reproducing only the direction-insensitive low tones. For steam-locomotive exhaust sounds the major problem which occurs when fixed speakers are used exclusively is synchronization of the sound with the rotation of the wheels. If a speedometer is provided at the cab (Section 16.8), its output could generate the necessary synchronization if combined with a manual switch providing information of the size of the driving wheels. Fortunately the exhaust sounds are essentially high frequency. If a central speaker is installed for the low frequencies, it need not be used for exhaust sounds; the small locomotive mounted speakers are adequate for realistic reproduction of these sounds.

19.24 Sound Generators

Because of the modern IC sound generators and the sound generating capabilities of microprocessors, by 1981 electronic generators appeared to be a most satisfactory idea. Much work remained to be done in this area, particularly publishing appropriate circuit information. The available IC sound generators required external capacitators and resistors to generate the desired sound. Earlier work in this area depended upon descrete transistors or IC operational amplifiers, but both of these required complex selection of connecting devices.

19.25 Amplifiers and Mixing

Amplifiers are generally required to drive the speakers. These do not need to be of greater fidelity than the speakers will reproduce. A 741 OpAmp with an amplifier connection may be quite sufficient. When fixed speakers are installed, supplying an amplifier per speaker permits signals from the various cabs to be sent to the speakers and mixed with each other at low levels. Only low power is required for realistic sound levels; operating sound effects at too high a volume destroy realism. Placing filters to kill the sound when a locomotive is in a tunnel, reducing the volume when passing under bridges, behind large structures, or in a cut enhances sound effects.

20 ELECTRIFIED RAILROADS

HO passenger motor E-10 sits under the high wire on the layout of Noel Holley. Overhead catenary and trolley wire systems are practicable for HO, TT, and larger scales. Outside third rail is also popular in O scale.

In the early days of model railroading it was not uncommon to see models of electrified railroads. This may have been due to the feeling that electric locomotives were more in keeping with the motors used in models or that the third rail or overhead wire had to be provided in any case. Whatever the reason, the advent of two-rail seemed to have all but eliminated catenary and third rail from the model scene except for traction and other specialized layouts. Nevertheless, there still remained interesting scenic items and the electrification of part of a layout offers operating possibilities.

Prototypes can be found for single overhead wire, catenary, or third rail but the figures show only catenary. It should be understood that the methods described apply equally well to wire or third rail.

There are three general approaches to model electrification. First is when the wire or third rail is only scenic and has no electrical function, the cars or locomotives running in normal two-rail fashion. The second method supplies power in the prototype manner with the rails serving as the ground return. The rails may be insulated from each other and be used for signaling. As it is easier to sectionalize rails than overheads, consideration should be given to making the wire common and sectionalizing the track. The third method takes advantage of the overhead to provide independent control for the electric locomotives with the others running standard two-rail.

The simplest case is where the same controls are used for both two-rail and overhead-powered locomotives. To prevent electric locomotives from operating off of the overhead or with their pantographs down, the wire can be grounded to serve as the common for electric locomotives as shown in Fig. 20-1. The electrics cannot be turned end for end as this would connect them to the common rail instead of the control rail. Virtually all electric locomotives are double ended so there is no need to turn them.

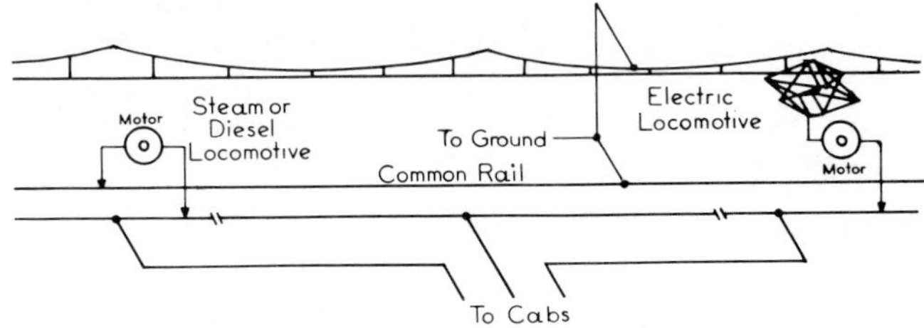

Fig. 20-1 Common control for wire and rail.

Catenary may be used to establish independent control over electric locomotives. Such control is particularly valuable when electrics are operated as helpers to steam or diesels. Under independent control an electric can move right up and couple to a steam locomotive with no problems. As shown in Fig. 20-2 the electrics operate

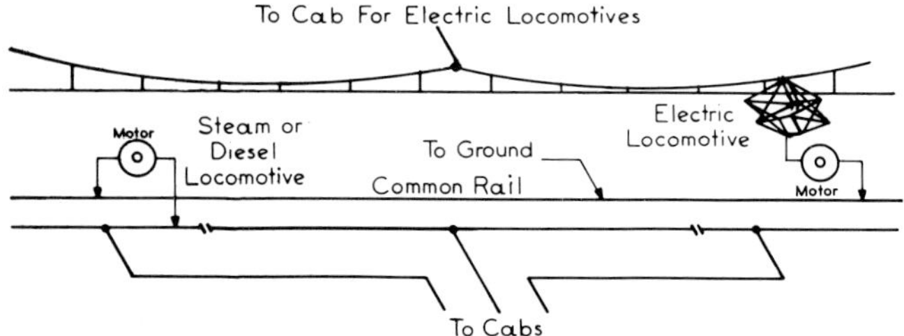

Fig. 20-2 Independent control of electronics.

between the common rail and the overhead, the steam or diesel between the common rail and the control rail. If only one electric locomotive is to be operated, the catenary can be all one section. Should more than one electric be required, the catenary can be sectionalized for any type of cab control system desired. Catenary sections need not conform to the track sections.

A variation on the idea of independent control was developed by the old Chatham, N.J., HO club as shown in Fig. 20-3. They had a long tunnel and it was desired to pull steam-powered trains through it with an electric locomotive. This could be done with the circuit of Fig. 20-2 but they did not want to string wire through the tunnel. Instead the electric locomotive was equipped with a relay which operated when the pantograph was in contact with the wire. This relay transferred the connection from the motor from the rail to the overhead. Thus when the locomotive was outside the tunnel, the relay was operated and the electric was controlled by its own special cab. Once the train entered the tunnel, the relay released and the electric operated from the rails as a simple double header.

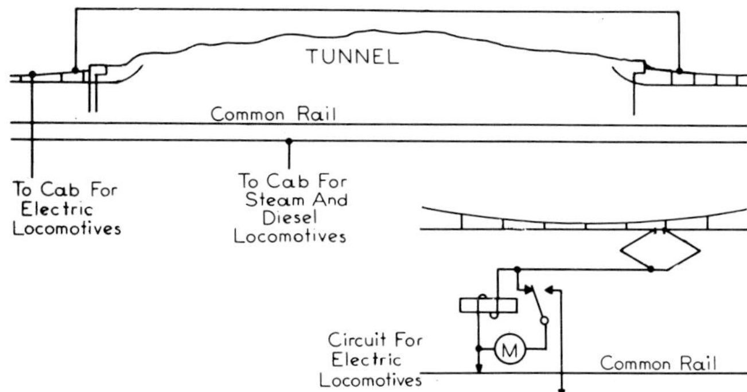

Fig. 20-3 Method of eliminating wire in a long tunnel.

21 TELEPHONES

21.1 GENERAL

Telephones serve three purposes on model railroads: to communicate between distant points, to reduce noise, and to avoid excessive calling for attention. The first applies only to large layouts or layouts which have some physical barrier between parts. But even on small layouts, if there are three or more operators, the noise due to conversations can be drastically reduced by the use of telephones. Probably the most important contribution the telephone can make is to enable one operator to gain the attention of another without calling. When an operator is concentrating on some activity, it often is difficult to get his attention without some aid. If the telephone system is arranged so each operator hears only what is intended for him, his immediate attention is commanded.

21.2 TYPES OF TELEPHONE SYSTEMS

There are several general types of telephone systems which have been used on model railroads. Each has its own advantages and meets certain requirements. The only general rule is to choose the simplest arrangement which will do the job.

21.21 Two-Party Line

The most elementary circuit is simply a pair of wires with a telephone on either end as shown in Fig. 21-1. It is the simplest telephone arrangement but also the most limited.

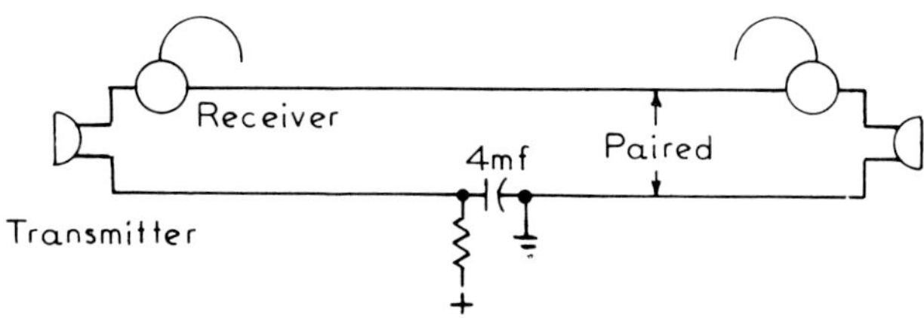

Fig. 21-1 Two-party line.

A direct current is supplied from a filtered power source (see Section 4.9) through resistor R1 and both carbon transmitters and receivers in series. Capacitor C1 serves us additional DC filtering and completes the voice-frequency loop. R1 limits the current to between .02 A and .03 A, the current required by carbon microphones, and its value should be calculated accordingly based on the talking-battery voltage supplied.

21.22 Multiple-Party Line

Several transmitters and receivers can be placed in series on a line as shown in Fig. 21-2 to form a multiple-party line. Such lines are often used on the prototype as dispatcher lines but suffer on model railroads due to the rapid-fire action of events. To avoid interference on the line from background noise and conversations not for the telephone, push-to-talk buttons are provided to short out the transmitters not being used.

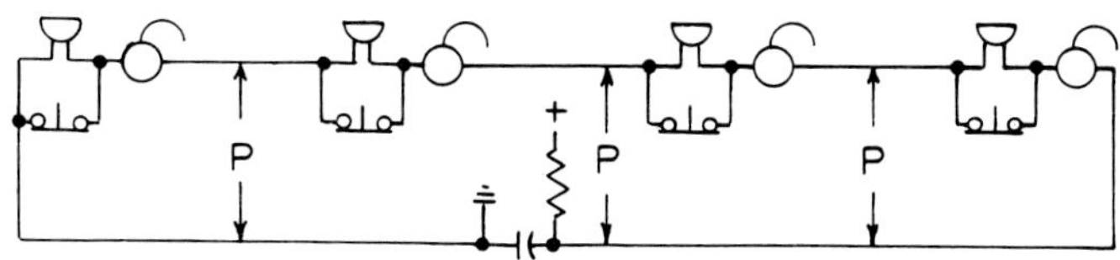

Fig. 21-2 Four-party line.

21.23 Selected-Line System

The selected-line system permits the establishment of two-party or multi-party lines as required and also permits several simultaneous independent conversations. Since telephones are connected only when needed, each operator hears only what is intended for him. For this a talking pair of wires is run from each telephone to all other telephones which can establish a connection tc that telephone. Switches are provided so that each operator can connect his telephone to the talking pair of the operator he wished to call. Fig. 21-3 shows an example of this type of system. Each line represents a pair of wires.

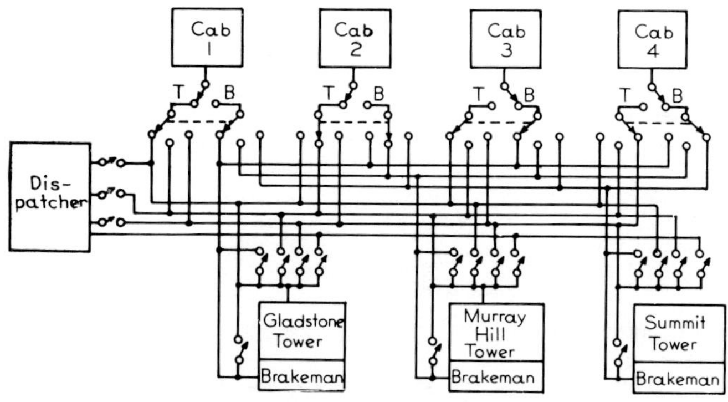

Fig. 21-3 Selected line system.

To keep a selected-line system flexible, the operators must not be permitted to tie all lines up into one big party line. In Fig. 21-3, part of the system which was installed at the Summit-New Providence HO RR Club, each engineer had the responsibility of keeping in telephone contact with the towerman *or* the brakeman at his station. He was provided with switches which permitted only one connection at a time so engineers could not establish a multi-party line. A towerman could not call any engineer but could connect to any adjacent tower, the brakeman at the tower, or the dispatcher. He was provided with non-locking keys so he would not leave a connection established when he was through with it. The brakeman could only call his towerman but the dispatcher could call all towers.

There can be as many independent conversations as there are available talking pairs. Often multi-party lines will be established, for example when the dispatcher connects to a tower with a cab attached. Priorities should be set up to facilitate operation. For example when the dispatcher calls, existing conversations should cease. The called party should always be mentioned first followed by the calling party, e.g., Summit, this is Murray Hill. Thus the called party is alerted to listen for who is calling.

21.3 TELEPHONE SETS

A telephone set consists of, as a minimum, a transmitter (microphone) and a receiver (headset). Carbon transmitters are used because of their sensitivity. If other types of microphones are used, such as ceramic, crystal, or dynamic, it probably will be necessary to add a one-transistor or IC amplifier per microphone.

Well filtered (smooth) DC, called talking battery, is passed through the transmitter and this current is modulated by the sound. The receiver is operated by the modulations on the DC to reproduce the sound. In the simple cases of Fig. 21-1 and 21-2, the DC is passed through the transmitters and receivers in series. In most cases, however, a transformer, often called an induction coil when so used, is added to separate the DC path through the transmitter from the receiver as shown in Fig. 21-4. Any voice-frequency (300Hz to 3.5 kHz) transformer with a turns ratio of about 2:1 will do, it is not critical.

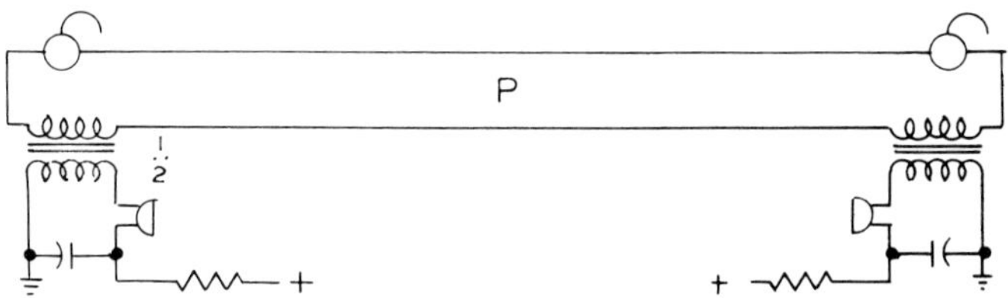

Fig. 21-4 Induction coils.

An advantage of the circuit of Fig. 21-4 is that the talking battery is not supplied over the talking pair but over a separate battery and ground lead to each telephone. This makes simple the application of the multiple-line system.

Note that the receiver at each telephone set reproduces the sound of its own transmitter, called side tone. With the circuits so far shown the side tone is too loud and tends to cause the speaker to talk too softly. This is no real problem on a model railroad but commerical telephones have antiside tone induction coils which lower the volume on the receiver at the transmitting set. Such commercial induction coils may be obtained from suppliers of used telephone equipment and it will be necessary to obtain information from the supplier as to how that particular coil should be connected as terminal designations are not standard.

21.4 TELEPHONE SIGNALING

Telephone signaling means sending an indication over the wires that something should be done, for example a ringing bell. Telephones during model railroad operation are usually so busy that it is best to provide each operator with a headset to wear in the manner of a telephone operator, see the photograph on page 2, Vol. I. Thus all that is necessary is to call the operator desired.

When telephones are employed that must be picked up, some sort of signaling device must be provided. In commercial practice a bell is rung or a lamp is lit over the same wires used for talking but this requires extra equipment. Since distances are short in model railroading it is generally preferable to provide extra wires to operate the signaling device. Lamps, because they eliminate noise, are generally preferred to bells or buzzers. A flashing lamp attracts attention better than a steady light.

21.5 TELEPHONE WIRING

Telephone wiring is unlike other model railroading wiring because DC insulation is not enough. The telephone system must not pick up AC signals to prevent any noise in the system other than that picked up by the transmitters. Several precautions must be taken. Above all, every talking pair must be a twisted pair of wires. This means the entire talking path between telephones except for any switches or terminals. Even at these points the wires should be kept as pairs as closely spaced as is practical. The DC ground and talking battery leads should be completely separate from those used by the railroad. For example do not use the common bus ground which feeds the rails to supply ground to the telephone sets. The ground for the railroad and that for the telephones should be connected together at only one point, normally at the talking-battery supply. This will be automatic if talking battery is supplied by a filter on one of the DC power sources for the railroad.

Run telephone pairs or cables separately from the cables supplying rails or other model railroad equipment. One method which has been used is to run all telephone wires on top of the benchwork grid and all layout wires under the grid.

When running several lines together, for example as when the multiple-line system is used, commercial telephone cable is convenient. It may be obtained from suppliers of used telephone equipment. Such cable is made in a wide range of number of pairs. Typically each pair has its own color or color combination but one wire of the pair has a tracer, usually a red stripe, so that the two wires can be told apart. Wire sizes range from 19 to 26 gauge with the smaller sizes most common.

Since telephones are most useful on large layouts, telephone systems tend to be built only when the need is for a reasonably complex system. Since the selected-line system is the best for large, busy layouts, there may be many talking pairs to install and keep straight. The liberal use of terminal strips is vital. They are needed for trouble shooting but, more important, for changes or additions.

The terminal strips should have two connecting points per terminal. Designate one side as the "cable" side and the other the "local" side as indicated in Fig. 21-5. Always connect pairs running to distant points to the cable side. Keep an accurate record of terminal assignment, one good method is directly on the schematic as shown in Fig. 21-5. Two circles are shown per terminal to illustrate the two connecting points but on an actual record only one circle need be drawn as the other is understood. Also note that only one lead is shown per pair to reduce drawing complexity, the other lead of the pair is always present and on the next terminal, in the drawing it is on the next higher even-numbered terminal. It is common merely to number the pair, that is pair 1 is on the first two terminals, pair 2 on the next two and so on. Show color and the designation of each lead.

Cable pairs are interconnected by strapping the local side of the block. This permits easy reassignment of pairs or the replacement of a failed pair by a good spare. If the cables have more pairs than are needed for the job in hand, it is good practice to connect a few spare pairs to the cable side of the terminal strip as shown for terminals 29 and 31 in Fig. 21-5.

The commercial telephone system is proceeding rapidly to the use of time-division multiplexing for handling telephone traffic. If computer cab control is installed, its CPU can automatically establish the telephone connection between each cab and the tower within whose jurisdiction the cab operates. Even without a CPU available, if there were several phones, a multiplexed system using only one transmission line would reduce wiring complexity and might also reduce costs.

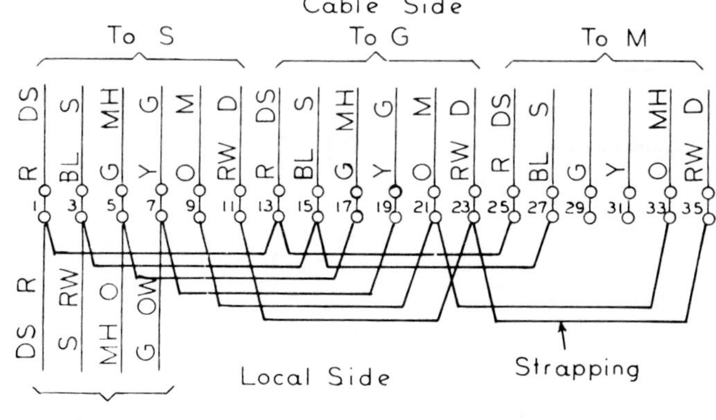

Fig. 21-5 Terminal schematic.

22 TROUBLE SHOOTING

22.1 GENERAL

Electrical troubles are different from most other types in that careful watching usually only shows the effects of the trouble, not the cause. When there is electrical trouble, follow these basic three steps: 1. Determine the type of trouble. 2. Isolate the trouble. 3. Be systematic. One of the pitfalls is to try to cure a trouble without knowing what it is or where it is located.

Trouble shooting transistor throttles is covered in Section 16.11.

22.2 DETERMINE TYPE OF TROUBLE

Most electrical faults can be placed in one of three categories: short circuits, open circuits, and crossed circuits. A crossed circuit is a special form of short circuit where one circuit is falsely connected to another.

Immediately a trouble develops, determine its category. For example, a train stops and cannot be started. Either an ammeter or a voltmeter at the cab will disclose immediately whether it was stopped by a short or an open, see Fig. 22-1. Crossed circuits usually show up as two things happening when only one should.

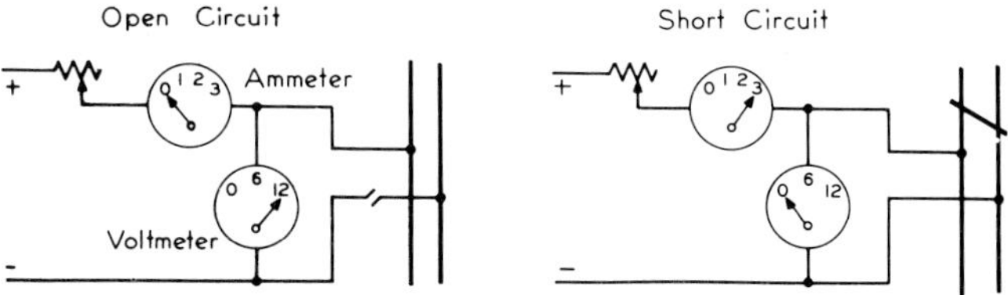

Fig. 22-1 Meter indications for shorts and opens.

22.3 ISOLATE THE TROUBLE

Once the type of trouble has been determined, isolate it so it can be found. An open circuit isolates itself as it must be between the power source and the device to be operated. It is only necessary to check along the leads involved with a voltmeter as shown in Fig. 22-2 or with a lamp. If a voltmeter is used, be sure to place a load on the wire being checked, a short circuit will do. Otherwise the meter may not disclose a resistance. For example, 100 ohms in a running power lead will stop a locomotive but will appear to be a continuous wire to a voltmeter.

Short circuits should be isolated by disconnecting as much of the circuit as is possible by the panel or other switches. With cab control it is often possible to isolate a short circuit to a single section of track.

Isolating a crossed circuit is exactly the same as for a short circuit except that both circuits involved should have the trouble spot isolated.

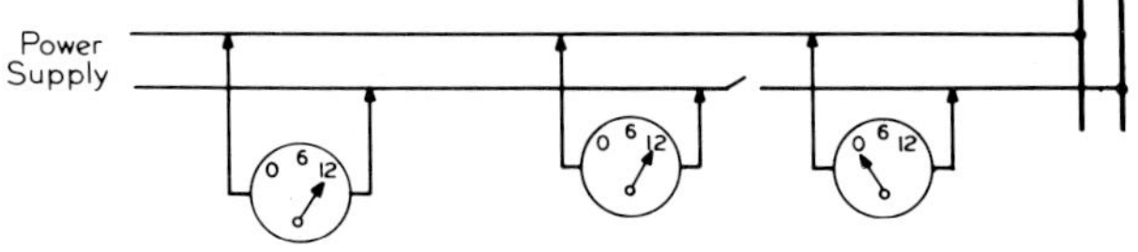

Fig. 22-2 Locating an open with a voltmeter.

22.4 BE SYSTEMATIC

In determining the type of trouble and its general location, a good start has been made on systematic trouble shooting. The method of finding the trouble depends to a large extent on the tools available. A lamp can substitute for a voltmeter but a multimeter which will read voltage, current, and ohms is very useful.

22.41 Locating a Short Circuit

The first step is to check everything movable but do so with care so, if movement eliminates the short, the exact cause will be known. Operate and release all switches and any other such items in the area of the short to see if that has any effect. Inspect all exposed wiring, especially at terminal strips and, if stranded wire has been used, for loose strands. Check insulated rail gaps if any are involved. Before starting to disconnect wires to further isolate the short, try running the maximum current possible into the circuit. Since seldom is a short circuit near zero in resistance, it may heat appreciably and be detectable by touch. If enough current can be supplied, the wires may become warm. If so trace the warmth until it disappears beyond the short.

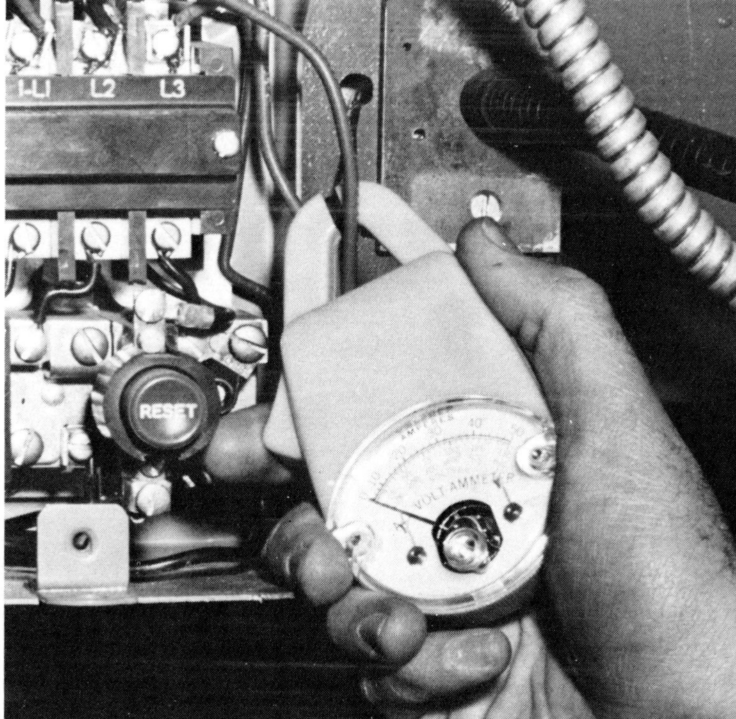

Fig. 22-3 Clamp-on ammeter.

An aid which has proven invaluable in locating shorts at The Model Railroad Club, N.J., is a clamp-on ammeter. As shown in Fig. 22-3, a clamp-on meter has two arms of magnetic material which open to accept the wire then are closed to measure the magnetic field set up by the current in the wire. Such meters are calibrated to read 60Hz sine waves so their reading in amperes is not accurate for full-wave rectified currents but that is not important. Clamping the meter on the wire with the short then following the current until it disappears will pinpoint the short. It is not even necessary to separate out the wire with the current, the meter can be clamped over an entire cable as long as the return flow of current is not also in the cable.

Amprobe Instrument, Lynbrook, N.Y. made a line of clamp-on ammeters in 1972, one of which is shown in Fig. 22-3. Some models also served as voltmeters and ohmmeters using conventional probes.

22.42 Locating Crossed Circuits

After the general area of the cross has been located, examine the two circuits involved to find all places where they could possibly touch. Often there is only one such location so a careful examination at that point may disclose the trouble. Failing to find the cross by examination, deliberately short circuit the heavier of the two crossed circuits as shown in Fig. 22-4 and apply the maximum safe current to the other. If that current can make the wires warm, the warm wires will lead directly to the cross and the cross itself might well be quite warm. Use of a clamp-on ammeter makes matters even easier and faster.

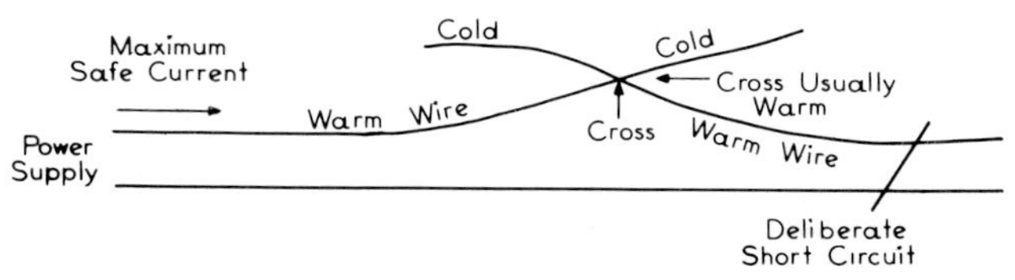

Fig. 22-4 Locating a crossed circuit.

22.43 Checking Devices

With the advent of the transistor and of ICs model railroaders have been presented with the problem of checking devices which cannot be inspected by eye. Fortunately transistors and many other electrical devices can be checked by an ohmmeter. A typical ohmmeter is simply a sensitive ammeter, .001A or less full scale, with an internal battery to supply current. Since the resistance being measured limits the current, the meter can read directly in ohms. Although separate ohmmeters are available, it is more useful to purchase a multimeter which can read ohms, volts both AC and DC, and current. Fig. 22-5 shows such a meter being used to check voltage on the rails. Even the lowest-priced multimeters are suitable for model railroad use but it is important to check the scales. Some meters have 10V, 100V scales. A 10V scale is too low for safe use, and 12V is difficult to read on a 100V scale. Also chose one with an Rx1 ohm scale, some of the cheaper meters have Rx100 or Rx1000 as their most-sensitive reading. In model railroading low resistances are often important.

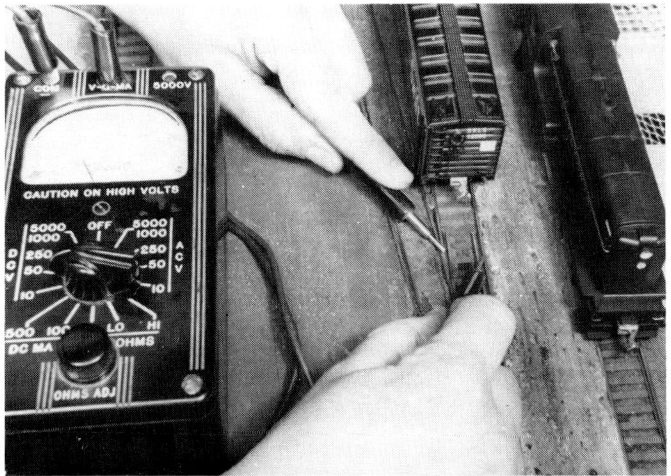

Fig. 22-5 Using a multimeter.

If any complex circuits exist such as transistor throttles, it is good practice to measure all voltages with a multimeter while the circuits are fully operational. Record these voltages directly on the circuit diagrams. Then when trouble develops, the existing voltages can be compared to the proper values. Almost always a failed device will cause a voltage reading to change on its terminals.

An ohmmeter can be used to check diodes and the diodes in a transistor, see Fig. 48, Chapt. 2 for transistor diodes. As shown in Fig. 22-6, a diode should measure high resistance in its blocking direction and low in its forward direction. On many, but not all multimeters the + terminal for its current when used as an ohmmeter is the − terminal when used as a voltmeter. Check your meter by measuring a diode of known polarity.

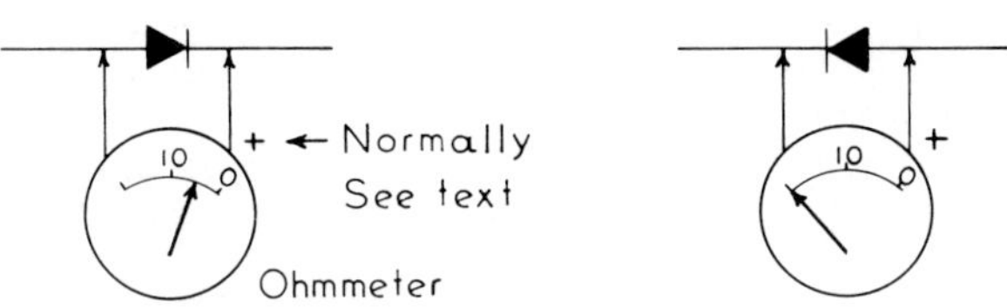

Fig. 22-6 Checking diodes with an ohmeter.

22.5 CLASSIC ELECTRICAL TROUBLES

Certain electrical problems occur over and over. Some are not even recognized as being correctable. A few of the most common faults are given below.

Shorts at Turnouts

When the open point is of opposite potential to the stock rail, a metal flange striking the stock rail as shown on the left in Fig. 22-7 will cause an intermittent short circuit difficult to locate because it may occur only on particular pieces of equipment operating in one direction at certain speeds. Either the throw of the point must be increased or, better yet, the point insulated from the frog and connected electrically to the stock rail. In the latter case the throw can be decreased to make a more realistic switch.

Some commercial insulated frogs depend on the taper of wheel treads to prevent the type of short shown on the right in Fig. 22-7 but not all wheels have sufficient taper. The metal rails can be filed down and a layer of insulation placed over them but this increases the length of the insulated section. The best solution is to substitute an all-rail frog, and to make the necessary circuit changes.

Shorts at Terminals

Four errors are often made when connecting to terminals which lead to short circuits. 1. Saving money by buying light weight terminals which can bend under the pull of the wire. 2. Stripping too much insulation so bare wire projects from the terminal which may be bent over to touch another terminal or similar bare wire. 3. Using stranded wire without taking great pains to assure that there are no loose strands projecting. 4. Using too much solder when soldering to a terminal.

Opens

A common cause of open circuits is dependence on the rail joiners to carry track current. Except on temporary layouts, always provide a soldered connection to each piece of rail, see Section 11.72. Use of flux other than rosin is likely to cause soldered connections to become open in a few years, see Section 11.43. Opens caused by broken leads are often due to nicking the wire when stripping the insulation and lack of neatness in the wiring so that the wires must be moved to get at other parts of the circuit. Use cabling or surface wiring.

22.6 SPECIAL PROBLEMS OF INTEGRATED CIRCUITS

Once integrated circuits (ICs) have been installed and proved operational for a period of several hours (a period called burn-in), they can be regarded as the most-reliable parts of the system. When a circuit with ICs fails, wiring problems should be suspected first unless it is known that the devices have received an excessive voltage surge or have been exposed to excessive heating.

The operation of an IC can generally be checked by stopping the circuit operation at the point of the trouble, and by observing the input and output voltage directly on the pins of the package. If the system is digital, a logic probe is more convenient than a voltmeter. Most commercial logic probes are made to illuminate an indicator when the logic level is high. There are commercially available test clips which can be clamped on a DIP and display the levels of all pins, usually illuminating an indicator for a low. Such test probes or test clips can be made by using inverters to drive LEDs. When such level indicators show proper levels but the circuit is not responding properly, possibly the voltage is above the maximum low or below the minimum high, the test probe makes one decision but the driven circuit the other. Check this with a voltmeter.

If the measurements indicate that a package is bad, if possible interchange the suspected package with another of the same type from elsewhere in the system. If the trouble follows the suspect package, assume it is a bad package.

It is advisable to keep a log of troubles and their cures. Even two failures of successive devices in the same position should be taken as a strong indication that excessive voltage or currents are involved with the failures.

Although the ICs are very reliable, not so the sockets into which they are plugged. If DIP sockets must be used instead of soldering the ICs directly to the conductors, it will probably be found necessary in time to disturb the socket contacts slightly now and then.

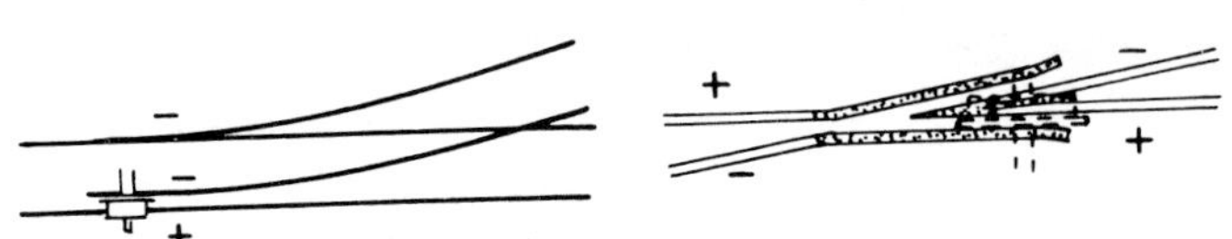

Fig. 22-7 Shorts at turnouts.

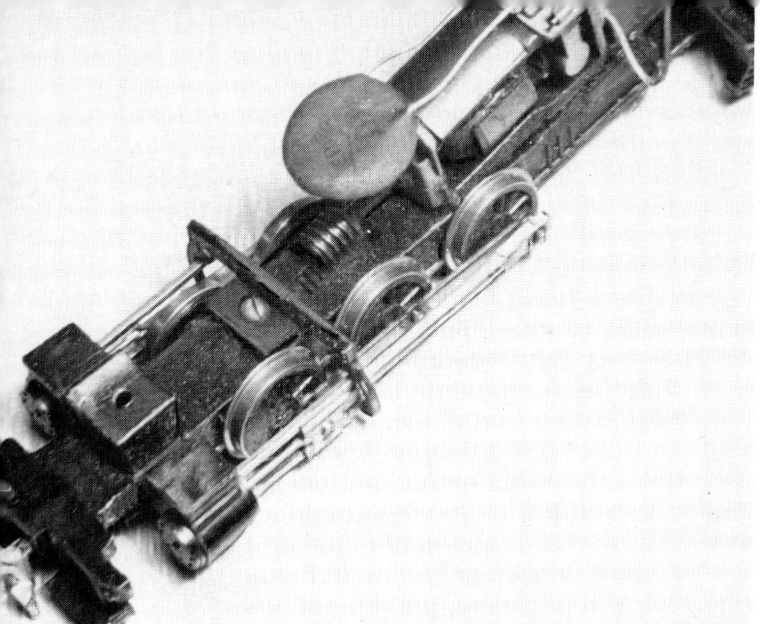

Fig. 23-1 Capacitor for inference suppression

23 RADIO AND TELEVISION INTERFERENCE

23.1 GENERAL

Any electrical device which makes or breaks current, particularly if accompanied by arcing, will generate radio frequency signals. Whether these signals will cause interference depends upon the strength of the signals generated, how well they are contained from radiating, and the strength of the radio and TV signals in the area. Whether interference signals must be suppressed depends upon their effects. Even if they are below the legal limits set by the FCC, should they cause trouble with neighbors, something should be done. Unfortunately there is no one set of procedures which will work in all cases. This Chapter describes several methods which should help but it will be necessary to try them to find out which one or combination will do the job.

23.2 IMPROVE RECEPTION

Often the easiest solution is to improve the reception of the radios or TVs affected. Install an outside antenna and, if necessary, use a coaxial lead in. Not only may increasing the wanted signal strength eliminate any need for suppressing the interfering signal, it may also build good will as the set will have better reception at all times.

23.3 GROUND THE LAYOUT

For safety reasons, a layout should be grounded, see Section 4.22. If the ground is a heavy wire led directly to a good physical ground such as cold-water pipe, it may materially reduce the radiated interference signal.

23.4 ISOLATE THE SOURCE OF INTERFERENCE

If interference still persists after grounding the layout, attempt to isolate the source of the interference. Operate each locomotive and other electrical equipment individually while observing whether or not it causes interference. Do not stop when one source has been found, there may be more. The worst situation is to find that almost everything causes some interference but at least it will then be known that the treatment must be general rather than specific.

23.5 INTERFERENCE SUPPRESSION FOR MOTORS

The prime cause of interference signals is arcing between the brushes and the commutator on motors. If the source of interference is only one or two motors, dressing the commutator and adjusting the brushes as described in Section 3.6 may bring such motors into line with the others. If all motors contribute excessive interference, try connecting a small capacitor directly across the brushes as shown in Fig. 23-1. The leads should be as short as possible consistent with permitting movement of the brushes. Check a range of values to find out which is the most effective, normally this will be found to be in the order of .001 to .01mf.

23.6 SUPPRESSION AT TRACK

Should capacitors at the brushes of motors not suffice as might be the case in extremely sensitive areas where arcing at the rails could cause unacceptable interference, it may be necessary to apply suppression along the track. Try connecting .01mf capacitors between the rails as indicated at the top of Fig. 23-2. If common rail is not used, connect both rails by capacitors to a heavy ground bus as at the bottom of the figure or connect capacitors between the rails and connect one rail to the ground bus through capacitors.

Note that a capacitor is indicated near both ends of each isolated rail. It may be found necessary to add even more in severe cases or perhaps fewer may be enough. In extreme cases it may be necessary to add radio-frequency chokes between the rails and the power leads. Capacitors such as the ones in Fig. 23-2 make the application of ultrasonic lighting and command control more difficult.

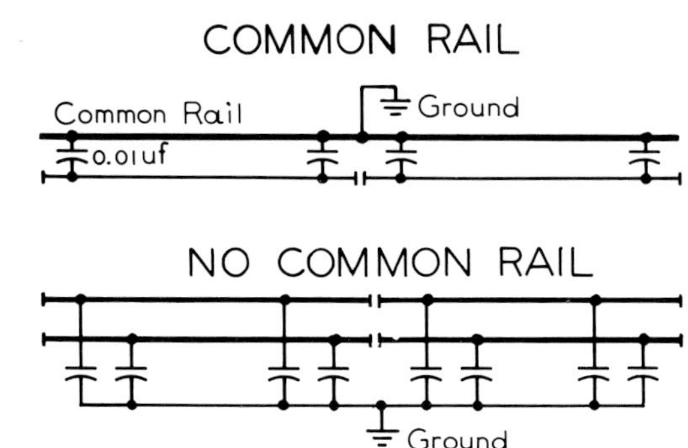

Fig. 23-2 Capacitators applied to track.

23.7 SUPPRESSION IN THE WIRING

The wiring of the layout serves as an antenna to radiate any interference signals generated. Most model railroad wiring is as shown at the top of Fig. 23-3 where the common (ground) is run separately from the feeders to the rails or other powered equipment. Thus the feeders serve as the antenna. This effect can be minimized to a major extent by running the leads in a tight cable with the ground return as shown at the bottom of the figure. This requires that the ground return wire follow each feeder to the point where it connects to the tracks, an unfortunate limitation which complicates the wiring but if simpler solutions do not cure the interference problems, it should be tried, perhaps with a test rewiring to the area of greatest trouble.

23.8 TRANSMISSION OVER WIRES

The interference signals may be transmitted to the radio or TV through the air or through the 110V AC house wiring. The latter is a distinct possibility if the sets being interfered with are in the same building. It is well to make this determination as it is easier to stop interference being sent over the line than interference broadcast into the air.

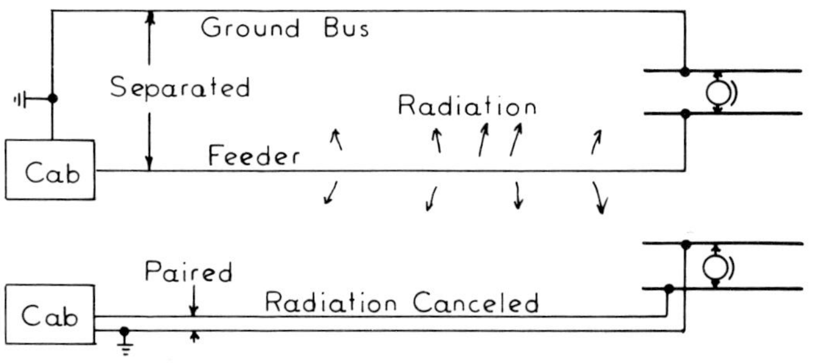

Fig. 23-3 Reducing radiation from feeders.

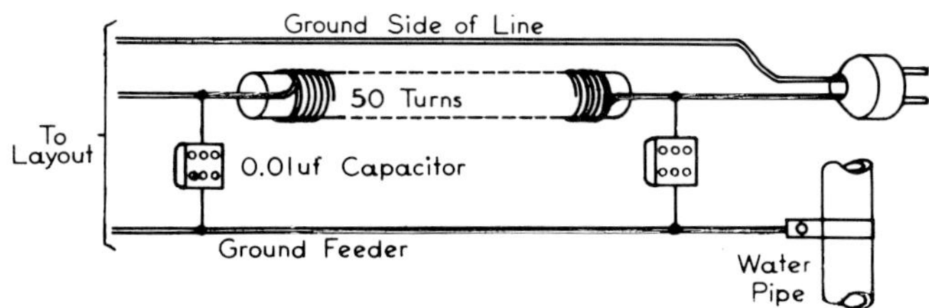

Fig. 23-4 Line feeders.

If possible, operate the railroad on batteries for a brief period. If this cures the interference, the probability is that it is being transmitted over the wires. Another possibility is to disconnect the antenna and place a short circuit across the antenna terminals of the TV or radio. If the interference persists, it is likely that it is on the wires. Commercial line filters are available, some of which can be plugged into the 110V outlet and the radio or TV plugged into the filter.

A commercial filter can be placed in the line powering the layout or one can be made as shown in Fig. 23-4. The radio frequency choke can be made by winding about 50 turns of No. 16 wire on a 3/4″ (1 cm) dowel. If a filter placed in the ungrounded side of the line helps but is not enough, put one in the ground side also.

24 INTEGRATED CIRCUITS

24.1 GENERAL

For model-railroad applications, an integrated circuit can be regarded as a "black box" which performs the function and has the inputs and outputs defined by its manufacturer. There is no need to understand the internal workings of the device. Particularly for digital systems, ICs have reduced circuit design primarily to the proper selection of an available IC and the determination of the interconnections between ICs. Because the great bulk of the interconnections are not external connections between packages, but are internal to the package, very sophisticated systems are now practical for model railroads. A single IC package measuring 6mm × 18mm (1/4″ by 3/4″), with only 16 external connections, requiring only miliwatts of power, and capable of operating millions of times a second for a virtually unlimited life can perform functions which, would require over 2,000 relays, kilowatts of power, much space, and tens of thousands of wired connections. Even if the relays were free, such a circuit would be totally impractical.

Designing for ICs starts with dividing the total system function into the largest possible functional blocks which can be performed by available ICs, counting, for example. Described in this chapter are the most-common functions performed by ICs, together with model-railroad applications of specific devices when such applications are known.

This is a rapidly-changing field, more powerful ICs are constantly being introduced. For example a function which in 1974 required 5 packages (a decoder and 4 FF packages) could, in 1976, be accomplished by one package. The only guide is when a needed function has to be determined; if the function seems to be one of general application, it is possible that it is available in a single package.

24.2 PACKAGES

ICs are available from the manufacturer either as bare chips (the IC itself) or with the chip mounted within a package. In the latter case the inputs and outputs of the chip are connected by the manufacturer to leads, also called pins, projecting from the package. Connecting wires directly to a bare chip is very specialized work, and hardly something a modeler would want to attempt, even with suitable bonding equipment. A possible exception might be when space is extremely limited, as for a receiver for a command control system such as that described in Chapter 17.

This chapter considers only ICs mounted in packages which permit one of the customary wiring methods, such as printed circuits or wire wrap, to be used. Because most ICs are sold and used after being mounted in such a package by the manufacturer, the terms "package", "chip", and "IC" are often used interchangeably. Technically, more than one integrated circuit may be on the chip of silicon and more than one chip mounted in a package. In this chapter, the package is considered the "black box." As long as the advertized functions are being performed, it makes no difference to the user what is inside the package.

Dual In-Line Package (DIP)

Although other forms of packages were available in 1981, by far the most common and useful was the Dual In-Line Package (DIP), shown in Fig. 24-1. This package gets its name from the two rows of

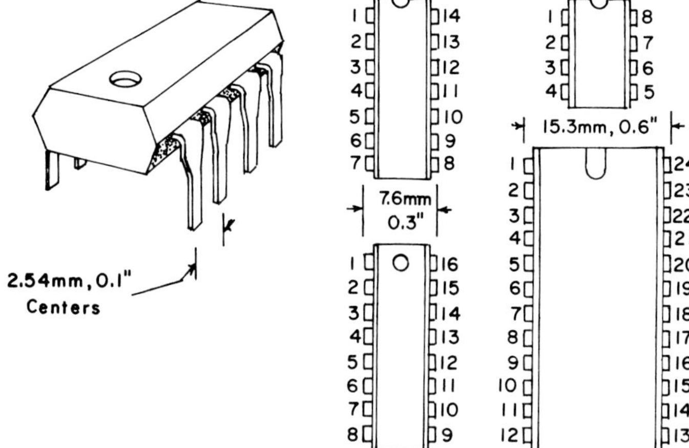

Fig. 24-1 Dual In Line package (DIP).

pins along the sides of the package. At one end of the package is a distinctive mark (not printing) in the package itself, usually a depression or a notch. This marks the end with the No. 1 pin. As shown in Fig. 24-1, if this mark is held at the top, with the leads projecting away from the viewer, the pin numbers start at the top left; count down the left side and then up the right side.

In Fig. 24-1 are shown dimensions and pin numbers for the most-common DIPs (8, 14, 16, and 24 pins). DIPs with other pin numbers are manufactured. Some memories have 18 and 20 pin packages and microprocessors usually have a large number of pins, 40 being a common number.

The package body may be made of plastic (N package) or of ceramic (J package). The plastic packages are less expensive and equally suitable for model-railroad applications.

24.3 LINEAR OR DIGITAL

ICs are divided into two major categories, linear (also called analog) and digital. Linear implies that the output of the device is proportional to the input. Analog means that any value of voltage (or current) is as valid as any other value. A common analog device in model railroading is a motor. The so-called 12-volt motors will operate just as well on 9V as on 12V, indeed the traditional way of controlling speed is to control the applied voltage. In contrast, digital means that only two values (often called states) are valid. For most digital ICs these two states are defined by a voltage above a specified value (this state being called "high" or "H"), or a voltage below a

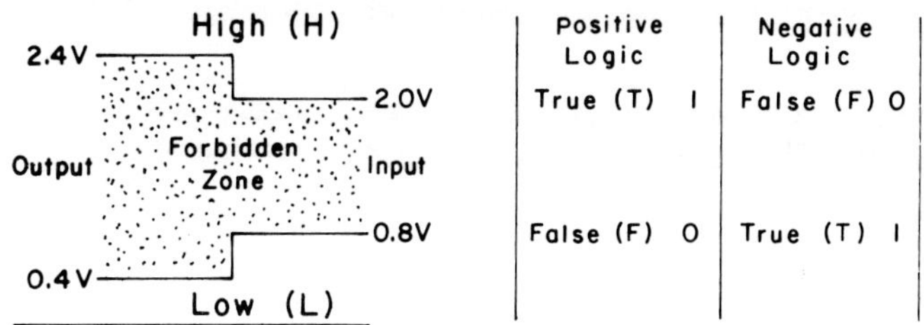

Fig. 24-2 Logic levels for TTL.

specified value (this state being called "low" or "L"). The exact voltage values depend on the family of logic, Fig. 24-2 shows those for TTL. The manufacturer of a TTL IC guarantees that, if the device is not overloaded, its low output voltage will not exceed 0.4V and that its high output voltage will not be less than 2.4V. The manufacturer further guarantees that an input voltage not exceeding 0.8V will be recognized as a low, and that an input voltage exceeding 2V will be recognized as a high. The difference of 0.4V between the specified limits for outputs and inputs allows for voltage drops in the interconnecting wiring. Note that any input voltage exceeding the minimum specification is simply a high, i.e., 5V is no better a high than 3V. Linear devices are quite different; 5V may yield entirely different results than 3V.

The voltages between the specified maximum lows and minimum highs are in a forbidden zone, as indicated in Fig. 24-2. If a voltage in this zone is applied to an input, that IC will determine whether that voltage represents a low or a high, and will act accordingly. There is no way of predicting what that determination will be. Fortunately, the problems of the forbidden zone are easily avoided by not exceeding the loading specifications of the device. As a general rule, most ICs can drive ten other (a "fanout" of 10) ICs of the same general type (family).

Although the ICs themselves respond to highs and lows on their inputs, the circuit designer is more often concerned whether the function, or desired action, is "true" (often called 1) or "false" (often called 0). If "true" corresponds to "high", it is called "positive logic" or "active high", as shown on the right of Fig. 25-2. If "true" corresponds to "low", it is called "negative logic" or "active low." This is also shown in the figure. Unfortunately there is no standard way of dealing with these conventions, and there is actual conflict among the different systems in certain cases. For the sake of clarity, only the functional method is described; other methods are not even mentioned. In the functional method, the action desired, i.e., lighting a lamp, is called true and it does not matter if the level commanding that action is H (positive logic) or L (negative logic). Economical circuit design requires the use of both positive and negative logic. The logic stages commonly alternate between positive and negative.

Before the advent of ICs, when the signal applied or delivered was analog in nature, for example the sound waves received and delivered by a telephone system, linear circuits had to be used for cost reasons. But digital functions are far more readily integrated than linear functions. Digital systems also do not have to be "tuned" or otherwise adjusted, and can have accuracy and reliability far in excess of that possible with linear systems. Therefore, by the late seventies the electronic world was going digital. As described in Chapter 17, the trend from linear to digital for command control was already underway by 1980.

Because digital systems are the wave of the future, this chapter is devoted primarily to digital ICs. Nevertheless the real world is full of analog devices such as motors and loud speakers. Consequently a need remains for ICs to work with such analog devices, so a few of the more important linear ICs are covered.

Even in a digital-logic system, some devices are linear or linear in part, examples of these are timers and oscillators. When such devices are manufactured specifically to work with a particular digital-logic family they are usually cataloged as digital circuits. For example, the 74123, a timer, is considered part of the TTL digital-logic family. On the other hand a timer or oscillator designed for general application is usually cataloged as a linear circuit. An example is the 555, an IC which can be used either as a timer or an oscillator, and often is included in TTL systems. Line drivers and line receivers are other classes of ICs which may be cataloged as digital if designed to work with digital logic, or as linear if general purpose.

24.4 LOGIC FAMILIES

A logic family is a series of ICs of essentially-standard internal construction which have been designed to work together by the simple interconnecting of outputs to inputs by conductors. All members of the same family share the same supply voltage and the same input and output specifications as far as voltage levels are concerned. There have been families which specified current levels rather than voltage levels but these are unimportant to model railroaders. In 1981 the following families had at least some devices available: DTL, RTL (both obsolete), ECL, TTL, CMOS, MOS, NMOS, and PMOS. ECL, an old family but, in 1981, still the fastest, is both expensive and difficult to use. In 1981 TTL dominated as far as availability and variety of devices were concerned. Many non-TTL devices, particularly memories, had TTL-compatable inputs and outputs; they could be wired directly to TTL ICs as if they were TTL. CMOS, which excelled with low power requirements (if operated at low speeds), suffered from high device costs and a limited selection. In 1980 new manufacturing methods were being applied to CMOS which promised a much better competitive position for that family.

In 1981 it appeared probable that TTL had reached its peak and, for future commercial circuits, would gradually be phased out. Nevertheless, at that time TTL by far dominated the field of devices available at low cost to model railroaders, and also had the greatest selection of devices available. Because of its widespread usage, TTL devices could be expected to remain readily available for several to many years to come. For that reason TTL is the family used primarily to illustrate functions in this handbook. Actually, as far as the logic design is concerned, there is no distinction among families. A block-signal circuit designed for TTL can have CMOS packages substituted for the TTL packages as far as the system functions are concerned. Changes of supply voltage and system inputs and outputs may be required. For example, CMOS cannot deliver as much output power as TTL and so may not be able to operate the same signal LEDs without providing output drivers. In some cases the devices of two families may even be alike in pin numbers, for example the 7400 (TTL) and the 74C00 (CMOS).

It is possible to design with mixed families. For instance, the obsolete DTL family can be used as if it were TTL, provided its reduced driving capabilities are kept in mind. With CMOS systems it is often necessary to include some TTL because a particular function is not available in CMOS. The interfaces between devices of one family and those of another must be done with care. When feasible, it is best to design using one family.

Within a single family there may be sub-families. This is particularly true for TTL, as illustrated in Fig. 24-3, for a NAND gate, base code 7400. These numbers designate the logical function of the device, that is a quad 2-input NAND gate in the commercial series 74. If the first two numbers were 54, the device would be logically the same but military grade good for an operating temperature range of −55°C to 125°C. The 74 series has a permissable range of 0°C to 70°C, quite broad enough for model railroad purposes. If no letter follows the 54 or 74, it is a standard unit and has the current and speed ratings which are given on the first line of Fig. 24-3. If an H follows the 54/74, it is a high-power unit requiring more input current, delivering more output current, and faster than a standard unit. An L in the code denotes a low-power unit which is much slower than a standard unit. An S denotes a Schottky-clamped unit (prevents saturation of the transistors) and is the fastest sub-family in TTL. LS denotes a combination of low power and Schottky-clamped units, yielding speed about the same as standard units, but with much lower current requirements. The trend in 1981 was heavily to the LS units. Not all codes were available in all of the sub-families. It is quite practical to mix sub-families, provided the current ratings are observed. For example, a 74L00 output can drive 20 74L00 inputs in parallel, but only three 74H00 inputs. Two letters representing the manufacturer preceed the type number on the packages themselves. A letter denoting the package type usually follows the type number. For example, a SN7400N is a 7400 quad NAND gate made by Texas Instruments. Other numbers of no significance to model railroaders may follow the package-type letter.

		Maximum Currents (mA)				Max. Switching Time (ns)	
		Input		Output			
		H	L	H	L	∕	∖
Standard	7400	.04	1.6	.4	16	22	15
High Power	74H00	.05	2	.5	20	10	10
Low Power	74L00	.01	.1	.2	3.6	60	60
High Speed	74S00	.05	2	2	20	4.5	5
Low Power High Speed	74LS00	.02	.36	.36	8	20	20

Fig. 24-3 Sub-families within TTL.

Regardless of the family selected, it is vital to obtain a good catalog of the devices available. For TTL, the best available book in 1981 was "The TTL Data Book for Design Engineers", by Texas Instruments, PO Box 5012, Dallas, TX 75222. A sizable book at low cost. Because it is such an excellent reference, its purchase is recommended even if a family other than TTL is contemplated.

24.5 INVERTERS

As shown by the truth table in Fig. 24-4 an inverter simply inverts, it performs no logic. The inverter changes an H input to an L output or an L input to an H output; it converts from positive logic to negative or vice-versa. When the functional system of logic is used, as in this Handbook, an inverter does nothing to the truth or false indication. This is shown by the circuit at the bottom of Fig. 24-4. In that figure the up position of the ON switch (connected to 5V for H) is designated as "true" and the LED illuminated is also designated as "true". The function to be performed is called ON as is the switch. When the switch is "false" (lower left in figure), i.e., connecting to ground (L), the output of the inverter is H so no current flows through the LED; it is off, the "false" condition. When the switch is "true" (lower right in figure), i.e., connecting to 5V (H), the output of the inverter is L sinking current from the LED and turning the latter on ("true"). The input to the INVERTER is said to be "active high", that is, when the action desired is to be performed, the level is H. The output of the INVERTER is said to be "active low", when

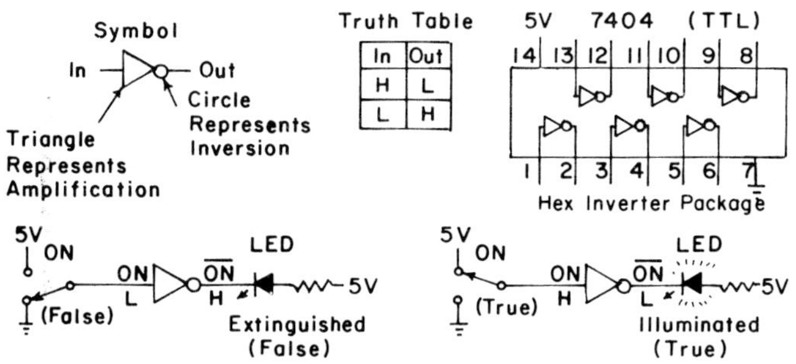

Fig. 24-4 Inverter.

the action desired is to be performed, the level is L. As shown in Fig. 24-2, active low is also called "negative logic". A common way of showing that L is true is to place a bar over the functional designation as illustrated at the INVERTER output in Fig. 24-4. Read that designation as ON bar. Sometimes a prime symbol is used instead of a bar, especially when typing, e.g., ON′. Note that, in the functional system, an INVERTER inverts the level, e.g., H to L, but not the function. A true input yields a true output and a false input yields a false output.

Good circuit design demands that the choice between positive or negative logic be made on the basis of economy. Some LSI (large-scale integration) devices force this choice by their input and output specifications. Nevertheless, the use of INVERTERS to convert between positive and negative logic often is a sign of poor circuit design, although a few usually cannot be escaped.

INVERTERS are often used as power amplifiers; the triangle part of the INVERTER symbol indicates amplification, the circle inversion. Examples are when the output of some logical device cannot drive all the loads requiring its output, or when a single load, such as an LED, requires more current than the logic device can supply. In such cases the logic device can drive one or more inverters which, in turn, drive the loads. Amplifiers, also called buffers, are also available without inversion, the 7407 (TTL) is an example. For reasons of cost, speed, and power drain, inverters are to be preferred to non-inverting buffers unless inversion is a problem. The circle of the inverter symbol always represents inversion and is used in conjunction with the symbol of many IC types other than inverters.

24.6 GATES

Gates are the basic building blocks of integrated circuits. At one time systems were assembled with nothing but gates. Today gates are used primarily as the glue to stick larger circuits together. It is necessary to understand gates and to have their truth tables committed to memory, to comprehend readily any system.

Unless otherwise specified, gates are always spoken of in positive logic terms (truth=H). The AND function is defined as being true when all inputs are true, as shown for the 2-input AND gate on the left in Fig. 24-5. In positive logic, when all inputs are H (true), the output of the gate is H (true). If any input is L (false), the output is L (false), no matter what level is applied to other inputs. An input which does not matter is called a "don't care" and is indicated by an X in truth tables.

AND gates are readily available with 2, 3 or 4 inputs as indicated in Fig. 25-5. To stay within the limitation of 14 pins, there are four 2-input AND gates (quad), three 3-input AND gates (triple), and two 4-input AND gates (dual) to a package.

The AND function (positive logic) but with a negative-logic output (true=L) is performed by a NAND gate, to the right in Fig. 24-5. The N for this and other gates, and the circle of the symbol at the output indicate an inverted output. It is as if the output of a AND gate was driving the input of an INVERTER. Gates in most logic families are naturally inverting so actually the NAND gate is sim-

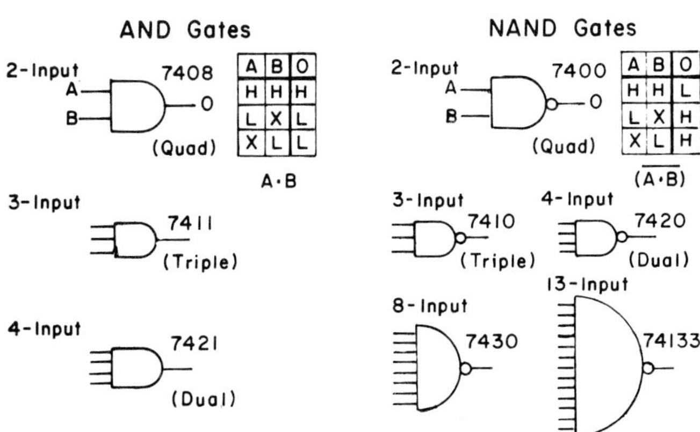

Fig. 24-5 AND and NAND gates.

pler, faster, and usually cheaper than the AND gate. Indeed, when there is a choice of gates, the NAND gate is always the one to select. Because it is preferred, it has the widest selection available, 2, 3, 4, 8, and 13 inputs in TTL.

When using the functional representation, it is important to remember that the function of a NAND gate is exactly the same as an AND gate, when all inputs are true the output is true but, in the case of the NAND gate, the output is negative logic so true is L.

In Boolean, the algebra of logic, the AND function is indicated by the symbol for "times". Therefore the function A AND B is indicated symbolically by A·B as shown in Fig. 24-5. If the output of the gate is inverted (NAND), a bar is placed over the expression for the AND function, also shown in Fig. 24-5.

The logical OR function is that the output is true when any input is true. As shown by the truth table on the left in Fig. 24-6 (for positive logic), when any input is H, the output is high. As the OR gate is the least-desirable type of gate, only a 2-input OR gate is readily available in TTL. Because gates naturally invert, the NOR gate, functionally an OR but with negative-logic output, shown in the right of Fig. 24-6 is preferred to an OR gate. Any input true (H) still yields a true output but, as it is negative logic, that output is L. TTL NOR gates are readily available with 2, 3, 4, and 5 inputs. Because NAND and NOR are the preferred gate functions, often circuit design results in alternating stages of positive logic-negative logic. Although it is customary to use positive logic gate names regardless of whether the inputs to a particular gate are positive logic or negative logic, the circuit designer must be aware that a negative logic OR or NOR function is performed by a positive logic AND or NAND gate. This can be seen in the truth table for the AND gate in Fig. 24-5. Any input true (L for negative logic) makes the output true (L), the functional statement for the OR function. Therefore the positive logic AND gate is said to be a negative-logic OR gate. If a NAND gate is used as a negative-logic OR gate, its output is inverted back to positive logic (H is true) as shown in the truth table for the NAND gate in Fig. 24-5.

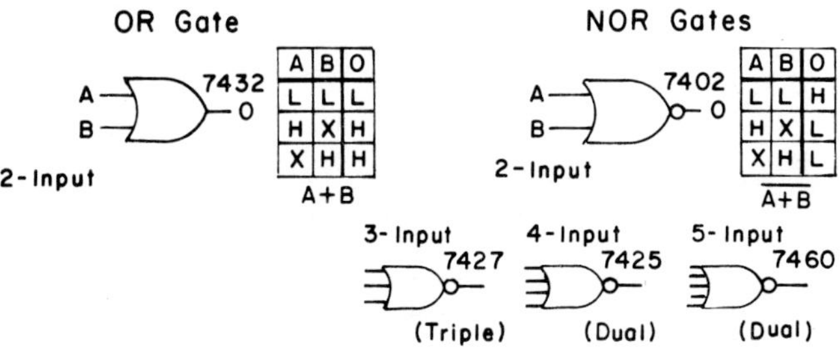

Fig. 24-6 OR and NOR gates.

By the same arguments, in Fig. 24-6, the AND function (all inputs true yield a true output) in negative logic is performed by the positive logic OR gate. If a NOR gate is used as a negative logic NAND gate, its output is inverted back to positive logic.

In Boolean, the algebra of logic, the OR function is indicated by the symbol for "add". Therefore the function A or B is indicated symbolically by A + B. If the output of the gate is inverted (NOR), a bar is placed over the expression for the OR function.

It is helpful, when reading a circuit diagram, to have some memory aid whether a gate is performing a negative-logic or a positive-logic function. Unfortunately, by 1981, no standard method has evolved. Some designers simply use the standard positive-logic symbol as the one at A in Fig. 24-7, leaving it to the reader to determine the function. Others use the logic symbol for the function in positive logic, adding circles to show conversions of negative to positive logic and vise-versa, as at B in the figure. With this method, the drawing symbol no longer represents the gate type which is installed at this point. The gate at B still is an AND gate as specified and purchased.

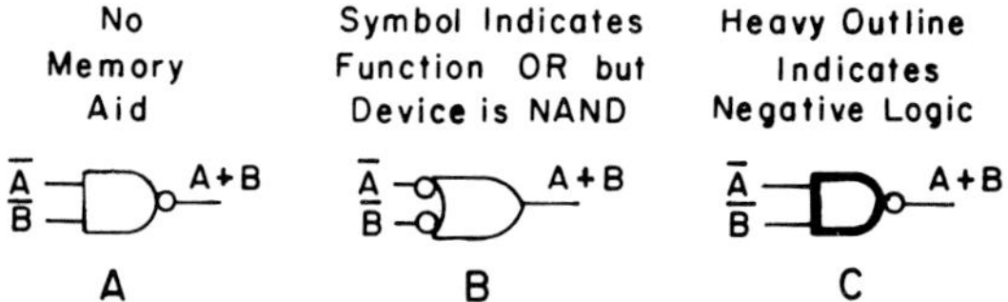

Fig. 24-7 Negative logic NOR representations.

Others use the standard gate symbol as at A, but somehow add an indicator that it is actually serving a negative-logic function. The convention adopted in this handbook to indicate that the gate is serving a negative-logic function is to draw the outline more heavily than gates serving positive logic. An example is given at C in Fig. 24-7.

The remaining gate type is one performing the exclusive OR (XOR) function; either input true, but not both true, will yield a true output. Fig. 24-8 gives the most-common symbol for an XOR gate and its truth table. Exclusive NOR (XNOR) gates are manufactured but are not as readily available.

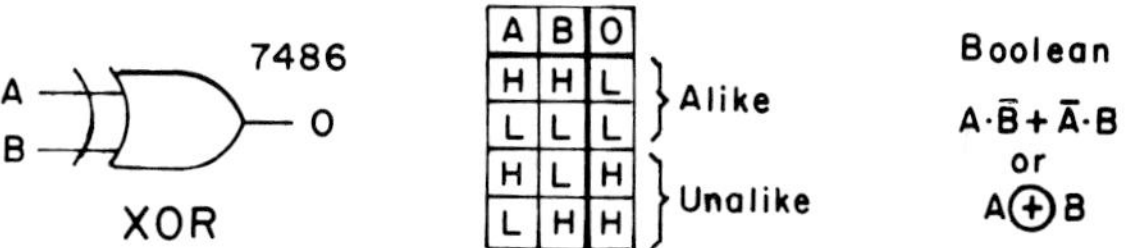

Fig. 24-8 Exclusive OR gate (XOR).

XOR gates do not have the general application of the other four types, but are useful as programmable inverters (the state on the program input determines whether the signal on the other input will be inverted or not), and to compare the state of two bits. An example of a controlled inverter is given in Fig. 24-42.

24.7 FLIP-FLOPS (FF)

A flip-flop (FF) is a circuit which will remember (store or lock-in are other terms used) a bit of binary information. The simplest FF, if only one is needed, can be made up of two gates suitably wired but, if two or more FFs are needed, packages containing a multiplicity of FFs should be used. The same is true if even a single FF of other than the simplest type is needed.

FFs have two states, SET and RESET, also called 1 and 0 respectively. FFs also have two outputs, usually called Q and Q bar although, due to pin limitations, often the Q bar output is not available as a package output. Except during the short interval when switching between states, the two outputs of an FF are of opposite levels. SET is defined as the state in which the Q output is H, RESET when Q is L.

24.71 Set-Reset (S-R) FF

The SET-RESET (SR) FF is the simplest and least-expensive FF. If otherwise suitable, this is the FF to chose. S-R FFs actually are the memory element within the more powerful FF types described further on in this Handbook. If constructed of two NOR gates, as shown in Fig. 24-9, this FF has positive-logic inputs, i.e., a active high on the SET (S) lead sets the FF and an active high on the RESET (R) lead resets the FF. When both inputs are inactive (L), the FF remembers which input had been active last. As shown at the top left in Fig. 24-9, if the FF had last been set, the H on its Q output applied to the opposite NOR gate holds the Q bar output L, and the L on the Q bar output combined with the L on the SET input holds the Q output H. To make it apparent that two gates form an FF, these two feed-back paths are almost invariably drawn slanting and crossed as shown.

After a S-R FF has been set, repeated pulses on the S lead will cause no further change. But, if the R lead is made active, as shown by the second circuit diagram in Fig. 24-9, the H on that lead will force the Q output low in turn forcing the Q bar output H, the reset state. After the FF has been reset, the R pulse can be removed because the feedback leads will hold the FF in the reset state. Repeated pulsing on the R lead will cause no further action.

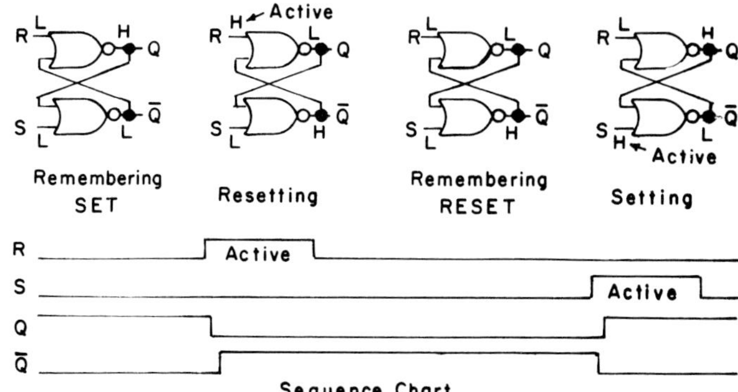

Fig. 24-9 NOR gate flip-flop.

When in the reset state, a pulse on the S lead will cause the FF to switch back to set, and it will lock up in that position until a reset pulse is received on the R lead.

At the bottom of Fig. 24-9 is a sequence chart showing circuit action as the inputs are made active and then restored to normal. Note that when R goes H, there is a slight propagation time (about 15 ns for TTL) until Q goes low then another propagation time until Q bar goes high. Thus, for a short interval, both Q and Q bar are low. Circuit design must take this into account.

Since a FF cannot be both set and reset at the same time, making both the S and the R input active simultaneously is an illegal FF operation. If they are both made active, both Q and Q bar will go H. As soon as one of the inputs is returned to normal, the FF will assume the state required by the input remaining active. Thus a S-R FF can be used to remember which input changed from active last, an ability used in the block-signal circuit shown in Fig. 15-47.

As shown in Fig. 24-10, an S-R FF with negative-logic inputs can be constructed using two NAND gates. The feedback action for remembering is exactly the same as that shown in Fig. 24-9, but of opposite levels. Since NAND gates are both cheaper and faster than NOR gates, FFs of NAND gates are to be preferred. Shown in Fig. 24-10 is the 74279, a TTL package containing four S-R FFs. Note that two of the FFs have two S bar inputs. There could be more inputs, as any input L to a NAND gate forces the output H.

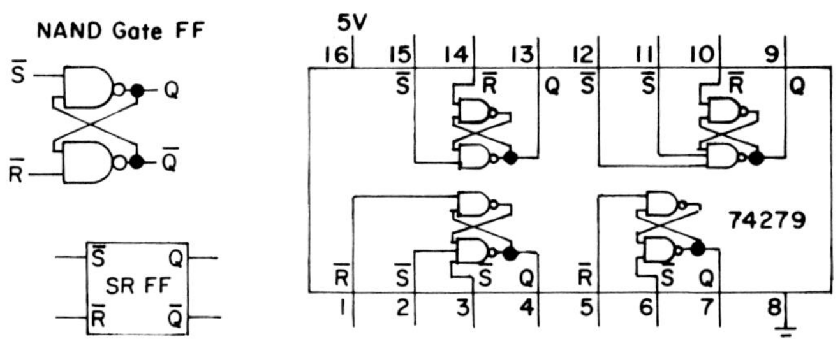

Fig. 24-10 NAND gate S-R flip-flop.

Also shown in the figure is a common "black-box" representation of an S-R FF for use on circuit diagrams.

The S-R FF is an asynchronous device since it changes its state as soon as the appropriate input is made active. Therefore it can be used in systems which are not provided with a clock, such as that shown in Fig. 15-46. For the same reason, it can register that at least one pulse has been received, regardless of when the pulse or pulses occurred with respect to the clock. But the requirement of separate set and reset inputs and lack of a clock input make it difficult to apply in many applications.

24.72 Latch FF and Master-Slave FF

Latch is sometimes used to mean a S-R FF or a D FF, but in this handbook latch FF or latch specifically refer to the gated FF shown at the left of Fig. 24-11. The state of the internal S-R FF of the latch is made to agree with the state of the input applied to D when the gate input is active, H is indicated in the sequence diagram of the figure. When the gate is L, any change on the D input is ignored. But, when the gate is H, any change in the level of F will cause an identical change in the level of Q. This feature is shown in the interlocking of Fig. 15-66.

Latches are the lowest-cost clocked FF, and are used primarily for temporary storage of information. For that purpose they are

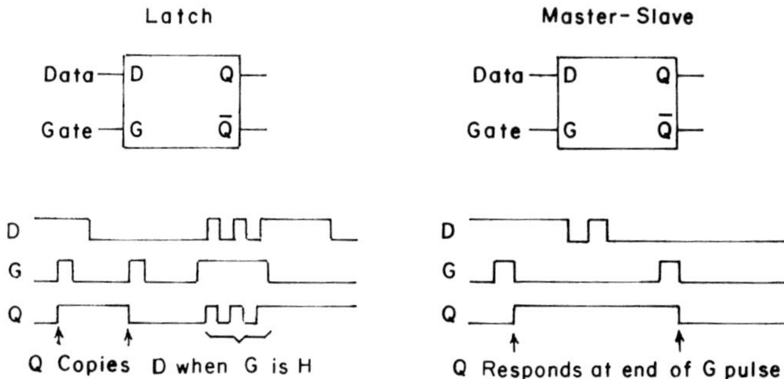

Fig. 24-11 Gated flip-flop.

packaged in groups of four (7475 and 7477) or of eight (74100) with gate inputs common to more than one latch FF. Due to pin limitations, latch packages often make only the Q output available from each FF.

The master-slave FF is actually two latch FFs so connected that when the gate goes H, one of the latches (the master) copies the state of the D input. When the gate goes low, the second latch (the slave) copies the state of the master. Thus the change of state of the Q output occurs after the end of the gate pulse. The advent of the D FF has made the master-slave FF almost obsolete.

24.73 D FF

The D FF is the most modern and most versatile of all the FFs. Like the latch it has a single D (data) input, but it is edge-triggered rather than level-triggered so its activating lead is called clock. As shown by the sequence diagram of Fig. 24-12, the Q output copies the D input when the clock input goes high, positive-edge triggered. The inherent delay in switching prevents the Q output from changing state until the activating point of the trigger edge has passed. With only a propagation delay this accomplishes the function for which the master-slave FF was developed. Because of this delay, the Q bar output can be connected directly to the D input of the same FF (the toggle connection) to make a T FF (Toggle FF) as shown at the right in Fig. 24-12. The D input, therefore, always stands at the state opposite to the state of the FF, each clock pulse causes the FF to switch to the opposite state. This connection is very useful for counting.

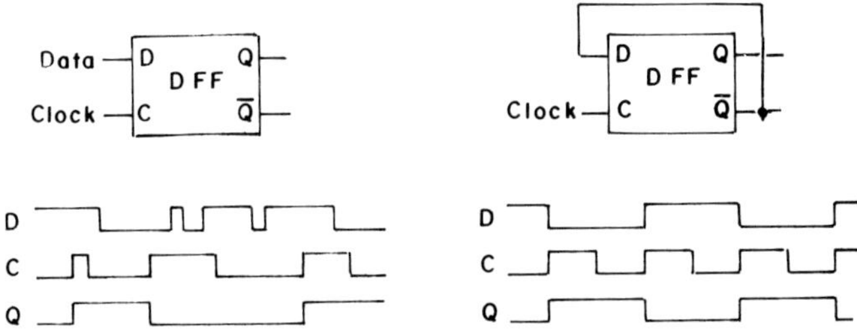

Fig. 24-12 D flip-flop.

Often preset and clear leads are brought out from the D FF and are active low as shown in Fig. 24-13. They are set and reset leads from the S-R FF which is the actual memory element within the D FF. Either the PS or the CL lead active will override the clock and the data inputs. D FFs are available in packages of 2, 4, 6 and 8 FFs. Examples of the use of a D FF can be seen in Fig. 15-58, 16-16, 24-32, and 24-42.

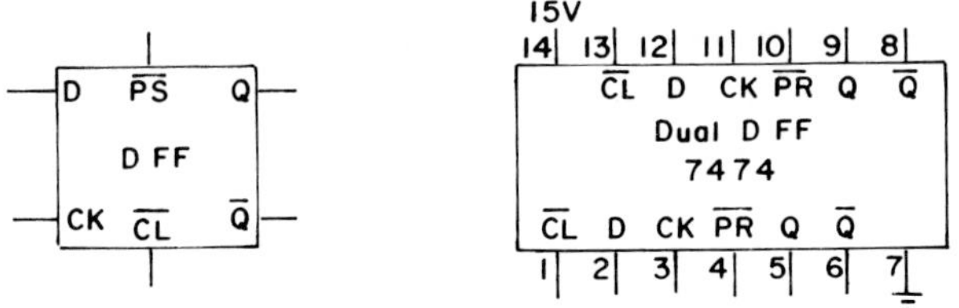

Fig. 24-13 D flip-flops with Present and Clear.

24.74 J-K FF

The J-K FF was the first integrated circuit to go beyond gates. It was extensively used in the sixties to construct counters, shift registers, and other functions now performed on single chips. Because of its extensive early use, the J-K FF became available in many variations of input gates and clocks. Fig. 25-14 shows one of the master-slave type, this particular code having a clear bar input, but not a reset.

As shown in the sequence chart of Fig. 25-14, when the CL bar input is active (L in this case), Q is forced L (reset). The gate input is not effective when CL is active. When CL is not active, the response of the J-K FF depends upon the state of the J and K inputs. If both are L, a pulse on the gate input has no effect. If J is H and K is L, the gate pulse will set the FF. If J is L and K is H, the gate pulse will reset the FF. If both J and K are H, the gate pulse causes the FF to toggle. For most applications the D FF, having but one data input, is more convenient than a J-K FF.

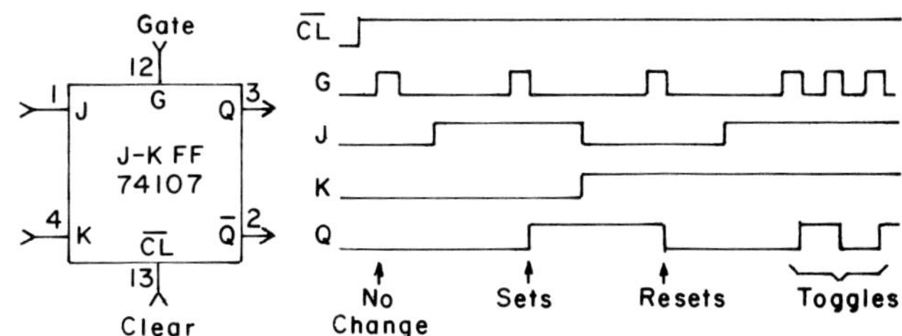

Fig. 24-14 J-K flip-flop, Master-Slave type.

24.75 Other FF Devices

Many LSI circuits include FFs and may be used to register data as though they were individual FFs. Examples are counters, shift registers, and memories. As such devices combine other functions with the function of a FF, the use of these larger circuits usually results in simpler design and in reduced wiring complexity. Also, FFs have been integrated with other types of functions, such as multiplexers and decoders. Such combinations should be used when available to reduce wiring complexity and to increase reliability.

24.76 Precautions Required by FFs and LSI with FFs.

When power is first turned on, except in special cases, the initial states of the FFs in the system are unknown. It is vital that every effect of initial states be considered. Often the initial state will be found to be immaterial; circuit action can start from any state. Otherwise it is necessary to bring FFs to their correct initial state before circuit action commences, to assure that no undesirable effect occurs, such as running a locomotive into the turntable pit.

Electrical noise may change the state of a FF unexpectedly, causing a change in circuit action. When possible, the system should be designed so that it can recover from false operations without human attention. If that is not possible, the system should fail safe while awaiting human corrective steps. Power, for example, should be removed by an error, not supplied.

24.8 LARGE-SCALE INTEGRATION (LSI), DIGITAL

The integrated circuits described so far in this chapter consist of only a few gates, and are often called SSI (small-scale integration). At one time entire systems were made of such devices, today major circuit functions consisting of hundreds, even thousands, of gates are available in a single package. The use of such complex circuit blocks, often called LSI (large-scale integration), greatly reduces design effort, wiring complexity, and cost. Where logic functions are concerned, gates and inverters have become the glue used to stick LSI packages together. The appearance of several interconnected gates and inverters should be a signal to examine the system at that point to determine if a better solution exists through the use of LSI.

The dividing line between SSI and LSI has shifted as technology improved to permit integrating larger and larger functions. At one time LSI was considered to start at about 100 gates or their equivalent. Other terms such as MSI (medium-scale integration) and VLSI (very large-scale integration) have found support to differentiate among degrees of complexity of ICs, but in this Handbook only SSI and LSI are used. Microprocessors are clearly LSI devices when integrated usually are considered as a separate class of devices. Microprocessors are covered in Chapter 25.

As technology improves, more and more powerful ICs are introduced. The primary rule in designing with LSI is to divide the system into functional units which can be implemented by the most powerful devices available. When dividing a system into functional units, consideration should always be given to adopting functional units which are likely to have wide applications, for example a counting function. If this is done, it is probable that a suitable IC will be found. In the paragraphs which follow, several of the most-useful and readily-available LSI functional units are described. The specific examples shown are TTL but, in many cases, similar functional units exist in other families.

24.81 Counters

Counting is one of the most useful of LSI functions. Its most-basic form is shown in Fig. 24-15. The pulses to be counted are applied to the clock input of the counter package. For a positive-edge triggered counter (the usual type), each time the clock input goes high, the contents of the counter are incremented as indicated by the table and by the sequence chart of Fig. 24-15. In the case of a binary counter, when the count reaches F hexadecimal (15 decimal, 1111 binary), the next input pulse increments the contents to zero. Also available are BCD (binary-coded decimal) counters which count 0 to 9 and then return to 0 on the next counting pulse.

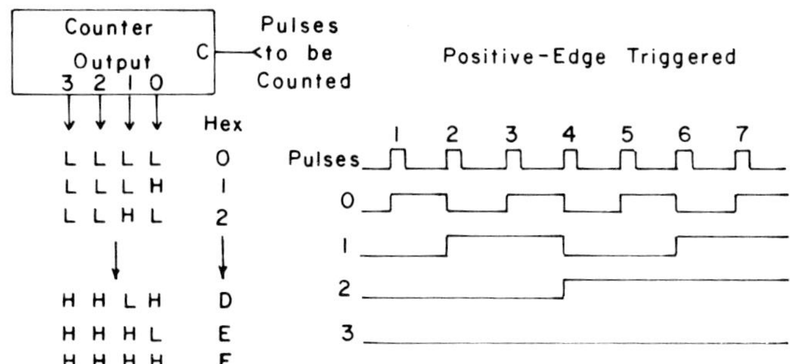

Fig. 24-15 Counting function.

In 1981 most of the readily available counters were of four bits, many could count either up or down (up-down or reversable counters). Also, most could be loaded so that counting could start at any desired point. The choice among the available types usually depends upon which has the most-convenient combination of inputs and outputs for the task at hand.

As a specific example of a commercial counter, Fig. 24-16 shows the 74193, a binary counter. The 74192 is an otherwise-identical BCD counter. Separate up and down counting inputs are provided. Like the set and reset inputs of a S-R FF, only one counting input can be active at a time, the other being held H. An example of the advantage of having two counting inputs can be seen in the check-out block signal circuits of Figs. 15-48 and 15-49.

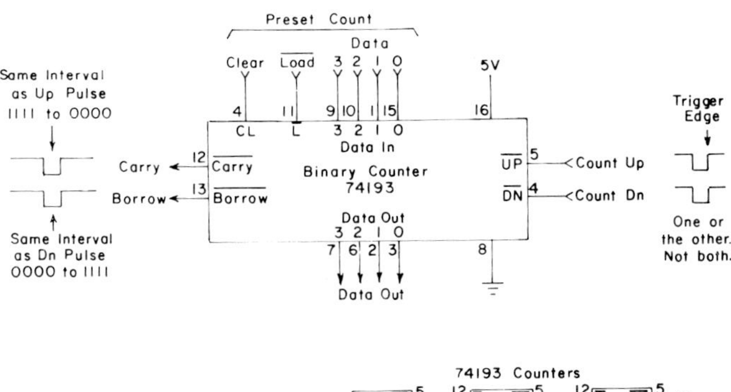

Fig. 24-16 Up-down counter.

When the content of the counter is maximum (1111), a pulse on the UP input increments the count to 0000 and, for the duration of the pulse on the input, develops a pulse on the CARRY output. In a similar manner, when the count is minimum (0000), a pulse on the DOWN input decrements the count to 1111 and, for the duration of the pulse on the input, develops a pulse on the BORROW output. As shown by the diagram at the bottom of Fig. 25-16, these outputs of one counter can be directly used to drive the counting inputs of another 74193 counter to construct a counter of more than four bits. Virtually all LSI counters have the capability of cascading counters of the same type number.

Most counters can be "loaded"; the internal FFs of the counter can be forced to states determined by levels applied to inputs of the counter, in the case of the counter shown in Fig. 25-16, the DATA IN inputs. When the LOAD input is made active (L in the case of the 74193), the states applied on the DATA IN inputs will appear on the DATA OUT outputs. Any counting inputs received while the LOAD input is active will be ignored. Thus counting will resume only after the LOAD input is once again inactive. Thus a counter can be used as a register which can be incremented or decremented, as shown in Fig. 24-17. Such a register could be useful in simplifying the programming of a microprocessor, an example is given in Fig. 25-4.

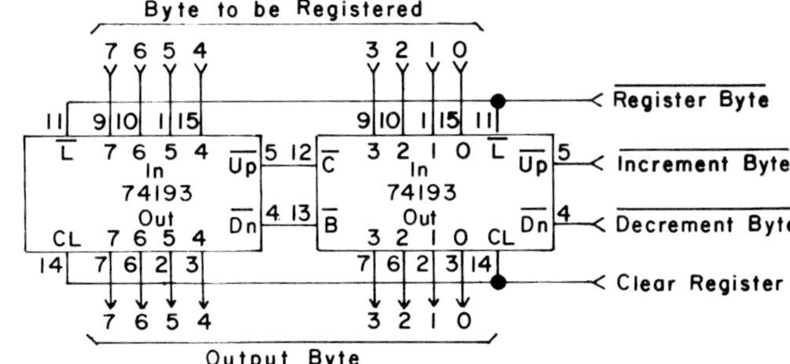

Fig. 24-17 Counters as an incrementing- decrementing register.

In addition to, or instead of, a LOAD input, some counters have a CLEAR input, as shown in Fig. 24-16. When this input is made active (H for the 74193), the counter is forced to 0000. The CLEAR input active overrides all other inputs, including LOAD. When the pulses to be counted are on a signal lead, and the signal "count up" or "count down" is on another lead, the 74191 binary counter (the 74190 in a BCD version) shown in Fig. 24-18 is convenient to use. The inputs, which differ from those of the 74193, are shown heavy in the figure. If the DOWN input is active (H in the case of the 74191) when a positive going edge is applied to the CLOCK input, the count will be decremented. If the DOWN is not active, the count will be incremented. If the ENABLE input is not active (L in the case of the 74191), a clock pulse will be ignored. The RIPPLE output develops a L pulse of the same duration as the CLOCK pulse when the count is 1111 and incrementing (or 0000 and decrementing). To cascade 74191 packages to build counters of more than four bits, this output is connected to the ENABLE input of the next higher order counter, as shown on the left in Fig. 2-18.

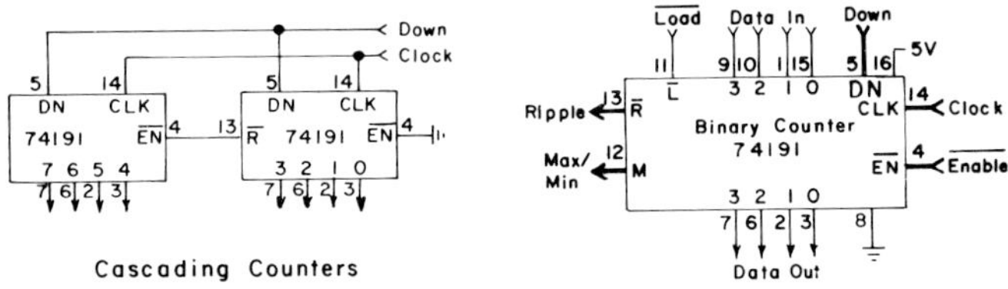

Fig. 24-18 Counter with a single clock output.

When counting up, an H output is developed on the MAX/MIN output during the time the count is 1111. When counting down, H is developed when the count is 0000. This output is very convenient in special cases. An example, a power-on delay taken from a computer cab control system, is given in Fig. 24-19. Another example, control of a clock, is shown in Fig. 24-20. Since the states of FFs are unknown when power is first turned on, it is often necessary to assure that critical FFs, including those in counters, registers, etc., are in their proper initial states before the system can be permitted to operate. Several machine cycles may be necessary to attain the required initial state. Although a time delay circuit could be used, it is better to count machine cycles, because then the power-on delay will always be the same as far as circuit action is concerned, even if the clock is running at a greatly reduced rate. In Fig. 24-19, when power is first turned on, the capacitor holds the LOAD input L, thereby loading all

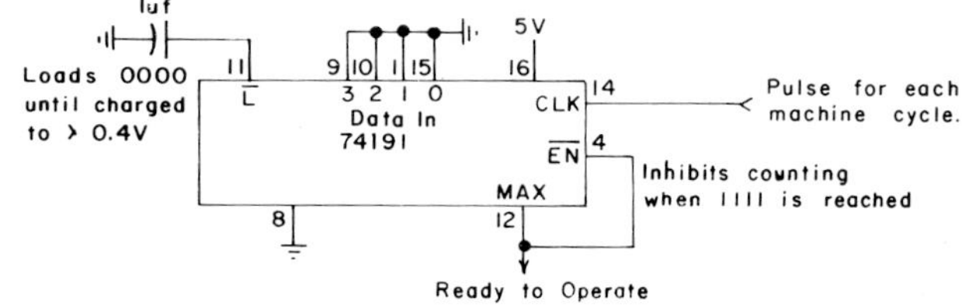

Fig. 24-19 Power-on counter.

zeros into the same counter. Current supplied by the L bar input will charge the capacitor, removing the LOAD signal. The counter then increments on each machine cycle until the maximum count is reached; the H on the MAX output then inhibits further counting, also serving as the ready-to-operate signal.

Counters are an extremely useful device for model railroad applications. Examples shown elsewhere in this book include the following:

1. Digital throttles, Fig. 16-14.
2. Turntable control, Figs. 13-29, 13-31.
3. Generation of Time Slots for a synchronous system, Fig. 24-20.
4. Recognition of synchronization interval, Fig. 24-33.
5. Block signal system, Figs. 15-48, 15-49, 15-56.

24.82 Synchronizers

In clocked systems, for the purpose of initially getting the system to run, and later for trouble shooting, it is desireable to admit clock pulses into the system one at a time or in bursts of a defined length. This is usually done by pressing a push button to admit the single pulse or to start the burst. To avoid malfunction, it is vital that the single clock pulse or the first pulse of a burst be of a full width. Some oscillators have enable inputs, see Fig. 24-46, which will start or stop the output pulses without shortening or lengthening a clock pulse. If an oscillator without this feature is employed, the use of a synchronizer as shown in Fig. 24-20 will assure that there is no splitting of a clock pulse. The constantly running clock output is applied to the IN input of the synchronizer. If the mode switch is set to RUN, L is applied to the mode input of the synchronizer and a constant stream of clock pulses appears on its output. If the mode switch is set to STEP, H is applied to the mode input and just one pulse will appear at the output of the synchronizer for each pressing and release of the STEP pushbutton. This pulse will be essentially the same width as that generated by the clock. In a particular case based on a computer cab control system, it was useful to generate a string of 16 pulses, called a cycle, to drive the cycle counter shown in Fig. 24-20 from 1111 (F) through its full count to stop again at 1111. When the mode switch is set on CYCLE, the H which appears on the MAX output of the counter will stop the count at 1111. Pressing the STEP button will index the counter to 0000. The MAX output will go low so the counter will be driven upwards again until it reaches 1111 and clock pulses cease, due to the H which is again developed by the MAX output.

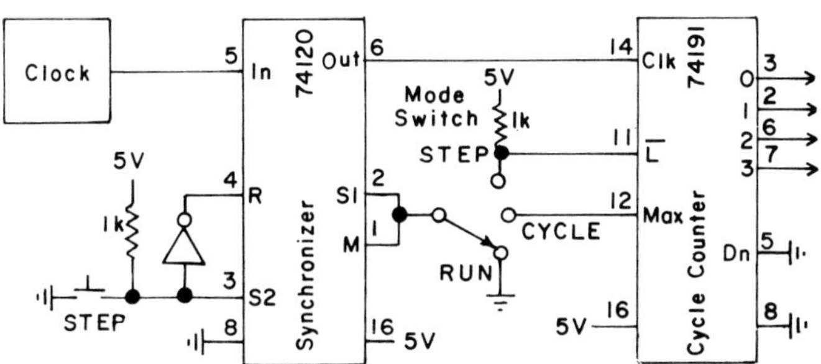

Fig. 24-20 Synchronizer.

24.83 Decoders

When used unmodified, a decoder is usually understood to be an IC which converts a binary input into one output L out of the total number of outputs. The term decoder is also used for any circuit which converts one code to another. The number of outputs depends upon the maximum number of combinations of the selecting input bits. For binary inputs, 2 inputs gives 4 possible outputs, 3 gives 8, and 4 gives 16. In the case of the 4-bit BCD code, there are only 10 outputs which have decimal significance.

Three different binary decoders are shown in Fig. 24-21, as well as the switch equivalent of each. The switch wiper is set to the position determined by the select inputs of the decoder. All outputs will be H except for the output selected. Even the selected output will be H unless the decoder is enabled (strobed, gated). Depending upon the manufacturer, the enable inputs may be labeled E, S, or G. As can be seen for the 74LS138, some enable inputs may be active H and others active L. The decoders shown in the figure must have all their enable inputs active in order to make a selection on the outputs.

A common use of a decoder is to decode the binary output of a counter into one-out-of-n. In Fig. 24-22 the clock decoders of a computer cab-control system are shown, and in Fig. 15-56 those of a

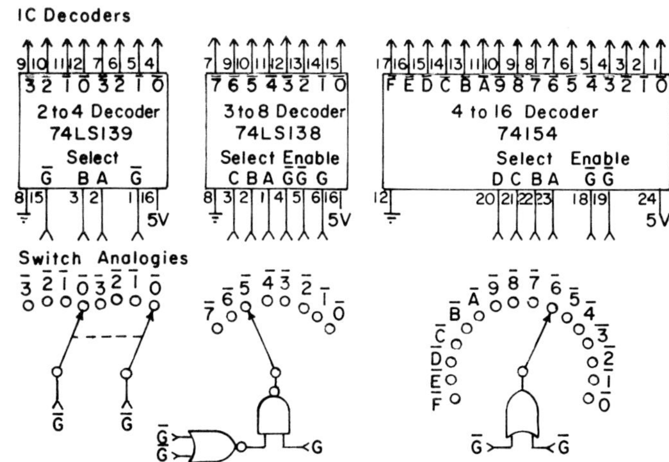

Fig. 24-21 Decoders.

block-signal system are shown. The 1MHz clock drives an 8-bit counter which is divided into four memory-count bits and four cycle-count bits. The 4-bit memory count is decoded into 16 (0 to F Hex) memory slots. Its outputs are used by the CPU (central processing unit) to process information to and from the memories. The 4-bit cycle count is decoded into 16 (0 to F) time slots, sometimes called phases. These are the basic timing intervals of the system.

In synchronous systems, it is useful to have a strobe pulse available near the center of each time slot. Such strobe pulses are generated by the strobe decoder of Fig. 24-22. Its select inputs are driven by the cycle counter so its outputs are selected in phase with the outputs of the cycle decoder. The strobe decoder is only enabled when the 8 output of the memory decoder is selected, thus the selected strobe output goes L only for the duration of memory slot 8, this slot appearing at the midpoint of each time slot.

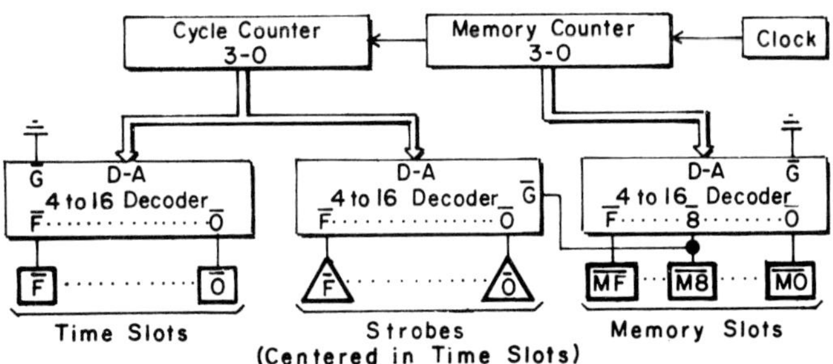

Fig. 24-22 Decoding of the clock.

It may be necessary to decode more than four binary bits, an example is in the I/O Unit shown at the bottom of Fig. 25-14. If this is so, some of the bits to be decoded can be applied as the select inputs to a first-rank decoder, as shown in Fig. 24-23, and the remaining bits as inputs to all of the second-rank decoders. Only the selected output of the enabled decoder will be L.

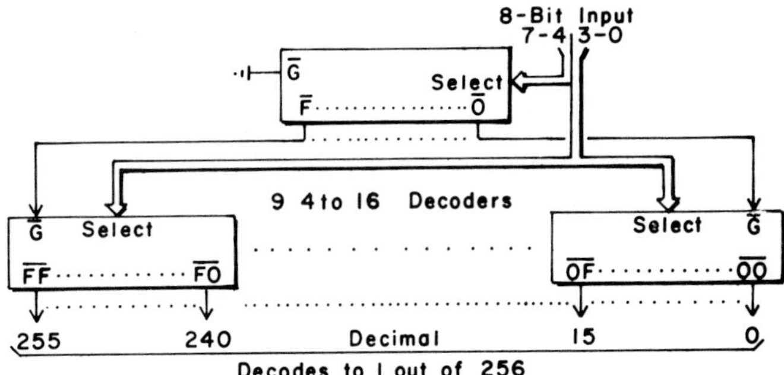

Fig. 24-23 Two-stage decoding.

When the full capability of an IC is not required for a single function, it may be possible to utilize the IC to perform more than one task. An example taken from a computer cab control system is given in Fig. 24-24. In that system when a cab was first turned on, four initializing digits had to be entered from the cab. After the cab was initialized, it was necessary to keep track of whether one, two, or

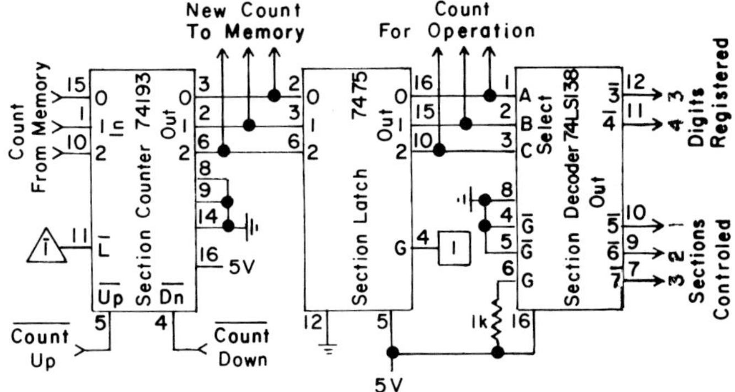

Fig. 24-24 Dual-purpose counting and decoding.

three sections were under its control. Since counting the initializing digits was always completed before it became necessary to keep track of sections, both jobs could be combined in the 3-bit section counter of the figure. The section count stored in memory for that cab was loaded into the section counter by the strobe pulse of time slot 1. Since the section counter would be incremented if necessary to register another digit, or either incremented or decremented if the number of sections under control of that cab were changed, the initial count was latched into the section latch at the end of time slot 1. If the section counter then was incremented or decremented, its new count was written into memory during time slot F. The original count held in the latch continued to be available for system use and was decoded by the section decoder. Note that the 0, 1, and 2 outputs of the decoder are not used. It is often the case that all outputs are not required. As a general rule, if more than one combination of inputs is to be decoded, it is better to use a decoder than gates.

Decoders can serve as demultiplexers; demultiplexer is, in fact, another name for a decoder. This use of decoders is covered in Section 24.85, multiplexing, see Fig. 24-32.

In addition to the general-purpose binary or BCD to 1-out-of-n decoders described so far, IC decoders are available to decode one type of code into another. These types of decoders may also be called converters or translators. One application is decoding binary or BCD codes into special codes used to illuminate displays. A decoder converting BCD into the code to generate the digits 0 to 9 using 7-segment displays is shown in Fig. 24-25. There are IC decoders available for this BCD to 7-segment conversion, but which also include internal counters and latches. TTL examples include 74143 and 74144.

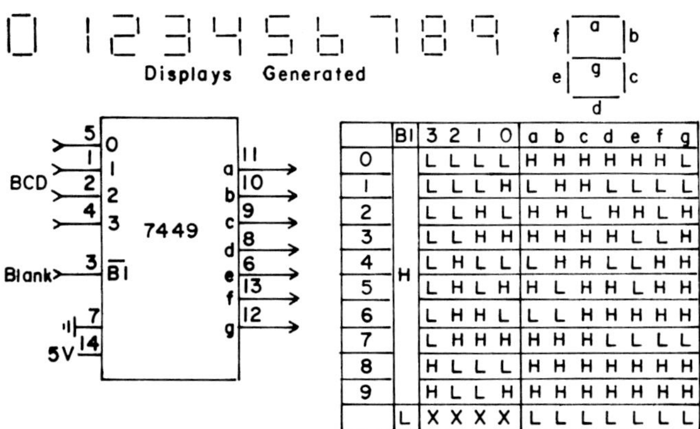

	BI	3 2 1 0	a b c d e f g
0	H	L L L L	H H H H H H L
1		L L L H	L H H L L L L
2		L L H L	H H L H H L H
3		L L H H	H H H H L L H
4		L H L L	L H H L L H H
5		L H L H	H L H H L H H
6		L H H L	L L H H H H H
7		L H H H	H H H L L L L
8		H L L L	H H H H H H H
9		H L L H	H H H H H H H
	L	X X X X	L L L L L L L

Fig. 24-25 BCD to 7-segment decoder.

Keep in mind that, if the decoding function required is one likely to be needed in many applications, there is an excellent chance it is available as a package. For example, ICs are available to convert BCD into binary (74184) and also binary into BCD (74185A).

24.84 Multiplexers

When used unmodified, multiplexer (Mux) is usually understood to be an IC which selects 1-out-of-n inputs to control its output, the selected input being determined by a binary select input. The number of selectable inputs depends upon the maximum number of combinations of the selecting binary code as follows: 1-bit select, 2 inputs; 2-bit select, 4 inputs; 3-bit select, 8 inputs; and 4-bit select, 16 inputs.

Five different Mux are shown in Fig. 24-26. Also shown is the switch equivalent of the three top ICs. The switch wiper is set to the position determined by the select inputs. If the Mux is not strobed (enabled, gated), H on the S bar input for all the Mux in the figure, all outputs will be false (L for Y, H for W) except in the case of the 74351. The latter has a 3-state outputs, all of its outputs will be high impedance when it is not strobed. When the Mux is strobed, the state of its output depends upon the state of the selected input, this is direct for a Y output, inverted for a W output.

A comparison of Figs. 24-21 and 24-26 shows that decoders and Mux are similar except that the signals pass through the devices in opposite directions. Nevertheless, Mux are more powerful logically than decoders.

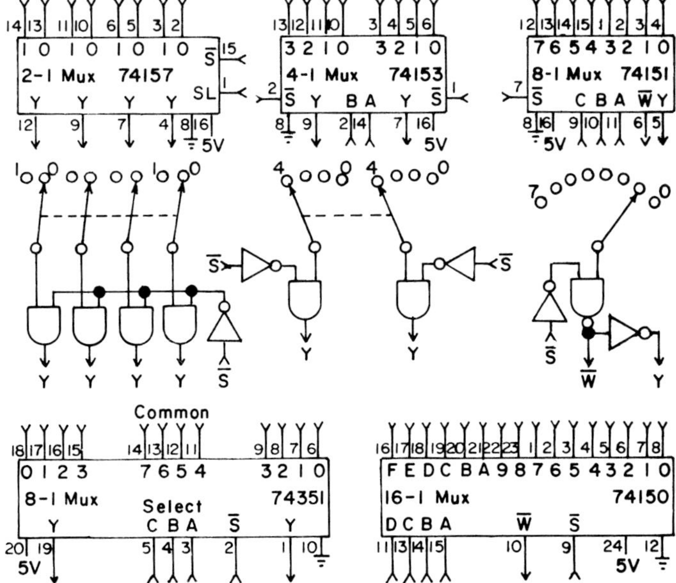

Fig. 24-26 Multiplexers.

Multiplexers can solve combinational-logic problems, often with a considerable saving of packages, interconnecting wiring, and design effort compared to using gates for the same function. Fig. 24-27 shows a comparison of a gate circuit and a Mux circuit for the same function. The savings of packages and wiring is obvious. The saving of design effort is not as clear, but the gate circuit requires the application of techniques to minimize the number of gates. Designing the Mux circuit only requires connecting three (any three) of the input variables to the select inputs of the Mux, and then determining one at a time what should be connected to each of the selected inputs of the Mux. If the function being performed is more complex than the one of the figure, even more gates may be required, but a single 8 to 1 Mux and a single inverter can solve any 4-input problem. A 16 to 1 Mux and one inverter can solve five inputs. A dual 4 to 1 and two inverters can solve two different 3-input functions provided two of the variables are common to both functions.

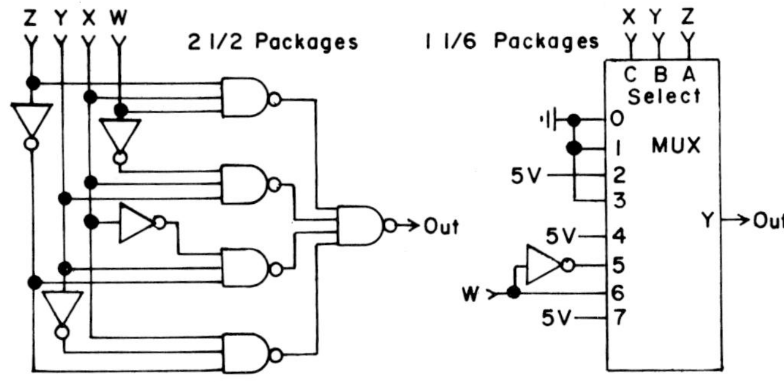

Fig. 24-27 Multiplexer vs. gates to solve a combinational logic problem.

The most usual application of a Mux is to select which of two or more sources of data are to be connected to the input of a using circuit. When applied in this manner, a Mux is often called a data selector. An example taken from the central processor of a computer cab control system is shown in Fig. 24-28. The section RAM of that figure stores the status information bits of each of the possible 1024 sections on the layout. During various periods of a cycle in which a cab is being served, the status information of the sections under control of that cab, and also the status of the next section on its route, must be made available. Multiplexers, one for each bit of the 10-bit section address, under control of the cycle count, select the section address which is to be connected as the address to the section RAM. Although there are 16 time slots in a cycle (O-F), since the addresses are selected for pairs of time slots (0-1, 2-3, etc.), only an 8-1 Mux is required. The zero bit of the cycle count is not used as a select input to this Mux. Examples of a Mux in a block-signal circuit can be seen in Fig. 15-57.

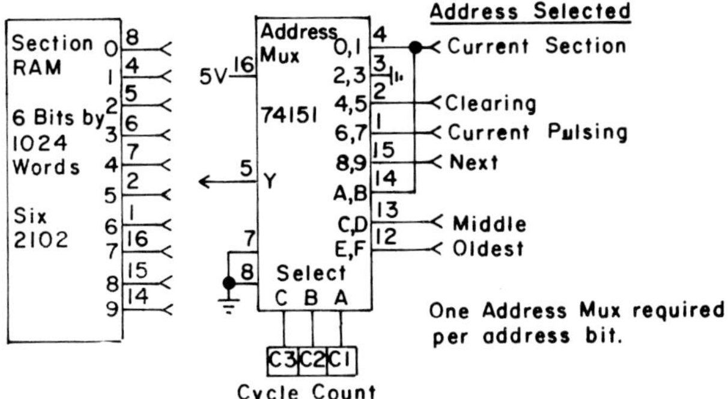

Fig. 24-28 Multiplexer as a data selector.

When the number of inputs to be selected exceeds the number available on the largest IC Mux, the Mux can be arranged in two stages as shown in Fig. 24-29. A possible application would be in the I/O unit for a microprocessor, see Fig. 25-14.

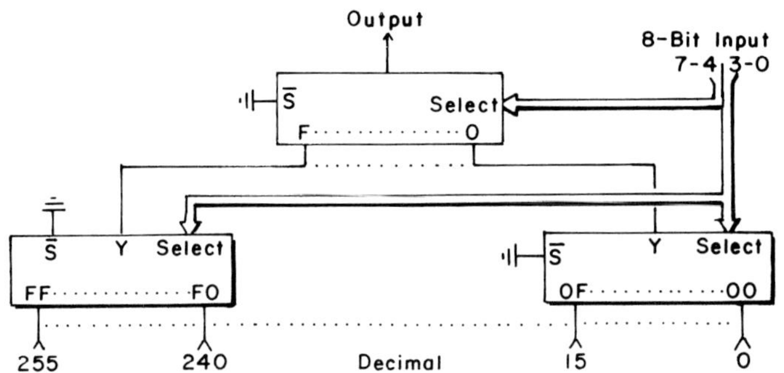

Fig. 24-29 Two-stage multiplexer.

In addition to using a Mux to select one of a multiplicity of inputs, it is possible to use either open-collector inputs or 3-state, also called tristate, outputs for the same purpose. The use of open collectors is shown in Fig. 24-30. In contrast with the conventional (totem-pole) output, which pulls up for a high or pulls down for a low, an open-collector output has only a pull-down transistor so its output is either a low or high-impedance. Therefore, several such IC outputs can be connected together, and to a common pull-up resistor to develop the system output. For multiplexing, only one of the ICs is enabled, in the case of Fig. 24-30 by time slots. The output of the enabled IC determines the system output. This type of multiplexing usually only has an advantage compared to using a multiplexer, when the selected inputs are physically separated. In this case, multiplexing the inputs to a single line may reduce wiring complexity. A 3-state output pulls up for a high, pulls down for a low, and has high impedance if its device is unselected. Most modern memories have 3-state outputs so two or more can be connected to the same output bus as shown in Fig. 24-31. When 3-state outputs are provided, they normally offer the most economical method of multiplexing.

An important class of ICs with 3-state outputs is that of line drivers, see Fig. 24-50.

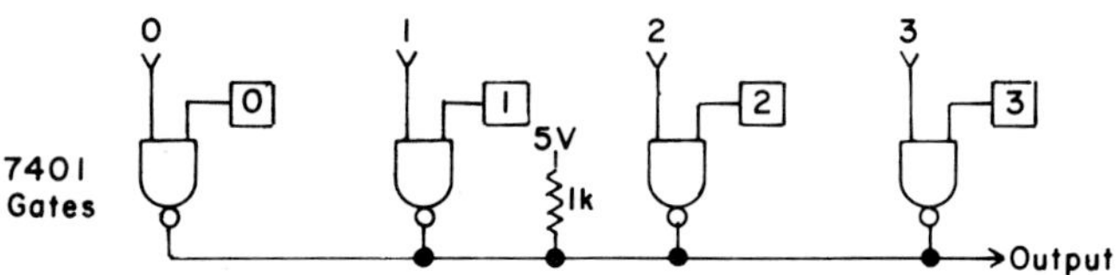

Fig. 24-30 Multiplexing using open collectors.

24.85 Multiplexing

Multiplexing is any means of sending several independent signals between two points. Signals can be sent over separate parallel

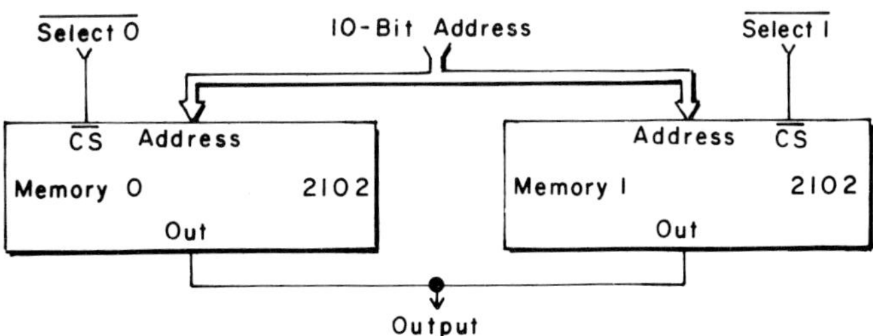

Fig. 24-31 Multiplexing using 3-stage outputs.

wires, (space-division multiplexing), as different frequencies (frequency-division multiplexing), or in successive intervals of time (time-division multiplexing). When used without a modifier, "multiplexing" normally (in this Handbook exclusively) means time-division multiplexing.

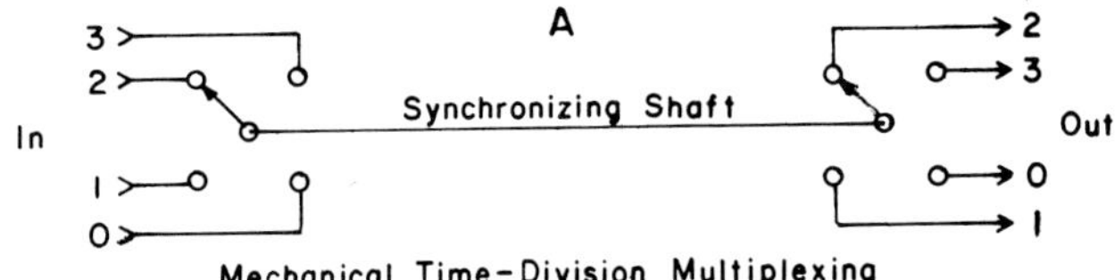

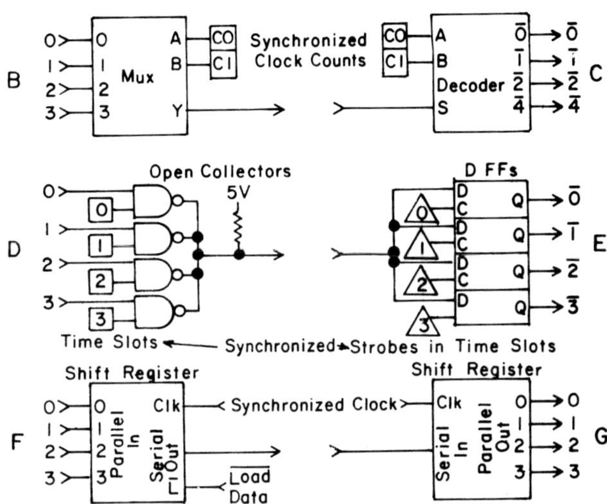

Fig. 24-32 Time division multiplexing.

A mechanical embodyment of multiplexing is shown at A in Fig. 24-32. Two wipers mounted at opposite ends of a rotating shaft establish, in sequence, connections between similarly-numbered inputs and outputs. The shaft could be replaced by a wire and the two wipers driven by synchronized motors to permit this method to be used over long distances. ICs now permit this multiplexing at the transmitting end, and demultiplexing at the receiving end, to be accomplished at high speeds both economically and reliably.

Three methods of multiplexing parallel inputs onto a line are shown in Fig. 24-32. At B a multiplexer selects the inputs in order, under control of a clock counter. At D the same function is performed by open-collector gates, under control of a decoded clock count; three-state outputs would serve as well. This method has advantages when the parallel inputs are separated in space or if the inputs are from various types of circuits. At F the parallel inputs are loaded into a shift register, then shifted onto the line under control of the clock. See section 24.86 for a description of shift-register operation.

When the series of pulses are received at the opposite end of the line, they must be assigned to their corresponding parallel outputs. At C a decoder controlled by a clock counter synchronized with the transmitting clock develops an inverted pulse on the corresponding output lead, this pulse is developed only during the time slot of the selection of that bit. When used in this manner, a decoder is often called a demultiplexer. See section 24.83 for a description of decoder action.

For an output level to be developed instead of a pulse of one time-slot duration, the incoming pulses can be latched into flip-flops (FFs) as shown at E, under control of a decoded clock counter synchronized with the transmitting clock. ICs which include several FFs and internal decoding are available. In TTL, the 74259 with 8 latches is an example.

For greater economy, if the parallel outputs are not needed immediately following the reception of each bit, this method can be applied by writing the bits as received into a memory.

As shown at G, the incoming bits can be clocked into a shift register (Fig. 22-34) by a clock which is synchronized with the transmitting clock. This method makes the parallel outputs available as levels instead of pulses, but it is necessary to wait until all the bits are clocked in before those levels can be utilized.

All of the time-division multiplexing methods require that the receiving circuit be synchronized with the transmitting circuit, so that the time interval in which a bit of information is received is precisely known. In a physically small system such as the multiplexed block-signal system shown in Fig. 15-53, no problem exists since the same clock counter and time-slot decoder can be used by all circuits involved. When the distance between transmitter and receiver is great enough to make the use of a common counter and decoder impractical, or when the transmission path is limited, for example the two rails to a locomotive, it is necessary to generate synchronized timing information at the receiving end. Many synchronizing methods have been used commercially, based on synchronizing a free-running oscillator at the receiving end to the master oscillator at the transmitting end. In model railroading, the most-successful approach has been to transmit the clock pulses from the transmitting end and to provide a method of synchronizing the clock counter at the receiving end. Two methods of synchronization for digital command control are shown in Fig. 17-4. In both cases, each clock pulse is transmitted over the rails. In the top example the clock counter is initialized when an interval is detected in which no clock pulses appear. In the bottom example, the clock counter is initialized when the A-C track power reverses polarity.

Unless constrained to use just one line, it is much easier to supply a separate clock line rather than transmitting clock and signals over the same line. A third line could be added to transmit a synchronizing signal, but adding a counter and controlling the pulses on the data and on the clock line is an economical method of obtaining synchronization. Fig. 24-33 shows the circuit used for synchronization in a computer cab control system. A separate clock line is used. Every clock pulse received clears (sets to zero) the reset counter. Therefore, regardless of the stagger between the data pulses and the clock pulses, as long as clock pulses are applied regularly the reset counter can never reach a count greater than one. During the synchronizing interval 8 clock pulses are suppressed on the clock line and at least 4 clock pulses sent in their place on the data line. These data-line pulses cause the reset counter to count to at least 100 (binary). The high on the No. 2 bit is the synchronizing signal which forces the receiving circuit to the correct synchronized state, ready to receive clock-line pulses when they are resumed at the termination of the synchronizing interval. In the particular system from which this example is taken, additional synchronizing information is required from the sending end. This information is sent by adding one, two, or three pulses (see Fig. 24-33) on the data line. These pulses are counted by the reset counter, and the resulting count is latched into the information latch for use after clock pulses resume.

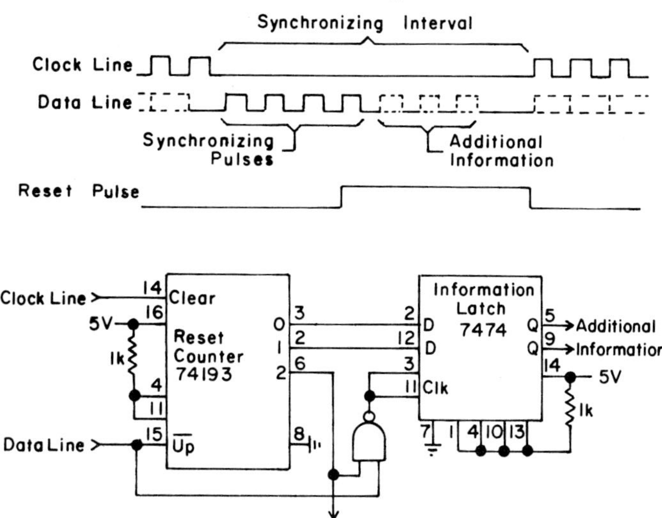

Fig. 24-33 Synchronizing counter.

Although a synchronizing interval can be detected by timing a period when no pulses appear, a method such as that shown in Fig. 24-33, which counts pulses during the synchronization interval, permits the system to operate at any clock rate. This is useful for getting the system into operation and for trouble shooting. Timing the interval requires the normal clock rate for proper operation.

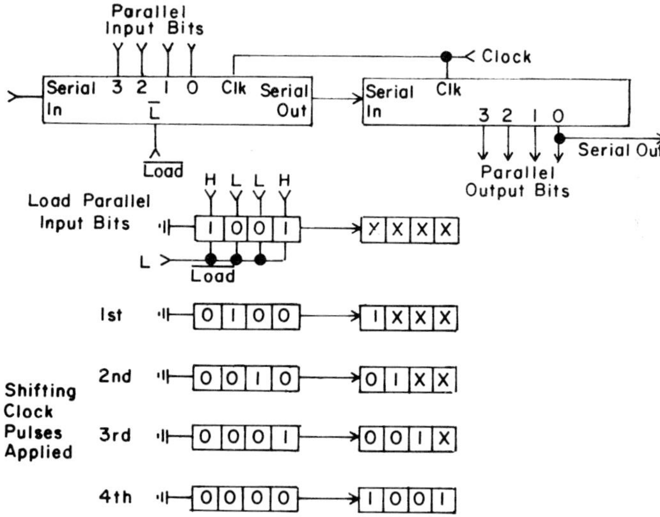

Fig. 24-34 Shift register operation.

24.86 Shift Registers

Available shift register packages contain four or more FFs which are internally connected. When a clock pulse is applied, the state of one FF will be copied by the FF to its right when shifting right, or to its left when shifting left. Fig. 24-34 diagrammatically shows two 4-bit shift registers shifting right. The shift register on the left has four parallel inputs. When the active-low load input is taken low, the levels applied to the parallel inputs force the internal FFs into the appropriate set or reset state. The serial out is the Q output of the right-most FF.

After the load input returns to inactive, a clock pulse applied to the shift registers will cause all FFs in both shift registers to copy the state of the FF to their left. After four clock pulses are received, the states originally loaded into the left shift register appear in the same order in the right shift register. Since the serial input to the left shift register is grounded, zeros are shifted into that register by each clock pulse.

Due to limitations of package pins, commercial shift registers with either parallel inputs or parallel outputs are usually limited to eight bits. Longer registers can be assembled merely by connecting the serial out of one shift register to the serial in of the next, a connection shown in Fig. 24-34. As shown in Fig. 24-35, shift registers with both parallel in and parallel out are available. This particular shift register is reversible, it can shift either right or left.

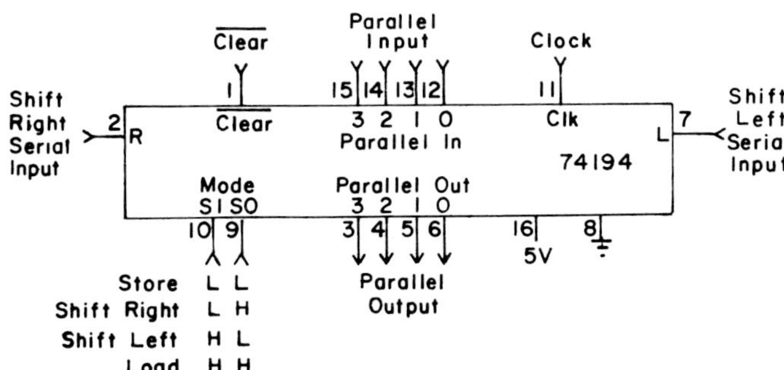

Fig. 24-35 Reversible shift register.

Since shift registers can convert serial inputs to parallel outputs or vice versa, they are well suited to multiplexing, see Fig. 24-32 F and G. They also can be used to multiply or divide by 2 for each shift pulse: 0001 (decimal 1) shifted left is 0010 (decimal 2), 0110 (decimal 6) shifted right is 0011 (decimal 3).

When serial information is to be stored for later serial retrieval, only serial inputs and outputs are provided. Very long shift registers of this type are available.

By connecting the serial out to the serial in of the same shift register, it is possible to rotate the bits; the left-most bit becomes the right-most bit. This is useful primarily for lining up data for the purpose of comparing the states of one or more bits. Applications of shift registers are shown in Figs. 15-58, 16-15, and 24-38.

24.87 Memories

Nothing has been more important to the success of modern electronic systems than the development of low-cost, high-speed, physically-small, low-power memories. Prior to 1974, the cost of memory was too high for it to be used in model railroading as a substitute for logic circuits. The largest memory in a single package at affordable prices was only of 256 bits. By 1981 memories of 4,096 bits were readily available, those of 64k bits were apparently soon to be available and work was progressing on packages with millions of bits. Because memory can always be substituted for logic, the advantages of having large memories available are reducing circuit complexity for the same function compared to previous methods, and making practical functions which were too costly or too complex to be implemented by previous techniques. See Figs. 15-65 and 15-66 for interlocking examples, and Fig. 16-14 for use with a digital throttle.

Some of the small memories, 16 bits for example, are implemented by TTL, a high-power technique. An example is given in Fig. 15-58. Large memories utilize low-power technology, such as CMOS, but often have TTL-compatable inputs and outputs so they can be designed into a system as though they were TTL. A static memory will store data with only DC applied to its terminals. A refresh memory requires the constant application of refresh pulses. For large memories, the refresh type is less costly but it is unlikely that their increased complexity of operation can be justified by lower first cost. Only static memories are covered in this Handbook.

Of the several types of memory available, the two of greatest importance are RAM (this stands for random-access memory but really means random-access read-write memory) and ROM (read-only memory, usually also random access). PROM (programmable read-only memory) differs from ROM only in that its contents can be changed, usually by some procedure external to the circuit in which it is used. The most inhibiting factor in the use of a ROM by a modeler is the problem of getting it coded. If the read-mostly memories ever reach the stage of being readily available at affordable prices, it will be a great boon to the hobby since their contents can be changed by circuit action yet they can serve as ROMs. Examples of PROMs to control signals is given in Figs. 15-65 and 15-66.

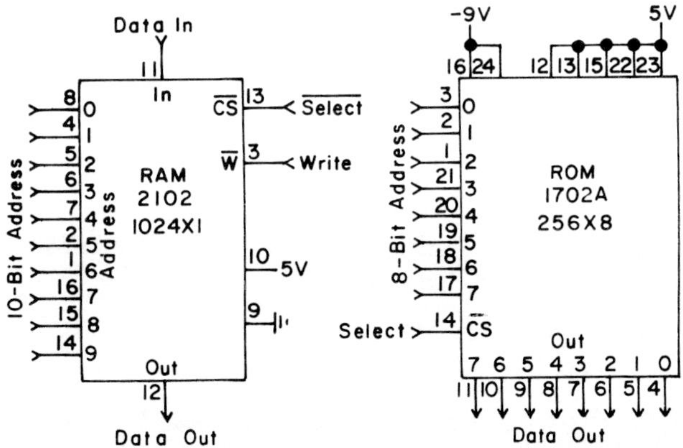

Fig. 24-36 RAM and ROM memories.

In Fig. 24-36 are shown an examples of a RAM and of a ROM. This particular ROM is a PROM which can be erased by exposure to ultraviolet light, and recoded. Both have 3-state outputs, the outputs are in their high-impedance state unless CS (chip select) is L.

Memories are known by the number of addressable words and the number of bits in each word. The RAM of Fig. 24-36 has ten address bits to access 1024 words, each word has just one bit, a 1024 by 1 memory. The ROM has only eight address bits and so has only 256 words, but each word has 8 bits, a 256 by 8 memory. When the package is enabled (CS bar L), the state of the bit(s) of the word addressed appears on the output lead(s). In the case of the RAM, when enabled and when a write pulse is applied, the state applied to the IN input will be written into the bit selected by the address input. It is necessary to consult the specification sheet for the particular RAM to determine the timing requirements for writing into that memory.

To minimize costs, memory organization (how the memories are arranged) is very important. Not only must the cost of the memories themselves be minimized but also the cost of the surrounding circuitry. As a general rule, the cost of the memory packages is likely to be lowest if the largest available memory devices suitable for the task are chosen and fully utilized. The cost of the surrounding circuitry is lowest when the outputs and the inputs to the memory packages make data handling simple. Fig. 24-37 shows how a change from parallel to serial-parallel organization for the cab RAM of a computer cab control system significantly reduces costs.

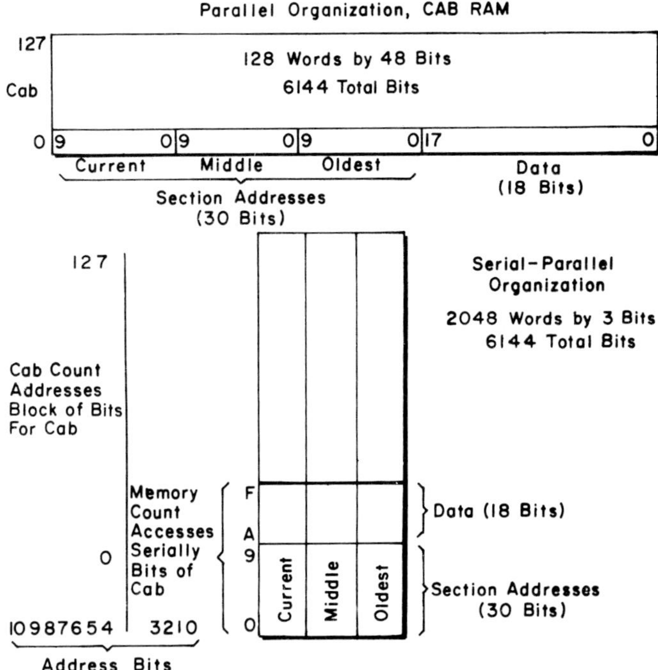

Fig. 24-37 Memory organization.

The cab RAM stores all the information which pertains to each of the maximum of 128 cabs of the system. Since all bits of the 48-bit word must be available in parallel, during the design phase it is easiest to think of this memory as being 128 words of 48 bits each, as shown at the top of Fig. 24-37. This organization requires many memory packages. Furthermore, during operation it is often necessary to transfer section addresses between two of the address locations. For example, when the cab reverses, the current section address (the previous head end of the train) must be interchanged with the oldest section address, previous rear of train, as well as to copy addresses as sections are released. Such transferring and copying requires handling all ten address bits in parallel, representing many multiplexers and registers for intermediate storage.

The organization actually constructed was the serial-parallel form shown at the bottom of Fig. 24-37. The 6144 total bits required exactly fill three 2048 by 1 memories so the cost of the memory packages has been minimized. Equally important is that the corresponding bits of each of the three section addresses appear at the outputs of the memories simultaneously, so to interchange or to copy addresses only one bit at a time need be handled by the multiplexers and intermediate storage. It was already known that a 16us time slot was short enough to meet operating speed requirements. By using a 1MHz clock, 1us memory slots were generated within each time slot, ample for modern memories for accessing, reading and writing.

Because the information now appears as three strings of pulses of 16 bits each, to make the information available in parallel form, the serial outputs are shifted into shift registers during the appropriate time slots. This equipment is shown in Fig. 24-38. These shift registers also shift addresses into the appropriate sections of the memory, under control of the transfer mux when section information must be written. They, therefore, also fulfill the role for which intermediate storage was required for parallel information. For data bits to be written, since they appear in parallel form, the three Mux at the top of the figure must be supplied for serialization. Nevertheless the number of packages surrounding the serial-parallel organized memory is considerably less than the number which would have been required for a parallel organization memory. This also applies to some detailed circuit operations not shown in Fig. 24-38. One of these, incrementing the section addresses for the housekeeping cab, is shown in Fig. 24-42.

The memories shown thus far require addressing the word to be read or written. When it is possible to design so that the word to be read is always the last that was written (last-in, first-out), an auto-

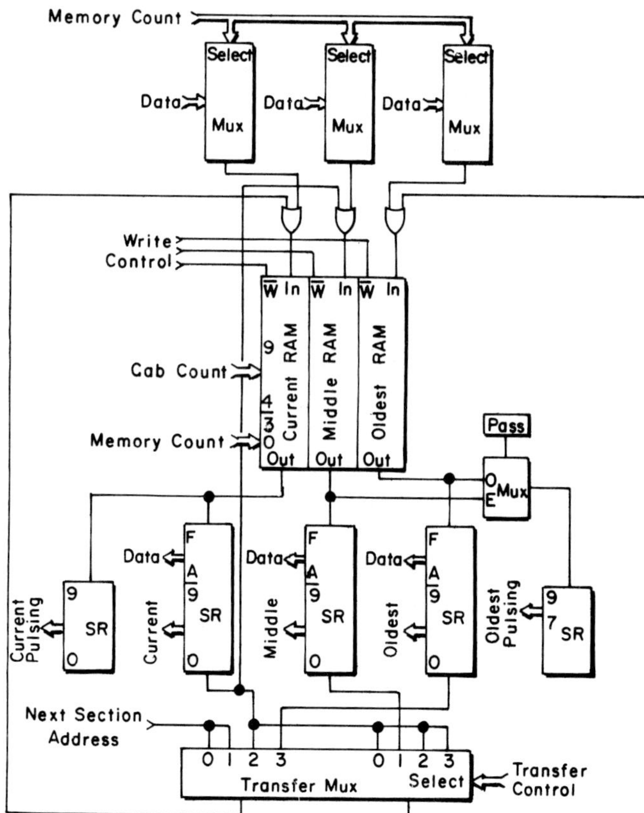

Fig. 24-38 Example of memory system.

matic addressing memory called a "stack" can be used. An example is given in Fig. 24-39. Every time a write pulse is received, the input data is written into the memory. At the end of the write pulse the address counter is incremented, making the next word in memory available for writing. To read the memory a read pulse is applied whose trailing edge decrements the counter; the most-recently written word is addressed and its contents appear on the out leads of the memory. An example of a memory in a multiplexed block-signal system can be found in Fig. 15-58.

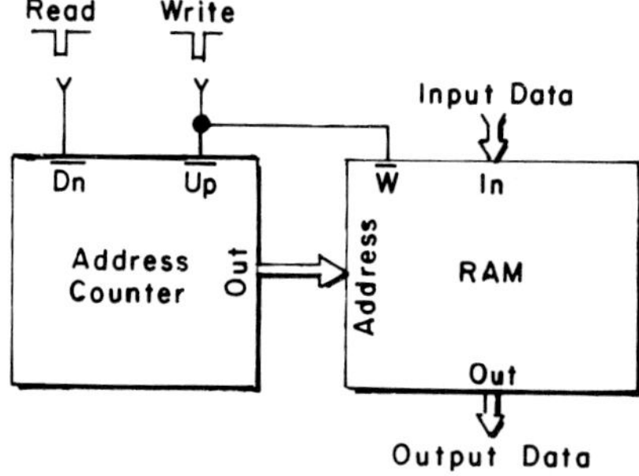

Fig. 24-39 Stack (Last-in, First-out) memory.

24.88 Addition, Subtraction, Multiplication, Division

Although modelers are more interested in control-type circuits than in number crunchers, it is not uncommon to need an arithmetical function in a processor, particularly adding and subtracting. ICs are available for performing these functions. Even in a microprocessor system which can add under program control, when only the sum of two inputs is needed and not the inputs themselves, program simplification may justify including a hardware adder, see Fig. 25-9.

IC adders are available which can add two 4-bit parallel inputs producing the sum, including the carry bit. These adders can be cascaded to sum words of more than 4 bits. An application of such adders, taken from a computer cab control system, is shown in Fig. 24-40. The lowest next section address of all the possible sections in the direction of movement of the train is obtained from the next section ROM. A 4-bit route code received from the tower contains either the information that there is no next section, no route through switches, section ends in a bumping post, or the amount that must be added to the lowest next section address to obtain the actual next section

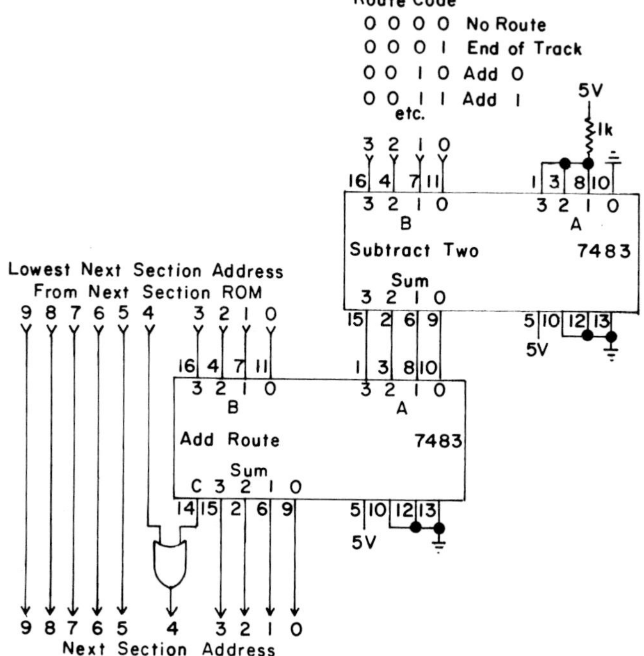

Fig. 24-40 Adders.

address on the route of the train. As can be seen at the upper right of the figure, route code 2 is "add zero". Therefore to obtain the proper addition, it is first necessary to subtract 2 from the route code. Since the 7483 only adds, the 2's complement of 2 is applied as the A input. To obtain the 2's complement, invert every bit, then add 1. Using 2 (0010) as an example, inverting yields 1101 and adding 1 gives 1110, the 2's complement.

The sum from the subtract two IC then is added to the least-significant 4 bits from the next section ROM. Since the 4 bits from the ROM must be zero if there is a possibility of a carry, the 4 bits and the carry from the add route IC are ORed. Examples of adders in a block-signal system can be found in Figs. 15-57 and 15-58.

More powerful ICs are available which can either add or subtract. An ALU (arithmetic-logic unit) is shown in Fig. 24-41. Whether the A and B inputs are to be added or subtracted depends

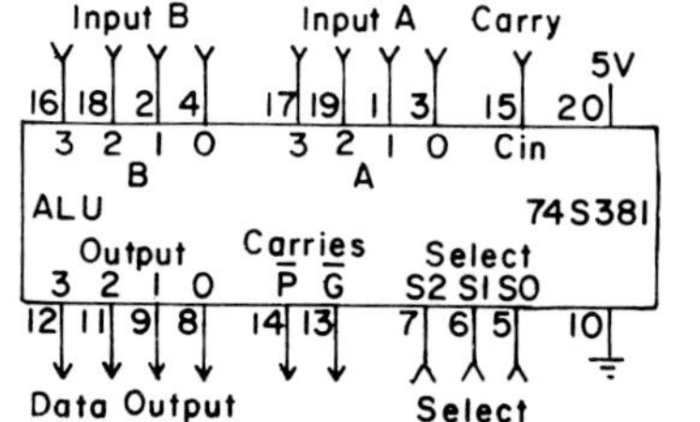

S2	S1	S0	Operation
L	L	L	Clear
L	L	H	B − A
L	H	L	A − B
L	H	H	A + B
H	L	L	A XOR B
H	L	H	A OR B
H	H	L	A AND B
H	H	H	Preset

Fig. 24-41 Arithmetic-Logic Unit (ALU).

upon the levels applied to the select inputs. Logical operations can also be performed on a bit-by-bit basis as shown by the table in the figure. More powerful ALU ICs than this one are available as well as ICs which can add, subtract, and shift either right or left.

When the bits to be added are in serial form, it is only necessary to add one bit at a time from each word together in a full adder, storing the carry bit in an FF for use when the two next more-significant bits are to be added. The special case of adding 1 to a serial word (incrementing), is shown in Fig. 24-42. This circuit is taken from a computer cab control system having the memory organization shown in Fig. 24-38. That system has a "housekeeping" cab, cab 6F, which accesses each section in turn to bring its status information up to date. For successive accessing, the section addresses stored in the cab RAM for cab 6F are incremented each time that cab is served. For this, when cab 6F is being served, during time slot 5 the D FF of Fig. 24-42 is preset. The high output of this FF will cause each bit of the previous section address to be inverted until the first bit in the zero state is received. That bit will be inverted and written into the cab RAM but immediately following the writing operation the FF will be clocked. Since its D input is now low, the FF resets and the remaining address bits will not be inverted. Since the FF will not be reset if the old address is all ones, it is reset in the following time slot 3.

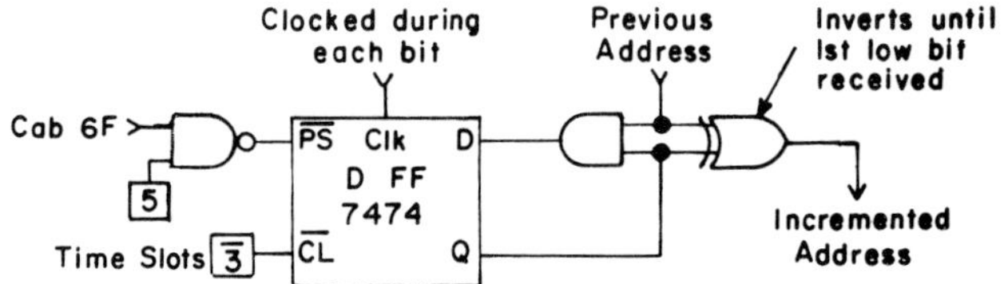

Fig. 24-42 Incrementing a serial word.

For multiplication or division by 2, as described in section 24.86, the binary number can be loaded into a shift register and shifted. Shift left for multiplication and right for division. Parallel binary multipliers and dividers were available by 1981. Most were of technologies other than TTL to reduce power dissipation. Chips designed for use in calculators also can be used but tend to be slow.

24.89 Comparators

Frequently the function of comparing two binary numbers is required. Often it is sufficient to determine whether or not the two numbers are equal, but sometimes it is necessary to know which number is larger. Parallel comparators are available as illustrated in Fig. 24-43, for comparing two 8-bit numbers. More packages can be cascaded if the numbers are of more than 8 bits.

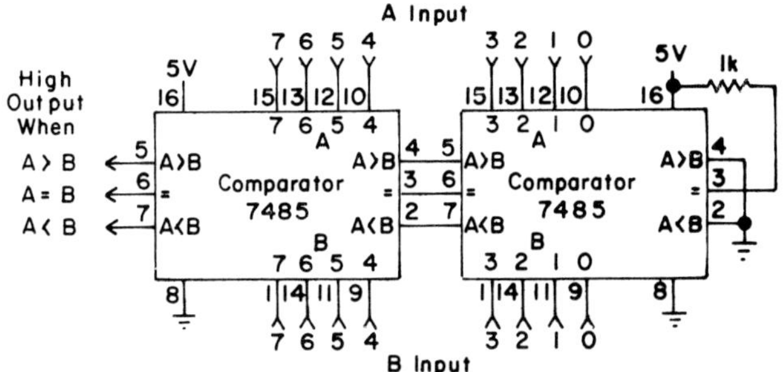

Fig. 24-43 Comparing two binary numbers.

Two model-railroad applications of comparators are to check the validity of data, see Fig. 24-45, and to determine whether or not a turntable has lined itself with the selected track, see Fig. 13-27.

24.90 Checking

When data is transmitted from one point to another there is a possibility that an error will be made. If that error is self-correcting the possibility of error can be ignored. (An example is an error which turns a signal red for a few miliseconds but regains its correct aspect the next time the data is transmitted.) Should the error result in wrong information to a memory or similar device, often the system cannot recover without human intervention. In such cases checking for an error should be considered. When an error has been detected in most model-railroad applications, operation based on the false transmission is blocked, the system awaits the reception of true information.

The key to any checking is redundancy; more bits must be sent than are necessary for the information. The easiest methods of adding the requisite redundancy are either to send an extra bit called the parity bit, indicating whether the number of "1" bits sent is even or odd, or to check that two successive transmissions are identical.

IC parity generator/parity checker packages are available as shown in Fig. 24-44. The 74L5280 is used both as a generator and as a checker. With the wiring indicated, the number of 1 bits in the 9-bit word to be transmitted, including the parity bit, is even. Therefore if an odd number of 1 bits are received, an error signal develops.

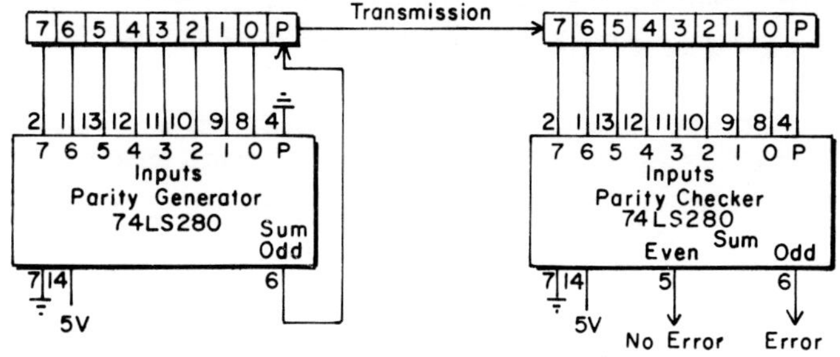

Fig. 24-44 Parity.

Checking that two successive transmissions are alike is shown in Fig. 24-45. Each time a particular piece of information is received, it is compared with the information received the previous time and stored in memory. If they are the same, a no-error signal is generated. Whether or not they are the same, the new information is then written into the memory for use the next time that data is received.

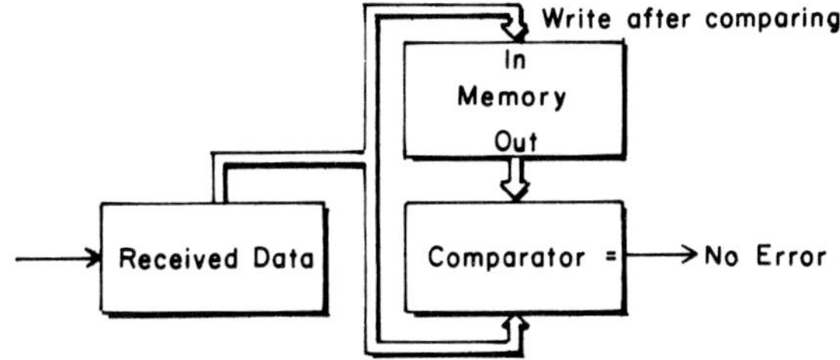

Fig. 24-45 Checking by comparison.

The choice between the two checking schemes above depends upon which is the more economical. Both may be used in the same system, for example in a computer cab control system. Direction sent from the central processor to the section circuit is critical information because even a momentary reversal of the motor may be noticeable. Therefore, in the system being used for the example, direction is always transmitted as two bits of opposite state. One of these bits may be regarded as the parity bit, making the number of one's received odd. If the received data does not check, the direction command received is ignored and no change is made in the polarity of voltage applied to the rails. This method is used to avoid providing memory for checking at the section circuits. For critical information sent from the section circuits to the central processor, such as the route code shown in Fig. 24-40, the comparison check is made because it is cheaper to provide extra bits in the cab RAM since there is only one such memory, see Fig. 24-38, than to provide parity generators at the many section circuits.

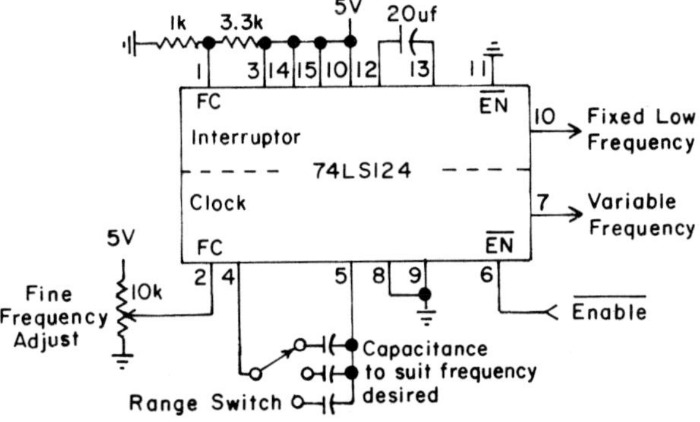

Fig. 24-46 Voltage-controlled oscillator.

24.9 INTEGRATED ANALOG (LINEAR) CIRCUITS

Analog systems make extensive use of linear amplifiers and of amplifiers which can perform operations such as integration, comparators, and timers. Even digital systems require some analog circuits. Specific applications of linear circuits in synchronous digital systems are oscillators for clocks and interruptors, line drivers and line receivers, I/O (input/output), and some timers. Asynchronous digital systems particularly tend to employ timers. When these types of linear circuits are manufactured for general purpose they are cataloged as linear ICs. Some are intended primarily for use with a specific logic family and are cataloged as part of that digital logic family. The 74-series circuits used for some of the illustrations in this section are so cataloged. All linear ICs, whether cataloged with a digital-logic family or as general-purpose, are covered in this chapter.

24.91 Clocks, Oscillators, and Interruptors

An oscillator is a free-running device which generates a repetitive, stable waveform. The oscillator of greatest interest today is one of alternating logic levels. If these alternating high and low levels are of approximately equal duration, it is often called a "square-wave" oscillator. A logic-level oscillator used to control a synchronous system is called a "clock". An oscillator of the same type, but used to generate flashing signals rather than for synchronication, is often called an "interrupter". Although "clock" and "interrupter" are really uses of an oscillator, these terms are commonly employed as the names for the devices performing those functions. An example of an interrupter driving a crossing flasher is given in Fig. 15-62.

An oscillator designed for use with TTL logic is shown in Fig. 24-46. As is the case with many IC oscillators, there are two independent oscillators in a single package. Such dual oscillators are well-suited for systems requiring a clock with a frequency which can be adjusted for testing, and also a constantly-running low-frequency interrupter so flashing signals will be unchanged and recognizable even at slow clock rates. Commonly, as indicated for the clock oscillator in Fig. 24-46, the timing capacitor is selectable by a range switch from the smallest capacitor which produces the normal operating rate of the clock, to the largest capacitor which produces a clock rate readily discernable by the visual indicators on the test panel. The particular oscillator shown is voltage-controlled, a variable voltage applied to the appropriate input can adjust the frequency over a considerable range. This is a convenient feature. The 74LS124 also has an enable input which permits the clock output to be stopped or started without splitting a pulse, see Section 24.82.

The 74LS124, being intended for use with TTL, uses only a single power source of 5V, the same as TTL. Many oscillators require other voltages, some even two different voltages. This presents a problem unless those other voltages are supplied for other reasons.

24.92 Timers

As a general rule linear timers should not be included in synchronous systems. It is almost always better to generate timing intervals by counting the clock, using the decoded clock to set and reset a FF, or by some other means controlled by the clock. Such methods not only are always synchronized with the clock, but also the interval generated is adjusted appropriately if the clock rate is changed. Nevertheless, there are some applications for linear timers in synchronous systems. An important application is when an interval shorter than any available from the clock must be generated. For example the memories of Fig. 24-38 require a 400ns write pulse delayed 200ns from the 1MHz clock. Two linear timers are used for this purpose, the first is triggered by the clock to generate the 200ns delay, the second triggered by the first at the end of the delay; the output of the second is the 400ns write pulse. Another important application is when synchronization of a remote unit is obtained by recognizing an interval when clock pulses are not received.

Timers are also known by other names such as one-shots and unistable-multivibrators. The most important classes of timers for model-railroad applications are "non-retriggerable" and "retriggerable". As shown on the left in Fig. 24-47, for a non-retriggerable timer the timing interval, of duration T in the figure, is started by the first trigger pulse. This timing interval expires after the designed interval whether or not additional trigger pulses are applied during the interval. The timing interval for a retriggerable timer, right, Fig. 24-47, also starts with the first trigger pulse, but if another trigger pulse is received before the timing interval expires, the timing interval will be extended for the designed time after that second trigger.

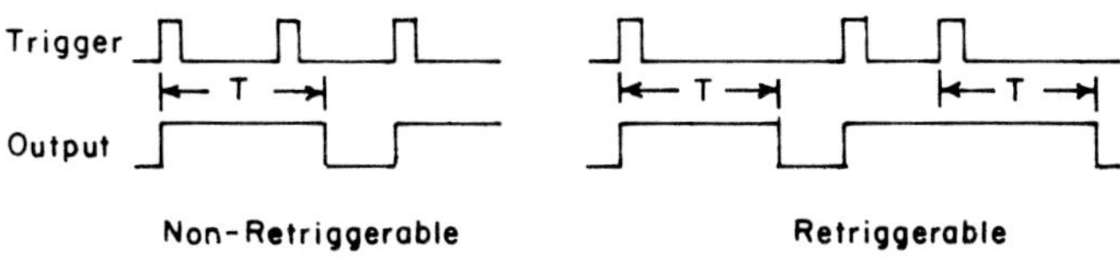

Fig. 24-47 Timer types.

There are many different IC timers on the market, some have a recovery-time problem. If they are triggered again shortly after their timing period expires, their next timing interval may be distinctly different than designed, usually shorter. This same problem occurs in some retriggerable timers; the timing interval extending after a re-trigger may be distinctly different from that designed. The specification sheets on timers seldom provide recovery-time information. Fortunately, in most applications in synchronous systems, recovery is of no importance.

Generally IC timers require an external timing capacitor, some require one or two external timing resistors. These external components determine the timing interval. For times in excess of 1ms, timers consisting of an internal oscillator driving an internal counter are the best since they offer the least variation in their timing intervals and are virtually impervious to electrical noise.

Timers are very useful for inputs to synchronous systems and in asynchronous systems. The debounce timer shown in Fig. 24-48 is an example. This figure shows the repeated openings and closings (bouncing) which occur when almost any type of a mechanical contact is closed. If the circuit to which such an input is applied is capable of responding to the bounces as if it were a succession of pushes of the push button, an error may occur. A solution is to apply the push button output as a trigger to a retriggerable timer whose interval is longer than the longest time between bounces. The timer output then will start with the first closure of the contact and produce a single output pulse extending beyond the last bounce. An application of this type is shown in Fig. 13-26. If the trigger inputs in Fig. 24-48 were clock pulses rather than contact bounces, the timer output going low would indicate clock pulses had stopped for the interval of the timer to provide a synchronization signal.

The trigger used in Fig. 24-48 is a negative-going edge. The timer shown has the capability of being triggered by either a positive- or negative-going edge as selected.

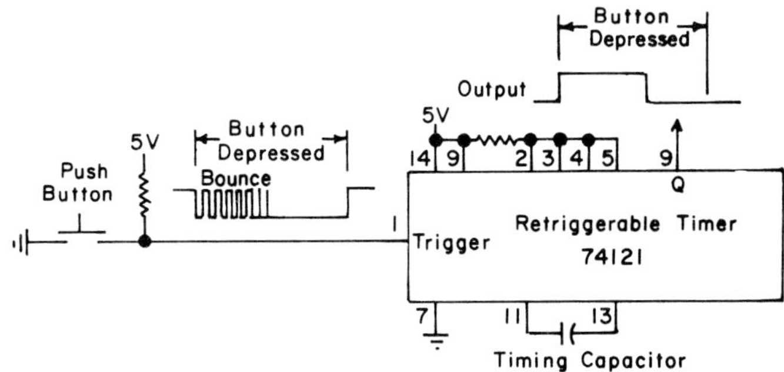

Fig. 24-48 Timer used for debouncing.

If only a short interval is to be generated, rather than using a timer with its attendant capacitor, it is often more convenient and economical to employ a delay line made up of inverters, as shown in Fig. 24-49. Each 74L04 inverter has a propagation delay of about 30ns. In Fig. 24-48 a three-inverter delay line has been used to generate a short pulse at the end of the timed interval T0-T1. Applications of this type of circuit in block-signal systems are shown in Figs. 15-49 and 15-56.

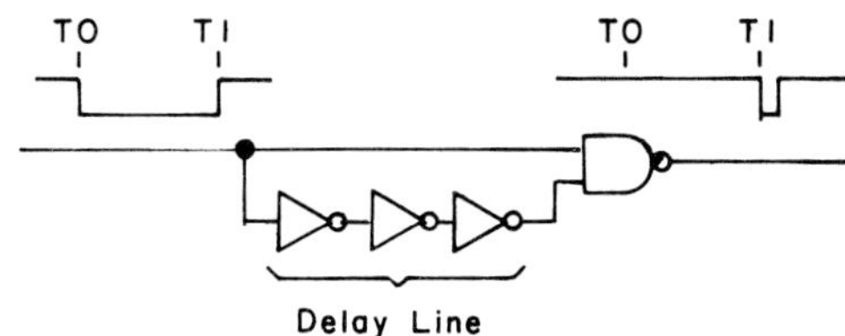

Fig. 24-49 Delay Line Timer

24.93 Line Drivers and Line Receivers

The use of simple interconnecting wires with modern ICs to transmit digital signals over distances greater than 1m (3') is often impossible due to electrical noise causing errors. For greater distances in such cases, a line driver can be used to convert the digital logic level to a signal on a transmission line, that signal is recognized by a line receiver which is capable of distinguishing the signal from electrical noise. The output of the line receiver is a logic level.

Many different types of IC line drivers and line receivers are available for various types of transmission lines and distances of transmission. The most reliable are of the differential type, an example being shown in Fig. 24-50. Differential means that the line driver generates a voltage between the two wires of the transmission line. A differential receiver responds only to the differential voltage between the two wires and ignores changes of voltage with respect to ground which appear on both wires equally (common-mode signals).

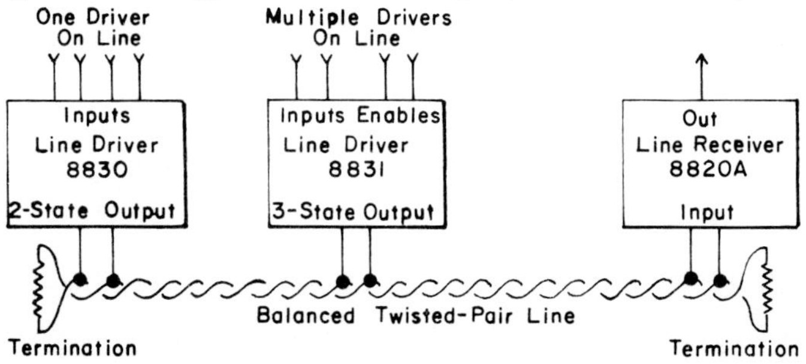

Fig. 24-50 Transmission lines.

Since electrical noise is usually picked up equally by both wires of the transmission line, a differential receiver can discriminate between signal and noise. Tests made in 1978 by The Model RR Club over a twisted-pair 30m (100') transmission line using the drivers and receivers shown in Fig. 24-50 showed negligible errors produced, the line was exposed to the most severe noise sources available. The line was of ordinary twisted pair. Better results could be obtained by using precision transmission line, but the latter is expensive and apparently unnecessary for model-railroad applications.

If there is only one line driver per line, it should be of a type such as that on the left in Fig. 24-50, which always places a signal on the line. If there is more than one line driver per line, the drivers must have 3-state outputs as the right line driver. In Fig. 24-50, only the driver which is to transmit is enabled, all the others are disabled, outputs in their high-impedance state. the line must be terminated in its characteristic impedance at each end. Most twisted-pair lines have an impedance of 100 to 130 ohms. If an oscilloscope is available, proper termination can be determined by observing the transmitted pulses at the receiving end of the line. If the line is properly terminated, these pulses will appear much like those observed at the line driver.

With a well-terminated line it is possible to send signals in either direction, but system design is usually easier and performance more reliable if a separate line is provided for each direction of transmission.

Totally impervious to electrical noise are light-fiber transmission lines. These have the additional advantage of electrically isolating the driving and receiving circuits thus eliminating any possibility of error due to differences of ground potential. For practical purposes these are one-way transmission lines from one driver to a single receiver. If the signal is to be sent to more than one receiver either separate fibers each with a driver must be provided or the signal received must be repeated onto another fiber extending to the next using circuit. A similar method must be used if several drivers are transmitting to a single using circuit.

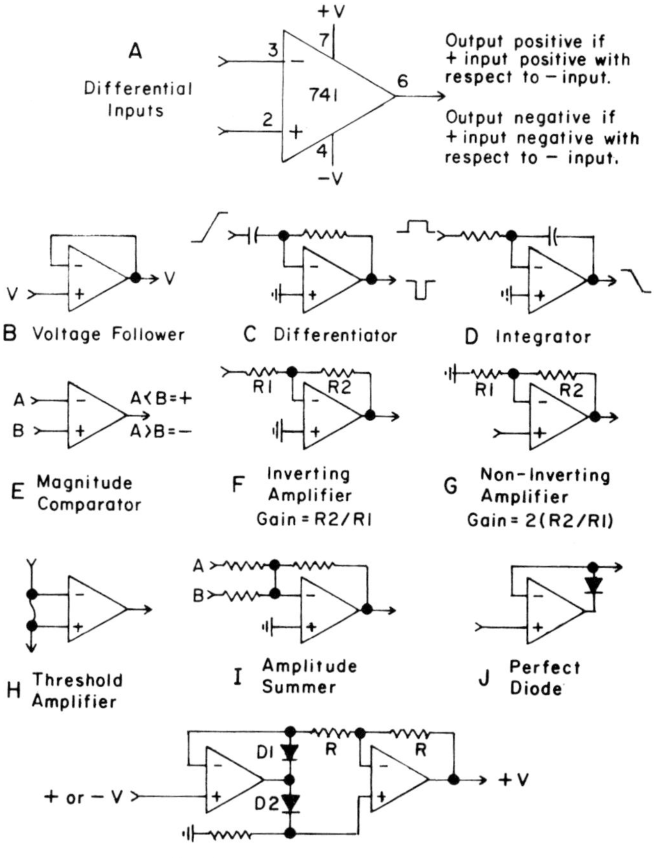

Fig. 24-51 Operational amplifiers.

24.94 Operational Amplifiers

Both digital and linear systems require many amplifiers. In the case of digital systems almost all are power amplifiers; the input and output logic levels remain the same. Linear systems have need of many types of amplifiers, for example those with a constant gain over a specified frequency range. The work-horse amplifier of linear systems is the operational amplifier, an example being shown at A in Fig. 24-51. An operational amplifier (OpAmp) is a differential amplifier, that is its output is determined by the difference of the voltages applied to its two inputs. Its output voltage will be positive if the + input is positive with respect to the − input, or negative if the relative polarity of the inputs is opposite. The two features of an OpAmp which distinguish it from other differential amplifiers such as line receivers, see Section 24.93, are that it has very high gain, typically 10,000 or more, and is designed for stable operation when part of its output level is fed back to its input. Several of the more-useful feed-back connections are shown in Fig. 24-51, but many more exist, including those which cause the OpAmp to generate useful tones such as those simulating a locomotive bell.

At B in Fig. 24-51, the output is fed back to the − input. Any voltage applied to the + input will cause an almost precisely equal change in the output voltage, the + and − inputs will be brought almost to the same level. Used in this way, the OpAmp is a power amplifier since microamperes supplied to the input can drive milliamperes at the output.

At C the differentiator connection causes the OpAmp to develop an output level proportional to the rate of change of the input level.

At D the integrator connection develops an output level proportional to the area under the input pulse. If the input pulse is of constant amplitude, this connection develops an output level proportional to the duration of the input pulse. This circuit is useful to create the momentum effect in throttles, see Fig. 16-13.

At E there is no feed back so even a slight change which reverses the differential voltage on the inputs will cause an output voltage change from one extreme to the other to indicate which voltage is higher. There are ICs called comparators which perform this function more rapidly than an OpAmp, but for most model-railroad applications an OpAmp is fast enough. Applications of an OpAmp in this mode are shown in Figs. 16-13 and 16-23.

At F two resistors are used in the feed-back path to control the gain of an inverting amplifier. The same basic circuit can be used for a non-inverting amplifier as at G, but note that for the same two resistances the gain of a non-inverting amplifier is twice that of an inverting amplifier. One use for such amplifiers is to operate meters, an example can be found in 16-22.

At H there is no feed-back path so the full gain of the OpAmp is used to detect current flowing though a low-value resistance. This connection makes possible sensitive series track circuits, see Figs. 15-13 and 15-14. At I the voltage-summing connection for an inverting amplifier is shown. This connection can be used to create a speedometer at a cab.

At J a diode is in the feed-back path and also in series with the output. If a negative-voltage input is applied, the output swings negative just enough to compensate for the voltage drop in the diode, so the output voltage is virtually the same as the input. But if a positive voltage is applied, the diode is back-biased and there is no output current. Thus this circuit operates as a perfect diode.

A combination of perfect-diode, inverting amplifier, and non-inverting amplifier circuits are used at K to form an absolute-value circuit, i.e., regardless of whether the applied input voltage is positive or negative, the output voltage has nearly the identical amplitude, but it always is positive. If the input is negative, D2 is back biased and the perfect-diode circuit (including D1) output is applied to an inverting amplifier with a gain of unity so the output voltage is essentially the same as the input voltage, but positive. If the input voltage applied is positive, diode D1 will be back biased and diode D2, the two feed-back resistors labeled R, and the two OpAmps make up a non-inverting amplifier of unity gain.

Unlike digital circuits, most circuits with OpAmps must be designed with adjustable resistances, capacitors, etc., since it is usually impractical to design a circuit which will operate properly without making fine adjustments. Some of these adjustments are due to the tolerances of the resistors. In general, if analog signals must be processed, it is better to convert them to digital signals (D to A convertor) before processing, particularly before storing in memory and to develop analog, outputs by converting digital signals to analog (D to A convertors).

24.95 Voltage Regulators

Many ICs operate over a limited range of supply voltage for example, the 74 series of TTL power source has the specified limits of 4.75 to 5.25 volts. IC voltage regulators such as that shown in Fig. 24-52 are convenient for obtaining such well-regulated voltages.

These are essentially OpAmps with internal voltage reference and feedback. They are available for positive and for negative voltages. Some have an adjustable output, but most are fixed. Unless the specific voltage needed is not available from the fixed type, it is safer to use only fixed-voltage regulators. For most model-railroad applications the supply voltage to the regulator is obtained from a full-wave rectifier with a large filter capacitor. This supply voltage must be sufficiently higher than the desired output voltage to permit the regulator to function. Two volts is generally sufficient, check the spec sheet for the regulator to be installed.

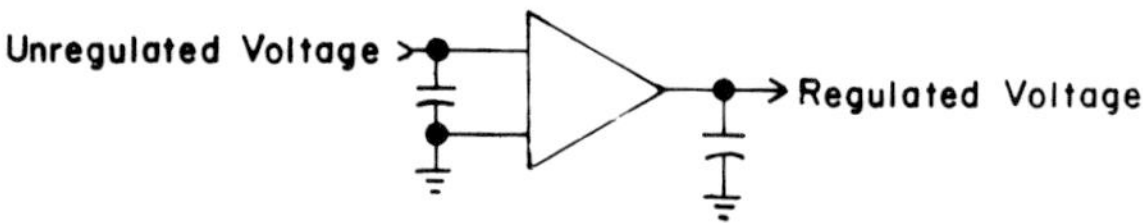

Fig. 24-52 Voltage regulator.

Most IC regulators are self-protecting; if their output is short-circuited to ground, only a stated maximum current will flow. Under such conditions the regulator will generate considerable heat. For example, a 1.5A 5V regulator operating from 7V will generate 10.5 watts of heat if short circuited. Even when operating normally at full load, 3w will be generated. Therefore voltage regulators should be mounted on a suitable heat sink such as a sheet of thick aluminum. Because of this heat dissipation, it is desirable to keep the unregulated supply voltage as low as proper operation of the regulator permits.

Some spec sheets require capacitors, as shown in the figure, at both the input and output of each regulator. Even if not specified, such capacitors are desirable to protect against surges, 0.5 or 1uf are appropriate values. These capacitors should be mounted very close to the regulator, for example soldered directly to the leads of the regulator.

For circuits which will require more current than can be delivered by one regulator, the supply buses should be divided so that the load on each bus is within the capability of a single regulator. For large circuits it is not necessary to determine how many regulators will be needed in advance. The simplest procedure is to wire all the buses together and monitor the current as the devices are added into the system. As the limit of the regulator is approached, the buses can be suitably divided and an additional regulator mounted on the same heat sink, if it is large enough, continuing the process until enough regulators have been provided for the maximum load.

It is vital that the ground connection to the regulator not be opened when the supply voltage is still applied. If it is opened, the full supply voltage will appear on the output of the regulator. A safe method is to make the ground connection from the unregulated power source by a separate wire to the heat sink on which the regulators are mounted. The heat sink providing the ground connection to the regulators; the ground connections to the system should then be made separately to that heat sink. An opening in the ground connection between the heat sink and the unregulated supply will effectively disconnect the unregulated supply from the system.

Since a single regulator can supply many IC packages, it is important that those packages be protected against overvoltage due to a failure of the regulator or a short circuit across the regulator terminus. For such protection a circuit called a "crowbar" is used. A crowbar is triggered by its input voltage rising above a selected value and, once triggered, short-circuits its input to ground. Commercial IC crowbars are available but serviceable crowbars can be made from bargain-basement SCRs as shown in Fig. 24-53. The SCR must have a current rating well above the maximum current rating of the regulator so if the regulator does not self-protect, it will be the regulator which will be destroyed, not the crowbar. The resistors of Fig. 24-53 which set the firing voltage of the crowbar, are best selected by trial and error since, with this simple circuit, there will be considerable variation between two SCRs even of the same code. Since, when fired, the voltage drop across an SCR is low, about 1V, even if high currents flow, the dissipation will be reasonably low. But, since it is

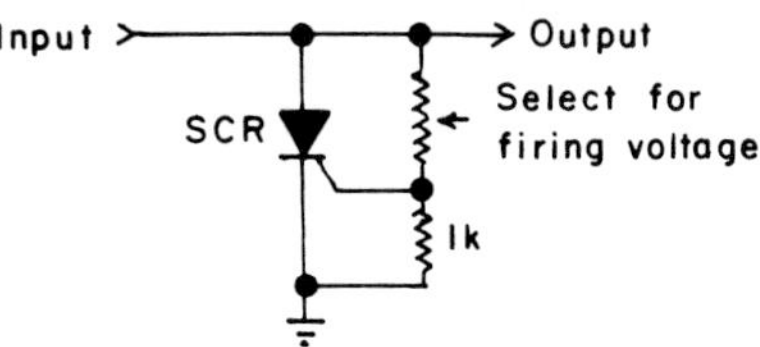

Fig. 24-53 Crowbar.

necessary to mount the SCR in any event, a small piece of angle is not only convenient but will serve as an adequate heat sink.

It is very important that the connections between the crowbar and the supply bus and the system ground be over separate leads from those to the regulator. This will minimize the likelihood that the protective circuit will ever be disconnected from the circuits it is protecting.

24.96 Phase-Locked Loop

Phase-locked loop (PLL) is an old technique for obtaining accuracy of tuning for frequency-selective systems. Until the days of IC PLLs, this technique remained too expensive for widespread use but today is used heavily for 40-channel CB, for the elimination of fine tuning of TV, etc. In model railroading PLLs are being used commercially in the recievers of the frequency-control Dynatrol command-control system of power systems. PLLs should be considered as the frequency-selective element for any model-railroad application of frequency control.

24.97 Sound Synthesizers

IC operational amplifiers with various tuned circuits in their feed-back loops have been extensively used to synthesize sounds such as bells and whistles. By 1981 special sound synthesizer ICs such as the 16477 were becoming available. This facilitated the design of electronic sound generators. Many of these devices required external capacitors and resistors. Digital as well as linear sound synthesizers were in the process of development, the digital types having the greatest promise for on-board sound generation in locomotives.

By 1983 microprocessors under program control were being used to synthesize sounds, even human voices.

25 MICROPROCESSORS

25.1 GENERAL

The essence of a microprocessor (uP) is that it performs operations one at a time under the control of a software program, the latter provides the instruction controlling which operation shall be performed. Thus only one set of equipment, such as an adder, need be included, thereby reducing circuit complexity compared to conventional logic.

Early uPs were constructed of many standard LSI packages. By 1981, however, a uP was generally understood to be a single IC package; this is the way a uP is considered here.

Although the various uPs available are much alike in principle, they differ in many details such as the numbers of registers provided internally and the instruction set. Manufacturers have available manuals for each of their uP types. Space permits only a discussion of the fundamentals which generally apply to microprocessors.

25.2 SINGLE PURPOSE OR MULTIPURPOSE

It is possible for a single uP to perform many tasks. They may even be equipped with a keyboard for entering new programs, or changing existing programs. Nevertheless, a multipurpose machine is always more complex than a single-purpose machine. I/O (input/output) devices and programming, two of the more costly and complex portions of a uP system, often can be simplified if the full power of the uP addressing and data capabilities are directed to one task only, instead of being made general purpose. Simpler equates to more reliable, and easier both to design and maintain. Furthermore, a single-purpose machine is not subject to the problems which can be introduced when some new task is being added to a multipurpose machine. Also of importance is that the test panel for a dedicated uP can display information in the form most useful for the specific function being performed. There may not even be a saving of cost when using one uP to handle two or more major tasks rather than using a separate uP for each task.

Although it is generally better to install single-purpose uP systems, there are two major exceptions. The first exists when a uP is being installed for some major purpose such as block signals and interlocking as well as some minor task, such as turntable control. Adding such a minor task to a uP system often will not adversely affect the major-task design. The second exception is when a complete, prepackaged general-purpose machine is purchased. Since such a uP system already has the complications required to be general purpose, that system may as well be used to handle all tasks within the limits of its capabilities.

25.3 METHOD OF OPERATION

A simplified block diagram of a uP system is given in Fig. 25-1. The block labled I/O (input/output) represents the circuits necessary to connect the inputs being received to the inputs to the uP package or memory, as well as to connect the outputs developed by the uP to the devices being driven (switch machines, signals, motors, etc.).

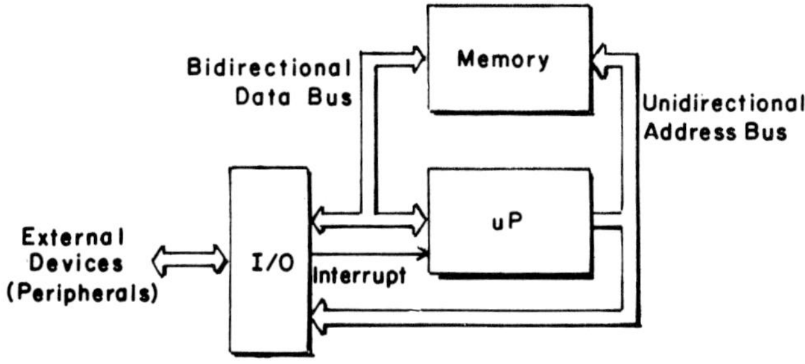

Fig. 25-1 Microprocessor block diagram.

The program of instructions which controls the action of the system is stored in the memory. The uP "fetches" these instructions in the proper order and "executes" each instruction as received. There are three general types of instructions. One is those causing actions internal to the system such as determining the aspect of a signal. The second is those causing a peripheral to be addressed and to send information to the uP over the data bus. The third is those causing a peripheral to be addressed and to take action based on commands sent on the data bus by the uP.

The memory usually consists of both ROM (read-only memory) and RAM (variable memory). Information in ROM cannot be changed by normal circuit action and so is the usual place to store the program, and to store data which does not change. Information in the RAM can be changed as required by the program or by the inputs received. One example of such information is the occupancy state of a block.

The amount of information which can be received, sent, or processed by the uP with one instruction is limited by the number of bits of the data bus. In 1981 the most common width of the data bus was 8 bits, an 8-bit machine, but uPs with 4-bit buses, 4-bit machines, and with 16-bit buses, 16-bit machines, were available. A 32-bit machine had been announced. As a general rule, the larger the byte, the easier it is to write the program.

Since a uP can handle only as many bits at one time as the width of its data bus, it is inherently a time-division multiplex machine. If the total information to be processed (the word) has more bits than the data bus, the uP must bite off parts of the word and process the word in pieces called "bytes". The size of the byte depends upon the width of the data bus (a 4-bit byte, an 8-bit byte, a 16-bit byte).

In addition to the memory addressed by the address bus, most uP types include registers within themselves. Such registers are highly useful because it is simpler and faster to place or retrieve information in or from a register than in or from memory. Again a general rule, the greater the number of internal registers, the easier it is to write the program.

Some uPs have special inputs or outputs. Only one such input, an interrupt is shown in Fig. 25-1. If an interrupt is received, the uP will stop processing is normal program, begin processing a special program, and upon completion of the special program resume its normal program at the point where it was stopped. The proper choice of a specific uP for a model railroad application may depend upon special inputs or outputs if they provide a simpler system than is possible with just the data and address buses.

25.4 PROGRAM

Within a microprocessor there is an internal data bus, there may be more than one, over which bytes can be transferred between internal elements of the uP and to or from I/O. The precise transfer or other action which takes place is controlled by the OpCode (operation code) of the instruction which has just been fetched from memory. The OpCode usually is contained in just one byte, but the byte may be followed by more bytes in the total instruction if additional information, such as a memory address, is provided by the instruction. The actual bytes, whether expressed in binary, octal, or hexadecimal notation, are called "machine language". To give an example of a one-byte instruction of the 8080 instruction set, 00000010 (binary), 02 (hexadecimal) causes the contents of internal register B to be incremented. As soon as an instruction is executed, the program counter or its equivalent is advanced, and the next instruction fetched. When taken as a whole, all the instructions necessary to complete the desired task are called the program.

It would be difficult to write a program directly in binary. Therefore the manufacturers provide a set of more readable notations called "mnemonics". The mnemonic for the binary instruction 00000010 given in the paragraph above is INR B, meaning increment register B. A program written in mnemonics is said to be in "assembly language". Each mnemonic instruction has a corresponding machine language instruction of one or more bytes.

A program which always ran through its program in the order in which instructions are placed in the program store would be most unusual. The ability to make decisions is a great power of software. For example, in a block-signal program, instruction 79 could be to test a block for occupancy. If it was found to be occupied, the program would continue on with instruction 80, but if it were found to be clear, the program would "jump" to instruction 155 and take entirely different action than if the block were occupied. An 8080 instruction which would perform this jump could be JZ 009B; read this as jump, if zero, to instruction 009B in hexadecimal, 155 in decimal. Note that as given this instruction calls for a jump to a specific address, a method which is difficult to use if we write the program by hand. In anything but a very short program it is extremely difficult to keep track of the address of each instruction. Even more difficult is determining how these addresses change when corrections or improvements are made in the program. Therefore, in assembly language, the jump is not to a specific address, but to the mnemonic of the instruction to which the jump is being made. For this, the target instruction of a jump is given a label. In this example, since a jump is made if the block is clear, the instruction to which the jump is made is labeled "CLEAR:". The colon separates the label from the OpCode for an 8080. If the instruction to which we are jumping is the INR B given before, the entire assembly-language code then is CLEAR: INR B. The jump instruction then calls for a jump to the instruction labeled CLEAR, e.g., JZ CLEAR. Once all the instructions are written in assembly language, they are processed by a program called an assembler which produces the machine language program required by the uP being used. The assembler program is prepared by the manufacturer of the uP. The user will have to find a computer on which that program can be run. Some uP manufacturers provide a service of converting a customer's assembly-language program into a ROM coded with the proper machine language.

If a model railroader has no alternative to hand coding, there is a technique which will avoid almost all renumbering of program instructions when corrections or additions must be made to the program. For this technique, the program memory must be at least twice, preferably four times the size required for a minimal program. This extra memory provides room to insert do-nothing insturctions called NoOps (no operations) among the executable instructions. When extra instructions are required, the appropriately located NoOps are replaced by the new insturctions, without changing the address of any previous instruction. If a NoOp instruction is all zeros, as is often the case, the ROM at NoOp addresses is simply not coded. Should a PROM such as the Intel 1702A be used for the program store, the addresses for the added instructions can be coded without disturbing the previously-coded executable instructions.

Some UPs include relative jumps in their instruction set, e.g. the 6502. Such UPs are easier to hand code as the jumps do not change if instructions are added or removed elsewhere in the program as is the case for an absolute jump, (a jump to a specific address). Such an instruction would be BEQ 09 which will cause the program to jump to the 9th following instruction if the result of the instruction being executed is zero. If relative addressing is provided, it should be used to the maximum possible extent.

Complete information for programing requires more space than is available here. The Intel 8080 Assembly Language Programing Manual, 1976, has 89 pages of information. The manual for the uP selected must be obtained. The factors influencing the choice of a particular uP are covered in section 25.5

It is possible to program by starting directly with the assembly-language codes. Many programmers, however, find it best to prepare a "flow chart" first. A flow chart clearly shows the decisions to be made and the actions to be taken. If prepared properly, the mnemonics can be written directly from information on the flow chart. An example of a portion of a flow chart and the corresponding mnemonics of assembly language (8080) are given in Fig. 25-2, for a portion of the block signal interlocking and CTC program described in Section 25.7.

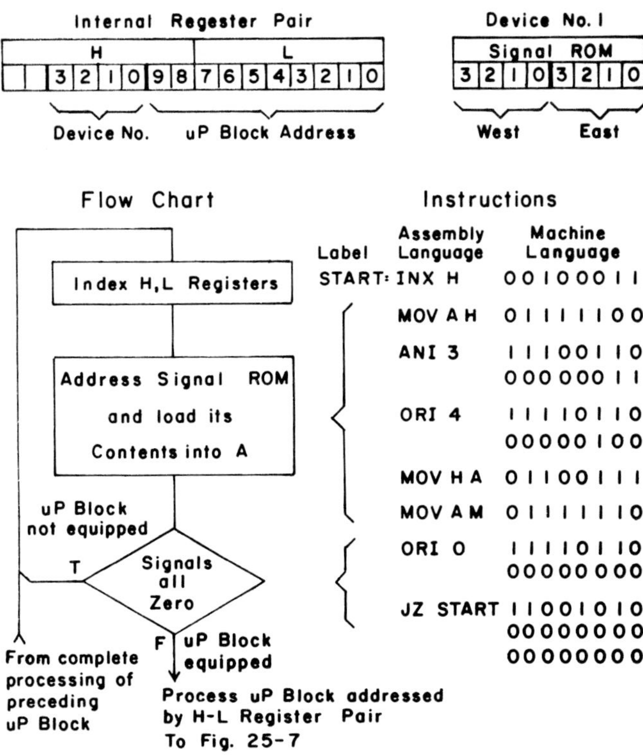

Fig. 25-2 Flow chart example.

In that program, when the processing of a uP block has been completed, it is necessary to select the next uP block address. If that address does not represent a working uP block, it is skipped over and the process is repeated until a working uP block address has been obtained.

The flow chart should use the capabilities of the uP chosen for the task. In the case of the 8080, the internal registers H and L are the ones best-suited to address memory. Therefore, they have been selected to store the address of the uP block to be served. As shown at the upper left in Fig. 25-2, the L register contains the eight least-significant bits of the uP block address, and the H register contains the two most-significant bits. Four more of the bits in the H register are used to store the device number of the device to be addressed. In this case, the signal ROM, device 1, is needed since the contents of this ROM will be all-zero if the uP block address does not represent a working block.

As soon as the processing of the previous uP block has been completed, the program will jump to START at the top of the flow chart, instruction address zero. The action required at this point is to index the uP block address. This instruction address is the point in the program where operation commences when power is first turned on; logically, the instruction at address zero should be the beginning of the program. This statement is labeled START so it can serve as a target for jump instructions. INX H, the zero address instruction, is the OpCode for indexing the H and L registers. This is a one-byte instruction, as can be seen by the machine language bits.

The next program step is to address the signal ROM, and read the contents of the word addressed into the A register. The A register, a common designation used in many different uPs, is the accumulator, a special register into which bytes must be loaded for most processing of data. Although this operation can easily be shown by a single box on the flow chart, five instructions are required for the 8080. Instructions 1 through 4 are needed to change the device number stored in the H register to 0001, the signal ROM. Mnemonic 5 causes the contents of the word in the signal ROM addressed by the contents of the H and L registers to be loaded into the A register. Mnemonics Nos. 2 and 3 are two-byte instructions. The OpCode (the first byte) informs the uP of this and the uP automatically causes the reading of the second byte. Note, however, that there is a separate address in the program store for each byte. Thus the address of the first byte of each instruction does not have a fixed relationship to the number of its mnemonic, one of the causes of difficulty in hand programing.

The next program step is to decide if the contents of the word read from the Signal ROM were all zero, indicating a non-existing uP block. If true, the program jumps back to START to index to the next uP block address. If false, the uP block addressed is a working block, and processing of that uP block commences. On flow charts it is customery to use the diamond symbol for decisions. The instruction set of an 8080 does not permit the direct testing of the contents of the accumulator to find out if it is all zeros. Such an instruction, if available, makes programing easier. Without this, in the case of the 8080, it is necessary to give an instruction which will set one of the status flip-flops, and then test the state of that FF. The 7th mnemonic of Fig. 25-2 causes the zeros of the second byte of the instruction to be logically ORed with the contents of the A register, but does set the Z flip-flop if the contents are all zero. The last mnemonic, JZ START, tests the state of the Z FF. If the Z flip-flop is found to be set, the program will jump to the instruction labeled START. In the example of Fig. 25-2, START is at address zero. The machine language instruction gives this jump address in its last two bytes. A major problem in hand programing is keeping track of the addresses to which jumps are made. This task is made easier through the use of relative addressing if such a capability exists for the uP selected.

Although the portion of the program shown in Fig. 25-2 is small, it can be seen that limitations of the instruction set often cause several instructions to be written for a single action. If a uP were chosen which had the capability of loading the device number contained in the H register from immediate data, data contained in a second byte of the instruction, and of testing the A register directly for all zeros, only three instructions would have been needed instead of the seven shown in Fig. 25-2.

25.5 CHOICE OF A MICROPROCESSOR

By 1981 there were many different uPs on the market and much work was being done on new types. Fortunately there are only a few main factors of importance in selecting a type suitable for the task at hand for most model railroad applications.

Established Design

An important factor of the uP is that it has been widely used and is well known. The 8080, the first of the modern uPs, has been popular since the mid-seventies; in 1981 the 8080 was still a viable choice since it was well supported by the peripheral equipment designed for it. Nevertheless, among the proven types of uPs, it would be prudent to select a design on the way in rather than one on its way to being replaced with more modern types.

Suitable Instruction Set

With the possible exception of waybilling processors, most model railroad applications are for control processors (cab control, block signals, interlockings, turntables, etc.). Therefore, mathematical instructions such as multiplying, square roots, etc. are not valuable. On the other hand, instructions which can test the state of a register for all zeros, or better yet, the state of any specified bit in a register, make easy the transfer of bytes between registers or to memory. They also can increment registers and are most helpful in reducing the complexity of the program.

Documentation

Instructions by the manufacturer on the uP, particularly a programing manual, are vital. If a uP has insufficient documentation it should be avoided by all except those skilled in its use.

Size

Most model railroad applications can be handeled by 4-bit machines, but this usually is at the cost of programing complexity. Unless the job is clearly one for a 4-bit machine, an 8-bit, or even better, a 16-bit uP should be chosen. In many cases the increase in system cost will be very minor, but even when there is an increased cost it is justified by the significant reduction in programing effort.

Internal Registers and Memory

The instructions required to handle data in internal registers and memory are far easier to program than those for use with external memory. As a general rule for model railroad applications, the more internal registers the better. The 8080 used in the example cited in section 25.7 has 6 internal registers. If it had more registers the programing would be much simpler; in the example, all available registers are used to store addresses, leaving no separate register available for any other use. Some uPs utilize the lowest-numbered bytes in RAM, often called "Zero Page" almost as though these bytes were internal registers.

Internal RAM, in effect, supplies several to many registers but usually does so without the program simplicity of internal registers. Some uPs have both internal registers and internal RAM. Internal ROM, unless changable by the user, is of little value in this hobby.

Cost and Availability

Older uPs often are widely available at a lower cost than the newer designs, but often the cost of the uP itself is overshadowed by the cost of memories and peripheral equipment. A modern uP may make more efficient use of memory, resulting in a lower system cost, or it may increase system cost by requiring more expensive new memory types. It is the total system cost which should be considered. In general ease of programming is more important than cost of hardware.

25.6 PROGRAM SIMPLIFICATION THROUGH HARDWARE

The most-difficult single thing when applying a uP to a model railroad application is preparing and debugging the program. It is true that connecting the various I/O devices to the address and data buses of the uP and then handling everything by the program will accomplish the task. This is the approach taken by the computer amateur since programing is "the thing" in the field. In contrast, model railroaders are interested in the end result, for example in seeing block signals operate properly, and not in programing for the sake of programing. Therefore, if it is possible to arrange the hardware, or even add hardware, so that the program or the system is made more simple or more easily understood, do so in most cases.

An example of simplification through hardware taken from the example cited in Section 25.7 is shown in Fig. 25-3. The maximum number of address bits required in the example system for any memory is 10 (1024 words), and the maximum number of I/O devices is 16. To make the system operation easier to understand, the 0 to 9 bits of the instruction bus are assigned as memory address bits. Bits 10-13 are assigned as the device No. (upper left Fig. 25-2). Bits 14 and 15 are assigned for special control. A 4-to-16 device decoder has been added so each I/O or memory can be controlled by a single lead. For example, the program store is enabled as device 1 and the signal ROM as device 2. In this case it is the system concept which is made simpler, not the program.

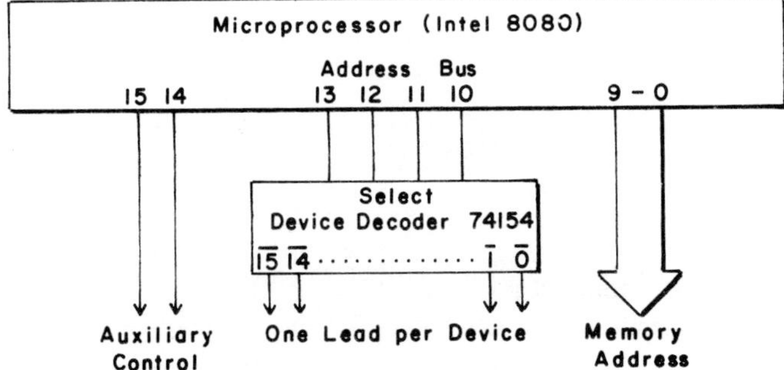

Fig. 25-3 Hardware address simplification.

Program simplification results if the added device eliminates a series of instructions which are often repeated. An example is if only the sum of two numbers is needed, and not the number individually; possibly it would be advantageous to add those two numbers in a hardware adder, making the sum available to the data bus. An example of such an adder is given in Fig. 25-9.

If there are insufficient internal registers to handle all the bytes which are in constant demand, it will be necessary to add the instructions to transfer such data into or out of memory. This may require many extra instructions, particularly if the information requires more than one byte. As a specific example, for the program shown in 25-2, assume there was no incrementable internal memory available to hold the 10-bit uP block address. It would be possible to use an external counter as shown in Fig. 25-4.

The 10-bit output of this counter is used to address the memories. The zero program instruction now becomes START: STA 3C00 which places the immediate address 3C00 Hex, 0011110000000000 in machine language, on the address bus selecting device 15, the number assigned to the new counter, thus indexing the counter and addressing the new uP block in the memories.

A very important hardware consideration which may yield program simplification, some would say this is a software consideration, is how the memories are arranged. This is called memory partitioning and, if there is just one large RAM, it is indeed a software problem. The example given in section 25.7, however, divides memory into hardware units to make system operation more obvious.

Choosing a data bus wide enough to handle with one instruction all the bits necessary for any given operation will save many instructions and much program complexity as compared to a program required to handle data in bytes. In 1983 it appeared as though a 16-bit uP was the proper choice for most known applications in model railroading.

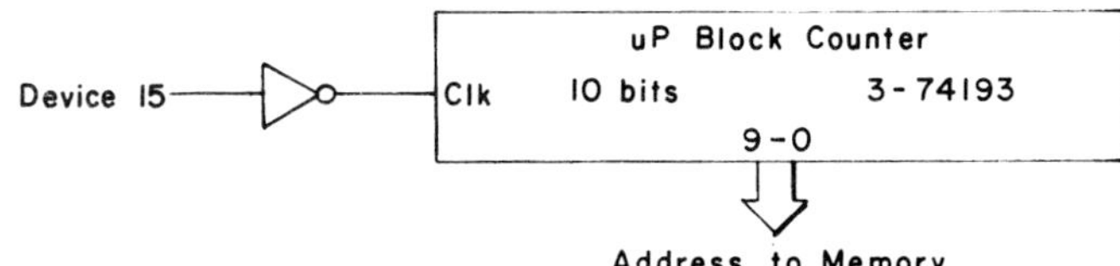

Fig. 25-4 External counter.

25.7 BLOCK SIGNAL, INTERLOCKING, CTC SYSTEM

Designing just one interlocking machine by conventional circuit methods is a difficult job (as described in Section 15.55). But, by designing a program which can be used for any track configuration, a single uP can serve as an interlocking machine for all interlockings on the layout, serve as a CTC machine for the entire layout, and on the side, operate all the signals. If designed for the largest conceivable layout, the program would be suitable for all layouts so that program would have to be debugged just once, then program ROMs could be copied from the final program and used by anyone. This is a task well suited to a uP since it does not matter if a signal changes its aspect in 1 second or 1 microsecond. Therefore, such a system is used as an example of a uP application on a model railroad. The specific system described is the result of a 1976-1977 study based on the use of an 8080 at The Model RR Club. This example shows the problems of handling a word in bytes (specifically 10-bit addresses in 8-bit bytes). A 16-bit machine would be easier to program for this task, particularly if it had more than three registers and more than one accumulator.

Algorithm

For virtually all complex tasks, it is desirable to find an algorithm, a method of reaching the desired result which enables a simple program to work its way through a complex maze of data. The secret of a successful algorithm is the breaking of the complex problem into small parts which appear very much alike to the program, the differences from one part to another being definable by just a few bits.

Bill Ridgway noted that, for signaling and interlocking purposes, any layout can be divided into uP blocks which contain only one switch used for routing. Such a block, as shown in Fig. 25-5, has only four possible positions. The program can deal with just one uP block at a time; the differences in treatment from one uP block to the next are controlled by just two position bits. There may be as many other switches as desired within the physical limits of the uP block on the layout as long as such switches do not control routing, but if reversed, merely make that uP block appear to be occupied. This

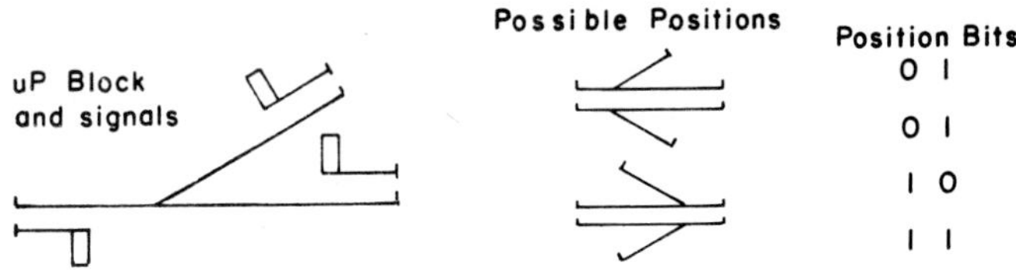

Fig. 25-5 UP block.

corresponds to prototype practice. If there is no actual switch used for routing in a uP block, the algorithm switch will be considered permanently set in one direction.

Each uP block is protected by a signal on each of the three possible approach routes. If the algorithm signal represents an actual signal on the layout, it is called a real signal. If it is purely an algorithm signal to pass information to the adjacent uP block, it is called a phantom signal. Phantom is the prototype name for similar signals assumed in an interlocking. The indications calculations for a phantom signal are, in general, different than for real signals, as is described later. But there are a few cases in interlocking and with signals opposing the current of traffic, in which phantom signal indications must be calculated as though they were real. This does not disturb the algorithm.

The signal on the diverging route is always a phantom. The type of signals on the straight route are defined by bits in the signal ROM, see Fig. 25-2. Code 0000 informs the uP that an actual uP block does not exist for that uP block address. Code 0001 indicates a phantom signal. The remaining codes indicate the type of real signal, such as semaphore, color light or position light, so that the calculated indication can be converted into the proper aspect for the signal at that location.

The algorithm must have a simple method of calculating the addresses of the next uP block on the route selected by the position of the switch in the uP block being processed (current uP block). To accomplish this, the uP blocks are constrained to the grid shown in Fig. 25-6. There are eight parallel routes, 0 to 7 in octal (000 to 111 binary) and 128 in horizontal sequence (0 to 177 octal, 0000000 to 1111111 binary.) This grid is large enough to meet the needs of the HO layout being built by The Model Railroad Club. Crossovers between routes must be between uP blocks of the same sequence number and differing by one route number. The next uP block on the straight route must have the same route number and must differ by one in sequence number. Thus the two position bits of Fig. 25-5, combined with switch position, determine whether bits should be added or subtracted from the current uP block address to find the addresses of the adjacent uP blocks on the route established by the switch (next uP block east and next uP block west).

Sequence Numbers

177	176	175		2	1	0	Route Number
177,7	176,7	175,7	– – – – – –	2,7	1,7	0,7	7
177,6	176,6	/	– – – – – –	/	1,6	0,6	6
177,5	/	175,5	– – – – – –	2,5	\	0,5	5
/	176,4	\	– – – – – –	2,4	1,4	\	4
177,3	176,3	175,3	– – – – – –	2,3	1,3	0,3	3
177,2	/	175,2	– – – – – –	2,2	\	0,2	2
177,1	176,1	175,1	– – – – – –	/	1,1	0,1	1
177,0	\	175,0	– – – – – –	2,0	1,0	0,0	0

All numbers octal. Total number of addresses: 1024 decimal.

Fig. 25-6 UP block designations.

Before attempting to process a uP block, the uP must determine that the uP block address held in the H and L registers is a working block, not a vacant address. This is done by testing the signal ROM for all zeros, as shown in Fig. 25-2. When it is determined that it is a working uP block, the next step is to calculate the next uP block east address, and store its address in the B and C register pair, also the next uP block west address, and store it in the D and E register pair. The flow chart of a program to accomplish this is shown in Fig. 25-7. At the top of that figure are shown the bits in the position ROM (device no. 2), and the bit in the data RAM (device no. 3), which are needed in this process.

Because there may be one or more vacant uP block addresses between the current uP block address and the next working uP block on the straight route, it is necessary to provide information of how many addresses must be skipped to reach the next working address. For this purpose, a 3-bit add west code and a 3-bit subtract east code are provided by the position ROM, see upper right in Fig. 25-7. Thus the next uP block can be up to seven addresses away from the current uP block.

The first action of the flow chart of Fig. 25-7 is to address the position ROM. This requires moving the contents of the H register into the accumulator, masking the previous device No., adding device No. 3, and moving the contents of A back into H.

With the position ROM addressed, its contents can be moved into A, and bit 7 can be tested by a masking instruction to find out if the switch in the current uP block faces east or west. If it faces east,

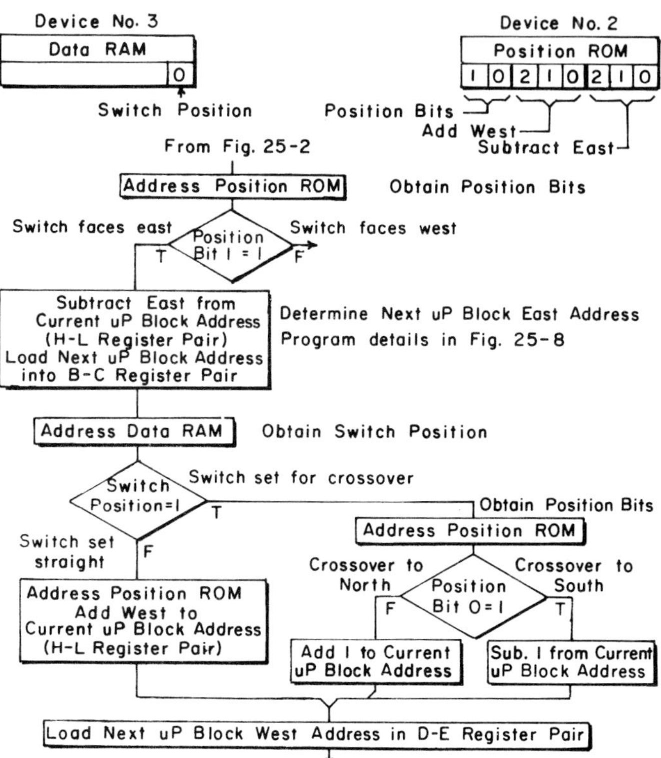

Fig. 25-7 Determining next UP block designations.

the next uP block to the east must be on the straight route so that the subtract east bits from the position ROM are subtracted from the current uP block address in the H and L registers, and the difference loaded into the B and C registers. The instructions necessary for this subtraction are described in detail later in this Chapter.

With the next uP block east address determined and loaded into the B-C register pair, the next problem is to determine the next uP block west address. Since this address depends in part on the position of the switch, the data RAM is addressed and the switch position bit is tested by the masking procedure described before. If the switch is set for the straight route, the position ROM is again addressed and its add west bits are added to the current uP block adress stored in the H-L register pair. Once determined, this address is loaded into the D-E register pair. The program instructions for this are much like those used to determine the next uP block address east.

If the switch was set to the crossover route, it is still necessary to address the position ROM, but this time bit 6 is tested to determine if the crossover route is to the south. If so, 1 is subtracted from the current uP block address, thus giving the address of the uP block on the parallel route to the south. If the crossover route is to the north, 1 is added to the current uP block address. In either case, the next uP block west address is loaded into the D-E register pair.

Although there are six-bits left over in the high-order register of each register pair, holding the uP block addresses in the registers has essentially used up all the internal registers of the 8080. It would be convenient to have more registers available for other uses; there would be advantages in choosing a uP type which has more internal registers than a 8080.

Each box or diamond on a flow chart usually represents several to many mnemonics in assembly language, and more than this in machine-language bytes. One set of assembly-language instructions to implement the determination of the next uP block address east of Fig. 25-7 is given in Fig. 25-8. Most operations which change data require that such data first be moved into the A (accumulator) register, necessitating temporary storage of bytes. This is common to most uPs, not just to the 8080.

Selecting a uP with two accumulators is very beneficial.

Several of the instructions of Fig. 25-8 are required because the uP block address has 10 bits, but the 8080 can handle only an 8-bit bite. This requires swapping bytes in and out of the A register. Choosing a 16-bit machine would simplify such programs.

A skilled programmer working with an assembler program on a computer would have no difficulty with actions such as those shown in Fig. 25-8. A model railroader, on the other hand, might prefer to eliminate a long series of instructions if they can be replaced by simple hardware. In this particular system, the add west bits in the posi-

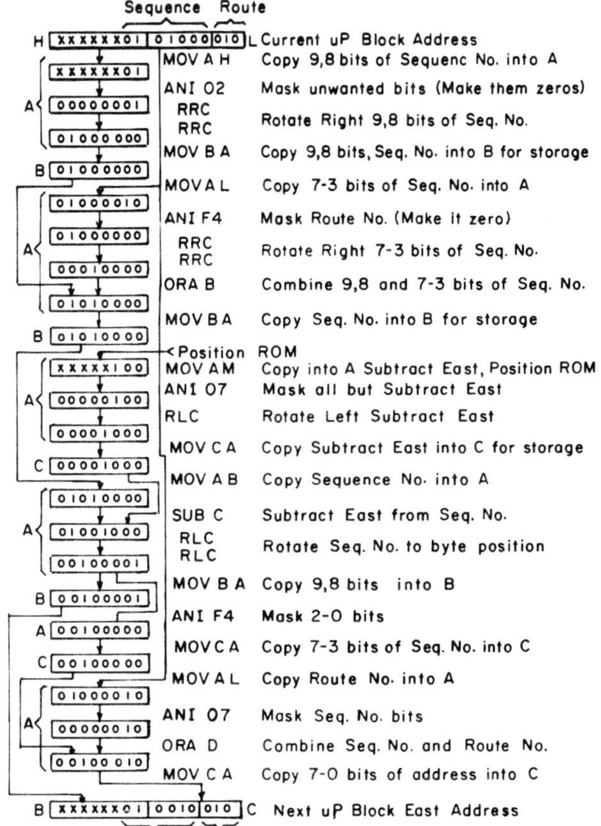
Fig. 25-8 Subtract east routine.

tion ROM have no value in themselves. What is needed is the sum of those bits and the most-significant 7 bits of the current uP block address. Therefore the bits from the position ROM, and the 3 to 9 bits of the current uP block address, can be continuously added in a hardware adder as shown in Fig. 25-9. The hardware-generated next uP block west is made available to the uP in two bytes as two device numbers. Exactly the same circuit can be used for the subtract east operation if the subtract east bits are in the two's complement form.

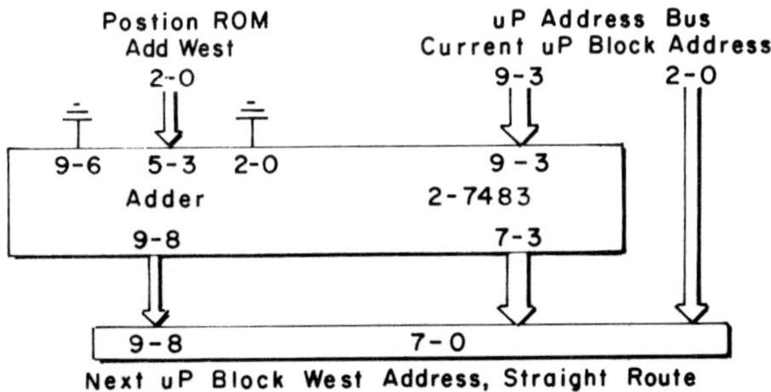

Fig. 25-9 Hardware adder.

At this point in the program, the current uP block address is known, as well as the addresses of the next uP blocks in each direction. The next step is to determine if there is a route established to the east, also to the west from the current uP block. This information, in the case of a 8080, can be stored in the spare bits of the high-order registers.

The system studied at The Model RR Club was based on the use of phototransistor presence detectors, as shown in Fig. 15-47. With the route known, occupancy of the current uP block can be determined by examining the condition of the detectors involved. The state of occupancy is then registered in the data RAM.

Automatic Block System

At this point, the bits representing levers of an interlocking or CTC machine are tested. If they are all zero, this uP block is not interlocked, and the program advances to the ABS (automatic block system) signal routine. For such operations signal indication, such as stop, approach, etc., is used. The signal protecting the route into the

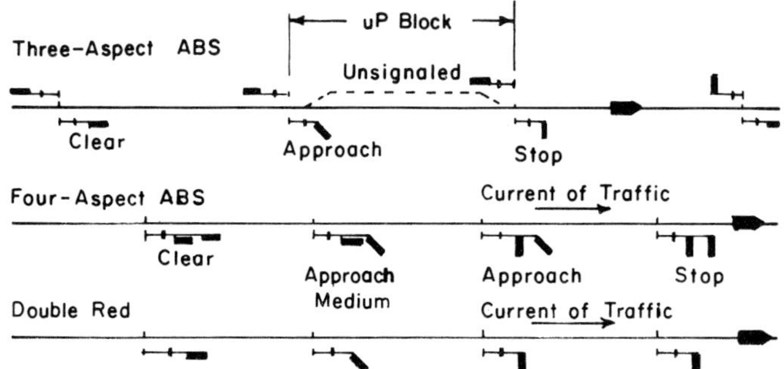

Fig. 25-10 Automatic block.

current uP block against which the switch is set is always given the indication of stop. The indications for the remaining two signals is stop if the uP block is occupied. As shown in Fig. 25-10, for ABS without overlap, the ABS block and the uP block coincide. The indication of the signal protecting an unoccupied uP block can therefore be determined by examining the state of the signal protecting the uP block in advance. The signal ROM has the information about whether the current uP block has three-indication signals operating in the usual ABS fashion, has four-indication signals, or is operating in the double-red system. In Fig. 25-10 it can been seen what these indications are. For the double-red system, there obviously has to be a different stop code stored in RAM for the two reds. This is because the signal protecting the uP block in the rear of the occupied block with its stop indication will display a stop indication on its scenery signal, let us call that stop indication in RAM stop 2. The uP block to the rear of the block with the stop 2 indication will display the approach.

Absolute Permissive Block

APB depends upon traffic being established by the train which first passes the headblock signal. In Fig. 25-11 the train shown in uP block 3 established eastward traffic when it first entered uP block 1. Two traffic bits then are placed in RAM, the 00 state of these bits indicating no traffic established. The first train to enter an unoccupied block at the end of single track between sidings will set the appropriate traffic bit. As each uP block making up the single track is processed, a traffic established indication present in the next uP block in either direction will be copied. All signals for opposing traffic then will be set to stop, while signals with traffic will operate in normal ABS manner. The program will not reset the traffic bit until all uP blocks on single track are unoccupied.

A routine very similar to that required for APB could be used for an automatic interlocking for a crossing. The essential difference is that all signals would be normally at stop. Any approaching train would clear its signal, and prevent the clearing of any other, until the cleared train had passed completely through the interlocking.

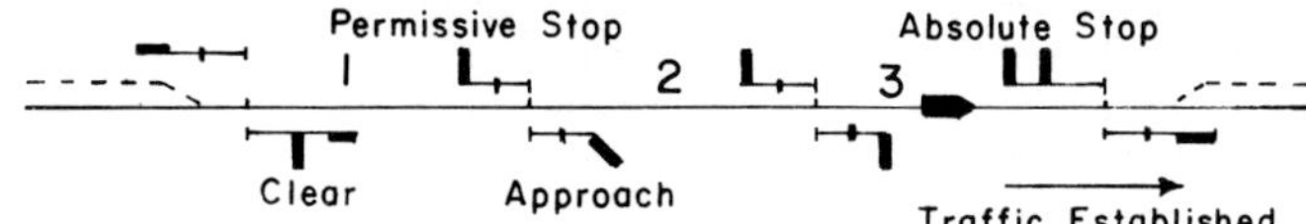

Fig. 25-11 Absolute-permissive block.

Overlap

Overlap is used in ABS to set the signal at the opposite end of a block to stop before an approaching train even enters the block being protected. This is to prevent opposing trains from entering a block from opposite ends without seeing a signal more restricting than approach. As can be seen in Fig. 25-12, a separate uP block is provided for the overlap. This uP block is protected by phantom signals. Either a real signal or a phantom to the rear of a real signal operates in normal ABS fashion. A real signal, or a phantom to the rear of a phantom signal, copies the indication of the phantom signal in advance. Since the signal ROM has already informed the uP

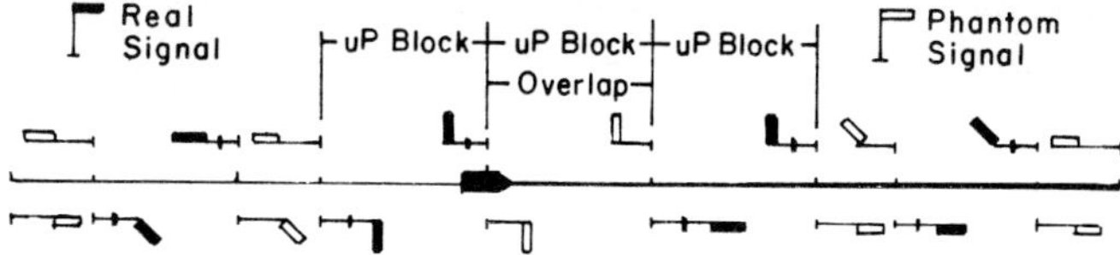

Fig. 25-12 ABS with overlap.

which signals are real and which are phantom, no further information need be provided for proper signal operation with overlap.

Once the indications of the signals are determined, information from the signal ROM is used to translate the indication bits into the proper commands for the real signal involved to set it to the proper aspect.

Interlocking

At the beginning of this section, a statement was made saying that designing a single interlocking by conventional means is very difficult. Therefore it is not surprising that the program which will provide interlocking, not just for one particular plant, but for any track configuration, would be complex. Signal indications depend upon routing, occupancy, and whether the next signal is real or phantom. Since the program processes every equipped uP block in the same manner, an algorithm is again needed. This algorithm must handle every conceivable interlocking or CTC condition, but here it will be described only for an interlocking controlling the junction between a single-track line and a double-track line, as shown in Fig. 25-13.

The real signals in Fig. 25-13 are placed as they would be on the prototype, with dwarf signals protecting against reverse movements over the crossover. Obviously there are not enough real signals to protect each of the uP block so several phantom signals must be used.

Fig. 25-13 illustrates an algorithm which will handle all model-railroad interlockings so far considered. At the top of the figure all real signals are set to stop by the position of the levers of the interlocking. If the switches are already set for the normal-speed routes and the blocks are unoccupied, the home signal can be pulled up as shown at A. A train entering the interlocking causes this signal to drop. This signal can then be made to remain at stop until again cleared by lever action (stick interlocking) or it can clear in normal block-signal fashion (non-stick or fleeted interlocking). Rather than being fixed, the action followed can depend upon an electrical switch on the interlocking panel.

To change the route, all the signals protecting the old and the new routes have to be set to stop by lever action, and the uP blocks involved need to be unoccupied before lever action can throw a switch. The program can even provide advance or approach locking; if a route has been cleared and a train has entered the approach block before the signal protecting that train has dropped, throwing the switch is prevented until a time delay had expired.

Assuming the switches have been set to the route shown at B in Fig. 25-13, and all uP blocks are unoccupied, the phantom signals act in normal block-signal fashion if there is a real signal in advance, or repeat the indication of the signal in advance if that signal is a phantom signal also. The real signal protecting the route repeats the indication of the phantom signal in advance as modified by the switch setting. At B the clear indication of the phantom is repeated as a medium clear since it is a medium-speed route.

At C the real signal protecting the block in advance on the single-track line is at stop. The phantom to its rear acts in normal block-signal fashion and displays approach. That indication is then copied by the phantom at the crossover, and finally as medium approach by the real signal protecting the route.

To cover the more-involved types of interlocking, such as the rare but not unknown case of having two home signals of the same direction protecting a single route, additional information must be provided in ROM.

The great power of uP controlling interlockings is that once the program is debugged and in ROM, any set of tracks can be interlocked merely by placing some easily-determined information in the data ROMs.

Once the indication of a real interlocking signal is calculated, the program jumps to the same routine that is used to translate a block signal indication into an aspect for the particular real signal in use at that point.

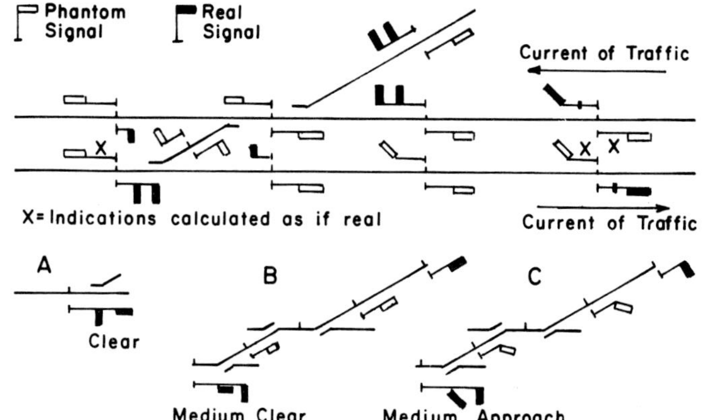

Fig. 25-13 Junction.

CTC

CTC (also called TCS) is really an interlocking which controls a considerable length of railroad. Therefore the controlled signals of a CTC machine use the same program that exists for interlockings. The intermediate signals use the same program as the non-headblock signals of APB, except that traffic is set by levers on the CTC machine rather than by train occupancy of uP blocks.

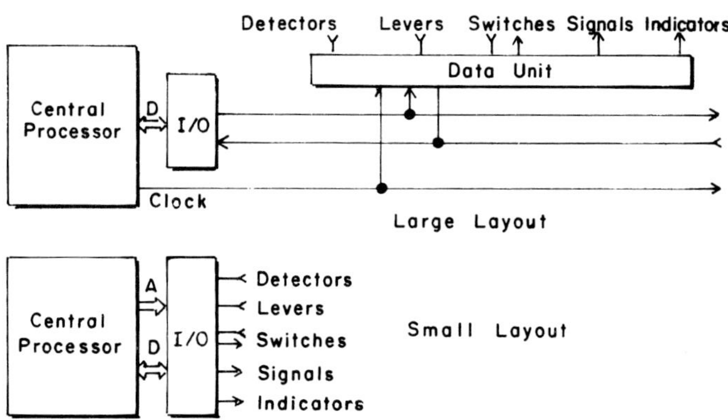

Fig. 25-14 Hardware considerations.

Hardware

Although a uP greatly simplifies the circuit design, there is still a lot of hardware design, particularly for the interfaces to detectors, switch machines, and other external devices. A simplified block diagram of hardware units is given in Fig. 25-14.

To a large extent, the hardware units within the central processor block are determined by the choice of uP. Even for a specific uP, there is considerable choice in how the memories are arranged. Furthermore, it is often possible to simplify programing complexity by simple hardware additions in this area. Nevertheless, the central processor is physically small and can be implemented with the usual IC logic techniques. This is not the case for the I/O equipment, which receives the data from external devices and sends the commands.

If the layout is physically large, it will probably be more economical to construct data units and locate them near the sources of data and the devices to be controlled. To save the number of transmission lines with their line drivers and receivers necessary to interchange information and commands between the central processor and the data units, this information can be transmitted in serial form over one line rather than over as many lines as there are bits in one byte. The uP can be programed to transmit or receive one bit at a time but the more promising approach is usually for the I/O unit at the central processor to make the conversion between parallel or serial. One bidirectional transmission line can be provided, but it certainly is faster, and probably simpler, to use a separate line in each direction, as shown at the top of Fig. 25-14.

The data unit responds whenever a uP block in its area is addressed; this address is sent over the transmission line before the data or commands. It then converts the commands received into outputs capable of driving the signals, switch machines, panel indicators and so forth. The data unit will also convert the DC levels received from levers, switch-machine contacts, and detectors into the appropriate synchronized pulses for transmission to the central processor.

A major advantage of data units distributed strategically around the layout is that the leads running to individual devices such as signals will never reach cumbersome concentrations in any one area. On small layouts when the number of leads to the individual devices permits them to be brought to one point, the I/O unit at the uP can handle them directly, as indicated at the bottom of Fig. 25-14. The program for either arrangement is the same, the differences are in the I/O unit.

On either a large or a small layout, the number of leads required between the individual devices, and the data unit or the I/O unit can be reduced by using the multiplex techniques shown in Fig 15-53.

INDEX TO VOLUMES 1 AND 2

This Index is complete for both volumes of the Electrical Handbook for Model Railroads, Vol. 1 Second Edition, and Vol. 2 Third Edition. Page numbers below 100 are in Volume 1, above 100 are in Volume 2. Pages 69-99 are deliberately omitted and are not missing.

Gil Freitag works the control panel at Stony Creek Yard on his HO Stony Creek & Western Railroad, one of three on the pike, which are in addition to a walk around throttle system. Houston, Texas, railroad was featured in April 1974 Railroad Model Craftsman, and is a top notch operating model railroad.